The Great Firewall of China

How to Build and
Control an Alternative
Version of the Internet

James Griffiths

ZED

The Great Firewall of China: How to Build and Control an Alternative Version of the Internet was first published in 2019 by Zed Books Ltd, The Foundry, 17 Oval Way, London SE11 5RR, UK.

www.zedbooks.net

Typeset in Sabon by seagulls.net
Index by John Barker
Cover design by David A. Gee

A catalogue record for this book is available from the British Library

ISBN 978-1-78699-535-3 hb
ISBN 978-1-78699-537-7 pdf
ISBN 978-1-78699-538-4 epub
ISBN 978-1-78699-539-1 mobi

Printed and bound by CPI Group (UK) Ltd, Croydon CR0 4YY

"Western anti-China forces have constantly and vainly tried to exploit the internet to 'topple China' ... Whether we can stand our ground and win this battle over the internet has a direct bearing on our country's ideological and political security."

Xi Jinping, speech to the National Propaganda and Ideology Work Conference, August 2013

Contents

Author's note   ix
Acronyms and abbreviations   xi
Map   xiii

Introduction: Early warnings   1

Part 1: Wall
1. Protests: Solidarity from Hong Kong to Tiananmen   15
2. Over the wall: China's first email and the rise of the   23
    online censor
3. Nailing the jello: Chinese democracy and the   35
    Great Firewall
4. Enemy at the gates: How fear of Falun Gong boosted   45
    the Firewall
5. Searching for an opening: Google, Yahoo and Silicon   61
    Valley's moral failing in China

Part 2: Shield
6. Along came a spider: Lu Wei reins in the Chinese   71
    internet
7. Peak traffic: Getting the Dalai Lama online   83
8. Filtered: The Firewall catches up with Da Cankao   89
9. Jumping the wall: FreeGate, UltraSurf, and Falun   95
    Gong's fight against the censors
10. Called to account: Silicon Valley's reckoning on   115
    Capitol Hill

Part 3: Sword

11. Uyghurs online: Ilham Tohti and the birth of the   131
Uyghur internet

12. Shutdown: How to take 20 million people offline   143

13. Ghosts in the machine: Chinese hackers expand   159
the Firewall's reach

14. NoGuGe: The ignominious end of Google China   165

15. The social network: Weibo and the last free-speech   175
platform

16. Gorillas in the mist: Exposing China's hackers to   185
the world

Part 4: War

17. Caught: The death of the Uyghur internet   195

18. Key opinion leader: How Chinese trolls go after   203
dissidents overseas

19. Root and stem: The internet is more vulnerable than   217
you think

20. The censor at the UN: China's undermining of global   227
internet freedoms

21. Sovereignty: When Xi Jinping came for the internet   239

22. Friends in Moscow: The Great Firewall goes west   247

23. Plane crash: China helps Russia bring Telegram to heel   259

24. One app to rule them all: How WeChat opened up   275
new frontiers of surveillance and censorship

25. Buttocks: Uganda's internet blackouts follow   285
Beijing's lead

Epilogue: Silicon Valley won't save you   307

Acknowledgements   319
Notes   321
Selected bibliography   369
Index   374

Author's note

Names: I have tried to use the most common spelling or usage for the names of people and places, even if this sometimes creates inconsistency, such as using the Pinyin transliteration system for mainland Chinese names (Zhou Enlai not Chou En-lai) but the older, less accurate Wade-Giles system for Hong Kong and Taiwanese names (Chiang Kai-shek not Jiang Jieshi). Where a Chinese or Hong Kong person commonly goes by an English first name, I have used it. Other naming rules, such as for Uyghur names, are explained in endnotes.

Chinese: Where non-English terms appear in the text, they are italicised unless the word has been adopted into the language or is a proper noun. For the sake of clarity, Chinese refers to the written language, in its simplified and traditional form, that is used in China, Hong Kong and Taiwan (and numerous other countries). Mandarin is the official spoken language of China and Taiwan. Cantonese is the primary language used in Hong Kong and in parts of southern China.

Quotes: Where text appears between double quotation marks, it comes from a primary source or a reliable secondary source, or was spoken directly to me in an interview. Dialogue or statements that were recounted to me by one of the participants appear in single quotation marks.

Acronyms and abbreviations

BBG   Broadcasting Board of Governors
CAAA   Chinese Civil Aviation Administration
CCTV   China Central Television
CDA   Communications Decency Act
CDP   China Democracy Party
CNC   China Netcom Communications
CNNIC   China Internet Network Information Centre
CQRS   China Qigong Science Research Society
DARPA   Defence Advanced Research Projects Agency
DDoS   distributed denial of service
DIT   Dynamic Internet Technology Inc.
DNS   domain name server(s)
DPI   deep packet inspection
EFF   Electronic Frontier Foundation
FAPSI   Federal Agency for Government Communications and Information
FSB   Federal Security Service
GIFC   Global Internet Freedom Consortium
IANA   Internet Assigned Numbers Authority
IAP   internet access point
ICANN   Internet Corporation for Assigned Names and Numbers
IETF   Internet Engineering Task Force
IP   Internet Protocol
ISP   internet service provider
ITR   International Telecommunication Regulations
ITU   International Telecommunication Union
KGB   Committee for State Security
LAN   local area network

MIIT   Ministry of Industry and Information Technology
NED   National Endowment for Democracy
NGO   non-governmental organisation
NSA   National Security Agency
PLA   People's Liberation Army, the armed forces of the Chinese Communist Party and the People's Republic of China
PRC   People's Republic of China
SCO   Shanghai Cooperation Organisation
SORM   System of Operative Search Measures
URL   Uniform Resource Locator
VPN   virtual private network
W3C   World Wide Web Consortium
WCIT   World Conference on International Telecommunications
WELL   Whole Earth 'Lectronic Link
WSIS   World Summit on the Information Society
WTO   World Trade Organization
WUC   World Uyghur Congress

Greater China, including the People's Republic of China,
Hong Kong, Taiwan and Macau

Introduction

Early warnings

Late on a Wednesday in March 2015, an alarm sounded in the offices of Github, a San Francisco-based tech firm. All exposed wood, open spaces and lots of natural light, the company's offices exemplified the kind of Scandinavia-meets-soullessness style which had spread out from Silicon Valley to take over modern workplaces. In the open-plan workspace, engineers tapped at keyboards under thick wooden beams and aluminium air-conditioning pipes. Most were preparing to leave, if they hadn't already. Outside, the sun had started to set and it was balmy and clear.

Alarms weren't uncommon at Github. The company, which maintained the largest repository of computer code in the world, had some 14 million users and prided itself on maintaining its service and staying online. Code stored on Github was used by developers around the globe, by companies big and small, with thousands of people in any given minute uploading projects, flagging issues and bugs, and releasing new versions to users. That is to say: people noticed when Github went down.

The first alarm indicated that there was a large amount of incoming traffic to several projects stored on Github. This could be innocent – maybe a company had just launched a big new update – or something more sinister. Depending on how the traffic was clustered, more alarms would sound if the sudden influx was impacting service site-wide. These sounded now. Github was being DDos-ed.[1]

One of the most frequent causes of any website going down is a sudden spike in traffic, as servers are overwhelmed with requests, causing them to crash or slow to a tortuous grind. In 2015, the website of the Eiffel Tower was knocked offline when Google linked to it from the search engine's homepage in honour of the tower's 126th birthday, sending millions of visitors to the site.[2] A distributed denial of service (DDoS) attack works in the same way, but maliciously. Such attacks have grown massively in frequency in recent years with the proliferation of botnets, hordes of zombified computers infected by malicious code that allows hackers to control them remotely.

"We are currently experiencing the largest DDoS attack in Github's history," senior developer Jesse Newland wrote in a blog post almost twenty-four hours after the attack had begun.[3] Public server status messages show that, over the next five days, as engineers spent 120 hours combating the attack, Github went down nine times.[4] The attack was like a hydra: every time the team thought they had a handle on it, it adapted and redoubled its efforts. Github wouldn't comment on the record, but a team member who spoke to me anonymously said it was "very obvious that this was something we'd never seen before".

In the company's internal chat room, Github engineers realised they would be tackling the attack "for some time". They had a problem, however: all previous strategies were based on attacks they or other targets had experienced in the past. But this was something different. As the hours stretched into days, it became something of a competition between the Github engineers and whomever was on the other end of the attack. Working long, frantic shifts, the team didn't have much time to speculate about the attackers' identity. As rumours abounded online, Github would only say: "We believe the intent of this attack is to convince us to remove a specific class of content." About a twenty-minute drive away, across San Francisco bay in Berkeley, Nicholas Weaver thought he knew the culprit: China.

Bespectacled, with receding hairline and a penchant for polo shirts, Weaver spoke in declarative, no-nonsense sentences. A one-time astrophysicist, he had switched over to specialising in computer security. At first, the Github attack didn't much interest him. Companies get DDoS-ed – it's a fact of life on the internet – and Github had been subject to many such attacks in the past. But as speculation grew online about the identity of the attackers, Weaver became intrigued. Communicating with other security researchers through Twitter and blog posts,[5] he helped pinpoint the targets of the attack as two Github projects connected to GreatFire.org, a China-based anti-censorship organisation that works to undermine that country's internet filtering. The two projects enabled users in China to access two censored websites: GreatFire's own, and the Chinese-language version of *The New York Times*. GreatFire, dubbed a "foreign anti-Chinese organisation" by the Cyberspace Administration of China,[6] had long been a target of DDoS and hacking attacks, which is why it moved some of its services to Github, where they were nominally out of harm's way.

As Weaver examined the attack, he saw something new, with massive implications for cybersecurity. In a paper co-authored with Bill Marczak and seven other researchers, published by the University of Toronto's Citizen Lab, Weaver revealed the existence of a previously unknown Chinese cyber weapon: the Great Cannon. The Citizen Lab team were able to track the Great Cannon to the same infrastructure as the Great Firewall, the colossal censorship apparatus that blocks off China's internet from the rest of the world, and controls what every user in the country can see or share.

"The operational deployment of the Great Cannon represents a significant escalation in state-level information control," they wrote: "the normalisation of widespread use of an attack tool to enforce censorship by weaponising users." For the Github attack, the Cannon co-opted the services of one of China's most successful internet companies: Baidu. Exploiting a vulnerability in Baidu's online advertising system, used by millions worldwide, the Cannon hijacked and redirected traffic to Github. Baidu, which denied any involvement in the attacks, was the fourth most visited site in the world at the time. When a user visited a site with Baidu's ads running on it, that code would request information from the company's servers in China. As the request was processed, the Cannon would intercept a small portion of it, and swap out Baidu's code with its own, forcing the user's browser to continuously load the two Github projects.

The attack went on for days. The Citizen Lab team said they were able to observe its effects until as late as 8 April, almost two weeks after Github's alarms first went off. GreatFire, whose own website was also targeted, estimated that during the attack it was running up bills of over $30,000 a day with its hosting service.[7]

Afterwards, as the Github developers struggled to make sense of the attack and come up with a roadmap for future incidents, there was confusion within the cybersecurity community. Why had China launched so public an attack, and in such a blunt force fashion? "It was overkill," Weaver told me. "They kept the attack going long after it had ceased working." The Citizen Lab paper showed an incredibly sophisticated system, equal even to the Great Firewall itself, but it had been used like a hammer to repeatedly bludgeon GreatFire and Github.

It was a message.

*

Around the same time as the Github attack, on the other side of the world, another kind of message was being delivered.

The police crowded inside the small apartment, bumping up against shelving units and the kitchen table. They wore light-blue, short-sleeved shirts with open collars, and their white and black peaked hats were pulled down over their eyes. Several smelled intensely of cigarettes, and they were sweating as the apartment's air conditioning struggled to keep up with the sudden increase in occupants.

One of them handed Li Gang[8] a notice. It was something the young computer developer had been dreading for months, ever since he had started moonlighting from his job to work on a remarkable anti-surveillance tool that let anyone easily pipe their internet traffic through an encrypted tunnel, preventing it from being spied upon or analysed. Just like the hugely popular BitTorrent protocol, which can be used for legal purposes even if most people use it for pirating TV shows and movies, Li's tool was nominally to boost privacy but had a major benefit for users in China: by encrypting and masking their traffic, it let them bypass the Great Firewall.

'If you do not comply with this notice, you will be arrested,' the police officer said, handing it to him. Li was ordered to stop work on his software immediately and, moreover, to delete all trace of it from the internet. He stammered an affirmative response, feeling a pit opening up in his stomach. Three years of work, gone. "I have no choice but to obey," he explained in a short blog post after the police had left, as he replaced the code with a message that it had been deleted "according to regulations".

Li wasn't the only Chinese developer to receive a visit from the police that month. Phus Lu, creator of GoAgent, another anti-censorship tool, also wiped his project from the internet. As he was doing so, he deleted all the posts on his Twitter account but one, a message linking to a Chinese translation of Russian dissident Alexander Solzhenitsyn's essay 'Live not by lies', written on 12 February 1974, the day Solzhenitsyn was arrested for treason.[9]

So in our timidity, let each of us make a choice: Whether consciously, to remain a servant of falsehood – of course, it is not out of inclination, but to feed one's family, that one raises his children in the spirit of lies – or to shrug off the lies and become an honest man worthy of respect both by one's children and contemporaries.

"Everything that has a beginning, has an end," Lu wrote on the GoAgent site. He had been working on the tool for four years.

Github, Phus Lu and Li Gang were among the first victims of a new front in China's war on the internet, launched by a new breed of censor determined to go after the country's enemies wherever they might be, using whatever means necessary. The Github incident was for many outside China the first hint they had of the ideology behind this resurgence in censorship, one that would come to define how China views the web both at home and globally: the doctrine of cyber-sovereignty.

*

It wasn't supposed to end up like this. The early evangelists of the internet preached absolute freedom from government control. The web, they said, would route around censorship, making it the ultimate Pandora's box for repressive regimes. As the late cyberlibertarian John Perry Barlow wrote:

Governments of the Industrial World, you weary giants of flesh and steel, I come from Cyberspace, the new home of Mind. On behalf of the future, I ask you of the past to leave us alone. You are not welcome among us. You have no sovereignty where we gather.

We have no elected government, nor are we likely to have one, so I address you with no greater authority than that with which liberty itself always speaks. I declare the global social space we are building to be naturally independent of the

tyrannies you seek to impose on us. You have no moral right
to rule us nor do you possess any methods of enforcement we
have true reason to fear.[10]

Despite the utopian language of Barlow and others, however,
walled gardens swiftly sprang up all over the early web, as a tiny
number of tech pioneers made billions from new internet monopolies. Silicon Valley, as it pushed the principle that "information
wants to be free", became a strident opponent of regulation and
anti-trust action, papering over the government-led and -funded
origins of the internet to claim a victory for private enterprise that
could be ruined if lawmakers attempted to rein it in.

Today, we are dealing with the failure of that ideology. Tech
giants dominate our media and politics. Those publishers they
do not increasingly own – hampering the media's vital role as a
watchdog over big business – they can make or break with the
tweak of an algorithm. The vast riches of Silicon Valley have
corrupted politics, leaving elected officials genuflecting in the
direction of tech billions in the hopes of replacing jobs disrupted
out of existence with data centres, company headquarters, and the
gig economy. Social media companies have refused to recognise
their role as publishers and gatekeepers, allowing propaganda and
malicious disinformation to propagate wildly on their platforms,
spreading lies and hatred, radicalising millions and potentially
even affecting elections.

That we are reaching a breaking point is obvious. More and more
voices are calling for regulation of the internet, for untrammelled
tech power to be kept in check. But just as capitalism has been so
tightly wedded to the concept of democracy that the problems with
the former are sometimes held up as reasons to abandon the latter,
so the values of an open and free internet risk being undermined by
the collapse of Silicon Valley's cyberlibertarian status quo.

Because there is another vision of the internet – one that is far more coherent and persuasive than many of us would like to admit. China's doctrine of cyber-sovereignty argues that the web is not a unique technology, transcending borders and international controls, but is like everything else, and should be regulated accordingly. We have border controls and import duties in the physical world, so why should the digital sphere be any different? The doctrine of cyber-sovereignty is a vision of total internet control, and emanates from a stance of deep suspicion about the web and its potential risk to state power.

For years, China's censors were mocked as analogue ostriches with their heads in the digital sand, but their vision has proven far more prophetic than that of the internet freedom advocates opposing them. China's censors are able to point to fake news, social media hate and hacking attacks, and to claim, not completely untruthfully, that these aren't serious problems in China. The Great Firewall, the colossal censorship apparatus that monitors all aspects of the Chinese internet, provides security and stability from the dangerous chaos of the unfiltered web, full as it is of terrorists, child molesters, hackers and scammers.

Just as the Communist Party itself has proven adept at handling any crisis that it faces – from the self-inflicted disasters of the Great Leap Forward and the Cultural Revolution, to the Arab Spring and the 2008 financial crash – so have the censors adapted, and outwitted those who opposed them. The system they built – the most sophisticated in the world for controlling, filtering and surveilling the internet – has gone from strength to strength. Technology giants, both foreign and domestic, have been brought to heel, and those who won't collaborate have been banished. Propaganda output has expanded into all walks of life, spreading an angry, xenophobic nationalism to drown out any criticism of state control.

The censors' success has not stopped the techno utopians heralding each new internet development – blogs, social media, instant messaging – as a panacea. Nor has it stopped them trumpeting any gap or loophole in the Great Firewall, no matter how short-lived, as proof of the ultimate futility of attempting to censor the internet. The utopians point to methods of jumping over the Firewall, such as proxies or virtual private networks (VPNs), as examples of the censors' weaknesses, and as reasons why such a system could never be implemented in another country. Never mind that many VPN services are unreliable and insecure and require credit card payments, the records of which could get any Chinese user (rather than the Facebook-addicted foreigners nearly all China-focused VPN services are targeting) in a heap of legal trouble.

A great deal of writing on Chinese censorship is based on a fundamental misunderstanding of both how the censors operate and what their ultimate goals are. The internet is a liberatory technology not because it can help share information, but because it can help build solidarity. It's why the Occupy movement spread across multiple countries, and how a small protest in Tunisia could spark a wave of pro-democracy demonstrations throughout the Arab world. At the same time, it's also how the Islamic State is able to spread its message and recruit volunteers from thousands of kilometres away, and how minor disagreements over representation in pop culture can evolve into the anti-feminist Gamergate movement.

Sceptics can point to individual websites and pages being uncensored in China to argue that the Great Firewall could never plug all its gaps, and so is doomed in the long run. Ultimately, however, this argument is facile and the airtightness of the Firewall is irrelevant. China's censors do not care about blocking content; they care about blocking solidarity. The number one target of censorship is not the Tiananmen Square massacre, or the banned religious movement Falun Gong, or news about official corruption, it is organisation outside the Party structure. Solidarity – such as that expressed by the hundreds of thousands of protesters in Beijing and other Chinese cities in 1989, or by the millions who took part in the Arab Spring – is the biggest threat to an authoritarian regime. China's leaders, as members of a Leninist and supposedly Marxist movement (even if, in practice, they act like ruthless capitalists), know this better than most.

When the internet came to China in the 1990s, it did not threaten the country's rulers because it risked undermining their control over information, but because it threatened to create a platform for organising against them. Tragically, for those who support a democratic, representative China, the censors were successful in stymying this threat. Terrifyingly, for the rest of the world, they have provided a blueprint for doing so for authoritarians elsewhere. And the censors are now taking their war against the internet overseas. Chinese diplomats are working at the United Nations and other international bodies to undermine and chip away at the norms and rules that underpin the global internet and help keep it free. State propagandists are extending their tentacles into Hollywood and the international media to control and suppress any criticism of China. And government-sponsored hackers are harassing dissidents and critics wherever they are in the world, sabotaging attempts to undermine the Great Firewall, and even targeting the very backbone of the web to try to give China a giant global internet off switch.[11]

In the past decade, China has begun exporting the technology used to power the Firewall to other countries. Russia has seen its internet, once freewheeling and dynamic, reined in and filtered, closing off one of the few remaining avenues for dissent against the Kremlin. Across Africa, from Zimbabwe to Ethiopia, China's allies on the continent have adopted Beijing's tactics of internet blackouts, cutting off access to whole regions during politically sensitive times, robbing people of their ability to organise or rally for change. Other countries across Asia, the Middle East and even in the West are increasing censorship of certain topics amid calls for greater internet regulation. At the same time, China has worked to undermine international protections for the open internet. Not only has Beijing drawn up the blueprints for any country to build a firewall of its own, but it is increasingly clearing the way of legal obstacles as well.

This book is about how we got here. How China did the supposedly impossible and built a controlled, warped version of the internet. How the vision of the web as a force for democracy and freedom failed, and the censors, far from retreating, are on the advance.

Part 1: Wall

Chapter 1

Protests

Solidarity from Hong Kong to Tiananmen

Bereft of people, Hong Kong's Civic Square is an ugly sight. Three concentric rings of concrete expand outward from a circular pedestal, on top of which sit two flagpoles with their banners hanging limply, the buildings looming on all sides preventing them receiving anything like a breeze. The entrance to the square is uglier still: a tall metal fence, sharp-tipped poles clustered close together, bookended by two squat, rectangular buildings with frosted glass windows inside which security guards take note of visitors.

The square, which sits in front of the central government offices in the busy business district of Admiralty, was intended as a way to bring the city's officials and people closer together. As a spot for protests and rallies, former Hong Kong chief executive Donald Tsang promised it would act as a reminder for future governments to "be liberal, open minded and proactively solicit public opinion at all times".[1] But when public opinion proved more often than not to be critical of government policies, and people used their proximity to power to complain about the numerous ways in which it was exercised poorly in the semi-autonomous Chinese territory, those in charge of Civic Square had a change of heart. And so Hong Kong's administrators, following a tried and tested pattern, looked at the hornets' nest sitting outside their windows –

annoying and potentially dangerous, but contained and predictable – and decided to kick it. By locking the square off from the public, they turned an ugly, boring stretch of concrete into a symbol of democracy and political participation, and created a magnet for future protests.

It was inevitable, then, that in September 2014, as the city was gripped by an upsurge of anti-government anger and desire for political reform, the square would be targeted. Despite this, and despite frequent calls in the preceding weeks for the square to be reopened, authorities were apparently taken by surprise when – on the night of 26 September – several hundred university and high-school students broke off from a larger pro-democracy rally and stormed Civic Square. The police responded with anger and violence, hitting protesters with batons and shields, and dousing their faces in pepper spray. Here, again, authoritarian overreach inadvertently created an icon that would be used against it. Many of the protesters were carrying umbrellas to protect themselves from the torrential rain that is an inevitable part of Hong Kong summers, and they unfurled them now to shield against the pepper spray. The protest had its symbol, and a name: the Umbrella Movement.

Throughout the following day, police and demonstrators fought for the square, and many protest leaders were dragged off and bundled into police vans. Images of the protesters defying pepper spray with spindly, fold-up umbrellas spread online, particularly on Facebook and Instagram, which was swiftly blocked in China. On WhatsApp and online bulletin boards, calls for support went out, and thousands more protesters began converging on Admiralty. Soon, the police at Civic Square found that they were the ones surrounded and in need of reinforcements. As the number of protesters grew into the tens of thousands, they shut down roads around the square, leaving the six-lane Connaught Road highway empty of traffic and seething with people.

At 5.57pm on 28 September, the first tear gas canister was fired. More followed in quick succession. By the end of the night the police had fired eighty-seven canisters in total, but the tear gas had the opposite effect to that intended.[2] Instead of dispersing the crowds, it bolstered and emboldened them. Those who were on the sidelines of the protest joined it in outrage at the use of the gas, including the parents of many students on the streets. The shock and fury over the police action was palpable. Many did not recognise the city they lived in. A middle-aged friend of mine, no bleeding heart liberal, wrote on Facebook that the gas was pointless as "we have no more tears left to cry", and others expressed similar feelings of dismay. Thousands of protesters flooded the streets and drove the police back.

When I arrived at the Connaught Road camp a couple hours after the first tear gas canister had been fired, the protesters were in full control. The street was an undulating mass of people, glistening with sweat and giddy with excitement. The occasional blast from a megaphone was the only thing to rise above the intense din of the crowd as people chattered excitedly in disbelief at what they had done, what they were doing. The summer heat in Hong Kong is oppressive and intense, sitting on top of your lungs and sucking sweat from every part of your body. As I passed through the crowd, I gratefully accepted a bottle of water from a man passing them out from a large plastic-wrapped pack. Others handed out goggles or scarves to protect from tear gas, and crates of umbrellas were scattered throughout the protest camp, like arrows for medieval archers.

I walked west towards Central district and the front line. On the way, I passed a double-decker bus that had been abandoned by its driver when he couldn't make it through the crush of people. Aside from its number, which had been changed into an insult against the city's leader,[3] it was unmolested. A few tired protesters sat inside; several were asleep. Following the highway up onto an overpass, I reached the edge of the protest camp and saw riot police for the first time. A line of shields stood across the bottom of the road, where the highway merged into regular streets again. Behind them, in dark-green uniforms, black gas masks and helmets, stood a hundred or so police. They had parked their vans behind them. The message was clear: this was as far as the protesters would come. They were wrong.

As I stood between the protesters and police, a tear gas canister flew over my head and exploded near the front of the crowd. As they screamed and moved back, their hands raised in the air in a show of non-violence, two more canisters were fired. Thick white smoke billowed out and I felt it begin to clog up my throat and burn my sinuses, nose and eyes. Tear gas doesn't so much make you cry as make your entire face expel liquid. I coughed as mucus poured out of my nose and my eyes streamed. I retreated back up the slope, where a protester helped douse my face with water. By the time I was free of the worst effects of the gas, the protesters below me had already rallied. The police had barely advanced at all, and those in the crowd with the foresight to be wearing goggles and masks walked calmly towards them again, making up the ground that had been lost.

Several more times, the police fired tear gas and tried to clear the crowd. But, maybe because they realised that a couple of hundred riot police were never going to be able to arrest the 30,000 or so protesters in between them and Admiralty, they never advanced far. Eventually they gave up and retreated entirely, leaving the streets to the protesters.

Those protesters would hold parts of the city for seventy-nine days. On the ground, they set up camps, classrooms, internet cafés and refreshment stands, while online, via instant messaging, Facebook and popular bulletin boards such as HK Golden, they planned the next stage of the occupation and organised against police actions and attacks by pro-China groups. Amid fears that the authorities would cut off telephone services, protesters installed apps such as FireChat, which allowed them to communicate via Bluetooth. Expressions of support and solidarity poured in from around the world, with one projector beaming messages submitted online onto a large wall near the main protest camp.

After their initial burst of violence backfired so spectacularly, the authorities switched to a gradual war of attrition, conducting sporadic clearance operations to chip away at the size of the camps that had sprung up in Admiralty, Causeway Bay and Mong Kok, and attacking the students in the media, casting them as enemies of normal Hong Kongers, disrupters of their lives. The last protesters were eventually cleared on 11 December, carried away singing pro-democracy songs, leaving behind a rough detritus of barricades, umbrellas and signs. A huge orange banner read: "It's just the beginning."

This was a common sentiment. And, indeed, despite the initial dejection over the sparse successes of the Umbrella Movement, it had a huge effect on Hong Kong politics, awakening a swath of young voters thought previously to be largely apathetic. Their influence was felt in parliamentary elections two years later, which saw a record turnout as more than 2 million voters in a city of just over 7 million returned a radically more pro-democracy and anti-Beijing legislature than ever before.[4] Three months after the September vote, Leung Chun-ying, the much loathed chief executive who was the focus of much of the Umbrella protests, announced that he would not run for a second term, a move hailed as a victory by nearly all pro-democracy activists.[5]

The protests had a profound effect on Hong Kong society and will be seen as a pivotal point in the city's history in decades to come. They were powerful not only because of the success of the organisers in getting hundreds of thousands to come out into the streets, but because the conversation around the protests and the expressions of solidarity with their demands were able to continue and evolve thanks to Hong Kong's relatively free media and, more importantly, the internet. Discussions of Hong Kong independence, which grew from a fringe idea before the Umbrella protests to a major influence on local politics, took place online, and a host of new publications catering to the 'Umbrella generation' were launched and thrived through social media. The new crop of young legislators, under near unceasing attack from the pro-Beijing establishment across a variety of fronts, was able to reach out directly to voters via Facebook and messaging apps, mobilising protests and shows of solidarity whenever needed.

Twenty-five years earlier, another group of students gathered on the streets of a different Chinese city.[6] The climate in Beijing in 1989 was similar to that in Hong Kong in the months before the Umbrella Movement, as young people gathered to debate political reform and plot the way forward. Just as the Hong Kong students were inspired by a freewheeling press and academic culture protected by the city's constitution and guaranteed by the 'one country, two systems' agreement that underpinned it, the Tiananmen movement sprang from a remarkable period of openness and reflection in China. Many students who gathered on the square were inspired by the 1988 television programme 'River Elegy', which argued that China had become backward and oppressive and called for Western-style reform and modernisation. "After the Cultural Revolution, liberal thought began to sprout," legendary Chinese journalist Yang Jisheng said decades later. "Liberalism was an attack on one-party rule – it was the wish for democracy, the wish for rule of law, the wish for respect for the constitution."

The Hong Kong protests began with the wildcat takeover of Civic Square and quickly spiralled into something far bigger. Tiananmen began in early 1989 as an expression of mourning, as thousands gathered in the square to mark the death of reformist

Party leader Hu Yaobang and use it as an opportunity to voice dissatisfaction with the government and the progress of reform. Students also took to the streets in Nanjing and Shanghai, as the unrest began to spread and anger grew. *The People's Daily*, the official Party mouthpiece, threw fuel on the fire with an editorial in late April denouncing the student movement, and accusing it of creating "turmoil". Just as the tear gas in Hong Kong years later would have the opposite effect to that intended, the Party's dismissal of the students' demands brought tens of thousands more demonstrators to the street. Protests continued into May, and the students became a permanent feature in Tiananmen. Without the internet, news about the struggle in Beijing spread much slower to the rest of the country, but it was carried by word of mouth and delegations sent to major cities to help 'spread the fire'. State media also did not take a consistent line against the students, with some reformist newspapers breaking with *The People's Daily* and voicing support for the protests. As the end of May approached, the turmoil that had begun in the capital risked spreading to the entire country, and the central leadership took an increasingly harder line. On 19 May, Zhao Ziyang, the popular reformist general secretary of the Party who advocated dialogue with the students, visited the square and apologised for having "come too late". Zhao was soon sidelined by the hardliners and placed under house arrest. The next day, Premier Li Peng declared martial law in Beijing.

On the square in late May, as numbers were dropping in the face of seemingly inevitable violence, student leaders discussed how to proceed even as the Party seemed to dither on taking action. Only years later did it emerge that paramount leader Deng Xiaoping and others who supported a crackdown faced defiance from within the Party leadership and the military, staying their hand for a time. Finally, on 3 June, more than 10,000 armed troops moved towards Beijing. "Their large numbers, the fact that they are helmeted, and the automatic weapons they are carrying suggest that the force option is real," a US State Department cable warned.

Hundreds were killed and thousands arrested as the People's Liberation Army (PLA) cleared protesters from the streets of the Chinese capital with tanks and sniper rifles. As the smoke cleared over Tiananmen Square, the Party machinery went into overdrive, ensuring that similar protests could never happen again. Hundreds of student leaders fled the country, either to Hong Kong, then still a British colony, or further afield; most would never be able to return. Many more were arrested or fired from their jobs – even people whose involvement in the protests was negligible. Zhao Ziyang stayed under house arrest in Beijing until his death in 2005.

In the years that followed, Tiananmen was stamped out of the historical record. Those who took part in it were obliged to forget, or face the consequences. They didn't talk about the protests with their children, who never learned anything of them in school. Even among those who lived through 1989, counterfactuals and half-truths were common, as propaganda spread false accounts to poison the historical record and introduce uncertainty. The students were denounced as violent anarchists who had attacked and murdered soldiers. The fact that no casualties occurred in the square itself, but in the surrounding streets as residents and protesters attempted to slow the PLA's advance, was given as supposed proof that the final death toll was exaggerated. Most of all, it was argued, even by those who recognised the horrors experienced in Beijing, that China's subsequent prosperity and modernity retroactively justified the crackdown; that without Deng's firm hand in 1989, he would not have been able to oversee subsequent reforms that led to an economic boom.

The Party's grip on history was near absolute. And then the internet came to China.

Chapter 2

Over the wall

China's first email and the rise of the online censor

In 1987, a decade after Mao Zedong's death, Beijing had seen better days. The city was still showing the scars of the Great Helmsman's final disaster, the Cultural Revolution. Over a ten-year period, Mao plunged China into unrest and eventually civil war in an attempt to preserve his increasingly shaky grip on power. Teenage Red Guards terrorised the capital, beating and torturing intellectuals, corrupt officials and 'class traitors', while in the countryside and provincial capitals, rival armed factions fought pitched battles and massacred each other as economic development ground to a standstill.[1]

Landing at Beijing airport in September 1987, one visitor was shocked to find "a few badly maintained structures, no larger than a small provincial airfield", with paint peeling from the walls, dim lighting and no signage.[2] Roads were crowded with bicycles and potholes were common. But there were signs of growing wealth as well. Those who could afford it drove gleaming Japanese cars (or at least cheaper domestic knock-offs), and tourists thronged the city's ancient sites, as new developments of gleaming glass and chrome sprang up among the dreary Stalinist architecture that dominated the centre of the city.[3]

In the Great Hall of the People, the blocky white palace to Party bureaucracy overlooking Tiananmen Square, Mao's successor Deng

Xiaoping welcomed 150 leading academics from fifty countries to the second conference of the Third World Academy of Sciences.[4] A tiny man – at under five feet he was regularly dwarfed by other world leaders – Deng had a round, lined face with deep-set eyes and a mischievous smile that gave him an elfin quality. Addressing the audience in his heavily Sichuan-accented Mandarin, Deng was keen to draw a line under the anti-intellectualism of the Cultural Revolution, lauding China's achievements in science and technology, and calling for more cooperation with Western institutions.

In a climate-controlled room in another part of the city, just such cooperation was taking place. A team of scientists, German and Chinese, were working on a state-of-the-art Siemens BS2000 mainframe computer.[5] That the computer was there at all was the result of years of negotiations, and a stipend from the World Bank, which had expressed concern that China was some twenty years behind advanced economies in terms of technological development.[6] One of the chief drivers of the project was Werner Zorn, a square-jawed and sandy-haired West German who worked tirelessly to secure funding for the computers, finding a loophole in Cold War-era restrictions on selling to Communist bloc nations in order to export them to China.[7]

Zorn had already seen success connecting his own country to the burgeoning global internet, and in late 1987 he flew to China to help his counterparts there do the same. In Beijing he met Wang Yunfeng, a professor at the snappily named Chinese Institute for Computer Applications of State Commission of Machine Industry. The pair were kindred spirits, working long hours with the unthinking optimism of many technologists of the era. Government restrictions and geopolitics were irrelevant; all that mattered was achieving their goal of connecting China to the world.[8]

On 14 September 1987, the team huddled around a small, boxy white terminal to see the fruition of their years of work. In

German and English (there were no ways of inputting Chinese at the time), Wang slowly typed out "across the Great Wall, we can reach every corner in the world", followed by a triumphant "this is the first ELECTRONIC MAIL supposed to be sent from China into the international scientific networks via computer interconnection". He added his own name, and those of Zorn and eleven other colleagues, and pressed send. Nothing happened – error. It would take another six days before the email was finally delivered, but history had been made.[9]

For Wang, the reference to the Great Wall may have been patriotic kitsch, but it had some historical resonance.[10] While the Wall was primarily a defensive structure, a procession of signal towers along its length also allowed it to act as a rudimentary semaphore, using coloured smoke signals to warn of attack or call to the capital for reinforcements.[11] But just as the Wall was built due to the fear of foreign invasion, so the internet would come to be seen as an outside threat.

Like their counterparts elsewhere, China's leaders initially saw the internet as primarily a tool for scholars and scientists to share information, not a particular source of concern.[12] Even by 1994, five years after mass pro-democracy protests had rocked Chinese society and the Tiananmen Square massacre had thrown a spanner in Beijing's claims of reform, only around 2,000 people, mostly academics, had access to the internet.[13] But change came rapidly. Within two years, the country's first commercial internet service launched and computer ownership exploded nationwide. Online bulletin boards began popping up on university servers – bringing with them discussion of sensitive topics and the sharing of forbidden information. While they may have been slow to realise the potential the internet had for fostering social change, both the Party and its detractors soon caught on. "If the students had email during the Tiananmen Square protests in 1989, student leaders in different cities could have been united," one activist said in 1998. "The news of the massacre could have spread overnight, the authorities couldn't block the news. It could have been a very different situation."[14]

The same thought was probably on the mind of Premier Li Peng – the much loathed conservative seen by most Chinese as the architect of the Tiananmen massacre – when, on 1 February 1996 he signed State Council Order 195: "Temporary regulations governing computer information networks and the internet."[15] This gave the state absolute control over the internet and its future development. A year later, the Ministry of Public Security promulgated a series of rules forbidding, among other things, the use of the internet for "inciting to overthrow the government or the socialist system".[16] It also placed regulation and supervision of the internet firmly under the remit of the security services.

*

The Party's predilection for controlling information has a long history that dates back well before the invention of the internet, when the censors would block books and films from being imported into China, or cut offending articles out of newspapers. But the internet, far from its boosters' optimism that it would act as a vaccine against censorship, gave the Chinese authorities the capability to control and surveil in a way that would be nearly impossible in an analogue world. From the beginning of the internet's development in China, censorship came built in, and the government has worked to expand its reaches ever since.

Internet censorship in China occurs on two main levels: internationally, as traffic passes from the global web into the country; and locally, within Chinese internet service providers and web companies. The first level is known as the Great Firewall, while the second has its origins in what was dubbed the Golden Shield Project. Increasingly, the term Great Firewall has also come to refer to all Chinese censorship, no matter the level at which it occurs. While this is not the most technically accurate descriptor for the multitude of interlinking and overlapping systems that result in content being censored on the Chinese internet, nor is it helpful to separate each function out too much, as they are all part of a whole and should be viewed as such. Equally important, 'Great Firewall' is a term coined by critics of the censorship apparatus and the one most widely used by dissidents and those who fight against online controls. Using it as a general descriptor is far preferable to adopting the propagandistic newspeak of terms such as Golden Shield or Green Dam, another proposed censorship system.

At the international level, the Great Firewall really is a firewall: a piece of software that blocks certain types of content and allows others. To do this, the Firewall inspects every piece of traffic, or packet, it handles, allowing most content but stopping anything forbidden. The process can be fairly simplistic: for example, if a user attempts to load the URL Twitter.com, which is blocked in China, the Firewall will cut the connection and all they will see is an error page. The same occurs for any IP addresses – designating the physical computer servers from which Twitter operates – associated with the service. This can also be done for URLs within websites. Until 2015, Wikipedia was mostly unblocked in China, but specific pages that discussed sensitive topics were censored. Most people will have experienced school or university firewalls that blocked access to 'inappropriate' web pages – many office workers still experience this – and this is also how those systems work.

Of course, the Great Firewall is considerably more advanced than office or school systems. If it wasn't, users could easily bypass it by setting up mirrors of sensitive sites on unblocked URLs or servers (although they would quickly end up in a game of cat and mouse with the censors) or by using proxy services – which route internet traffic through another website, concealing its true purpose – to access banned sites. The Great Firewall, however, has shown itself adept at defeating almost any tool invented to get around it. It does this by inspecting the traffic itself, not just its source or destination. For example, if a user is trying to visit a hitherto unblocked website containing information about the banned religious movement Falun Gong, the Firewall can detect keywords related to the group and drop the connection (and flag the website for more thorough review). While encrypting traffic, or the use of proxies and other more sophisticated tools such as virtual private networks (VPNs), can prevent this inspection to a greater or lesser extent, this is by no means a perfect method for avoiding the censors. If a user in Beijing is encrypting all their traffic and piping it through a VPN server based in California, they probably have something to hide from the censors. Although the Firewall cannot block the individual websites they are visiting, because it can't see their traffic, it can slow or block their internet access entirely, or prevent them from connecting to the VPN servers next time they log on. More perniciously, it can also prompt a follow-up, a face-to-face interview by security agents, who may discover what exactly the user is trying to hide. At times of heightened political sensitivity, the censors have even blocked the protocols that allow VPNs to function entirely, preventing anyone from accessing them, despite the fact that many businesses use such services for completely innocent purposes, such as connecting to a work intranet or increased security for sensitive transactions.[17]

The Great Firewall exists at multiple levels, disseminated across the routers and switches that make up the backbone of the Chinese internet, and at the consumer level within internet service providers (ISPs).[18] When a user in China tries to load a web page, their ISP pings a list of forbidden URLs and types of content. If the page is not banned, the request is passed to an internet access point (IAP), which handles routing traffic to servers all over China and around the world. It's at this stage that packet inspection takes place, looking for keywords and suspicious flags. When the destination server sends the web-page data back to the user, it is inspected again. Only if it clears all these hurdles is the internet browser able to load anything. (This is why loading sites hosted outside China, even completely innocent ones, can take an age.)

Such inspection and filtering is no easy task – there's a reason why school firewalls settle for just blocking URLs – and is made possible only thanks to the physical structure of the Chinese internet, and the vast sums the government has shown itself willing to spend on internet censorship. Nearly all connections between China and the global internet occur at three choke points where vast internet exchanges route traffic to the huge fibre-optic network that forms the global internet backbone, and eventually to websites and servers in other countries. These choke points are located in Beijing in the north, Shanghai on the east coast, and the southern city of Guangzhou, near Hong Kong. Blocking at this level is often deliberately obfuscated: when loading a forbidden website, users are presented with an error page similar to the one they see when a website is down, or their wifi connection has dropped, making it difficult to state unequivocally that something has been censored.

While these filters are important, the centrepiece of the Great Firewall is the system of internal controls that operates within the country's borders. Most Chinese users aren't visiting overseas websites – the majority of them aren't in Chinese for a start. Chinese and Russian state media both have large English-language operations, but few internet users in Iowa are checking them to see if they're reporting information censored by Washington. While the border filters are there to keep check of anyone attempting to stray outside China's walled garden, the important pruning work is going on within.

That the system works so well is in part thanks to US corporations and engineers, particularly the Silicon Valley-based multinational Cisco, which began supplying filtering and surveillance equipment to Chinese censors in the early 1990s. In 2001, the Canada-based International Centre for Human Rights and Democratic Development estimated that China was buying as much as $20 billion worth of telecoms equipment every year,[19] mostly from US firms, and accounting for up to 25 per cent of the global market. In the words of internet historians Tim Wu and Jack Goldsmith, the Great Firewall was originally built "with American bricks".[20]

One of those American bricklayers was Michael Robinson.[21] He had been working as a computer engineer at the University of California Berkeley when he was suddenly laid off in 1993. "I literally didn't have anything better to do," he told me. "So I went to go teach English in China for a year."

One year turned into two, and he got a job at a research lab in Beijing. Robinson's supervisor asked him to help connect the lab to the internet, which was just beginning to be available in China. "I read in the local English-language paper that the post and telecoms office was handing out free internet accounts for a pilot programme, so I went down and signed the lab up," he said. "Immediately it became apparent there were a lot of problems with this internet service." Robinson dug into the connections and discovered that a lot of the system was not set up properly. He managed to find the email address for an administrator and began sending suggestions – "If you change this config file here this is going to start working, add this here, this thing is broken this way." He didn't know it, but he was applying for a job.

In the early 1990s, Sprint, the American technology giant, had been contracted by China Telecom to build China's first commercial internet.[22] Sprint in turn enlisted the help of a pair of US-educated Chinese scientists, Edward Tian and James Ding. The pair built the backbone of what would become ChinaNet, the first non-educational Chinese network, beginning with linking up computers in Beijing to the global internet. At the time, there were very few experienced network engineers in China, so when Robinson began emailing suggestions on how to improve his lab's connection, Sprint leaped at the chance to hire him.

"I already had twelve years of experience using the internet and internet technology; for everyone else in the world, practically speaking, this was a brand new thing," he said. It worked out well for both parties: Robinson received a significant increase on his meagre academic salary, and Sprint got a world-class engineer who knew China and was happy get paid comparatively nothing next to what his counterparts made in the US. He helped the company put together a demo for senior Party leadership in Beijing and got approval for the project to roll out nationwide. "It was on the same sort of justification Al Gore had used: national infrastructure," he said. "The Chinese were thinking, 'Well, if the Americans are building this, maybe we should get in on that.'"

At the time, there were only a few thousand Chinese internet users, but the bandwidth still struggled to keep up, with the entire country sharing the equivalent of what was a home connection in the US. Chinese-language support was also pretty spotty, and most users were forced to use English interfaces and websites. There was also no unified system of displaying Chinese characters, which meant that messages which appeared fine on one system could be unreadable on another.

In January 1995, Sprint launched two dedicated lines connected to the US, through Beijing and Shanghai, and two months later dial-up access began to expand throughout China.[23] In May of that year, China Telecom began plans for a national internet backbone, and Sprint attempted to cut its local partners out of the new, extremely lucrative, deal. In response, Tian and Ding launched their own company, AsiaInfo, which was able to beat Sprint to the contract.[24] A few years later, Tian launched China Netcom Communications (CNC), with direct support from the Chinese leadership, including Jiang Zemin, whose son sat on the board. CNC began importing millions of dollars' worth of Cisco routers and switches, and by 2002 it had connected seventeen of China's largest cities with more than 8,600 kilometres of fibre-optic cable, in trenches dug by tens of thousands of workers.

Even as Chinese companies took over the core infrastructure contracts, there was still plenty of money to be made. "The internet was wildly successful beyond anybody's imagination," Robinson said. "You couldn't believe how it took off and how profitable it was. There was definitely an alignment of political will and profit motive to expand internet access throughout the country as rapidly as possible." For a time in Beijing, the internet was everywhere – on billboards and the sides of buses – as the country followed the government's lead on going all in on the new technology.

The Party wasn't completely sold on the internet, however. "For some time I was the only Westerner who had access to the global blocking list," Robinson said. "There was definitely a concern that they did not want to install something that they couldn't control if they needed to." Content that attracted the censors' ire was not always the most obvious: two of the first three sites to be blocked were run by Maoists. For a long time, the censors were happy to have a relatively light touch, safe in the knowledge that if they needed to control things they could. Nor was the censorship network Robinson and other engineers put in place particularly ground-breaking. It utilised the same basic filtering technology Cisco and other companies were providing to major firms across the US. "Nobody questions the authority and the right of a corporation to very tightly manage and control and monitor the communications in and out of a company's network," Robinson said. "That tech had been built from the very beginning to serve the market of corporate customers. All China did was turn on those switches for the entire country."

As China neared the turn of the century, the censors were thoroughly established. But a new generation of internet activist was arising as well – seasoned pro-democracy fighters who recognised better than the authorities the potential of the internet as an engine of solidarity and dissent. It was only a matter of time before things came to a head.

Chapter 3

Nailing the jello

Chinese democracy and the Great Firewall

Li Hongkuan was a spammer extraordinaire.[1] Beginning in 1997, he built up a database of hundreds of thousands of email addresses, collecting those available online or trading them with others in the same business. Particularly useful were university servers, which often had little to no security, allowing Li or one of his assistants to grab the email addresses of all the staff and students who ever signed up for an account.

That year, he launched his newsletter, *Da Cankao*, known in English as *VIP Reference*. Compiled by Li and a team of volunteers, *Da Cankao* collected articles that had been censored in China and translated sensitive stories from the foreign press before dumping them into the inboxes of thousands of unsuspecting users. By spamming people with the newsletter, it not only spread far and wide, but also gave recipients plausible deniability if they were found in possession of a copy. One exceedingly unwilling subscriber was Qing Gang, head of the Shanghai police computer security supervision department. In a spectacularly over the top interview with a US newspaper, Qing described the newsletter as "spiritual pollution".

"If there was something you didn't need, and I sent it to you by force, could you accept that?" he said. "Would you be disgusted or not?"[2]

For those who received it willingly, *Da Cankao* could be revelatory, opening their eyes to a world of dissident thought and alternative sources of information they never knew existed. Zhao Jing, who would go on to become a famous dissident writer himself, under the pen name Michael Anti, was twenty-three when he first received a copy of the newsletter, in 1998. He was living in Nanjing, a large but still somewhat provincial city in eastern China. "It was like a culture shock," Zhao told me. "I thought, 'Oh my god,' all this news is very sensitive." Before discovering *Da Cankao*, he knew almost nothing about Chinese politics, beyond what was in state media, which contained no critiques or debate. "Suddenly you see there's this discussion going on. It really opened your mind."

The name of the newsletter harkened back to the turmoil of Li's childhood in the 1960s and 1970s. Classified reports had always been written for the country's top leadership, filed in secret by state media reporters across the country, giving a critical view of goings-on that would never be permitted in the newspapers they normally filed for. Outside the privileged world of those who received the uncensored reports, they were known as '*da cankao*', or 'big reference'. The nickname was derived from *Cankao Xiaoxi*, a newspaper collating foreign news reports that was available only to Party members, and known popularly as 'little reference' (*xiao cankao*).[3] During the Cultural Revolution, normal communication networks broke down, and the *da cankao* reports became one of the few remaining reliable sources of information.[4] Titbits would seep out to the general public through the children of senior officials, who would sneak a look at their parents' briefings and tell their friends of the chaos spreading around the country.

For Li, the name was also a way to insult the old men in charge of the Party, who needed their reports printed out in extra-large type. "For my generation, whoever experienced the Tiananmen massacre, we all hated the government," he told me.

Li had been in the square himself, hours before the tanks rolled in. An assistant professor at Beijing Medical University, he had been taking photographs on 3 June with a camera borrowed from a colleague. The mood among the protesters was tense and noisy. Many leaders of the movement and older intellectuals had already urged the students to vacate the square, to consolidate their victories and prepare for the next stage of the struggle, before the government moved to wipe them out completely. There were signs that such a decision was coming: Deng Xiaoping had declared martial law two weeks earlier, and throughout 3 June state television broadcast warnings to stay off the streets, saying that troops would use "any and all means" to enforce order.[5] Thousands of People's Liberation Army troops were already at the outskirts of the city, and scuffles were breaking out between them and local residents. Concerned more for the safety of his colleague's camera than his own person, Li reluctantly decided to leave the square and go home at around 9pm. Unbeknownst to him, as he moved away from the square, shots had already been fired in the western parts of the city, and the tanks were rumbling towards Tiananmen. He slept through the first parts of the massacre, and woke up to find the world had changed.

While he escaped the bullets, Li did not come out of the protests unscathed. Weeks before 4 June, he had volunteered to go to his graduate school in Shanghai to help "spread the fire". Li's speech was recorded so that it could be passed on to other universities in the city, but after the protests ended, one of those tapes made it back to Beijing and to his employer. He was lucky, in that the school's Party secretary was not much of a true believer; Li was dismissed from his teaching duties but allowed to keep his staff accommodation while he searched for another job. 'There's no way we can employ you with this material,' the Party secretary told him, gesturing to a transcript of his speech. 'But you're young and bright; you should go to America.'

Two years later, aged twenty-eight, Li did just that. He landed a visa for a research job at the Albert Einstein College of Medicine in New York. The Party had hoped to shuffle him out of the way, like so many other dissidents and independent thinkers who were encouraged (or forced) to go into exile. But freed from the watchful gaze of the authorities, and still seething with anger about Tiananmen, Li became far more of a problem for the authorities than he ever was in Beijing. In New York in the mid-1990s, he reconnected with other members of the student movement, volunteering his time and a burgeoning expertise in computers, which he had first become interested in a few years before. Li was particularly keen to find ways to get uncensored information into China, and worked with others to translate and publish stories about the country online. But dissident groups attract intense personalities, and their shared commitment to democracy could not paper over the many other ideological differences. Inevitably, there were disagreements, as members clashed over what should be published and what shouldn't, splitting into rival factions and organisations. Eventually, Li did what so many others were doing and decided to start his own publication, free from the 'suppression' not only of the authorities, but also of his fellow dissidents.

This could have been the start of a slide into irrelevance, but Li's timing was impeccable, coming after a much hyped 'year of the internet' in which the new technology had received breathless media coverage in China, massively expanding the number of people buying computers and getting online.[6] Thousands had signed up for email addresses through universities and the handful of semi-private providers springing up at the time, and pro-democracy websites were beginning to be blocked en masse, making them impossible to read without going through a proxy service, details about which were hard to come by, and which also slowed down the already clunky late 1990s internet speeds to a crawl. On 17 September 1997, Li delivered the first issue of *Da Cankao* into thousands of inboxes across China.

To build up his database and help spread the newsletter – subscribers were encouraged not to forward issues of *Da Cankao* in order to avoid getting into trouble with the authorities – Li and his volunteers searched for email addresses wherever they could, including trading with other spammers. "I had a policy that if you give me 10,000 email addresses I'll give you 10,000 as a swap," Li said. "People with an entrepreneurial spirit loved to get in touch with me."

One of those entrepreneurs was Lin Hai, a baby-faced thirty-year-old with deep-set eyes and a mop of thick, black hair. A born capitalist, he recognised before many in China the potential of the internet for making money.[7] In the late 1990s, there were just over 2 million Chinese online, concentrated in major cities and on university campuses,[8] but while the number of internet users was growing rapidly, the amount of businesses catering to them was limited. Lin founded a company in Shanghai offering basic web design and software-engineering services. With search technology still in its infancy, he advertised his products via email, and it was through this that he came into contact with Li Hongkuan.

It proved to be an unfortunate connection. On 25 March 1998, police barged down the door of the apartment Lin shared with his wife and young child, and began ransacking it.[9] They seized his computer, floppy disks, modem and other equipment.[10] Lin Hai had inadvertently become China's first internet dissident.

In a fast-tracked trial held behind closed doors, he was charged with "subversion of state power and the socialist system".[11] Even his wife, Xu Hong, was blocked from attending. In an emotional letter to the court, she said Lin had simply been providing public information by trading email addresses with Li and was not involved in the delivery of subversive materials. "If someone is killed with a knife, should you arrest the knife maker, or the murderer?" she wrote. Both she and Lin maintained throughout the process that he was a simple businessman, and unpolitical, although emails introduced as evidence in court suggested that he had a more than passing familiarity with the content of *Da Cankao* and may have sympathised with its pro-democracy message. Li said that whether Lin was explicitly political was beside the point; he saw Lin as another member of the Tiananmen generation, with the same 'natural' loathing of the government as him.

Despite the best efforts of Lin's lawyers, and his wife's pleadings, the Shanghai No. 1 Intermediate People's Court found Lin guilty after just four hours of deliberations, and sentenced him to two years in prison. The trial, which was covered widely in the international press, was indicative of much of what was to come, both in the authorities' ruthlessness in cracking down on online activism, and the foreign media's smug eye rolling at China's parochial attempts to control the internet. A *Wall Street Journal* report from the time was typical:

> China may be fighting a losing battle. While it blocks some websites, Chinese internet users have no trouble reading a variety of political views online ... Pornography is also easily accessible. And a growing number of Chinese internet users maintain web-based email accounts that can't be accessed by Chinese security organisations.[12]

Within years, the term 'Great Firewall', which had been coined by *Wired* magazine in 1997, was famous worldwide. Some Chinese even welcomed the advance of the censors. One internet café owner told reporters that an internet which allowed individuals "to do as they please, lets them go brazenly wherever they wish, is a hegemonist network that harms the rights of others". The man, who put a banner reading "Information Industries of China Unite!" atop his business's homepage, said the internet at the time was an "English hegemony" and needed to be challenged by "an exclusively Chinese-language network".[13]

*

On the morning of 28 June 1998, Wang Youcai entered the Civil Affairs Bureau in Hangzhou, the old imperial capital a couple hours south-west of Shanghai. A former Tiananmen student leader who was imprisoned for several years over his role in the protests,[14] Wang was one of a number of pro-democracy activists who hoped to take advantage of a sudden relaxation of political suppression in the late 1990s, as China assumed control over the British colony of Hong Kong and sought to join the World Trade Organization (WTO).[15] The so-called 'Beijing Spring' saw the release of pro-democracy icon Wei Jingsheng[16] and the signing – though not ratification – of the International Covenant on Civil and Political Rights.[17] A state visit by US President Bill Clinton was thought to be the perfect time to push the boundaries even further, and so Wang and two others walked into the government building near Hangzhou's famous West Lake and attempted to register, legally and openly, a new political organisation: the China Democracy Party (CDP). As the stunned registrar was refusing to accept the registration and ushering them out of the building, the new party's manifesto was posted online and sent out to the hundreds of thousands of *Da Cankao* subscribers around the country.[18]

Wang was swiftly arrested and the CDP banned, but in the months that followed, other dissidents set up regional branches of the Party throughout the country, and continued to organise online.[19] In November, members took it a step further and sought permission from the State Council to form a 'national preparatory committee' ahead of a formal Party congress. This was too much for the authorities, and a crackdown was ordered. Dozens of CDP members were arrested, and in December 1998, Wang Youcai and two other leaders, Xu Wendi and Qin Yongmin, were imprisoned on charges of "endangering state security".[20] Wang would not be released until 2004.[21] With characteristic disregard for foreign opinion, Premier Li Peng told a German newspaper matter of factly: "[I]f a group is designed to negate the leadership of the Communist Party, then it will not be allowed to exist."[22]

While some foreigners may have been put off, the jailing of Wang Youcai and subsequent crackdown on the CDP, which included intense censorship of the group's materials online, did little to shake Washington's confidence in China. In early 2000, the Clinton administration normalised trade relations with China, clearing the way for Beijing to join the WTO. The president and his supporters were confident not only about the benefits free trade would bring to the world, but that more open markets would also open up China politically. Speaking in Washington, Clinton hailed the new century, in which "liberty will be spread by cell phone and cable modem".[23] China, whose leaders he had denounced eight years before as the "butchers of Beijing", was changing.[24]

"In the past year, the number of internet addresses in China has more than quadrupled, from two million to nine million," Clinton continued in his easy Arkansas drawl. "This year the number is expected to grow to over twenty million. When China joins the World Trade Organization, by 2005 it will eliminate tariffs on information technology products, making the tools of communication even cheaper, better and more widely available. We know how much the internet has changed America, and we are already an open society. Imagine how much it could change China."

Clinton paused for applause. "Now there's no question China has been trying to crack down on the internet – good luck," he said, his eyebrows arched, to laughs from the crowd, as he neared the punchline. "That's sort of like trying to nail jello to the wall."

In the years since Clinton's speech, China's censors have mostly proved him wrong. They have nailed the jello to the wall more securely and easily than even the most hardened cynic would have imagined in 2000. Throughout this effort, though, they have faced intense opposition both within and from outside China. No group has proven the difficulties of instituting comprehensive censorship, more shaken both the censors and the Party, and inspired a greater crackdown than a collection of mostly middle-aged followers of a mystic from northern China who encouraged healthy living and breathing exercises. The effort to stamp them out online would see the Great Firewall built to new heights, and open up a new front in the war for China's internet.

Chapter 4

Enemy at the gates

How fear of Falun Gong boosted the Firewall

To the west of Beijing's Forbidden City, Fuyou Street snakes between a cluster of traditional *hutong* courtyard residences and the sprawling government complex known as Zhongnanhai, which is abutted north and south by two lakes, with the old imperial seat to its east. Along one side of Fuyou Street runs a tall red wall topped with faux Qing dynasty crenellations, and it was this people gathered next to now, clustering together to avoid stepping into the road and blocking traffic. They had begun to arrive in the early hours of the morning of 26 April 1999,[1] talking softly with one and other, and occasionally passing bottles of water around. Spring in Beijing is chilly and brisk, and the crowd wore puffy jackets and big coats. Most were middle-aged, and many spoke with accents indicating that they were from outside Beijing, come to the capital from China's industrial heartlands in the north-east.[2] By 8am, there were thousands on the street, and the line of protesters stretched up Fuyou Street and around to the northern side of Zhongnanhai. Some of the protesters sat on the ground in the yoga-like poses of Falun Gong, a religious movement based on traditional Chinese practices that had emerged a few years earlier, attracting millions of followers. Others stood, waiting. There were no banners, no shouted slogans; they had come there with a purpose and were determined to see it through. As one protester told a reporter: "You cannot solve our problem, only the government can do this. Therefore, we want to talk only to the government."[3]

At the height of the protest, more than 10,000 people had gathered around Zhongnanhai. Ten years after Tiananmen, in the heart of Beijing, a mass protest had broken out on the government's doorstep, seemingly out of the Party's control and to the complete shock of the security services. It was an unheard of, impossible challenge to the central government, and it demanded a reaction.

When that reaction came, in the form of an intense crackdown that saw hundreds killed and thousands arrested across China, it was accompanied by extreme levels of censorship. Falun Gong founder Li Hongzhi's books were banned, as was disseminating copies of his speeches or other Falun Gong material.[4] Online, positive references to Falun Gong were scrubbed and all of the group's websites were blocked by the Great Firewall. Early studies of Chinese internet censorship found that terms and websites relating to Falun Gong were among the most filtered, along with the homepages of human rights organisations.[5] Such was the verboten nature of any mention of Falun Gong that the group became something of a baseline measure of censorship, mentioned in seemingly every article about the Great Firewall. When *New York Times* columnist Nick Kristof joined Chinese microblogging platform Weibo in 2010, one of his first posts to test the service was to ask "Can we talk about Falun Gong?" His account was quickly deleted.[6] Falun Gong practitioners within China were also the earliest targets of a massive surveillance apparatus, built in part by Western companies, which has since expanded to threaten all dissidents and critics of the Party. From outside China, Falun Gong practitioners would also become some of the most important enemies of the Firewall, working to undermine and destroy it.

*

Falun Gong began in Jilin in China's far north-east, on the border with North Korea, in late 1992. Once part of the Japanese puppet state of Manchukuo, industrialisation policies started by Tokyo were enthusiastically adopted by the Party once it came to power, and the province, along with neighbouring Heilongjiang and Liaoning, became China's factory belt, home to much of the country's heavy industry. Under Communism, hundreds of thousands of workers in the province had 'iron rice bowl' jobs with state enterprises: guaranteed employment, housing, and social benefits. Under Deng Xiaoping's reforms, however, as China moved towards market capitalism, the iron rice bowls were broken, and thousands were left without work, forced to compete in the new privatised economy.

The loss of their jobs and healthcare left many in the region dejected and disillusioned, and Jilin became a hotbed for new religious movements, traditional medicine revivalists, and snake oil salesmen. Li Hongzhi mixed elements of all of these when he invented Falun Gong, which emerged out of a surge in enthusiasm for qigong in the 1980s and 1990s that saw hundreds of prospective masters battling it out for followers.[7] Elements of qigong date back to ancient China, but the practice itself was invented and popularised in the 1950s, before being integrated into the developing field of 'traditional Chinese medicine' promoted by the Party as a substitute for its abandoned promise of free healthcare for all.[8] The term refers to the practice of cultivating or balancing one's *qi*, a life force or energy flow, using yoga-like exercises and clean living, and by following various spiritual teachings. Suppressed during the Cultural Revolution, qigong did not really take off until Deng's reforms kicked in, at which point it exploded, becoming a nationwide obsession. It was practised by millions of ordinary people in parks and squares, and even by the country's leaders, in their exclusive seaside resort of Beidaihe.[9]

Li Hongzhi was born in the early 1950s, around the start of the first qigong craze, in Jilin province.[10] Like many of his cohort, his schooling was interrupted by the chaos of the Cultural Revolution, and he completed his secondary education years later by correspondence course. According to his official Falun Gong biography, which was initially widely publicised but is now largely absent from the group's websites, from the age of eight Li studied with two great masters, learning to cultivate "truth, compassion, and forbearance" and becoming a master of the Chinese martial art, gongfu.[11] This likely fictional – or at least heavily embellished – origin story is in keeping with those of other contemporary qigong masters, but it became a key point of attack for the Chinese government when it began the anti-Falun Gong campaign, with Party researchers interviewing Li's family, childhood friends and schoolteachers in an attempt to debunk its claims;[12] this may explain why it no longer appears in most group sources.

What no one disagrees about is that Li began teaching his version of qigong in Jilin in the early 1990s, before moving to Beijing as his fame grew. He named his movement Falun Gong to reflect its Buddhist elements, such as the dharma wheel, or *falun*. By the end of 1992, Li and his teachings had been endorsed by the official China Qigong Science Research Society (CQRS),[13] and he began touring the country, giving lectures and establishing practice centres and training schools.[14] At this time, Li was just one of many qigong masters, and there was nothing to indicate that his group would be singled out for a government crackdown. Indeed, for much of the early 1990s, his books were printed by government-linked publishing houses, and he was regularly invited to speak to prominent officials.

Just as Li was becoming more and more popular, however, official opinion began to turn against qigong. While there had always been critics of the movement, including in prominent government positions, they had previously been outvoted by its supporters. The most prominent of these backers was Zhang Zhenhuan, a former People's Liberation Army general, veteran of the wars against Japan and the Guomindang, and the director of China's early nuclear weapons programme.[15] In his retirement, Zhang directed the CQRS and was a fierce proponent of the health benefits of qigong practice.[16] After his death in March 1994 at the age of seventy-nine, qigong lost one of its most strident defenders, and criticism of the practice increased. Much of this backlash was well deserved: qigong masters frequently made absurd claims and performed supposedly miraculous feats that were little more than magic tricks. During the boom, qigong rallies and teaching sessions resembled those of televangelists in the US, replete with practitioners dissolving into fits of reverence and claiming to be healed of long-term ailments. Many of the tricks performed by qigong masters were similar to those of self-proclaimed psychics in the West, such as bending spoons or breaking bricks with their heads. At the height of the craze, those who questioned or criti-cised qigong masters could find themselves hounded by followers, and even attacked. Sima Nan, a former qigong practitioner turned fervent critic, claimed that he was attacked, detained and suffered "two crushed vertebrae, a crushed trachea and other injuries" at the hands of qigong defenders,[17] before the tide turned and he became a much sought-after cult-buster, praised by the Chinese government and prominent Western sceptics including Christopher Hitchens.[18] Other anti-qigong intellectuals, such as He Zuoxiu, a leading member of the Chinese Academy of Sciences, compared the practice to the Japanese Aum Shinrikyo cult, which carried out the deadly Tokyo subway sarin attack in 1995.[19]

Li initially attempted to harness some of this anti-qigong sentiment by casting Falun Gong as its more scientific, less huck-sterish form. Despite his bombastic claims about Falun Gong giving followers supernatural abilities, Li largely avoided the demonstration of these powers himself, unlike other qigong masters who frequently performed magic tricks and faith healing in public. As Falun Gong scholar David Palmer writes:

> [Li] redefined his method as having entirely different objectives from qigong: the purpose of practice should be neither physical health nor the development of extraordinary powers, but to purify one's heart and attain spiritual salvation.[20]

Breathing exercises could help towards this goal, but they had to be combined with study of Falun Gong texts, particularly *Zhuan Falun*, published in 1994 and still Li's most important work. There was also a strict moral code, akin to a cross between Christianity and Buddhism, with a focus on purity, absolution of one's sins, and attaining enlightenment. In *Zhuan Falun*, Li writes:

> It was Dafa – the Great Way of the universe – that created the cosmic body, the universe, life, and all of creation. Any life that turns away from Dafa is truly corrupt. Any person who can align with Dafa is truly a good person, and will be rewarded and blessed with health and happiness. And any cultivator who is able to become one with Dafa is an enlightened one – divine.[21]

While Li would consistently deny that he was leading a religion – only five of which are officially recognised in China, and all are strictly regulated – it was this transformation from a health practice into a faith movement that enabled Falun Gong, which followers began increasingly to refer to as Falun Dafa, to survive in the face of growing opposition. Other qigong groups, unable to find funding and publish their materials as the government turned against the practice, lost followers in droves, but the millions of Falun Gong practitioners were resilient. Their struggles were seen as necessary to redress the karmic balance and achieve enlightenment, just as a Christian martyr is defiant in the face of oppression, knowing their reward will come in heaven.

Wary of the growing opposition, and perhaps sensing a coming crackdown, Li left China in early 1995 and moved to the United States. For all his genius as a teacher and salesman, once outside the country and dependent on his advisers for information, Li showed himself to be a severely lacklustre tactician. His first major misstep was in withdrawing Falun Gong from the CQRS in November 1996, reportedly in order to avoid paying the organisation dues as revenue from *Zhuan Falun* and other texts skyrocketed. Attempts to register the group as a 'social organisation' in order to avoid being swept up in the growing anti-qigong campaign failed, however, and Falun Gong was left without any official imprimatur or institutional defenders.[22]

Li's worst mistake would prove almost fatal for his movement. Throughout the mid-1990s, as criticism of qigong in general and Falun Gong in particular grew, Li encouraged a blistering public relations strategy akin to the Party's own regular protestations that countries or businesses have "hurt the feelings of the Chinese people". Between June 1996 and April 1999, Falun Gong practitioners staged some 300 peaceful demonstrations outside newspaper offices, TV stations and universities, calling for the retraction or 'correction' of negative reports about the group.[23] Emboldened by the easy success of these protests (which were also carried out to a lesser extent by other qigong groups), Li and other Falun Gong leaders were ill prepared for any pushback, and, when it came, they massively overplayed their hand.

*

In 1999, Shi Caidong was a twenty-eight-year-old postgraduate student at the Chinese Academy of Sciences.[24] The day before the Zhongnanhai protest, he had gone to his usual practice site, where he and other Falun Gong adherents met to do exercises and discuss Li Hongzhi's teachings. One of the women there told him about a protest in Tianjin, a city about ninety minutes east of Beijing, where hundreds of practitioners had gathered outside the offices of a magazine after it had published an article critical of Falun Gong. The demonstration had been peaceful, but as more and more people began joining and it stretched into a fourth day without any sign of the magazine caving in to the protesters' demands, riot police were sent in to disperse the crowd and arrest dozens of protesters. The article was part of a growing swell of criticism against Falun Gong, which had already seen the group's main text, *Zhuan Falun*, banned from publication. Shi and his fellow practitioners were incensed: the actions taken against the group were unconstitutional, but officials wouldn't listen to their protests or attempts to explain the matter. As aggrieved Chinese citizens have done for centuries, they decided to take their complaints to the highest authority, the central government offices in Beijing.

Now in his late forties and living in the US, where he emigrated in 2002, Shi told his story slowly and purposefully, as if he had done so many times in the past. At first we spoke in Mandarin, but when my Chinese failed and his English couldn't fill in the gaps, his wife offered to translate, speaking in lightly accented English and occasionally hurrying her husband when he repeated himself or misunderstood a question.

When Shi reached the central government compound at Zhong-nanhai, at around 7am, the pavement was already thronged with people, and nervous-looking police officers were pacing the length of the crowd, unsure of what to do. Shi was at something of a loss as well; he walked along the road looking for any practitioners he knew. As he neared the junction with Xi'anmen Street and the compound's western entrance, Shi heard a rumble of applause and saw Premier Zhu Rongji coming out to meet the crowd. A sprightly, no-nonsense seventy-year-old, Zhu had recently returned from a trip to the US, and had to be woken early to deal with something that wasn't supposed to happen in Beijing: a mass protest.

'Why have you come here?' he asked the crowd, flanked by several security officers. Greeted with a clamour of eager voices, he raised his hands and protested he couldn't talk to so many people at once, and asked to speak to the protest's leaders. When the reply came back that there were no leaders, he requested the crowd nominate some.[25] Shi was near Zhu and was one of the first to step forward. Along with two others, he was led inside Zhongnanhai to a reception room, where he was instructed to sit and wait to meet with representatives from the petitions office, the bureau tasked with hearing the complaints and grievances of all of China.

After an extended delay, several officials came and demanded that Shi and the other representatives write down their names, addresses and places of employment before their complaint would be heard. When the interview started, the officials were inundated with injustices both actual and imagined, just as Zhu had been outside. They were eventually able to whittle it down to three main demands: that the protesters arrested in Tianjin be released; that the ban on publication of *Zhuan Falun* be reversed; and that people be allowed to practise Falun Gong freely and without interference.[26] As the conversation continued, however, the officials realised that they weren't talking to protest leaders, only participants, with a loose idea of what the huge demonstration was intended to achieve. They sent Shi and his fellow representatives back outside to find someone more 'senior', and he eventually returned with a man who had been practising Falun Gong since 1994, only two years after Li Hongzhi first began teaching. Leaving Zhongnanhai, Shi gave the officials copies of *Zhuan Falun* as gifts.

According to Kang Xiaoguang, a Chinese academic and Falun Gong critic, the officials met with several groups of protesters, none of whom were able to give a clear set of demands until Li Chang and Wang Zhiwen, leaders of the Falun Gong Research Society, one of the group's top bodies, were called in.[27] Kang, citing government sources, said Li and Wang had not been at the protest themselves but were instead tasked with feeding information back to Li Hongzhi, who was then in Hong Kong.[28] The talks lasted late into the evening until the Falun Gong representatives re-emerged and told the crowd to go home. The authorities, they said, had promised to release the Tianjin protesters and listen to the group's other complaints. Many who had gathered outside Zhongnanhai saw this as a victory for the protesters, as did some Western journalists. An article in *Asiaweek* published two weeks after the protest noted approvingly that the Chinese authorities had, so far, "treated the group with a notably light touch".[29] According to Kang's account, however, other senior Falun Gong figures were frustrated with the lack of any concrete agreement, and Li Hongzhi was angry that the protest had not continued into a second day, as the Tianjin demonstrations had. There was also frustration that neither Li Chang nor Wang Zhiwen had met with any senior Party figures, but had been fobbed off onto lower-level petitions officials.[30]

The Falun Gong leadership's fears turned out to be well founded. The Beijing protest did not spark a reconciliation with the government; instead, a huge crackdown was launched, along with a propaganda campaign the like of which had not been seen since the heights of the Cultural Revolution.[31] In the decade after 1999, hundreds of thousands of Falun Gong practitioners were detained or arrested across China, suffering abuse and torture. Hundreds more were executed, often extrajudicially, or died as a result of their treatment in custody.[32]

As online censorship of Falun Gong ramped up in the early days of the crackdown, offline there were orders for state media to go hard after the group and its founder. Chinese journalists tracked down Li Hongzhi's relatives, friends and teachers to denounce him, and critics of the group claimed that more than 1,400 people had died as a result of practising Falun Gong. In his review of this material, academic David Ownby concluded that while some of the stories are plausible – elderly people stopping certain medications because they believe that qigong exercises will provide the same benefits – little evidence was provided for the total figure, and many stories are repetitive, and suspiciously feature prominent Falun Gong figures, even Li himself, intervening to prevent practitioners seeking medical help or going back onto their medication. Practitioners also told Ownby that there is no injunction against using medicine, particularly life-saving medicine, in Falun Gong teachings.[33] In my own interviews with Falun Gong practitioners, I have been told the same thing. As well as seeking out critics of Li and his followers, state media also ridiculed the group's beliefs, lampooning the same supernatural claims that had once been cheerfully and readily promoted by the Chinese press.

Despite this, many ordinary Chinese were not wholly convinced, and public opinion did not decisively turn against the group until almost two years into the crackdown. This may have been influenced by a lingering belief in the benefits of qigong – which was practised by tens of millions of people at the height of the boom – or by the fact that most people's picture of a typical Falun Gong practitioner was an earnest middle-aged woman doing dorky exercises in the park. This changed radically on 23 January 2001, after one of the most controversial and hotly disputed incidents of the entire crackdown.

As the backlash to the Zhongnanhai protest began, Li had taken a backseat in the hope that he could reach a private settlement with Chinese leaders. In 2001, however, in a New Year's message to his followers, he took a more strident tone than ever before. In what many interpreted as a call to abandon the type of passive non-resistance that had characterised the crackdown until then, Li said followers facing persecution could justifiably "go beyond the limits of forbearance".[34] Weeks later, five alleged Falun Gong practitioners entered Beijing's Tiananmen Square, where they doused each other in petrol, adopted qigong poses, and set themselves alight.[35] A CNN crew happened to be in the square at the time and witnessed the incident from start to finish, before the journalists were dragged away by police. According to an account by CNN Beijing bureau chief Rebecca MacKinnon:

> [The crew] witnessed four more people immolating themselves. They raised their hands above their heads and staggered slowly about, flames tearing through their clothing.
>
> The crew witnessed one of the victims being driven away in a police van. He appeared to have serious burns on his face, and CNN producer Lisa Weaver could smell burning flesh as the van slowly passed. Four other bodies lay on the pavement after authorities put out the flames. Shortly afterward, portable screens were erected in two spots to shield the bodies from view.[36]

Shortly after the incident, the state-run news agency Xinhua issued a short report on its English service (but not the domestic Chinese wire) identifying the five people – a man, two women, and their young daughters – as Falun Gong practitioners from Kaifeng in Henan province, who had been "hoodwinked by the evil fallacies" of Li Hongzhi.[37] Immediately, the official account was contested by Falun Gong spokespeople, who pointed out that Li's teachings forbade suicide.[38] After gory videos of the immolations were broadcast by state TV, as well as footage of the surviving victims in hospital – one immolator died in the initial incident, another passed away later – Falun Gong spokespeople continued to contest the official account. They pointed to a number of anomalies in state media reports, particularly the presence of fire extinguishers in the square at the time of the immolations,[39] and the speed at which Xinhua produced a report on such a sensitive topic, which usually would have taken hours of vetting and authorisation before it could be put out to foreign audiences.[40] Questions were also raised over why there was apparently a state media camera crew on hand to record the incident. While officials said that the footage was confiscated from the CNN team, the US broadcaster denied this, saying its staff were unable to record anything before they were detained.[41] *The Washington Post* also failed to find any friends or relatives of one of the victims in Kaifeng who knew that she had been a Falun Gong practitioner or had ever seen her performing Li's exercises.[42]

As with many incidents in China, barring a sudden decision by the Party to open its archives, the truth may never be known. While scepticism over the official account was expressed outside China, within the country the incident was the final blow to whatever positive reputation Falun Gong still had, and public opinion turned decisively against the group.[43] Attempts by Falun Gong to cast doubt on the official line became increasingly strident, indicative of just how devastating the incident was to its image. Almost two decades later, one of the most prominent sections on Minghui, a major Falun Gong website, was still devoted to debunking the "self-immolation hoax", which it said "remains the single most influential factor in garnering disgust or hatred toward Falun Gong among the Chinese people".[44] Whether state agents orchestrated the incident, as Falun Gong practitioners claim, or the protesters were acting out of desperation and a misunderstanding of a faith that banned suicide, it was a huge win for the government. The Tiananmen incident helped create the caricature common today of Falun Gong practitioners as crazy, brainwashed cultists capable of anything.

That the anti-Falun Gong campaign was so effective was in large part due to the Great Firewall. In turn, the supposed threat posed by the group acted as a defence of the Party's internet control policies: who could argue that a dangerous cult such as Falun Gong, which encouraged children to burn themselves alive, should not be censored and suppressed? To this day, anti-Falun Gong propaganda is so effective both in and outside China that much reporting on the group by foreign media repeats the Party line, or, if it relies on the testimonies of Falun Gong practitioners, is dismissed as overly credulous and unreliable. In my own reporting on the group, I have seen otherwise staunch critics of the Party dismiss Falun Gong claims outright, even if they are supported by objective, verifiable evidence, and self-described Chinese and Western liberals who bemoan the bulldozing of churches or restrictions on Ramadan fasting but cheer the banning of foreign Falun Gong practitioners from coming to China or Hong Kong.

Falun Gong practitioners have not always helped this impression. Understandably desperate to bring attention to the oppression they suffer in China, they often wilfully exaggerate and fabricate claims in order to do so. In Hong Kong and other cities around the world, they stage gory mock demonstrations of the live organ harvesting they allege occurs in Chinese hospitals,[45] which do more to scare away passers-by than concern them. I have even come across some people who assumed that it was Falun Gong themselves who were doing the organ harvesting. The self-immolation incident goes a long way to explaining the increasingly desperate, ham-fisted messaging from the group. If you think the government staged the incident and has everyone convinced that it was your fault, restraint and a commitment to absolute truth probably aren't your top priorities.

Despite the public protests in Hong Kong and elsewhere, Falun Gong's main role in fighting the Party and the Firewall is largely unknown, even to those who benefit from it. For years, Falun Gong practitioners have been among the most active in undermining the Firewall and working to reverse the censorship it carries out. To do so, they have relied on an alliance of conservative anti-Communist US lawmakers, internet freedom advocates and software engineers. One group of allies they could not enlist – indeed, who often worked against them, hand in hand with the censors – was Silicon Valley's biggest companies.

Chapter 5

Searching for an opening

Google, Yahoo and Silicon Valley's moral failing in China

The small crowd wore heavy coats, hats and scarves to guard against the bitter cold of the Beijing winter. Snow was on the ground as they gathered outside the ten-storey concrete and glass building that housed Google China on 12 January 2010. Some laid flowers around the multicoloured sign showing the company's logo, while others read tributes. At night, candles were put on top of the sign, in a sign of mourning.[1]

Inside the Google offices, the atmosphere was even more funereal. The team had been aware of ongoing disputes between Google management and the Chinese government, but the news, dropped that morning, had hit them like a bombshell. Most were still asleep when frantic calls from colleagues in the US woke them and told them to look at the company's official blog.[2] In a post titled 'A new approach to China', senior vice president David Drummond wrote that executives had concluded "we should review the feasibility of our business operations in China".[3]

"The decision to review our business operations in China has been incredibly hard, and we know that it will have potentially far-reaching consequences. We want to make clear that this move was driven by our executives in the United States, without the knowledge or involvement of our employees in China who have worked incredibly hard to make Google.cn the success it is today," Drummond said.

While he was optimistic a solution could be found to allow the company to continue to operate, for anyone with knowledge of the Chinese government the writing was on the wall: Google China was finished. Employees gathered at the company's Beijing head-quarters, unsure whether they had jobs anymore, or if Drummond's careful language meant that there was a chance of legal blowback from the government.[4] Eventually, an executive told them to leave and gave them tickets to see *Avatar*.[5]

When they returned to the offices the next day for a teleconference with Google co-founder Sergey Brin and other senior leadership, staff urged the Silicon Valley higher-ups not to give up on China. Government relations head Julie Zhu compared them to generals, safe at home, who were abandoning their soldiers in a theatre of war. Within weeks, Google began redirecting traffic to its Chinese search engine through its Hong Kong subsidiary instead, "the most significant and embarrassing retreat in the company's history"[6] and an ignominious end to a four-year experiment that had hurt Google's reputation both in China and at home, seen it lose market share, have executives dragged before Congress, and be subjected to one of the worst, most intense cyberattacks its security team had ever experienced.

*

Google launched a Chinese-language version of its search engine in 2000, a year after the company was founded.[7] Right away, it ran into problems with the Great Firewall, and was often slow or inaccessible as the censors tried to push users towards domestic search engines that did not include results for sensitive topics such as the Tiananmen Square massacre or Falun Gong.[8] But Google's Chinese site was never fully blocked, and despite major hurdles, by 2002 the company controlled about 25 per cent of the Chinese market, a level of success never achieved by other foreign search engines.

In August of that year, however, Google was blocked for two weeks, and it was completely banned the following year. Brin told reporters he thought the ban "might have been at the instigation of a competitor", and although he did not name any names, many others pointed the finger at Baidu.[9] The Chinese search engine had been struggling to compete with Google, but it had good connections with the government and on a number of occasions traffic was directed from Google to Baidu during politically sensitive periods.[10] "Basically, some Baidu people sat down and did hundreds of searches for banned materials on Google," one tech executive said at the time. "Then they took all the results, printed them up and went to the government and said, 'Look at all this bad stuff you can find on Google!' That's why the government took Google offline."[11]

Baidu vehemently denied the charge, but no one could deny that it was the greatest beneficiary of the Great Firewall blocking the US search engine. Ahead of the ban, the Chinese search engine also benefited from Google's inability to play as fast and loose as it did with copyright, and users flocked to Baidu to search for illegal MP3s to download. Faced with its first major defeat, Google nonetheless doubled down on China, first by acquiring a minority stake in Baidu,[12] and then by sending a team of executives to the country to scout out when and whether Google could open operations there.

Google was not the only Silicon Valley firm to try to break into China. Nor was recent history for American companies particularly positive in this regard. On 24 September 1999, Yahoo, once the hottest tech company in the world before Google surpassed it, launched a Chinese subsidiary. At the time, Yahoo was still an online directory rather than a search engine, and it promised "an internet guide designed specifically for web users in China".[13] To this end, the Chinese site included headlines from government-friendly sources such as *China Youth Daily*, Xinhua and the Guangzhou Communist Party mouthpiece *Nanfang Daily*, as well as stock quotes and weather forecasts.

While the Chinese offering was initially just one of many rapidly rolled out international versions of Yahoo, the emergence and quick success of Google were eating into its US market share, and Yahoo China became a lot more important to the firm's bottom line. This left Yahoo vulnerable to pressure from the government to play ball, lest it lose access to potentially vital revenue. In 2002, the Internet Society of China, a nominally non-governmental body that nevertheless has strong ties to the security services and official censorship bodies, propagated the 'Public Pledge on Self-Discipline for the Chinese Internet Industry',[14] and Yahoo, along with every major Chinese web firm, signed.[15] The document obliged signatories to refrain from "producing, posting or disseminating pernicious information that may jeopardise state security and disrupt social stability, contravene laws and regulations and spread superstition and obscenity". They also promised to "monitor the information publicised by users on websites according to law and remove the harmful information promptly".[16]

As Yahoo transformed from directory to search engine, it readily censored results just as its Chinese competitors did. Chat rooms, still a major part of online life at the time, filtered phrases such as 'multi-party elections' and 'Taiwanese independence'.[17] Reporters Without Borders labelled Yahoo a "Chinese police auxiliary" in 2004, a designation that would become darkly prophetic. That year, Yahoo provided information about a Chinese journalist to the authorities that would result in his arrest, abuse and years-long imprisonment.

In April 2004, Shi Tao was working for the *Contemporary Business News* in Changsha, Hunan province. Square-jawed and bespectacled, with thick black hair parted in the middle, the thirty-five-year-old often pushed the boundaries of what was permitted at a state-controlled newspaper, pursuing corruption cases and other sensitive issues. Under a pseudonym, he also published essays online advocating for political reform and multiparty democracy, and attacking the government. That month, he had published a blistering criticism of the recent arrest of a member of the Tiananmen Mothers, an organisation of activists whose children had died in the 1989 protests, the fifteenth anniversary of which was approaching. The essay was titled 'The most disgusting day'.[18]

His emotions were already running high, therefore, when he was called into a staff meeting on 20 April and advised, along with all the other reporters, of a censorship notice the paper had received from the Party's central propaganda bureau. It warned against covering any potential protests or other activity around the Tiananmen anniversary, or mentioning the historical event at all. Shi was outraged, and after most of his colleagues had gone home that night, he logged into his personal Yahoo account and emailed his notes from the meeting to the administrators of the New York-based dissident site *Democracy Forum*, which posted an excerpt from the censorship notice online:

> This year will see the 15th anniversary of the 'June 4th event,' and overseas pro-democracy activists have been busy, and are preparing to commemorate the day by adopting very intrusive activities, and preparing to infiltrate China …
>
> Overseas antagonistic forces are trying to draw young people and teenagers through such channels as religion (printed matter and internet), or developing academic activities and assistantships to study in schools, and engaging in illegal activities.[19]

Reporters and editors were warned to "take strict precautions against the 'Falun Gong' evil cult organisation sabotaging events" and instructed to "never say anything that is not in line with the policies of the central government".

While Shi's notes were posted under the pseudonym 198964, thanks to surveillance methods built into the Great Firewall itself, and Shi's and the website administrators' own lack of security awareness, the authorities were able to track an email to *Democracy Forum* that most likely contained the post in question. While they knew the address, they could not link it to a particular person, and so they turned to Yahoo, demanding the company turn over information about the account holder. According to a lawsuit Shi and others later filed against the company, which Yahoo eventually settled, the data provided not only included the contents of the email itself and Shi's identity as the account holder, but also showed that he had logged on from his workplace at the time the incriminating email was sent.

On 23 November 2004, as he was walking home in the middle of the day, a hood was placed over Shi's head and he was bundled into a vehicle. At the same time, his house was searched, and his computer and papers seized. He was kept in detention for almost a month before he was formally arrested, during which time he was subjected to stress positions and otherwise abused. Before his trial the following year, Shi's lawyer was harassed and eventually placed under house arrest. A court-appointed replacement entered a guilty plea on Shi's behalf, and, on 30 April 2005, he was sentenced to ten years in prison for leaking state secrets. In the judgment, the court referenced "account holder information" furnished by Yahoo as helping to prove Shi's guilt.

Following Shi's sentencing, Yahoo was widely castigated by rights groups and democracy activists. Dissident Liu Xiaobo, who would himself be jailed in 2009, wrote an open letter to Yahoo founder Jerry Yang, saying that the company's "evil deed cannot be explained in any way but to say it was pandering to the communist dictatorship".[20] Liu wrote:

I used to be a customer of your company, but after learning about the case of Shi Tao, I no longer use the two email accounts I have with Yahoo. I also will never use other internet products provided by your company, and I will call on all netizens with a good conscience to reject your services until you break off your cooperation with the [Party's] net police. The case of Shi Tao is a warning: those who put profit before all else may not have the luck of gaining a profit. Most likely they will lose both profit and credibility.

Its credibility may have been shot, at least with observers in the West, but Yahoo was on the verge of some serious profit, even if it meant the company essentially exiting China. In 2005, Yang transferred control of Yahoo China to a fledgling e-commerce and online service company founded by a thin, gangly former English teacher called Jack Ma. At the same time, Yahoo bought a 40 per cent stake in Ma's company, Alibaba.[21] That investment would prove to be the most lucrative in Yahoo's history, as Alibaba grew into a global internet powerhouse with a market cap in the hundreds of billions of dollars, eclipsing Yang's company. In time, the Alibaba stake would essentially prop up Yahoo as it suffered huge losses in other parts of its business and stumbled on towards ultimate irrelevancy. But that was many years in the future. In 2005, the repercussions of the Shi Tao case were not yet over, and Yahoo's credibility still had several more hits to take. At least this time, however, the company would not be alone.

Part 2: Shield

Chapter 6

Along came a spider

Lu Wei reins in the Chinese internet

Internet censorship in China is both pervasive and unobtrusive. Pervasive, because everything that is published or discussed online is subject to the whims of the censors and can be deleted at a moment's notice; and unobtrusive because the regime's efforts to control what makes it onto the Chinese internet and to popularise alternative domestic versions of banned services have been so successful that most people are unaware of, or unconcerned by, the borders of their digital world. Even in the early days of the Chinese web, when it was an inferior imitation of the global internet rather than the booming, controlled colossus it is today, only some 10 per cent of users said they regularly used tools to bypass the Firewall. By the mid-2000s, that number had been cut in half,[1] and in 2010 an extensive study by researchers at Harvard University found that only 3 per cent of users took advantage of circumvention tools.[2] This drop in attempts to jump over the Great Firewall is a result of two things. Firstly, while they may have evolved in an environment of naked protectionism, and are subject to pervasive censorship, many Chinese social media sites and search engines are just as good – if not better in some ways – as their Western competitors, reducing the need to bypass the filters. This period also saw a massive upgrading of the Firewall itself, making proxies, VPNs and other methods harder and harder to use.

Because they are not attempting to leap the Firewall, the censorship that the vast majority of Chinese internet users experience is carried out not by the government but by the websites and internet services they visit. As journalist Rebecca MacKinnon argues in *Consent of the Networked*, these internet companies are "the stewards and handmaidens, the tools and enforcers, of China's inner layer of internet censorship".[3] Internet content providers – blogging platforms, publishers, social media, bulletin boards – are required to register with the government and are held liable for all content appearing on their websites, regardless of who created it.[4] Companies are expected to keep their own houses in order, albeit with close supervision from the government. While regulations and laws set out certain types of content that are absolutely illegal – such as calling for the overthrow of the state, or promoting terrorism – much of what is forbidden is obfuscated by Party speak and meaningless buzzwords such as 'harmony' and 'public order'.[5] Failure to follow these unwritten rules can result in heavy fines, temporary suspensions of service, or even a website being banned altogether.[6] To this end, most internet businesses in China, particularly social media and others that allow user-generated content, employ teams of hundreds of in-house censors, who are generally far more vigilant and draconian than their government overseers in order to protect their own backs, and those of their employers.

Unlike the Great Firewall, which is intended to hide information from view, including its own existence, internal censorship is often far more transparent. Some sites carry notices when content has been removed, or if a search term is not in accordance with national regulations.[7] In January 2006, the internet surveillance division of the Shenzhen public security bureau (PSB) introduced the world to

Jingjing and Chacha, two cartoon police officers with big, manga-style eyes designed to "let all internet users know that the internet is not a place beyond the law".[8] Images of the two mascots were posted on all government-run websites and bulletin boards in the city. Speaking to the *Beijing Youth Daily*, the official newspaper of the Communist Youth League, a Shenzhen PSB officer was open about their intended purpose; despite their cutesy names and perky smiles, Jingjing and Chacha were designed "to intimidate".

Along with deletion notices and banned keywords, Jingjing and Chacha form part of what China expert Perry Link, writing about thought control in Chinese academia, dubbed the "anaconda in the chandelier".[9]

> Normally the great snake doesn't move. It doesn't have to. It feels no need to be clear about its prohibitions. Its constant silent message is "You yourself decide," after which, more often than not, everyone in its shadow makes his or her large and small adjustments – all quite "naturally." The Soviet Union, where Stalin's notion of "engineering the soul" was first pursued, in practice fell far short of what the Chinese Communists have achieved in psychological engineering.

One of the most surprising things to outsiders about the Chinese internet is how free it can seem in the right light. Political problems are discussed, corruption is exposed and criticised, national leaders are lampooned, and air pollution is discussed endlessly and at length, like the British discussing the weather. This can lead some observers to doubt the severity of Chinese censorship – it's not North Korea, after all. But as well as the anaconda in the chandelier, reminding everyone beneath it of the dangers of crossing the unmarked lines, there is a nest of vipers slithering over the carpets, darting in to kill certain thoughts before they gain hold. Some forays across the limit of acceptable behaviour may involve only the vipers, as posts are wiped from existence and accounts deleted. But repeated pushing, a refusal to accept the 'natural' way of things, will soon bring the anaconda crashing down.

Nothing will attract the attention of the censors and security services like calls for solidarity or collective action, and it is here where the true boundaries of the Chinese internet lie. An influential Harvard study found that, far from simply deleting or blocking specific content, the goal of the Chinese internet controls is "to reduce the probability of collective action by clipping social ties whenever any collective movements are in evidence or expected".[10] One app for sharing short comedy videos was reportedly blocked not due to any particularly dangerous content, but because its userbase was too cohesive, organising meetups, and sending secret messages to each other in public by, for example, flashing their car headlights in a specific pattern.[11] Although their fandom never went beyond a sports team level of shared identity, even this was deemed too subversive. Nor does collective action need to take place for it to be punished; just the suggestion of it can be enough. In 2010, Cheng Jianping, a human rights activist from eastern Jiangsu province, was arrested and imprisoned for sarcastically encouraging protests at an international trade fair in Shanghai with a three-word tweet: "Charge, angry youth."[12]

This sensitivity makes a perverse sense. The Chinese Communist Party is, after all, a revolutionary movement, and its leaders are still steeped in Marxist and Maoist ideology, even if they rarely put it into practice. Party officials therefore are more aware than most of the power of solidarity, and the dangers to them of anyone organising outside the Party's absolute control. This is why even calls for rallies expressing support for government policies are sometimes censored, whereas a series of vituperative posts excoriating government officials for the poor air quality and accusing them of corruption might not be. The shadow of the Soviet Union looms large over the Party, and China's leaders remain terrified of sharing the same fate as their Russian counterparts. Despite constant speculation by foreign pundits over who will be 'China's Gorbachev', perestroika is a dirty word in Chinese political circles and Mikhail Sergeyevich is a villain with no equal.[13] This is not ideological: Gorbachev's mistake was not in moving away from socialism – he was partly inspired by China's own "reform and opening" after all[14] – but in giving up control. By allowing groups to organise and agitate from outside the Party structure, by tolerating nationalist sentiment in the Soviet republics and the rise of figures such as Boris Yeltsin, Gorbachev unleashed an unstoppable wave of discontent and agitation for change that was previously contained and filtered through the Soviet bureaucracy, or crushed by state power.

When speech steps over the boundaries of acceptable criticism into calls for action, the reaction is swift and absolute. The chief censors, based in Beijing, communicate their instructions to counterparts at the provincial level, and in the country's top internet companies and semi-independent media. These range from orders not to 'hype' certain stories to a 'no tolerance' policy of absolute deletion. Private individuals – celebrity microbloggers and other social media stars – may also be warned to shy away from certain topics, or encouraged to communicate the government line to their millions of followers.[15]

While a great degree of censorship – particularly on social media – is automated, for truly important subjects the task becomes a manual one, with thousands of censors scouring bulletin boards, blogs and social media for 'harmful' content. Compliance is expected in seconds. When censors at Sina Weibo, China's largest social media platform, were slow to delete posts about a censored New Year's Day editorial by a liberal newspaper, their supervisors were dragged into a lecture by their government minders and reminded sternly of the importance of "running the internet in a civilised manner".[16]

Censorship orders are usually delivered by phone and expected to be obeyed immediately. Despite the potential dangers of sharing them exposed by Shi Tao's case, the sheer number of organisations that have to be instructed in this fashion means that many instances are inevitably leaked. For over a decade, the main recipient of such leaks has been the US-based *China Digital Times*, founded by Xiao Qiang in 2003.

Like many of his generation, Xiao had been radicalised by the Tiananmen protests. He was studying in Ohio at the time and watched in horror with other overseas students as the crackdown unfolded, seeing the photographs and video of soldiers attacking students on the streets of his home town.[17] He wanted to find a way to express his solidarity with the goals of the Tiananmen movement, so, following a brief period back in China, where Xiao spent weeks interviewing those who had been on the square, he dropped out of his physics PhD programme and moved to New York, where he joined Human Rights in China.[18] After almost a decade at the head of that organisation, in 2001 he received a MacArthur Genius Grant,[19] and he used some of the money from that award to found *China Digital Times* two years later, running it out of a small house in Berkeley, California.

Through a vast network of contacts and tipsters in China, *China Digital Times* collates censorship instructions issued to the media by various levels of government and publishes them as directives from the 'Ministry of Truth'. The site's vast archives give an invaluable insight into the motivations of the censors, and show two clear priorities: preventing collective action, and wiping out any criticism of the censors themselves.

Criticism of censorship is such a sensitive topic that it doesn't even necessarily matter where the critique came from. In March

2017, during a meeting of the Chinese People's Political Consultative Conference (CPPCC), a mostly useless Party rubber-stamp body that is supposed to advise on legislation, delegate Luo Fuhe complained that continued censorship risked harming the country's economic and scientific progress by hampering researchers' access to information and slowing down internet speeds. The censors' reaction was immediate: "All websites, please find and delete reports and posts on Luo Fuhe's 'proposal to improve and increase speed of access to foreign websites' as soon as possible," said a leaked order.[20]

Similar commands are issued for protests and demonstrations, even when their motivation is patriotic and in support of Party goals. After China lost a landmark international court ruling in July 2016 over its sprawling territorial claims in the South China Sea, spontaneous protests broke out targeting the Philippines – the other party in the case – with calls for boycotts of Filipino products and of KFC, which served as an easy representative for the US, Manila's main ally.[21] As the protests threatened to get out of control, however, with some calling on the government to take military action to enforce its claims, a leaked censorship order told website owners "for the near future, do not hype or spread information related to illegal rallies and demonstrations. Pay close attention and delete inflammatory information."[22] In the wake of this order, according to Weiboscope, a monitoring service at the University of Hong Kong, the phrases 'KFC' and 'South China Sea' were heavily censored on social media.

When censorship alone is not enough to stymie calls for collective action, state media can be drafted in to help. During the anti-Philippines protests, a Xinhua editorial said that while feeling anger over the ruling was "the embodiment of patriotic feeling ... if that feeling leads to illegal behaviour that destroys social order, then it is mistaken to label it 'patriotic'".[23]

That Xinhua would be used in this fashion is no surprise. After Jiang Zemin became Party general secretary in 1989, during the Tiananmen protests, the news agency's role was expanded drastically, and it was given a key role in setting the Party line on sensitive issues.[24] During the protests on the square, several key newspapers had come out in support of the students; divergence on such issues would no longer be tolerated. Even as China's newspapers were increasingly encouraged to generate revenue for themselves rather than depend on state funding, expanding their coverage to attract more readers, including by doing investigative journalism, top-down control over certain content was increased. During particularly sensitive periods – such as political transitions, key anniversaries or natural disasters – newspapers often ran identical front pages, all carrying the official Xinhua line.

In the early 2000s, the man tasked with overseeing Xinhua's evolving role was Lu Wei, a young newcomer to the Party who would go on to become one of the pivotal figures in Xi Jinping's clampdown on the internet.[25] Lu was born in 1960 in Chaohu, a small city in Anhui, an impoverished province in eastern China. Appropriately enough for a future censor and propaganda chief, his home town was wiped from existence in 2011 to help juice the GDP statistics of the provincial capital, Hefei, into which Chaohu was absorbed.[26] In Anhui, Lu worked a variety of jobs, including as a substitute teacher and factory machinist, before he joined the Party in 1991, at the relatively old age of thirty-one, after which he was dispatched by Xinhua to serve as the news agency's correspondent for the south-western province of Guangxi.

Since its formation, Xinhua has served two roles, both as a traditional, albeit highly controlled, newswire and as a secret intelligence-gathering apparatus, with reporters across China and overseas filing dispatches back to Party headquarters for the eyes of only the highest-ranking officials.[27] Sometimes this political role was clearly stated, as when Xinhua's bureau in Hong Kong served as China's unofficial embassy to the British colony prior to 1997,[28] but more often it was an open secret, one that gave Xinhua correspondents – and their counterparts at the Party's official mouthpiece, *People's Daily* – no small amount of power.

These reporters often fulfilled the traditional press role of watchdog, performing valuable investigative journalism and muckraking, but with the key difference that their findings were never made public. Xinhua correspondents produced "internal reference materials" on matters "detrimental to the image of the Party or the government, that affect social stability and unity, or that are inappropriate for open publication, such as graft and corruption, social unrest, and major business fraud".[29] The most important of these internal references, the *Guonei Dongtai Qingyang*, or 'final proofs on domestic trends', was issued once or twice a day, classified top secret, and distributed only to the central Party leadership, provincial secretaries and governors. Those deemed worthy of receiving the dispatches – whose nickname *Da Cankao* was later borrowed by Li Hongkuan – had to return them within a set period, and they could be punished if they lost their copies or allowed an unauthorised person to see them.[30]

A position as Xinhua correspondent was therefore an ideal role for someone as politically ambitious as Lu. Stocky and short, at around five feet, Lu was possessed of a huge self-confidence and had an easy smile and an instinct for which way the political winds were blowing. Within Xinhua, he developed a reputation as a highly driven workaholic, and his rise within the agency was rapid.[31] He was soon promoted to leadership roles, first at the provincial level and then in Beijing. By 2001, he was the news agency's secretary general, and he would become its vice president within three years.[32] According to some reports, Lu also served as personal spin doctor for Wen Jiabao, who became China's premier in 2003.[33] During his tenure, 'Grandpa Wen' carefully cultivated a 'man of the people' image, with the bespectacled sexagenarian posing for photographs after one natural disaster wearing a waterproof jacket and carrying a bullhorn to direct rescue workers.[34] A former protégé of the purged liberal reformer Zhao Ziyang, Wen also gently departed from Party lines on some issues, serving as the good cop to other leaders' bad cop and giving the impression of dissent, or at least debate, at the top. His liberal inclinations never seemed to have much of an effect on policy, however, and dissident Yu Jie spoke for many when he released his book-length denunciation of Wen: *China's Best Actor*.[35]

As Xinhua vice president, Lu demonstrated a keen eye for advancement and a willingness to take on big targets that would help him rise in the ranks. In 2006, he spearheaded new rules that would have forced foreign news agencies to partner with a Xinhua subsidiary if they wanted to operate in China. Many observers saw the move as an attempt by Xinhua to muscle in on the lucrative financial news business then dominated by Reuters and Bloomberg.[36] Eventually, facing a World Trade Organization suit over Xinhua's dual role as censor and competitor to foreign media, the rules were relaxed.

The dispute marked the beginning of an aggressive push by Xinhua to expand its commercial offerings, which began during Lu's time at the organisation. At first this only saw it competing for business within China, but then Xinhua began to compete with and undercut foreign newswires such as Reuters and the Associated Press overseas too, expanding China's influence and weakening competitors seen as unsympathetic to Beijing. As many media companies have struggled financially, Xinhua's offerings, particularly its photo wire, have become more and more attractive, and its competitors have increasingly cut staff overseas as they face their own revenue issues. Xinhua has been particularly successful in Africa, where many media organisations are less able to afford the services of the major international wires.[37]

Lu helped spearhead this transformation, and in leaked US State Department cables, diplomats reported how they had threatened Lu with a potential WTO complaint if China followed through on the new rules, only for him to pugnaciously insist that the issue was one of "Chinese sovereignty".[38] Lu told the US representatives that "any company that wants to conduct business in China must obey Chinese laws". He then launched into a tirade about the fickleness of foreign media. Reuters, he complained, had broadcast an item saying Taiwan was an independent country, while the Dow Jones newswire had published an article "supporting a call for Chinese citizens to overthrow their government and calling on the United States government to fight against the Chinese dictatorship".

These were arguments he would roll out again years later, after Xi Jinping tapped Lu to lead his war on the internet.

Chapter 7

Peak traffic

Getting the Dalai Lama online

In the summer of 1988, Dan Haig was feeling directionless.[1] Born in Milwaukee, Wisconsin, on the shores of Lake Michigan, he grew up in nearby Glendale, and went to university in the state capital, Madison. After graduation, he wanted to see the world and have the types of experiences you couldn't get in the Badger State, so, in 1987, he uprooted and moved to Taiwan to teach English. The trip didn't turn into the life-changing experience the twenty-four-year-old had been hoping for, however. Taiwan was both too familiar, not exotic enough to challenge him and expand his mind, and too strange, leaving him with a feeling of constant, gentle alienation, and an inability to be truly settled. So after almost a year, he flew to southern China and made his way to Tibet. Haig, who had long, wavy brown hair and a short beard, making him look like someone following the hippie trail decades earlier, began hitchhiking and bussing around the plateau, having conversations in shaky Mandarin with people who by and large didn't speak that language, but feeling a deep relationship with the land and those who lived on it. For several days, he travelled with a Buddhist monk and the man's father, the three of them communicating almost exclusively in hand gestures and facial expressions, enjoying themselves heartily.

After he returned to Wisconsin, Haig was surprised to find Tibet waiting for him in the form of Geshe Sopa, a Buddhist monk and professor of Tibetan language and culture. Haig enrolled in a four-year course that completely failed to turn into a PhD but gave him a decent set of language skills and the germ of an idea not yet ready to be realised. In 1994, having tried going east, he now went west, moving to California just in time for the first dot-com bubble. He joined a start-up run by his little brother's best friend from high school, and learned to build websites.[2] He helped code the first CNET. com, and, in a sin that still haunts him, some of the first banner ads ever put on the internet. The dot-com bubble was still inflating – Pets.com, which would go on to be one of its most notable failures, had not even been founded – but Haig was put off by the rush to commercialisation and the ever increasing focus on money.

He decided to return to his Tibetan studies, and signed up for a course in Tibetan medicine at a school in Dharamsala, in the Indian Himalayas, the de facto capital of the Tibetan government in exile, and where the Dalai Lama had fled in 1959. It was the first time the course had ever been offered to non-Tibetans, a reflection of how isolated Dharamsala was at the time, a small town some 1,400 metres above sea level with little contact with the rest of India, let alone the wider world. It was a trip that would create a lifelong connection between Haig and the Tibetan community, and help bring the internet to Dharamsala, something that would prove to be both a blessing and a curse.

Arriving in the Himalayas in 1995, Haig wasn't able to completely shed his Silicon Valley habits, and soon found his way to the town's computer centre. That somewhere like Dharamsala would even have such an institution was hardly guaranteed in the mid-1990s, but Haig had read an article in *Wired* that described how two Canadians had arrived a few years earlier and connected the Tibetan enclave to the internet, albeit in a fairly rudimentary fashion.

One of those Canadians was Thubten Samdup, a member of the Canada Tibet Committee and another unlikely internet pioneer.[3] Samdup was born in the Tibetan capital of Lhasa in 1951, a year after the People's Liberation Army (PLA), victorious in the Chinese civil war, invaded Tibet and ended a brief period of self-rule. The Tibetan leadership, unable to resist militarily, signed an agreement with Beijing recognising Chinese sovereignty over Tibet and welcoming the PLA as liberators from foreign imperialism.[4] Many Tibetans regarded the agreement as one made under duress, a last-ditch effort to maintain the region's autonomy from direct Chinese rule and uphold the authority of the Dalai Lama and other religious figures who had historically run Tibet.[5] This effort was unsuccessful, and resentment against increasing Chinese encroach-ment bubbled under the surface for years before finally exploding in 1956 into armed conflict between Tibetan militants and PLA forces. In 1959, the unrest, which was backed covertly by the US government and the CIA, reached Lhasa and soon spiralled into a "full scale rebellion".[6] As PLA shells struck near the Dalai Lama's palace in Lhasa, the religious leader and his retinue, disguised as peasants, fled the city amid a dust storm, eventually crossing into India, where they were granted political asylum.[7] Samdup's family followed the Dalai Lama several months later, and he came of age in the growing exile community in Dharamsala.

In Dharamsala, Samdup studied traditional Tibetan music and eventually won a scholarship to Brown University in the US to study ethnomusicology. After he graduated, he returned to India, where he took over the Tibetan Institute of the Performing Arts and got involved in the Tibetan Youth Congress. Around this time he met his wife, Carole, a Canadian specialist in religion who was studying in Dharamsala, and in 1980 the two of them moved to her home town of Montreal. Strong-jawed, with thick black hair and round glasses, Samdup looked like a Tibetan Clark Kent, with a smile that crinkled up his entire, freckle-flecked face. In Canada, he continued to be involved in Tibetan politics, and set up the Canada Tibet Committee to spread awareness the situation in Tibet and lobby the Canadian government.

In the late 1980s and early 1990s, much of this work was done by long-distance telephone and fax, at substantial expense. At the time, there were no commercial internet service providers in Canada, and few people had access to the web, but a university professor friend of Samdup's gave him an unused email address. Samdup began communicating with other Tibetan activists around the world, but it soon became apparent there was a big gap in this burgeoning online network: the Tibetan community in Dharamsala. In 1994, Samdup returned to India with three computers, which he installed in the newly created Tibetan Computer Resource Centre and hooked up to the Indian government-run Education and Research Network (ERNET).

At that time, the entire subcontinent was running off a 128-kilobit line to Europe, close to a billion people sharing the equivalent of a household connection in the West, although the vast majority had no access to computers.[8] When Haig first visited the computer centre years later, he was shocked by the bootstrapped rudimentariness of it all. Sending an email required "incredibly arcane voodoo" using Pegasus, an early piece of email software the instructions for which had to be written out next to the computer, they were so user-unfriendly. After an email had been laboriously composed and sent, it was then transmitted down a phone line to another computer in Delhi, where it would join a queue of other emails sent in the past few days. At some point, according to his own schedule, the systems administrator in Delhi would connect the machine to the internet and the emails would finally be sent. Receiving emails was like getting a telegram in the 1900s. They would pile up on the machine in Delhi, which would eventually transmit them to the computer centre in Dharamsala, where a volunteer would print them out and distribute them to their recipients. This was all too much for a man who had lived and worked at the heart of the technological revolution, and Haig decided something must be done.

After extensive preparations in Dharamsala, including measuring the distances between buildings, Haig returned to the US and began gathering supplies. In April 1997, accompanied by four friends, he landed in Delhi with hundreds of metres of steel cable, stacks of network cards, routers, modems and power converters, and began the forty-hour trek to the Himalayas. Arriving back in Dharamsala, the team was raring to get started, but before they could, they had to meet with endless government officials, explaining over cups of tea what each piece of hardware was and what it did. Most of the officials did not comprehend what the project was, but they were satisfied at least that it wasn't dangerous, and passed the five Americans up the line to the next level of bureaucracy. Eventually, they got an audience with the Dalai Lama himself, who was fascinated by the project and peppered them with questions, even donning stereoscopic glasses to check out a 3D tattoo Haig's colleague Rick Schneider, a telecoms engineer from San Francisco, had on his arm. With the Dalai Lama's blessing, all obstacles faded away and the team got to work.

Soon they discovered a whole host of other problems, the biggest one being the lack of anything approaching health and safety in India. The state of wiring in most of the buildings left Schneider in a near constant state of freak-out. Blackouts and brownouts, both planned and not, were also a frequent occurrence. Visiting a bank to change money one day, Haig and Schneider noticed a water boiler with two naked wires plugged into the back which led out of a window. After exchanging their dollars for rupees they followed the wires, and were appalled to see them lead directly into a tangle of cables atop a high-voltage power line.

Haig's team went around the Tibetan community, installing computers and network cards in public buildings, and switching out Pegasus for Eudora, then the cutting edge in email clients. While his four compatriots returned home soon afterwards, Haig remained in Dharamsala for several months, training staff and volunteers at the computer centre and writing documentation for the equipment they had installed. When he finally left, there were about ten computers connected to the internet; within a year or two, there would be more than 100, with demand far outstripping Dharamsala's rudimentary bandwidth, meaning that usage had to be rationed by the computer centre. But as the millennium rolled around, the Tibetan exile community was as firmly connected to the web as anyone else. That's when the real trouble began.

Chapter 8

Filtered

The Firewall catches up with Da Cankao

In August 2001, *The New York Times* publisher Arthur Ochs Sulzberger Jr sat opposite Chinese leader Jiang Zemin in a gaudily decorated meeting room inside the West Mountain Compound, a government building overlooking Beidaihe.[1] A beach resort on the Bohai Sea east of Beijing, Beidaihe had served as a retreat for Party leadership for over four decades. It was where plans were laid for Mao's Great Leap Forward in 1958, and where, thirty years later, paramount leader Deng Xiaoping dismissed reformist general secretary Zhao Ziyang and set the stage for the Tiananmen crackdown. A foreigner in the Beidaihe compound was a rare sight, a foreign journalist rarer still – even state media was permitted inside only for official photoshoots. The *Times* team had come in numbers, and Sulzberger was flanked by a coterie of the paper's journalists, columnists and translators. Jiang, wearing his iconic large square glasses and a dark suit, was frank and occasionally combative, demonstrating an easy comfort with the press that none of his successors would ever match, or, for the most part, even attempt.[2]

Responding to a series of questions about US missile defence systems, Taiwan and the Dalai Lama, Jiang peppered his answers with quotes from ancient Chinese poems and English idioms. The only question that seemed to stump him was about the *Times* itself.

Columnist Tom Friedman asked Jiang why the paper's website was censored by the Great Firewall, "and how do you square China's incredible progress with information technology with its practice of blocking some important information sources on the web, such as our newspaper's own website?"

"Everything has two aspects, pros and cons. The pros of the internet are that it makes it very easy for people to communicate, to share advances, expertise and information about science and technology. But that aspect is affected by some unhealthy things," Jiang said, but then he seemed to falter in his boilerplate response to a censorship question. "You raised a very specific issue about *The New York Times* website in particular, I cannot answer this question. But if you ask my view of *The New York Times*, my answer is it is a very good paper."

According to Craig Smith, the paper's Shanghai bureau chief who accompanied Friedman and Sulzberger to the meeting with Jiang, "within days, nytimes.com was accessible again in China". It remained unblocked for almost a decade, before reporting about the finances of China's elite, including Jiang's own family, caused it to be censored once again.

In the early years of the new century, this was a rare win. In July 2001, as China neared 26 million internet users, Jiang complained that existing legislation was "inadequate" for tackling the challenges posed by the web. In a speech to the Party Central Committee, he said that the internet had "contributed a lot to the economic growth of China [but] the development of information technology has also brought new problems", in particular the spread of "superstition, pornography, violence and pernicious information" that could "harm the mental health of the population and of youth".[3] This was the start of many crackdowns on porn and other 'harmful' material that would greatly expand the powers of the censors both technologically and legally.

The Party issued dozens of new regulations, including provisions which stated that the purpose of news websites was not to inform the public but to "serve socialism" and "safeguard the nation's interests and public interest". Online content was to be "healthy" and "civilised" and help raise "the quality of the nation".[4] Particular attention was paid to pornography, and, in the wake of the crackdown on Falun Gong, which Jiang himself ordered and largely oversaw, "propagating evil cults and feudal superstitions".

On 11 December 2001, China joined the World Trade Organization (WTO). It was hailed as a victory for reform and opening, but having achieved a goal they had spent decades working towards, acquiescing to onerous demands from the US and the WTO, the Party now doubled down on internal controls. The following year, Google was blocked outright for the first time, as investment in the Golden Shield project reached $770 million, with an estimated 30,000 security officers working within the censorship apparatus.[5] A 2002 study by researchers at Harvard found that China had the most restricted internet in the world.[6]

One of the first people to notice the uptick in censorship was Li Hongkuan, as it became harder and harder for people to access *Da Cankao*. "Around the time China started to join the World Trade Organization, they really spent money to build up the Great Firewall," he told me.

We met in early March 2018, when, with the skies threatening rain, I walked from my hotel just off Capitol Hill, in Washington DC, to a restaurant on a quiet shopping street nearby. At fifty-four, Li had short hair that stuck up from his head, and an easy, broad smile. He had lived in DC for almost two decades, and had become comfortably wealthy buying and selling houses in the surrounding area, as the capital's population boomed and the commuter belt spread.

Over a lunch of Serbian food with too much cheese, Li told me about how he had devoted most of the previous year to online battles with another Chinese exile, the billionaire Guo Wengui. Li had been an early supporter of Guo when the latter fled Beijing for New York, promising to take down the Chinese leadership with revelations of corruption at the highest levels, but Li had turned against him after several of Guo's major predictions had failed to come true. The fight had turned ugly, with Guo suing Li for assault, libel and slander.[7] When I spoke to Li, he shrugged off the court case from a billionaire with potentially limitless resources. He had spent years feuding online with various antagonists: from pro-China trolls and other dissidents to US government agencies and the entire Chinese internet censorship apparatus.[8]

"I had this belief, this vision, from the beginning: I believe the free flow of information will overthrow the dictatorship in China ultimately," he said. "I thought it would come quicker, somehow China struggled on. Membership of the World Trade Organization saved the Chinese regime; they became so rich and invested so heavily in the Great Firewall that it delayed the effectiveness of the free flow of information to overthrow the regime."

It took several years, but just as they stamped out the China Democracy Party, the censors were finally able to defeat *Da Cankao*. As the Firewall was upgraded, it became impossible to spam the newsletter into people's inboxes as before. Li and his team tried ways of getting around the filtering, switching out sensitive words for acronyms and homonyms, using images instead of text, and even writing emails vertically, so that each line had only one word on it, but it was never enough. He struggled on for years, but by 2005 Li was almost out of money, and delivery was getting harder and harder. A promised $40,000 grant from the National Endowment for Democracy never appeared, and it began a protracted dispute that left Li feeling embittered and disillusioned. The last full issue of *Da Cankao* was published on 30 May 2005.

Michael Anti, the blogger who was inspired by *Da Cankao* as a young man, said Li's project was also a victim of its own success. Not only did its wide readership attract the intense focus of the censors, but it also sparked a flurry of similar sites and newsletters. Blogging also took off in China in the early 2000s, and while writers in the country often had to self-censor or had their posts deleted, the variety of topics being discussed increased dramatically. *Da Cankao* no longer seemed so vital. "As the years went you could see a more serious debate happening on the Chinese internet," Anti told me. "One guy, one editor, cannot compete with hundreds." Even so, he and many others were disappointed to see *Da Cankao* go. Li's newsletter had once set the agenda for a huge swath of the dissident community, and while there were alternative sources of news and commentary in the wake of its closure, both censored and uncensored, they "could never catch up to the influence that *Da Cankao* had for us".

The censors had taken down one of their biggest antagonists, but the fight against the Firewall was just beginning, and they were about to face their biggest test yet.

Chapter 9

Jumping the wall

FreeGate, UltraSurf, and Falun Gong's
fight against the censors

On a day in May 2005, Li Yuanlong sat at his computer in an apartment on the western edge of Bijie, a rainy, humid city in north-western Guizhou, on the borders of Sichuan and Yunnan, surrounded by rolling green hills. Short, with bowl-cut hair, prominent ears and a square jaw, the forty-four-year-old reporter for the state-run *Bijie Daily* booted up a blocky Lenovo desktop he had bought a year earlier and loaded FreeGate.[1] His son had got a copy of the software from a friend shortly after Li registered the family for the internet,[2] allowing them to bypass the Great Firewall and access sites run by Chinese dissidents overseas.

Li was seething as he typed. He had been outraged by the recent dismissal of a journalism professor at the prestigious Peking University. Jiao Guobiao had been removed after he had written a series of essays critical of the government, including one titled 'Denouncing the Central Propaganda Department'.[3] He had also lauded American foreign policy, including in a cringeworthy poem praising the war in Iraq and a later essay in which he hoped to sell China to the US "for one cent".[4] These had been roundly attacked online by other intellectuals, even after Jiao's firing.[5] This reaction appalled Li, who shared Jiao's right-wing, pro-America views.

He wrote a long essay, 'Becoming an American citizen in spirit', praising US democracy and interventionism, and criticising the Party and its supporters as a "rotten corpse allowing maggots to live".[6] Using FreeGate to bypass the Firewall, he uploaded the essay to the website of the *Epoch Times*, a US-based Chinese-language dissident newspaper, under the pseudonym 'Night Wolf'.

Four months later, Li's seventeen-year-old son Alex was heading home from school when his stepmother called and told him to stay away because the police were at their house.[7] She had been picked up at her work and driven home so that they could search the property. At the same time, agents had raided Li's offices and arrested him.[8] Alex eventually returned home to find his stepmother weeping and his father's computer gone. Li was charged with "inciting subversion of the state" and sentenced to two years in prison. Alex was forced to testify against him at his trial.[9]

While Li's writings were inflammatory enough on their own to get the censors' attention, he had inadvertently waded into one of the fiercest battles being fought on the Chinese internet, part of a wider crackdown that had already claimed hundreds of lives and seen thousands more imprisoned. The fight between Chinese nationalists and America-loving neoconservatives was just a sideshow by comparison. *Epoch Times* and FreeGate were both run by followers of Falun Gong, which had by then become one of the Party's most loathed foes, and a verboten topic on the Chinese internet.

*

While it began as a distinctly Chinese phenomenon, after founder Li Hongzhi left China in 1996, Falun Gong's base shifted to North America, particularly the US and Canadian east coasts. Since before the crackdown, the group had made use of the internet to disseminate materials, making all of Li's books available for free in multiple languages online and encouraging members to join mailing lists to keep them updated about Falun Gong activities in their area. After the practice was banned in China, this existing organisation, while significantly hampered by the Great Firewall, helped Falun Gong practitioners continue to spread their message, often adopting the same spamming methods as *Da Cankao*, as well as sharing illicit CDs and floppy disks.

According to the group's teachings, anyone could practise Falun Gong, with or without a wider organisation – just do the exercises and read Li Hongzhi's teachings. While it is true that there is far less of a top-down management structure than in other religions, there is still a hierarchy of sorts guiding the faith. Many of the most important bodies or figures in Falun Gong are based in the US, not least Li himself. Falun Gong's main media outlets, *Epoch Times* and New Tang Dynasty (NTD) Television, as well as the classical Chinese performance group Shen Yun, are based in New York, which alone hosts thirty-five Falun Gong practice sites.[10] Websites Minghui.org and FalunDafa.org, which serve as the primary information and organisational repositories for practitioners around the world, go a long way to obfuscate their structure and where they are based, but archived records suggest that they were both registered in the US.[11] One of the group's major organisations, the Eastern US Buddhas Study Falun Dafa Association, is registered as a public charity in New York, according to IRS records.[12] Based in a red-brick building on a tree-lined street in Queens, the organisation reported total revenue of almost $200,000 in 2014–15, against expenses of $250,000.[13] Its stated purpose is "to promote and advertise the practice of Falun Dafa (Falun Gong) and to facilitate the national conference and meetings for practice of the principles". It owns the two major trademarks for Falun Dafa in the US, used on publications, clothing and other goods.[14]

A 2006 congressional report estimated that there were several thousand Falun Gong practitioners in the US.[15] According to researcher David Ownby, who conducted fieldwork with North American Falun Gong practitioners, around 90 per cent were Chinese, mostly well-off, highly educated immigrants living in major cities, who came to the country in the 1980s and 1990s, before the crackdown began.[16] They had been bolstered since by practitioners fleeing China, many of whom have claimed asylum on the grounds of religious persecution.

In Manhattan's Chinatown, bright yellow newspaper vending machines emblazoned with the Chinese name of *Epoch Times* are the most visible sign of Falun Gong, along with regular protests by practitioners outside the large grey building that houses the city's Chinese consulate, near the Lincoln Tunnel. When I visited in mid-2018, there was a long line of visa applicants stretching up the block, while opposite them across the busy road a small group of Falun Gong practitioners held banners and performed exercises. On important dates, larger protests are staged outside China's embassy in Washington DC and consulates in other major cities across the US. In private, Falun Gong practitioners have formed an effective lobby in Washington, where they have found a ready audience for their pro-religious freedom, anti-Communist message. This audience has included many neoconservative politicians, who advocate for internet freedom policies and have embraced Falun Gong as a victim of the Great Firewall.

Censorship circumvention was a natural fit for Falun Gong. Following the crackdown, Falun Gong became one of the most sensitive and most censored topics on the Chinese internet, outdoing Tiananmen Square and Tibet. Leaked documentation for the 'Green Dam Youth Escort' – software developed as part of an abandoned plan to install active censorship tools on every computer in China – contained hundreds of Falun Gong-related terms, including 'Zhuan Falun', 'Epoch Times', '6.10 Office' (an alleged Chinese government bureau tasked with crushing Falun Gong), 'Jiang Zemin', and the faith's key tenets of 'truthfulness, compassion and forbearance'.[17] The blocking of Falun Gong is granular and near absolute, with the censors going so far as to ban the Cyrillic character used in mathematics to represent a multiplier of 1 million because of its similarity to a Falun Gong symbol.[18]

Beginning in the early to mid-2000s, as censorship ramped up, knocking *Da Cankao* and others offline, groups of Falun Gong engineers in the US began developing software to punch through the Great Firewall and allow practitioners inside the country – and potential converts – access to Falun Gong materials.

One of these engineers was Bill Xia, who moved to the US in the 1990s, before Falun Gong was banned.[19] From his home in North Carolina, Xia debated with other Falun Gong members in online chat rooms about what could be done to fight the intense censorship they were facing. It was in these chat rooms that he met David Tian, a researcher at Nasa's Goddard Space Flight Center.[20] Initially, they used tactics similar to Li Hongkuan and *Da Cankao*, sending out Falun Gong news and study materials to millions of email addresses in China, dodging the still-rudimentary Great Firewall by converting text to images and constantly switching servers. This tactic's effectiveness was decidedly finite, however, and it also treated users in China as passive recipients of information. People could not go out and search for the truth about Tiananmen or Li Hongzhi's latest writings; they could only hope it was dumped into their inboxes by one of the Falun Gong team's many email blasts.

In 2001, Xia and others began looking into the FreeNet project, with the hopes of converting it for Chinese users. FreeNet was developed by Irish programmer Ian Clarke while he was a student at the University of Edinburgh.[21] Released in early 2000, it allowed users to host censored or sensitive content on the dark web, that part of the internet not visible to search engines or indexing services. The dark web is now far better known thanks to the proliferation of illegal drug markets such as Silk Road and Agora, which existed parallel to the world wide web but were accessible only by using specialised software, such as the Tor Browser. Tor was originally developed by the US government to help agents avoid detection overseas. It remains one of the most popular anti-surveillance tools, although its effectiveness at avoiding censorship is limited, and both NSA and independent researchers have found serious vulnerabilities that could expose users.

FreeNet differed greatly from modern censorship circumvention tools in that its primary function was to share files, not allow access to blocked sites. While in theory you could set up a FreeNet version of a blocked site, just as there are Tor mirrors of *The New York Times*[22] and the frequently banned white supremacist publication *Daily Stormer*,[23] you would have to share links to it on the mainstream internet, putting yourself at risk of censorship and surveillance. Sites also load considerably slower than they do on the open web, an inevitable result of bouncing requests through multiple layers of servers to anonymise them and bypass any restrictions.

FreeNet China launched in late 2001.[24] "We tried to adapt it for Chinese users," Xia told me. "We customised the interface, made underlying modifications to the software." Like FreeNet itself, the Chinese version focused on providing access to banned materials, including the '*Tiananmen Papers*', a compilation of purported secret Chinese government documents relating to the 1989 crackdown, and back issues of *Da Cankao* and other pro-democracy magazines. While in theory a huge online collection of samizdat is a valuable thing, in practice the type of person who would seek out the Tiananmen Papers is probably already not a fan of the Communist Party. To learn the means of accessing those papers, they also had to have a connection to online dissident communities, or at least someone who could get them a copy of FreeNet China, which was swiftly blocked shortly after its release. According to a study of Chinese peer-to-peer software, FreeNet China had a "core, dedicated group" of a few thousand users in 2002, and was mostly spread by email or, thanks to its small size, by illicitly shared floppy disk. It is doubtful whether it ever grew much beyond this; it was replaced by Tor, which is more widely used and faster, and with more full-featured circumvention tools, which allow for the visiting of blocked sites on the open web as well as sharing files.

Within a year of launching FreeNet China, Xia and his colleagues "started to feel increasingly strongly that we needed to build a different software from scratch". In 2002, they launched DynaWeb, which was rudimentary as an anti-censorship tool, but so was the Great Firewall at the time. Early filters worked like a blacklist, preventing access to specific websites and IP addresses. A user would type a banned URL into their browser; before loading it, their ISP would check it against the record of prohibited sites and decide whether or not to allow the connection. The same was true of IP addresses, the numbers that correspond to an individual server; so if a user set up a dummy, unblocked domain that pointed to the same place, it too would be filtered out.

The initial way around such techniques was to use proxies, safe havens through which traffic was tunnelled, so from the Firewall's perspective the user was loading an approved website. Rather than load the banned URL directly, the user would send the request via a proxy service that forwarded it, loaded the page, and sent it back to the user. As far as the censorship software was concerned, the user only ever interacted with the proxy service, not the banned website, so there was nothing to block. Of course, since the proxy service had to be publicly accessible in order to function, with a domain and IP address attached to it, there was an obvious problem with this approach, and proxies used by Chinese internet users were blocked in droves. In the early years of the Great Firewall, new proxies were shared on a daily basis, quickly adopted, and just as quickly blocked by the censors.

DynaWeb, and its successor software FreeGate, took this approach and supersized it, giving users access to dozens, if not hundreds, of proxy servers running concurrently. If one was blocked or otherwise inaccessible, the software switched the user to another without their knowledge, allowing them to surf the internet unmolested, albeit at a significantly slower speed than if they weren't tunnelling all their traffic through a proxy. "The government would try to block any website or mirror website you started, so we needed to keep moving around and stay dynamic for the whole network," Xia told me. "So the software would connect users to this dynamic proxy network instead of needing to type in a proxy URL or to keep updating what's blocked and what's not."

In 2006, Xia and his team partnered with Alan Huang, a Silicon Valley-based engineer and Falun Gong practitioner behind UltraSurf, which worked in a similar fashion, to create the Global Internet Freedom Consortium (GIFC). They also registered a number of companies related to their products in order to bid for US government contracts and other funding.

A fundamental goal for the team behind FreeGate and its related tools was to make it "really, really easy" to use. Given that the initial users were Falun Gong practitioners in China, most of whom were middle-aged, if not older, and had little technical knowledge, this wasn't just a point of principle, it was a necessity. The difficulty in using anti-censorship tools for the average person was a common complaint, especially for anonymising services such as Tor, although its developers too have since released the far easier-to-grasp Tor Browser. Having used FreeGate extensively myself when I first moved to China in 2010, I can attest to its relative user-friendliness. It also kept ahead of the censors fairly well in those days, and was able to update itself and keep its servers from being blocked, although there would occasionally be a complete blackout that couldn't be fixed except by connecting to the open web by another means and down-loading a new version of the software (or by acquiring the update from someone else). This was relatively easy for a foreigner who left the country intermittently and had access to VPNs and friends overseas who could download the software and email it to me, but for regular Chinese internet users it was a far bigger headache.

The biggest problem for FreeGate, which remains the most signif-icant stumbling block for any and all anti-censorship software, was getting the word out. Tools are no good if no one they are designed to help knows they exist, and it is naturally difficult to spread the word about ways to fight censorship on a censored network. "One channel we relied on heavily at the beginning was to use mass mailings," Xia said. "We included the proxy URL in the emails." One advantage his software had over others was its connections to the Falun Gong community, who were already illicitly sharing Li Hongzhi's texts and other banned materials and were able to spread the word to other practitioners and non-believers alike about FreeGate. Xia and his team also benefited from the fact that, in the first month of FreeGate's release, it largely went unnoticed by the censors, which meant that it could be downloaded freely from within China, helping to build an initial userbase who, once it did start getting censored, could help share it to others and spread the word. "They always focus on the most popular software and tech-nologies," Xia said. "It makes it harder for any new technologies to become popular, but on the other hand if any new technology can stay low key they may survive for a long time." After this initial grace period expired, "we started to see active blocking of our IPs – throughout the years they keep upgrading their technology, and we keep evolving to match it".

While the proportion of users of any censored internet who attempt to bypass the blocks is very small, by most measures

FreeGate and UltraSurf were astoundingly successful. This was despite their websites looking like they were designed in the 1990s and putting out ugly, sometimes atrociously buggy software. Between them, the two apps claimed millions of monthly users at their height,[25] and UltraSurf in particular was lauded as an effective anti-censorship tool, with a 2011 Freedom House report saying that it was "small in size, easy to hide [on] a computer, and discrete during usage ... performance is excellent, and it does not require any installation".[26] However, the same report pointed to problems with analysing the company's software and how it worked, due to its closed nature and scant technical documentation; these problems were also raised about FreeGate and other products put out by its parent company, Dynamic Internet Technology. "DIT's technology and its internal expertise are impossible to evaluate from an outsider's perspective," the report's authors said. "While DIT claims that their software constantly circumvents the Chinese Golden Shield Project, it offer [sic] no scientific or other evidence of this."

This lack of openness and transparency has long been one of the primary criticisms of FreeGate and UltraSurf. In 2012, Jacob Applebaum, a lead developer on the Tor project and one-time WikiLeaks spokesperson, wrote a caustic takedown of UltraSurf, based on his reverse engineering of the software. Most damning, given the fundamental purpose of the product, Applebaum found "that it is possible to monitor and block the use of UltraSurf using commercial off the shelf software".[27] He claimed that UltraSurf was "nearly worthless" as a privacy tool, and presented numerous security concerns for users, particularly that dummy copies of the software could be used to attack unwitting installers.[28] "UltraSurf does not provide meaningful anonymity and their security claims are false, misleading or entirely incorrect. It seems reasonable to stress that users who require any kind of security should avoid UltraSurf," the Tor report concluded. "We recommend against the

use of UltraSurf for anonymity, security, privacy or internet censorship circumvention."

In a response, UltraSurf accused Applebaum of basing his
assessment on an outdated version of the software and of misrep-
resenting or misunderstanding other features. They implied that
Tor was self-interested in attacking UltraSurf, as it also competes
for funding from government agencies. "Tor and UltraSurf
represent fundamentally different approaches solving the censorship challenge," the statement said. "As a result of these different
approaches, Tor simply cannot handle the number of users or scale
of activities that UltraSurf can."

It continued:

The Chinese government in particular has spent considerable
resources and has purchased high-end equipment from top
vendors around the world in an attempt to block software
like UltraSurf, yet it has never successfully blocked us for any
extended period of time; neither has there been any evidence of
monitoring. The same cannot be said for the Tor system, which
has been successfully blocked in China on many occasions for
extended periods.[29]

For many internet freedom activists, who tend towards a kind of
libertarian hacker ethos, one of the most damning things about both
FreeGate and UltraSurf was that they themselves blocked users from
visiting websites deemed undesirable by the developers. UltraSurf
admitted to employing filters to "block access to pornographic
material, illicit websites, and other sites deemed offensive". Like
the functioning of the software itself, however, this blocking was
not done transparently. While a service such as UltraSurf might
argue that it should be able to block pornography for bandwidth
or religious reasons, the definition of what exactly constitutes

pornography is pretty fuzzy, and "other sites deemed offensive" was fuzzier still. In a 2010 *Wired* article, an UltraSurf programmer, coming across a transgender porn site in the system's logs, told the reporter: "We don't want to spend our money supporting that."[30]

*

Years of fighting the Great Firewall costs money, and securing enough funding to keep going was always a key problem for Xia and his fellow developers. In 2001, he registered Global Internet Freedom Inc. as a corporation in his home state of North Carolina,[31] changing the name later that year to Dynamic Internet Technology Inc. He also set up the DynaWeb Foundation (also initially called Global Internet Freedom Inc.) as a non-profit organisation to take in donations and apply for charitable grants. A 2003 annual report gave DIT's area of business as "computer consulting" and listed eight board members, including Xia. Tax returns showed the non-profit bringing in around $6,500 in its first year. By 2003, revenue was up to $30,000, against around $23,000 worth of expenses to, according to that year's return, "provide connections to prohibited websites via computer home pages".

Beginning in late 2002, DIT partnered with Voice of America (VOA) and Radio Free Asia (RFA) to help break their content through the Great Firewall. Products of World War Two and the Cold War respectively, VOA and RFA are funded by Washington and for decades were banned from broadcasting in the US itself under anti-propaganda laws.[32] While both broadcasters profess objectivity and impartiality, by their very nature they tend to be pro-US in a broad sense and lean heavily on dissidents and critics of countries they cover. Often this serves as a counter to domestic propaganda, which may feature little to no criticism of the government. RFA in particular produces some excellent reporting from local journalists, often at great risk to themselves, out of Tibet and

Xinjiang, areas of China from which most Western journalists are locked out. According to its charter, the broadcaster's mission "is to provide accurate and timely news and information to Asian countries whose governments prohibit access to a free press".[33] Following the Tiananmen crackdown, funding for VOA broadcasting into China was ramped up, and in 1994 RFA was launched with an initial Mandarin-language broadcast in order to "promote democracy and human rights" in China.[34] Within a year, Beijing was investing heavily in jamming signals from the two US-funded broadcasters, and state media denounced them as tools of the CIA. Their websites and email newsletters were also heavily blocked and censored, a problem that Xia's company helped them solve.

Already sending mass emails containing Falun Gong tracts, DIT began transmitting newsletters for VOA and RFA with links to proxy servers and copies of banned reports. These emails had a limited period of effectiveness before the links were blocked by the Firewall. In order to get around the extra-sensitive spam filters built into Chinese email clients, the DIT team monitored which messages were getting through and which weren't to try to reverse-engineer the censors' blacklist. The solution was similar to that followed by early spammers, using letter substitutions, images instead of text, and other tricks. So VOA became V0A and homonyms were substituted for sensitive Chinese characters.[35] These partnerships (DIT also provided services for Human Rights in China and a few other NGOs) brought in some money, but not much: the foundation's tax returns for the early 2000s report revenue in the low tens of thousands, with often little left over after expenses, mainly server and other technical costs.

At the same time, demand for FreeGate and UltraSurf was increasing, and in 2006 Xia and others met with Michael Horowitz, a long-time China critic and member of the right-wing Hudson Institute, and Mark Palmer, a former US diplomat.[36] The two helped connect the Falun Gong practitioners with conservative lawmakers and lobby for government funding. In 2007, DIT secured a $4.47 million contract with the Broadcasting Board of Governors (BBG), which oversees VOA and RFA, for "mailing and distribution services", with an initial payment of $900,000.[37] Palmer became a key supporter and lobbyist for DIT and Falun Gong more generally. A former speechwriter for Henry Kissinger, he co-founded the National Endowment for Democracy (NED), which funnels US government cash to dissident and civil society groups in autocratic countries and has been heavily criticised for its lack of transparency and for promoting regime change. NED is so toxic in some countries that groups actively avoid it despite being eligible for funding, for fear that they will be viewed as agents of US imperialism.

The BBG wasn't the only US government entity funding internet freedom efforts. In 2001, In-Q-Tel, the venture capital arm of the CIA, invested $1 million in SafeWeb, a California-based start-up founded by thirty-five-year-old Stephen Hsu.[38] SafeWeb's software Triangle Boy promised to give users everywhere "free, private and secure access to an uncensored web".[39] In 2003 the company was acquired by anti-virus firm Symantec,[40] and Triangle Boy was later quietly discontinued.

In May 2008, an employee of the GIFC, FreeGate's and UltraSurf's parent organisation, appeared before the US Senate Subcommittee on Human Rights and the Law to argue for more funding for internet freedom programmes. "The companies and organisations that make up the [GIFC] have maintained the world's largest anti-censorship operation since 2000," Shiyu Zhou told lawmakers.

> The battle of Internet freedom is now boiling down to the battle of resources. It is our belief that $50 million – enough to allow [GIFC] programs to scale up their operations through purchasing equipment and expanding network capacity – will

be enough for us to reach the critical mass of ten percent of the 230 million Internet users in China. Importantly, the time for doing so is this coming year, given the current political dynamic in China and the upcoming Olympics. We hope and trust the Senate and the Congress will grasp what we believe to be a historic opportunity.[41]

Zhou's testimony, along with lobbying from Horowitz and Palmer, was effective. In 2008, a number of conservative members of Congress successfully amended a House Appropriations Bill to put aside an extra $15 million for the State Department's Human Rights and Democracy Fund, to be "made available for an internet freedom initiative to expand access and information in closed societies, including in the Middle East and Asia".[42] At least initially, however, the money did not go to the GIFC as intended, as government officials expressed concern at Beijing's reaction to giving such a large payout to Falun Gong practitioners.

Nevertheless, this was the start of a boom in funding for GIFC projects: government records show that FreeGate and UltraSurf received almost $12 million from the BBG between 2007 and 2017. Some continued to question the decision to fund a Falun Gong-backed group, especially one that was actively working to undermine Chinese national policy. China's ambassador to the US, Wang Baodong, was unsurprisingly outraged, saying that the GIFC and Falun Gong were "bent on vilifying the Chinese government with fabricated lies, undermining Chinese social stability and sabotaging China–US relations".[43] Anytime there was any suggestion of cutting or redirecting funding from the GIFC, however, Horowitz, Palmer and their allies in Congress and the media would ferociously lobby the State Department to keep the money tap turned on. As a 2010 report said: "in the past year, columnists at the *New York Times* and the *Wall Street Journal* and the editorial page of the

Washington Post have called" on the State Department to support the GIFC.[44]

Their cause was greatly helped by the 2009 Iranian election, which saw mass protests and an increase in internet censorship, leading to a spike in downloads of UltraSurf and FreeGate by users in Iran. Anti-Iran hawkishness is a bipartisan position in Washington, and the pro-internet freedom lobby were boosted by the growing narrative which permeated the media that the protests were a 'Twitter Revolution'. In a series of blog posts in June 2009 about Twitter's role in the demonstrations, Andrew Sullivan, an influential Iraq War supporter turned critic best known for pushing bunk race science in the pages of *The New Republic*, wrote for *The Atlantic* that Twitter was the "critical tool for organising the resistance in Iran".[45] Speaking to NPR, *The Wall Street Journal*'s Yochi Dreazen went even further, saying that "this [revolution] would not happen without Twitter".[46] Former George W. Bush national security adviser Mark Pfeifle even argued for Twitter to receive the Nobel Peace Prize.[47]

While it is undeniable that Twitter helped connect millions of people in the West with protests they might not otherwise have been that invested in or informed about, its actual effect on the ground was negligible. As journalist Evgeny Morozov wrote in a damning takedown of the 'Twitter Revolution' myth, on the eve of the protests, less than 0.027 per cent of the population was on Twitter, and many of the most popular 'Iranian' Twitter accounts during the uprising were people tweeting from the diaspora, sharing information sent to them by relatives and friends on the ground. Twitter was used to publicise the protests, but mostly in the West, in English. On the ground, the Farsi-speaking protesters were using more traditional communication methods, and the vast majority weren't paying any attention to Twitter.[48] This reality didn't stop *The Wall Street Journal* editorial page arguing in early 2010, months after the protests had begun to fizzle out, that Twitter had done "more for regime change in the Islamic Republic than years of sanctions, threats and Geneva-based haggling put together".[49]

One group of Iranians were paying attention to Twitter, however: the censors. From the beginning, they were suspicious about the motives of this Silicon Valley firm, which all the usual suspects in the Western media were holding up as instigator and guardian of the protests roiling the nation. Their suspicions were confirmed when, in a hugely misguided move, a twenty-seven-year-old State Department official, Jared Cohen, emailed Twitter co-founder Jack Dorsey to request that the company delay a scheduled global maintenance period that would have seen the service go offline for a few hours. In an even stranger move, the State Department then publicised that it had done so, with Assistant Secretary of State for Public Affairs P. J. Crowley telling *The New York Times* that "this was just a call to say: 'it appears Twitter is playing an important role at a crucial time in Iran. Could you keep it going?'"[50]

For those looking for evidence of US involvement in the Iranian protests, the admission that the US had directly intervened to keep Twitter online was pretty damning, and it was seized upon by the censors in Tehran, Beijing and elsewhere as evidence of why these American social media companies could not be trusted. Twitter didn't win the Nobel Peace Prize,[51] and Mahmoud Ahmadinejad went on to serve a second term as president of Iran, but the supposed 'Twitter Revolution' and its supporters in the West did succeed in providing abundant ammunition for censors the world over, resulting in the blockage of many social networking sites and other services, including those that could actually be used to easily organise protests.

The 'Twitter Revolution' showed the danger of direct government – particularly US government – involvement in internet freedom initiatives. The censors' argument is often predicated on the fact that foreign technologies and services are a danger to state security, that blocking them is akin to blocking terrorist groups. This means that proponents of internet freedom must walk a rhetorical tightrope, advocating for technologies and policies that could undermine autocratic regimes while avoiding appearing to do so in order to promote the interests of other governments. The internet is not a weapon of US imperialism, but that does not prevent it from being wielded in this way, or characterised as one.

This means, despite the terrible oppression that Falun Gong has received and the continued vicious propaganda campaign against it, that direct US government funding of Falun Gong's attempts to bypass the Great Firewall can be counterproductive to the cause of global internet freedom. Whether because it recognised this risk or because more recent administrations have been less willing to annoy Beijing, Washington appears to have realised this as well. Xia was very much aware of the problem, telling me he had seen "media reports mention that the State Department may feel pressure about the potential impacts on the US–China relationship and may want to avoid supporting our technologies". The Iran protests were very much a high point for FreeGate and UltraSurf, and funding to GIFC projects has lessened, with the most recent government contract ending in 2016, according to official records. "In recent years that collaboration has stopped," Xia said. Unfortunately for him, and for users of his tools, the amount of money flowing to the censors has only increased, and accessing the software from within China is now harder than ever.

While FreeGate and UltraSurf do not release detailed user figures, from my own reporting and knowledge of the internet freedom community, the number of people accessing the services from China appears to have dropped, even as they continue to be popular in countries with less effective firewalls, such as Iran and other Middle Eastern nations. In the last decade, more and more

Chinese users have turned to virtual private networks (VPNs) to get around the Firewall, helped by a boom in commercial services catering to those seeking privacy from government and employer surveillance. While VPNs as an anti-censorship solution have their own problems and have become less reliable as the Great Firewall continues to grow, for a long time they were a much more reliable means of accessing the open internet, even though the best services were often cost-prohibitive for the average Chinese internet user.

Others have simply abandoned censorship tools altogether. Since FreeGate was first released, China's internet has completely transformed, going from a walled-off garden with lots of ladders out of it to an increasingly impenetrable bubble with heavily censored alternatives to popular sites and little relation to the rest of the global internet. In part, this metamorphosis has been driven by ever-escalating censorship, but it has also become easier as a user in China not to miss the global web. The companies that dominate the internet in the rest of the world – Amazon, Facebook and Google – have all tried and failed to succeed in China. In the early years, the absence of such big players would be painfully obvious and a reason to jump the Great Firewall, but in their stead has arisen a crop of Chinese tech giants offering equivalent services, with the only difference being that they are all too willing to play along with government censorship, and they benefit hugely from doing so.

Chapter 10

Called to account

Silicon Valley's reckoning on Capitol Hill

In 2006, Google was still working on improving relations with Beijing when its executives in the US were dragged before their own government. In a congressional building on the south side of Capitol Hill, representatives of Google, Microsoft, Yahoo and Cisco faced a barrage of questions from the House Subcommittee on Human Rights and International Relations, which had called a hearing on whether the internet in China was "a tool for freedom, or suppression".

"While the internet has opened up commercial opportunities and provided access to vast amounts of information for people the world over, [it] has also become a malicious tool, a cyber-sledgehammer of repression of the government of the People's Republic of China," said Chris Smith, a large, square-jawed Republican congressman with intense blue eyes and thin-rimmed reading glasses, as he leaned forward in his seat.[1] "As soon as the promise of the internet began to be fulfilled, when brave Chinese [users] began to email each other around the world about human rights issues and corruption by government leaders, the Party cracked down."

Of the four companies arrayed before Smith, Google had faced the most criticism from the US media, thanks to both its fame and the company's well-known, and often mocked, 'Don't be evil' slogan. Of the four, however, Google's time operating in China was the shortest, and its conscience was the cleanest. Google was accused of collaborating with the creators of the Great Firewall, but Cisco had helped build it. In 2004, Yahoo provided user records that helped lead to the arrest of journalist Shi Tao, who was later sentenced to ten years in prison.[2] The following year, Microsoft had deleted the blog of dissident author Michael Anti after the authorities complained, censoring him not only in China but around the world.[3] This sparked instant outrage and criticism, but a Microsoft spokesperson defended the move on the grounds that it was the cost of doing business in China: "While this is a complex and difficult issue, we remain convinced it is better for Microsoft and other multinational companies to be in these markets with our services and communications tools, as opposed to not being there."

This was a view shared by Google's top management, particularly co-founders Sergey Brin and Larry Page, who had an evangelical view of their product. In this they were forerunners of what would become a Silicon Valley stereotype: the start-up founder who thinks they're going to save the world. All Google's executives understood that going into China would mean acquiescing to government censorship, which would seem to contradict the company's much vaunted founding principles. From their headquarters in Mountain View, however, it did not seem that clear-cut. In the words of chief executive Eric Schmidt, perhaps the biggest proponent of the company's China strategy, "We actually did an 'evil scale' and decided not to serve at all was worse evil."[4] Even years later, after everything fell apart, Page defended the decision: "Nobody actually believes this, but we very strongly made these decisions on what we thought were the best interests of humanity and the Chinese people."

The man Mountain View chose to help save China from life without Google was Taiwanese computer scientist Kaifu Lee. A cross between Steve Jobs and Dale Carnegie, he was such a popular public speaker that touts once sold tickets to one of his events in Beijing for $60 apiece.[5] Lee would be a huge boost to Google's brand in China, which had suffered due to the difficulties using the site caused by the Great Firewall. "I all but insist that we pull out all the stops and pursue him like wolves," Google senior vice president Jonathan Rosenberg wrote in an email to his fellow executives. "He is an all-star and will contribute in ways that go substantially beyond China."[6]

Stops were pulled out, and Google poached Lee from Microsoft with a $13 million contract, including a $2.5 million signing bonus. Lee quickly showed his worth as a public relations tool, writing that his decision to leave Microsoft was due to Google's youth, new way of doing things, and unmatched commitment to freedom and transparency. "I have the right to make my choice," he wrote. "I choose Google. I choose China."[7] Lee landed in Beijing on 17 September 2005 and immediately set about touring the country, recruiting students from top universities and building up the company's reputation with the wealthy Chinese elite.

On 25 January 2006, the censored Google.cn search engine went live, and brought with it a barrel load of criticism. In a post on the company's blog, senior policy counsel Andrew McLaughlin tried to explain Google's reasoning and rebut some of the critiques:[8]

> Google users in China today struggle with a service that, to be blunt, isn't very good. Google.com appears to be down around 10% of the time. Even when users can reach it, the website is slow, and sometimes produces results that when clicked on, stall out the user's browser ...
>
> This problem could only be resolved by creating a local presence, and this week we did so, by launching Google.cn, our website for the People's Republic of China. In order to

do so, we have agreed to remove certain sensitive information from our search results. We know that many people are upset about this decision, and frankly, we understand their point of view. This wasn't an easy choice, but in the end, we believe the course of action we've chosen will prove to be the right one ...

We ultimately reached our decision by asking ourselves which course would most effectively further Google's mission to organize the world's information and make it universally useful and accessible. Or, put simply: how can we provide the greatest access to information to the greatest number of people?

For some employees, particularly Lee in Beijing, the decision to comply with censorship was an easy and obvious one. In his plodding autobiography, *Making a World of Difference*, he devotes just one page to the controversy, around the same amount of space he gives to discussing the cushy amenities at Google's Silicon Valley headquarters. Describing a meeting with top executives in the US, Lee writes that he "spent a lot of time and effort to help them understand why it was necessary to abide by Chinese laws in China. Finally, I saw most of them nodding."[9]

In the US, Google's success had come from the fact that it was objectively superior at finding more relevant results than its rivals. Now it turned out that the company was equally skilled at burying content. When the Chinese search engine launched, in the words of Google biographer Stephen Levy, the company's engineers "had done a scary good job in preventing Chinese citizens from accessing forbidden information".[10] The first page of results for 'Falun Gong' listed only sites criticising the practice, while searches for 'Tiananmen Square' produced lots of nice tourist photographs and none of tanks.

Unlike its local rivals, however, Google.cn let users know when they weren't getting the full picture. Without seeking permission from the government first, the search engine had decided to include a message hinting that censorship had taken place: "These search results are not complete, in accordance with Chinese laws and regulations." It was a sop to critics in the US, and a way for those inside the company with doubts about the China strategy, particularly Brin, to alleviate them somewhat. But this tiny dose of transparency would later come back to haunt Google.

*

That Chinese users were better off with a censored version of the American companies' services than none at all was a common refrain on Capitol Hill, as Smith and other lawmakers tore into the tech giants, accusing them of collaborating with the Chinese regime and throwing dissidents under the bus. The New Jersey congressman came out guns blazing, comparing the companies' role in China to that of IBM under Nazi Germany. Google, Yahoo, Microsoft and Cisco, he said, had helped the Chinese authorities prop up two essential pillars of a totalitarian regime – propaganda and a secret police – by "propagating the message of the dictatorship unabated and supporting the secret police in a myriad of ways, including surveillance and invasion of privacy, in order to effectuate the massive crackdown on its citizens".[11]

Michael Callahan, Yahoo's general counsel, was the first to attempt to rebut the lawmakers' barrage of criticism. He defended Yahoo's role in the Shi Tao case, saying that the company "had no information about the identity of the user or the nature of the investigation" when they provided data which condemned him to years in prison.

"When we receive a demand from law enforcement authorised under the law of the country in which we are operating, we must comply," Callahan said. "Ultimately, American companies face a choice: Comply with Chinese laws or leave."[12]

Google communication chief Elliot Schrage, a curly haired, clean-shaven Californian, made a similar argument. Google, he said, had been forced to choose between compromising its mission by failing to serve users in China or by collaborating with Chinese censorship. "Self-censorship, like that which we are now required to perform in China, is something that conflicts deeply with our core principles," he said. "Our hope is that the decision will prove to be the right one. If, over time, we are not able to achieve our objectives to continue to balance those interests in China, we will not hesitate to reconsider doing business in that market."[13]

The Google executive did not falter until Jim Leach, a white-haired Iowa Republican, drilled down on how the company had worked out what to censor. "You indicated that self-censorship was required, as I understand it, but it is my understanding that it was voluntarily undertaken, and you did not have any negotiations with the Chinese government," he said. "Is that valid or invalid?"

"Congressman, it is a condition of the licence to do business in the country that you comply with the law, and it is a condition of complying with the law that you restrict the content available," Schrage said, before Leach interrupted him.

"So it is not true that you did this in anticipation of the Chinese government objection. You had the government objection prior," Leach said.

Schrage responded that if the company had not agreed to restrict content, it would never have been able to acquire a licence to operate in China. Looking tired, his voice dripping disapproval, Leach asked: "Did they cite exactly what it is you were to block in this licence that you have, and then if it did not, how do you know what to block, if it is not that you are anticipating government actions? I mean, how do you know?"

"My understanding is, and, again, I do not have the licence in front of me, but I did have a conversation with my colleagues about this very issue, the licence makes reference to the laws that need to be respected or complied with, and that is the basis," Schrage said.

"So you interpret these laws on specific things?" Leach asked.

"Based on the practices," Schrage said.

"Did you check with Yahoo? How do you know what the practices are? Did you check with your competitors? They have to do this, so we are going to do this?"

"What we did was we set up a computer in China and started performing searches, and as the chairman demonstrated rather powerfully, we learned from using other services and comparing the results of other services to our own."

"So you just put down what others did – for example, your Chinese competitor – and decided to do the same thing without being asked. That makes you a functionary of the Chinese govern-ment," Leach sounded astonished, as Schrage tried and failed to interject. "You have asked yourself the questions of what if I am a censor, what would I want to censor? You go to the practices of others, and then you follow them. Is that a valid description? This is an amazing description, I want to tell you. This is using your technology to learn how to censor."

His voice rising, Leach continued: "In all industries, we have all heard this term 'best practices'. I think you just have affirmed a novelty in American commerce: worst practices you have studied and adopted. That is an astonishing circumstance ... So if this Congress wanted to learn how to censor, we would go to you, the company that should symbolise the greatest freedom of information in the history of man. This is a profound story that is being told."[14]

"This was not something that we did enthusiastically or not something that we are proud of at all," Schrage said, his voice cracking slightly. He pointed to Google including a statement on all results highlighting when censorship had taken place.

Tom Lantos, a Democrat with deep-set eyes and swept-back white hair, asked Schrage if he could say he was "ashamed of what you and your company and the other companies have done?"

"Congressman, I actually cannot."

"Cannot?"

"I cannot say that. As I alluded to earlier, I do not think it is fair to say that we are ashamed of what we have done."

"I am not asking for fairness; I am asking for your judgement," Lantos said. "You have nothing to be ashamed of?"

"I am not ashamed of it, and I am not proud of it. We have taken a path ... that we believe will ultimately benefit our users in China," Schrage said. "If we determine, Congressman, as a result of changes in circumstances or as a result of the implementation of the Google.cn programme service, that we are not achieving those results, then we will assess our performance, our ability to achieve the goals, and decide whether or not to remain in that market."[15]

Lantos, a Hungarian Jew who survived the Holocaust and whose family were killed in concentration camps, turned to the other witnesses to ask whether they were ashamed. "IBM complied with legal orders when they cooperated with Nazi Germany," he said forcefully. "Those were legal orders under the Nazi German system. Since you were not alive at that time, in retrospect, having a degree of objectivity which some of you are incapable of summoning up with respect to your own case, do you think that IBM, during that period, had something to be ashamed of?"

Jack Krumholtz, Microsoft's youthful general counsel, had the misfortune of attempting to respond: "Congressman, we think that, on balance, the benefit of providing the services that Microsoft provides ..."

"My question relates to IBM and Nazi Germany," Lantos interjected.

"I cannot speak to that."

"You have no view on that?"

"I am not familiar in detail with IBM's activities in that period."

"Did you hear our Chairman's opening remarks on that subject?"

"Yes, I did."

"Do you think those are accurate remarks?"

"I take the Chairman at his word, certainly ..."

"I also take the Chairman at his word. Assuming that his words were accurate, is IBM to be ashamed of that action during that period?"

"Congressman, I do not think it is my position to say whether or not IBM is to be ashamed of its action in that period."

Robert Wexler, a young Democrat from Florida, was the only lawmaker to really dissent from his colleagues, drawing a comparison between IBM's complicity in the Holocaust and the US government's failure to take action against Nazi Germany to slow down or stop the implementation of the Final Solution. The US, Wexler pointed out, could have taken far more stringent action to pressure China on internet censorship; instead, it had normalised relations with Beijing and increased bilateral trade.

Then he threw the tech firms a lifeline: "Could somebody tell us, if the four of you got together ... and tomorrow said, we are packing our bags, what do you reasonably believe would be the consequences to the development of the internet in China? Would these poor victims of the Chinese policy of this type of persecution, do you think they would be any better off?"

Schrage was the first to respond: "I think that there would be less information, less available to people in China."

"I believe it would be a lose–lose," Microsoft's Krumholtz said. "I believe that Chinese citizens would lose, and I believe that all of those of us who would like to promote greater democracy, greater freedom of expression in China, would also be at a loss."

It was an eloquent summary of how the companies saw their role, amid a blistering hearing that left the witnesses reeling and appalled some within Google, who felt that they had got a raw deal. While Schrage's uneasy, grudging acceptance of the ickiness of doing business in China was perhaps the norm inside the company, a few, like Lee in Beijing, found the criticism utterly bizarre.[16] Eric Schmidt, the company's narrow-eyed, pale-haired executive chairman, was another. "I think it's arrogant for us to walk into a country where we are just beginning to operate and tell that country how to operate," he told reporters at an event in Beijing a few weeks after the hearing.

*

If US lawmakers thought Google was acting too much like a Chinese company, the search giant's biggest problem in China was that users saw it as an American interloper. Baidu, which had been the biggest beneficiary of Google's brief ejection by the Great Firewall, sought to capitalise on this attitude with an intensely hostile advertising blitz.[17] In one commercial, a tall, bearded white man in a top hat, accompanied by an Asian woman in a wedding dress, speaks heavily-accented Mandarin while a Chinese man in traditional garb taunts him with a series of word games. Eventually the foreigner collapses, vomiting blood, as his bride and supporters jeer and run to the victorious Chinese master. "Have a problem? Just Baidu it," a voice says over the company's logo.[18]

Baidu, like many companies in China facing foreign competition, sought to make the choice of business a matter of patriotism, emphasising its local knowledge and understanding of the Chinese market. This was in spite of Google.cn being staffed and run by some of the country's brightest technologists and engineers, who were at least as experienced in dealing with the unique challenges of Chinese searches as their competitors.

"To be competitive here, you must understand the local culture," Baidu's handsome, youthful-looking chief executive Robin Li said in

2014, when asked to reflect on why Google.cn had failed. "If you don't understand local circumstances, it's difficult for you to survive in the market."[19] He gave the example of a gaming portal that chose the Chinese name 'More Rice to Come', which Li said was intended to evoke China's agricultural past but had the opposite effect, offending the young, urban Chinese who made up the majority of internet users at that time. "They definitely were not starving, so they felt no connection to the name. Instead, they may even have felt insulted, and thought to themselves, 'I am not a peasant,'" he said.

In the eyes of Robin Li and many other Chinese, Google made the same mistake when it adopted the official Chinese name Gu Ge, two characters meaning both 'valley song' and 'song of the harvest'. The name was suggested by the company's Chinese staff and deliberately chosen to avoid any potential negative connotations (a previous transliteration of Google, 'Goo-go-a', was seen as overly cute and childish), but when it backfired it was held up as an example of the search firm's innate foreignness. "It didn't have any negative meaning, and the priority was to get a Chinese name as soon as possible," said Dandan Wu, one of the founding members of Google.cn.[20] "We phonetically translated the company's name into two Chinese words with a nice meaning, 'a song from the valley'," Kaifu Lee wrote in his autobiography, which does not mention the controversy surrounding the company's Chinese moniker.[21] Perhaps for Lee and Wu, wealthy, upper-class sophisticates generations removed from toiling in the fields, the name was quaint and pleasant, but for China's middle-class strivers it seemed patronising – and a video advertising the new name, done in traditional ink brush style, didn't help:

In this sowing season Google takes the name Valley Song. Using the grain as a song, it is a song of sowing and expectation. It's also a song of harvesting with joy. Welcome to Gu Ge.[22]

"They thought people would feel happy about such a good harvest. But at the time, Chinese netizens couldn't care less about any harvest," Baidu's Li said years later. A website was launched, NoGuGe.com, which urged the company to reconsider, saying the name had a 'negative impact' on users and would hurt Google's image in China. It attracted thousands of signatures and suggested alternative transliterations. But it's hard to imagine that Google wouldn't have suffered a similar backlash if it had chosen the top-voted suggestion, Gou Gou, or 'Dog Dog'.[23]

Google was damned whatever it did – not because it lacked Chinese staff with local knowledge or understanding of the country's unique circumstances, but because it lacked the government connections and support that Baidu had cultivated for years. Baidu was able to present itself to officials as the reliable, trustworthy and, most importantly, patriotic alternative to the suspicious, US-operated, anti-censorship Google. Between 2002, when Google was blocked by the Firewall, and the launch of Google.cn in 2006, Baidu grew from a single-digit market share to well over 50 per cent.[24] The American search engine managed to claw its way back to around 30 per cent within a couple of years, mainly at the expense of smaller Chinese search engines, as the market became a two-horse race. But as it began to threaten Baidu, some Google employees said they hit an artificial ceiling: "It was as if the government was sending Google a message: you can be in our market, but you must not be the leader."[25]

Despite its initial stumbles, Google appeared to be finally making headway in China. Eric Schmidt, the company's chief executive, who remained the biggest supporter of the China strategy even as his fellow executives' doubts grew, visited the Beijing offices in April 2006. In a fancy hotel hired for the occasion, he joined the China team in celebrating the company's new name. Schmidt and Lee built a large puzzle showing the two characters, Gu Ge, as audience members applauded.[26] In meetings later, Schmidt said, "We will take a long-term view to win in China. The Chinese have five thousand years of history. Google has five thousand years of patience in China." He did not realise just how much that patience would be tested.[27]

Part 3: Sword

Chapter 11

Uyghurs online

Ilham Tohti and the birth of the Uyghur internet

On 23 September 2014, Ilham Tohti sat before the People's Intermediate Court in Urumqi, capital of Xinjiang, a region in China's
far west. He was thousands of kilometres from his home in Beijing,
where Ilham,[1] a university professor and founder of the politics and
culture website Uyghur Online, had been arrested eight months
before. Ilham was charged with using "malicious fabrications and
distortions of the truth to incite ethnic hatred", encouraging violence,
and working with a "vile criminal clique" to split the country.[2]

Ilham wore a red and orange checked shirt he had been wearing
the day he was arrested, but otherwise his appearance had changed
dramatically. Most of the forty-four-year-old's hair had gone grey,
and a large bald patch had appeared on top of his head. Slumped in
his chair, he looked tired, his once plump features now gaunt, with
large bags under his eyes. And yet, as the day's proceedings began, he
greeted the court with a smile, and paid close attention as the hearing
continued. In his closing statement denying all charges against him,
Ilham told the court that he had "always opposed separatism and
terrorism, and not a single one of his articles supported separatism".[3]

"I love my country," he said, speaking in both Mandarin and
Uyghur, his native language and that of the ethnic group of the
same name which makes up the majority in Xinjiang.

Outside Xinjiang, Uyghurs are a tiny minority, making up less than 1 per cent of China's total population.[4] Speaking a Turkic rather than Sinitic language, and mostly Muslim, Uyghurs are darker skinned than most Han Chinese, with Eurasian features and oval eyes. Male Uyghurs often wear traditional *doppa* headgear – a square skullcap common among Turkic peoples – while many women choose to be veiled. Although most Chinese Uyghurs live in Xinjiang, there are thousands who have moved to the country's major cities, particularly Shanghai and Beijing, where many began migrating in earnest in the 1980s.[5] Because of their small numbers and Xinjiang's geographic isolation, their representation and perception within China are often based on Han stereotypes.[6] These can range from being depicted as an exotic if somewhat quaint and backwards culture of dancers and musicians[7] to a pervasive image – particularly of young male Uyghurs – of dangerous vagabonds prone to theft and violence.[8] The fact that many early Uyghur migrants to big Chinese cities spoke little Mandarin, and that they lived in segregated neighbourhoods, only compounded their alienation and the Han majority's distrust.

Ilham was born in 1969, in Artux, at the western edge of the Tarim Basin, near the ancient oasis city of Kashgar and the border with Kyrgyzstan. Unlike the capital Urumqi, or other parts of north-eastern Xinjiang, Han Chinese were still a tiny minority in the area around Artux, less than 10 per cent, with Uyghurs being the predominant ethnic group.[9] Twenty years earlier, the People's Liberation Army (PLA) had marched into Xinjiang, cementing the Party's control over the region. Ilham's family was both a beneficiary and a victim of the new China.[10] His father, Tohti, was sent to the Chinese interior for high school and later studied at two prestigious universities in Beijing. After graduation, Tohti returned to Xinjiang to work as a civilian official for the PLA, a prominent role for a Uyghur at the time. He held this role throughout most of the Mao era, weathering the ideological storms of the Anti-Rightist Movement and the Great Leap Forward. But then, in 1966, the Cultural Revolution came to Xinjiang.

At the beginning of the Great Proletarian Cultural Revolution – the decade-long civil war that paralysed China and caused the deaths of tens of thousands of people – provincial officials were initially successful in preventing the chaos spilling into Xinjiang.[11] But the Red Guards could not be kept out forever, and along with a fervent loyalty to Mao and his desire to cleanse the country of 'reactionary' elements, they brought with them a vicious Han supremacist ideology. In Beijing and other major cities, foreigners were targeted and ethnic minorities suffered throughout China. A straw figure with a black face was hanged outside the Kenyan embassy,[12] while the British mission was stormed and burned. In Inner Mongolia, tens of thousands of ethnic Mongols were detained and horrifically tortured.

"Red Guards just off the train from Beijing," writes historian James Millward, "knew and thought little of traditional Uyghur culture."[13] They shared this with Jiang Qing, Mao's wife and one of the leaders of the Cultural Revolution. Jiang was quoted as saying she "despised" Xinjiang and openly regarded minorities as "foreign invaders and aliens".[14] The Guards revelled in destroying Uyghur culture: ancient customs were banned, Muslim graveyards desecrated, Qur'ans burned, and mosques turned into pigsties.[15]

In 1971, Ilham's father was swept up by the violence and killed.[16] An intellectual, a member of the local Party elite and a Uyghur, Tohti was damned thrice over in the eyes of the Guards. Being a model minority was not enough to save him, just as it would not be for his son. Ilham was two when Tohti died, and he grew up not really knowing who his father was. Few who lived through the terrible days of the Cultural Revolution, in which even the non-believers were often forced to compromise themselves by participating in denouncements and violent struggle sessions, wanted to discuss it afterwards. Ilham felt proud of his father, but his idea of him was vague, seen mainly through the eyes of his mother, who raised Ilham and his three brothers while working in a car repair shop.

Ilham and his siblings thrived. His eldest brother joined the army, and later the Party, going on to hold a series of high-ranking positions in local government and in provincial Party bodies. Another brother became a public security officer, and also a Party member. In 1985, aged sixteen, Ilham left for Beijing, where he studied at Minzu University, the country's top school for ethnic minorities. After graduation, he stayed on campus, first as an administrative worker before eventually joining the faculty of the economics department.

At that time, China was undergoing great change, as the policies of reform and opening up initiated in the late 1970s really took hold, transforming the country from a backwards, closed-off nation dominated by the cult of Mao to an outward-looking, capitalist power. As his family had risen to the heights of Xinjiang society, and as he was ensconced in the elite circles of Beijing academia, Ilham could have thrived as a representative of the new, multi-ethnic, meritocratic China. Over time, he would likely have been invited to join one of the numerous political advisory bodies that, in theory, provide input on legislation, but more often act as old boys' clubs, furthering members' stature and prestige.

Ilham was acutely aware of the privilege he possessed and his unique situation compared with most Uyghurs from Artux. He began writing about the challenges facing Xinjiang, such as pervasive unemployment among Uyghurs, and the need to reform the region's economy, which was dominated by state-run entities such as the Bingtuan, a colossal paramilitary production and construction corps set up in the 1950s that still controls most agricultural business in Xinjiang. Ilham did not see himself as a political figure – indeed, he vociferously rejected attempts by others to cast him as such. He was an academic, studying the problems and making recommendations to the government to help it achieve its self-stated goals of improving the situation of ethnic minorities, reforming the economy, and fighting extremism.[17]

This effort was not appreciated by the authorities. To Xinjiang officials, always on the lookout for separatists, a Uyghur Muslim academic speaking publicly about the region's problems, and even giving interviews to the international media, could not be tolerated. Almost immediately, Ilham began experiencing harassment and pressure from officials in Xinjiang. Within the relatively more liberal environment of Beijing, he was somewhat protected, but when he launched his multilingual website Uyghur Online in 2005, that pressure extended to his family and friends. Some of them reached out to Ilham, begging him to keep his head down and focus on making money, the mantra of post-Tiananmen China. But he couldn't stop; in particular, he felt Uyghur Online was too important.

The website, half discussion forum and half news site, covered Xinjiang politics and culture, building a large community of authors and commenters. It was strictly moderated, and anything close to extremist or separatist thought was quickly deleted by a team of volunteer administrators, but it did not shy away from discussing sensitive issues. In Uyghur, Chinese and other languages, Ilham hoped that the discussion and debate would help build connections between ethnic communities and lead to greater understanding and empathy.

*

Xinjiang sprawls. Stretching from the Tibetan plateau in the southeast to Kazakhstan on its north-western border, the Xinjiang Uyghur Autonomous Region[18] is China's largest administrative region by far, at more than 1.6 million square kilometres. At the same time, it is one of the country's least densely populated regions, with around 22 million people,[19] half of whom are clustered in the areas around Kashgar, Yining, and the capital Urumqi.[20]

The Heavenly Mountain range bisects Xinjiang west to east, dividing it into distinct northern and southerly regions. In Dzungaria in the north lies Urumqi, most of the region's manufacturing, and the majority of its Han population.[21] Dzungaria, originally peopled by nomadic Mongol tribes, also contains most of Xinjiang's grasslands and arable land.[22] This is in stark contrast to the southern Tarim Basin, which is dominated by the Taklamakan Desert, a vast, arid expanse lying in the rain shadow of the Himalaya and Pamir mountain ranges, dotted with the occasional oasis fed by snowmelt.[23] Tarim is where most Uyghurs live.

Although invading Chinese armies rampaged through what is now Xinjiang and controlled parts of it for centuries, the modern administrative unit dates only to the mid-nineteenth century.[24] The name Xinjiang – its Chinese characters translate as 'new territory' – was bestowed on the region by the Manchu authorities in 1884, bringing it formally into the Qing Empire.[25] Before then, Xinjiang had been known by the vague term 'western regions'.[26] With more than 2,000 years of documented history, spanning khanates, petty kingdoms and empires, it is perhaps understandable that many Uyghurs and other non-Han groups in Xinjiang object to the region's Chinese name. Uyghurs in particular tend to prefer the term East Turkestan, which, though newer – popularised during the early twentieth century – better reflects the region's proximity to, and kinship with, the 'West Turkestan' of Uzbekistan, Kazakhstan, Tajikistan, Kyrgyzstan and Turkmenistan, whose peoples share histories and ethnicity with those native to Xinjiang.[27] East Turkestan was also the name of two short-lived breakaway republics in the 1930s and 1940s[28] and is strongly associated with the Uyghur independence movement today.[29]

Just like 'Xinjiang', the term 'Uyghur' is also one with a history steeped in politics. As journalist Nick Holdstock argues, while the term itself appears to date back centuries, "not only do the peoples the term originally referred to have little or nothing in common with Uyghurs in the modern era, there were also centuries when no such identity existed".[30] In modern parlance, Uyghur refers to the Turkic-speaking, largely Muslim ethnic group that has traditionally formed the majority in what is now Xinjiang,[31] although significant Hui, Mongol, Kazakh and Han minorities have long existed there as well.

Following the founding of the People's Republic of China, Beijing moved quickly to shore up control of its westernmost regions, both militarily and rhetorically. In 1959, a Party journal stated that "Xinjiang has since ancient times been an inseparable part of the motherland", a view shared by few historians.[32] As Holdstock writes:

> Only a very selective historical view allows the present Chinese government to claim that the region has *always* been a part of China, one which requires glossing over the eight centuries when the area wasn't part of any regime based in that territory, either in part or as a whole.[33]

James Millward, one of the most respected historians of the region, has written that the idea of Xinjiang as an essential part of China was "something no Chinese would have argued before the nineteenth century".[34] Even then, as Justin Jacobs demonstrates in his history of republican-era Xinjiang, the region was still viewed as a thing apart from China proper, under the control of Beijing but always at risk of being lost, becoming another 'Outer Mongolia' or Manchuria.[35]

History shows that, regardless of how rulers in Beijing concep-tualised Xinjiang, local administrators from the Qing Empire to the republican period through to today have always regarded it as fundamentally different to the *neidi* (interior). In 1916, Governor Yuan Zengxin wrote to Beijing to remind his superiors of the need for flexibility and alternative tactics in Xinjiang, which, he noted, "absolutely cannot be managed in a fashion similar to that of the inner provinces".[36] At times, the 'special conditions' of Xinjiang have played to its residents' advantage. Until relatively recently, Uyghurs and other ethnic minorities in Xinjiang were largely spared Beijing's draconian family-planning policies.[37] The "need to maintain social and political stability" meant that Xinjiang, while not unscathed, was spared the worst of Mao Zedong's disastrous Great Leap Forward.[38] As famine caused by catastrophic misman-agement and corruption hit parts of the Chinese interior, millions of refugees fled to the comparative abundance in Xinjiang.[39]

Sensitivity over Xinjiang's place within China and its inherent Chinese-ness, or lack thereof, continues today and is key to under-standing Beijing's policies towards the region and the harsh treatment of those within it. While the Party may claim that Xinjiang has been a part of China eternal, its actions reveal an ongoing paranoia that the region could break away entirely. Only in Tibet are policies as draconian and crackdowns on dissent as hard as they are in Xinjiang. While Uyghurs bear the brunt of this – facing discrimi-nation in employment and education, and restrictions on practising their culture, religion and language – Han residents of Xinjiang are also stigmatised and often regarded as 'others' by the wider popu-lation of the *neidi*.[40]

*

When I visited in May 2017, the Niujie mosque in western Beijing was sleepy and quiet. Inside its grand courtyard, reminiscent of traditional Chinese temples, a young couple posed for wedding photos draped in elaborately embroidered gold cloth. The oldest and largest mosque in Beijing, Niujie could hold around a thousand worshipers at peak times, such as Friday prayers, but few were visible now. The only other people in the mosque were a handful of veiled middle-aged women and an elderly caretaker on a seemingly endless loop between his guard post and a backroom where a kettle brewed large batches of tea. The surrounding Muslim quarter was far busier, as crowds of people queued in the hot sun outside holes in the wall where sweaty cooks grilled meat and served snacks in small white plastic bags. Most Beijingers' dealings with Uyghurs begin and end at the *chuanr* (pronounced ch-wah-rr) stand, the triumph of northern Chinese street food, where skewers of chicken, lamb and vegetables are roasted over a charcoal brazier and served with warm circles of seasoned, crispy flatbread.

In a Starbucks near the Ministry of Foreign Affairs in Beijing, I met a woman from Xinjiang, who asked that I call her Gu Li, the Uyghur equivalent of Jane Doe. Gu moved to the capital shortly after she was born, in 1985, and has lived there ever since. She grew up in a Han community, was not particularly religious, and was as integrated into Chinese society as anyone can be. But her experiences of daily discrimination and micro-aggressions were characteristic of life for many Uyghurs. Seeming more exhausted than angry, she told me about baristas writing 'foreign friend' on her cup rather than bothering to try to spell her Uyghur name, and the time when she was ordered to come to the front of class in kindergarten so the teacher could point at her facial features to show other students "what a Uyghur looked like".[41]

Gu also expressed frustration with the depiction of Uyghurs in the Chinese media: as backwards, overly religious, and dangerous. This was what Uyghur Online was intended to combat, and other Uyghurs had also attempted to change this, launching blogs and video series showing their daily lives, or the difficulties of integrating into general Chinese society as a Muslim, such as the pervasiveness of pork in Chinese cuisine and the pressure to drink alcohol at professional networking events. But all too often state media focused on the alleged risk of terrorism from Islamist groups that had targeted Uyghurs for recruits, or it simply ignored them altogether. Uyghurs such as Gu – who, on paper, embodied the government's model for how ethnic minorities should integrate into Han society – were represented even less.

In talking to Gu and others like her in the capital, I was hoping to get a better understanding of how things had been for Ilham and his family, particularly his daughter Jewher Ilham, who now lives in exile in the US. Growing up in Beijing in the early 2000s as the child of a successful, well-off academic, Jewher enjoyed a rare level of privilege but still experienced the type of daily discrimination Gu described. Other Beijingers often didn't know how to place Jewher. With a prominent nose, round face and large, wide eyes, she was obviously not Han, but in her formal boarding school uniform she did not fit most people's stereotype of what a Uyghur was supposed to look like either. Often, in shopping malls or markets, Han sellers would assume that she was a Westerner and call out to her in English in the hopes of a big sale.[42]

'Hello? Miss? Miss? Come and look please,' they would say, but when she responded in fluent, Beijing-accented Mandarin, her ethnicity would become clear and they would give up. The stereotype of Uyghurs as poor and untrustworthy took precedence over the sellers' first impression of her as a wealthy potential customer.

This sense of alienation was compounded by how out of place Jewher felt in Xinjiang whenever she visited family with her father and stepmother. Although she was born in Beijing and grew up in a mostly Han community, like many Chinese whose families have migrated within the country, Jewher still thought of her *laojia*, or home town, as being that of her parents. But when she visited, her relatives viewed her as an outsider. They saw her as a Beijinger, a guest to be treated with generosity and love, but not one of them.

She felt stuck between two worlds, at home in neither of them, a sense of confusion and isolation that only increased as she got older and gradually became aware of her father's position within the Uyghur community, and his vulnerability because of it.

At her elite boarding school, not far from her parents' home, at first Jewher was only peripherally aware of who her father was becoming. In her absence, Ilham had turned the family's apartment into a halfway house for homeless Uyghurs he met on the streets of Beijing, giving them food and shelter until they could find a more permanent place to live. At the weekend, when Jewher returned from school, the house would often be bursting with people, and she would sit and talk with these strangers, hearing about their lives and struggles.[43] She would often know more about them than she did about Ilham himself. While he was loving and affectionate, her father maintained a level of distance from his children, particularly regarding his political work, encouraging them to focus on their schooling and get ahead.

Jewher could nevertheless sense that something was wrong. While children will accept most situations as normal, as she became a teenager, she began to realise that her family was anything but. Police officers did not visit her friends' apartments to meet with their fathers. Nor did anyone else's father have to take sudden 'vacations' during which he could not call or write. During this time, the situation in Xinjiang was worsening, becoming more and more tense. An explosion was coming, one that would engulf her father and set him on a path he could not control.

Chapter 12

Shutdown

How to take 20 million people offline

The fire that would engulf Ilham Tohti and the Uyghur internet was sparked in mid-2009. A five-hour train ride north of Hong Kong, on the border of Guangdong and Hunan provinces, lies the small and ancient city of Shaoguan. Dating back to the early years of the Tang Dynasty, the city is surrounded by some of the most stunning landscapes in China: sprawling red sandstone hills, lush greenery and giant outcrops carved by centuries of erosion.

With just over a million people living within the city's three main districts,[1] Shaoguan was tiny by the standards of Guangdong province, less than a tenth the size of Shenzhen, the sprawling megacity to the south. Like its much larger neighbours, however, the city had been transformed by an influx of migrant workers from all over China, who moved from the provinces to seek employment in the hundreds of factories that sprang up in Guangdong as its GDP grew almost fivefold between the start of the millennium and 2010.[2]

In 2009, the Xuri Toy Factory in Shaoguan's central Wujiang district employed around 16,000 migrant workers.[3] Mostly in their teens or early twenties, they lived in cramped dorms, working long hours and sending much of their meagre paycheques home. Unlike factories in Shenzhen or Dongguan, which were filled with migrants from the interior, most of the Xuri workers were from rural Guangdong or neighbouring provinces. They spoke Cantonese, Hakka and a smattering of other languages and dialects, but Mandarin, China's official language since 1956, was their common tongue. They were also nearly all Han, the ethnic group to which 91 per cent of China's population belongs.[4]

In May, a new group of workers arrived at the factory.[5] They did not fit in with the other employees. They dressed differently, their skin was darker, and many had beards. Most did not speak Mandarin, and none were Han. The almost 800 men and women were Uyghurs. They had travelled 3,800 kilometres from Shufu county, near Kashgar and the border with Tajikistan, to make toys for export overseas, part of a government plan to develop their home area by sending migrants out to the coastal provinces, where they could earn up to seven times the annual salary in Shufu.[6]

From the beginning, the Shufu workers were kept at a distance from their new colleagues: housed in separate dormitories and placed in all-Uyghur teams. One official justified the segregation on the grounds that Uyghurs had "different living and eating habits" to Han workers.[7] This separation only served to deepen the suspicion with which the Han workers viewed their new colleagues. Within weeks, rumours began to spread that the Uyghurs were thieves and rapists. "Some young Xinjiang boys are involved in many robbery cases," one Han worker said in a characteristic account. "They are bad. You know, they don't know Chinese and we don't know their language. We can't communicate with each other."[8]

As the rumours multiplied, in canteens and on internet bulletin boards, some began claiming that management was ignoring or covering up criminal behaviour by the newcomers. "The first rape occurred in the woods behind the factory and the perpetrators were three Uyghur male workers," according to one account posted online. "One week later, another girl went out for a midnight snack and was dragged into the Uyghur dormitory and gang raped. When the security guards brought her out, she was stark naked. The factory offered her 10,000 yuan [around $1,400] to keep quiet."[9] While sexual harassment and assault is a real and pervasive problem within Chinese factories, with as many as 70 per cent of women in one area reporting being propositioned or otherwise harassed by their male colleagues,[10] there is little evidence to support the claims that Uyghur men were preying on their Han colleagues. The author of a widely shared bulletin board post saying that six Uyghur men had raped two Han girls later confessed to fabricating the account because he blamed the newcomers for taking his job.[11]

Late in the evening of 25 June, as Shaoguan sweltered in the muggy summer heat, Huang Cuilian, a nineteen-year-old trainee line worker, was making her way back to her dormitory after a night out with friends. Huang had been at the factory for only a few weeks, and in the dark she missed her building and stumbled inside another of the identical blocks. As she walked to what she thought was her room, Huang found several young Uyghur men sitting on their beds. Perhaps influenced by the rape rumours, or simply shocked to suddenly be alone in a room full of strange men, she screamed and ran out of the door.[12]

For the testosterone-filled young Han men who made up the bulk of the factory's workforce, this was the last straw. Although Huang later said that she told no one about entering the wrong room, her scream was heard across the campus. At around 11pm, a mob formed carrying knives and iron rods pulled from bed frames.[13] Hundreds of Han men converged on the Uyghur dormitory, smashing windows and hurling rubbish through the holes. Inside the building, Uyghur and Han workers fought in the corridors as others attempted to barricade themselves in their rooms or flee into the hills behind the factory grounds. Any Uyghurs unlucky enough to be caught outside the dormitory were savagely beaten and left for dead. "People were so vicious, they just kept beating the dead bodies," one witness said later.[14]

Two Uyghur men – Aximujiang Aimaiti and Sadikejiang Kaze – were beaten to death,[15] and at least a hundred others were injured in the violence, which took more than 400 riot police five hours to stop, according to official reports.[16] The Uyghur workers not in hospital or the morgue were moved to an empty dormitory in a neighbouring factory. Many simply left, forgoing any outstanding pay, and returned to Shufu.[17] In October 2009, the alleged ringleader of the violence, Xiao Jianhua, was sentenced to death for his part in it, while five others were given prison terms ranging from seven years to life. Three Uyghur men were also jailed for "participating in group affray".

Sparked by ethnic hostility and out-of-control rumours, spread largely over the internet, the Shaoguan Incident, as it would come to be known, was only the first in a series of events in the summer of 2009 that would drastically alter the lives of all those living in Xinjiang and further drive a wedge between Uyghurs and the Han majority.

*

The demonstration started peacefully.[18] Early in the afternoon of 5 July 2009, several hundred Uyghur university students converged on People's Square in central Urumqi, carrying the Chinese flag and signs reading 'We are Chinese citizens'.[19] The square, all cement and neatly manicured trees, was centred around a 32-metre-tall monument to the People's Liberation Army (PLA). On the northern edge sat the Xinjiang regional Communist Party headquarters. Protesters demanded a meeting with Nur Bekri to discuss the Shaoguan Incident. A Uyghur government official, Nur Bekri was the nominal head of Xinjiang, but as with most Chinese political positions, the local Party secretary, a Han named Wang Lequan, held the real power.[20]

The protesters were angry. The Shaoguan Incident had largely been ignored by state media, but enough information – from the international press, bloggers, witnesses and the rumour mill – had made it to Urumqi that many felt the government was, at a minimum, ignoring the incident, if not engaging in a full-blown cover-up. Videos showing mobs of Han workers attacking their Uyghur colleagues were shared widely online, increasing the outrage and calls for an investigation. One Guangdong official threw fuel on the fire by dismissing the violence in Shaoguan as being like a spat "between husband and wife".[21] According to Human Rights Watch, "many Uyghurs in Xinjiang saw the footage as emblematic of the discrimination they suffered within China, and of the government's unwillingness to protect them".[22]

Unlike in Shaoguan, where police dithered at the edge of the violence for hours before finally intervening, the response to the People's Square protest was near immediate. Riot police converged on the demonstrators, arresting as many as seventy on the spot and pushing those remaining out of the square and south towards the junction of Lonquan Street and South Heping Road, where another large group of protesters had already gathered. Witnesses told Radio Free Asia, the US government-funded broadcaster, that riot police chased and beat them during the clearance of the square.[23]

As the police pushed the crowd further south into the predominantly Uyghur areas around the Grand Bazaar, its numbers swelled. Denied the ability to stage even a minor demonstration, the mood among the crowd was turning, and many began to shout insults at the police. At the same time, police behaviour became more aggressive as the crowd grew in size, and shock batons, tear gas and water cannon were deployed to try to disperse the protesters, who began throwing stones in response.[24] Large, angry protests are often hovering on the edge of riot, as those in front are pushed into the shields and batons of the police by the swelling of the crowd behind them, their frustration and fury growing by the second. That fury spilled over now, as protesters began attacking the police in earnest. Overwhelmed by the crowd, which by now numbered well over a thousand, the police pulled back.[25] Gangs of rioters rampaged through the streets south of the Grand Bazaar, armed with clubs, knives and stones. They randomly attacked and in many cases beat to death any Han they found in the streets, including women and elderly people, and set cars, houses and shops on fire.[26] Despite their heavy-handed tactics earlier in the day, security forces were apparently caught completely off guard by the outbreak of violence and many neighbourhoods were left at the mercy of the mob for hours before some 20,000 paramilitary police and PLA soldiers poured into the city to restore order.[27]

When the smoke cleared on 6 July, with hundreds of soldiers and armoured vehicles patrolling the streets, Xinhua reported that 129 people had been killed in the riots, and many more injured.[28] The number of dead would later rise to 156.[29] Hundreds of vehicles and shops were damaged by the fires, and dozens of police cars were vandalised, Nur Bekri said in a televised speech days later.[30]

While the police were initially slow to react, the censors were not. Within hours of the violence breaking out, all phone, text messaging and internet services in Xinjiang were cut off. As the PLA entered Urumqi, reports and videos emerging from the riots were being scrubbed from Chinese websites, forums and social media.[31] Newspapers and news websites were ordered to parrot only the Xinhua line, and not to do any independent reporting on the riots.[32] Urumqi Party chief Li Zhi justified cutting off internet to the Xinjiang capital "in order to quench the riot quickly and prevent violence from spreading".[33] Why this meant that the rest of the Xinjiang Uyghur Autonomous Region – even Kashgar, more than a thousand kilometres away – had to be cut off as well, he didn't explain.

Unlike during similar unrest in Tibet the year before, foreign reporters based in China were allowed into Urumqi, although many complained of being harassed and followed by authorities, their access to Uyghur parts of the city and non-Han witnesses strictly restricted.[34] Nor was this apparent openness necessarily altruistic: journalist Nick Holdstock argues that the authorities were likely hoping that "pictures of the wounded, and the damage to the city would evoke sympathy and thus support for the authorities' version of events".[35]

This did mean, however, that dozens of foreign reporters were on hand to witness a second major outbreak of violence, as mobs of Han residents rampaged through Uyghur neighbourhoods carrying out revenge attacks. A US embassy official in the city at the time reported seeing groups of dozens of Han men holding clubs moving towards the city's Uyghur quarter, unmolested by police or security forces.[36] "The Uyghurs came to our area to smash things, now we are going to their area to beat them," one man told reporters.[37] Despite the heavy police presence in the city, the mob met with little resistance, and set about attacking Uyghur businesses and homes. While some overseas Uyghur groups claimed that many were killed in the violence, most other reports said injuries were limited.[38] The police eventually moved in with tear gas and flash-bang grenades to disperse the mob, though few arrests were made. This would mark an end to the violence in the city, but the fallout was only just beginning.

*

Even before the 2009 internet blackout, Uyghur websites were tightly controlled by the authorities. Makanim.com, an early popular site launched in 1998, was shut down after repeated postings on its bulletin boards calling for independence for East Turkestan aroused the ire of the Public Security Bureau.[39] In the years that followed, website administrators learned to toe the line on politically sensitive topics, self-censoring in order to stop the sites being closed completely. In 2005, Dilshat Perhat launched Diyarim.com while a student at Xinjiang University. Diyarim took advantage of new technologies that allowed it to display the Uyghur script, and it would go on to become one of the most popular sites on the Uyghur internet. It was also strictly self-censored. When Dilshat registered the site, he signed an agreement "not to permit any postings that might undermine the peace or harm the unity of the motherland".

For many younger Uyghurs, who grew up in an environment of marginalisation and surveillance, even the limited freedoms offered online could be revolutionary, particularly when it came to matters of identity. As Iranian sociologist Masserat Amir-Ebrahimi wrote in 2004 about her own country's tightly controlled internet:

> In democratic societies, cyberspace is often viewed as an 'alter' space of information parallel/complementary to public spaces/ institutions. In countries where public spaces are controlled by traditional or restrictive forces ... the internet has become a means to resist the restrictions imposed on those spaces.[40]

In a society that was becoming ever more (Han) Chinese, where the Uyghur script was often limited to badly translated signs,[41] the internet provided a space for the realisation of a distinctly Uyghur identity. But more than that, especially for Ilham Tohti and others like him, it offered an avenue for greater understanding between all Chinese peoples, a forum to discuss the problems facing Uyghurs and potentially find a solution that didn't involve greater repression or the same old calls for independence.

As news of the Shaoguan Incident spread in late June 2009, administrators of the most popular websites were left uncertain how to act. Enough information had spread via limited state media reports for Urumqi to be "simmering with the news", according to Rachel

Harris and Aziz Isa, two academics who were in the city at the time. Videos of the attacks at the Xuri factory "spread swiftly around the Uyghur community, testament to the speed and efficiency of new media, bypassing and filling the void left by the state media".[42]

Diyarim, the largest and most popular site, changed its colours to black and white in mourning for the Uyghurs killed in the violence. This would later be cited as justification for the site's administrator being sentenced to five years in prison for "endangering state security". Diyarim's bulletin boards were flooded with posts about the Shaoguan Incident, which quickly gave way to anger over official inaction, and later to calls for demonstrations. While administrators tried to delete as many of these posts as possible, keenly aware that anything related to mass action was well beyond the bounds of permissibility, they were often overwhelmed.

"If the administrator doesn't allow this post, I will keep posting it," one commenter wrote around this time. Not all were negative: on Uyghur Online, one Chinese-language post that survived the censors called for an official investigation into the Shaoguan Incident, but added that it "could be an opportunity" for improved interethnic relations. "I believe that under the guidance of the government and with everyone's joint efforts, this matter will be properly resolved," the poster wrote.[43] Following the violence in Urumqi, the government did seek a resolution, but it was not one the poster would ever have dreamed of.

In the days after the Urumqi riots, as all internet access was cut off in Xinjiang, state media seemed to recognise the Shaoguan Incident as an immediate cause of the unrest. A Xinhua article published on 8 July – '"Unintentional scream" triggered Xinjiang riot' – downplayed the violence at the Xuri factory as a "row between young men", but nevertheless drew a direct link between it and the Urumqi riots. This reading was short-lived. Accepting the Shaoguan Incident as the primary cause of the Urumqi riots would have required acknowledging the frustrations felt by Uyghurs about the discrimination and abuse they suffered throughout China. While a more nuanced view might have been possible elsewhere, in Xinjiang, where everything was seen through the lens of separatism and terrorism, blaming the Party's policies even partially for the violence that unfolded was unthinkable. Provincial authorities wasted no time in finding the true culprits behind the riots, which they said had been "instigated and directed from abroad, and carried out by outlaws in the country". Party secretary Wang Lequan took it a step further, shifting the blame to one organisation, and one person: Rebiya Kadeer. The riots, Wang said, were a "profound lesson in blood" which revealed the "violent and terrorist nature" of Rebiya's World Uyghur Congress (WUC).

Rebiya Kadeer was once China's richest woman and a darling of state media, before, like Ilham Tohti, her activism on behalf of her community stepped over an invisible line and the Party turned against her, eventually forcing her into exile. At the time of the riots, she was a relative unknown in Xinjiang; since she had left China in 2005, mention of her and the WUC, a Washington-based pressure group, had been strictly censored, and it's doubtful that many knew of her, let alone looked to her for guidance.[44] Writing after Wang turned her into the household name he claimed she had always been, Rebiya said that he had only confirmed for many Uyghurs "that Chinese officials have no interest in observing the rule of law when we are concerned".[45]

Pinning the unrest on Rebiya and the WUC served two purposes. It recast the riots within the familiar lens of separatism: the WUC, while a completely non-violent organisation, does call for a democratic solution to the 'East Turkestan question', which is tantamount in Beijing's eyes to calling for Xinjiang independence. Casting blame outside China for inspiring the riots – which shattered the tenuous peace between Uyghurs and Han in Xinjiang, devastated tourism, and threatened the region's economy[46] – also retroactively justified the actions that were already being taken to cut Xinjiang off.

A month after the riots, an editorial in the military newspaper *China National Defence Daily* would set out this justification in its clearest terms. Unrest in Urumqi, the paper said, "once again demonstrates that it is becoming urgent to strengthen internet control. This is to avoid the internet becoming a new poisoned arrow for hostile forces."[47]

All governments have been accused of exploiting moments of national trauma to push through unpopular policies, be it in the name of national security, reconciliation, or just because they hope no one is paying attention. In China, where the censors and security services are hugely powerful, there is rarely an incident the answer to which is not more censorship, more control. Such was the case in Xinjiang. In response to half a day of rioting, more than 20 million people in China's largest administrative region were left without access to the internet, long-distance phone calls or text messaging for almost a year.[48]

*

The internet blackout began with no warning. Jesse, an English teacher living in northern Xinjiang at the time,[49] had been up until the early hours of the morning the night of the Urumqi riots, checking the news and emailing with friends to let them know he was OK. The following morning, when he woke up, he was surprised to see that he had no new emails, before he realised nothing was loading. "Between 3am and 8 or 9am, things got cut, and then we couldn't access anything outside," he said.

For Jesse and his wife, the blackout was more of a personal annoyance, but for many around them it was "extremely disruptive". While the blackout would have been a devastating overreaction no matter where it happened, the effect was compounded in

Xinjiang by the region's geographic isolation. Even Urumqi, with its 3 million-strong population in 2009, tiny by Chinese provincial capital standards, was almost a thousand kilometres from the border with Gansu province, itself a sparsely populated, cripplingly poor part of China. The nearest major city was Xi'an, in Shaanxi province, 2,500 kilometres away, or, for those Xinjiang residents fortunate enough to have the documents required to fly, a three-hour plane ride.

Some of Jesse's neighbours would take a train from Urumqi late on Sunday evening to Dunhuang, the nearest city across the border in Gansu, where they would work from Monday to Friday in a hotel room, before returning to their families for the weekend. "I knew a lot of Chinese people and even a number of foreigners who would do that every week," he said. It was that or go out of business, as many internet cafés and other companies that couldn't relocate staff to Gansu soon did.

Unlike in the early days of the internet, when dial-up modems spent several noisy minutes connecting and could be knocked offline by someone trying to use the phone, mobile data and high-speed wifi have made it easy to forget how fragile the connection we have to the web actually is.

When someone types a URL into their browser and presses enter, a request is sent to their internet service provider (ISP), which parses the URL they typed through its domain name servers (DNS). These translate the URL – google.com, for example – into the numerical IP address of a physical server where the web page requested is hosted. Large sites may have many servers to choose from, or be hosted on a set of cloud-based servers with a single IP address representing data stored across multiple machines or virtual machines, but the principle is the same. Once the ISP knows the location of the server it needs to connect to, it attempts to route the request to it in the fastest way possible. To do so, the request is sent to an internet exchange, where it joins a wave of other web traffic moving to and from the backbone of the internet, a huge physical network of routers and fibre-optic cables.[50]

For example, if I am trying to load a website from my home in Hong Kong, the server of which is based in the US, my request is first sent to my local ISP, Hong Kong Broadband, whose DNS convert the URL into an IP address. Since that IP address is across the Pacific, my request is passed to the local internet exchange, which routes it to the fibre-optic cables that make up the Asia–America Gateway,[51] the 20,000-kilometre underwater cable system that stretches from Hong Kong to the Philippines, then to Guam, Hawaii, and finally to San Luis Obispo in central California, 'the Happiest Place in America'.[52]

After my request has passed through another internet exchange point and a couple more routers, it reaches the server, which retrieves the information requested and sends it back along the path just travelled. On a fast, unfettered broadband connection, this transcontinental journey is completed mere milliseconds after I type the URL and press enter, but the speed of the journey belies how vulnerable this process is. There are numerous points in the path from computer to modem to ISP to DNS to internet exchange to internet backbone to exchange to ISP to server where the request could be blocked, dropped, or slowed down. The ones most people will be familiar with is when a personal modem isn't working and the request never leaves the house, or (less often today than years ago) the ISP's servers are down and the request can't be converted into an IP address. But disruption can also happen at the other end of the equation. In 2008, millions of users across the Middle East were cut off from servers in the US when several undersea cables were damaged by unknown causes.[53]

While that outage was accidental, the Xinjiang internet blackout the following year showed that the same effect could be achieved

155

intentionally. China is particularly vulnerable in this regard, as all internet backbones and major exchanges are owned or controlled by government entities.[54] China Unicom, the colossal state-owned telecoms company that administers much of the country's internet infrastructure, has three major 'national-level' exchanges in Beijing, Guangzhou and Shanghai,[55] from where traffic is routed to the rest of the world. Similarly, China Telecom connects users in Xinjiang via an Urumqi–Beijing link and a smaller exchange in Xi'an.[56] It is at the national level, as traffic moves in and out of the country, that the Great Firewall operates, inspecting packets and blocking or throttling undesirable content.

Cutting off internet access to an isolated part of China like Xinjiang was fairly easy,[57] requiring only a few engineers at China Telecom and China Unicom to disable services that carried internet traffic for that region of the country, as defined by IP addresses.[58] To cut off more than 20 million people from the internet took only a few actions, completed in minutes. The ease with which the internet was cut off to Xinjiang was in stark contrast to the effects of the blackout. As one Chinese blogger joked darkly, "Xinjiang has finally achieved independence in one way, independence from the internet."[59]

Tourism, wholesalers, and anyone else dependent on email or online orders suffered what one described as a "fatal blow", forced to rely on phone business or make the 1,000-kilometre, twenty-four-hour drive to Gansu.[60] As a tone-deaf Xinhua article described after the lifting of the blackout, one family had to drive their teenage son to Gansu every week for months on end to get updates on his college application.[61] It wasn't all bad, Xinhua reassured readers, quoting a woman who said that she was relieved she no longer "had to worry about my son's net addiction".

While limited service, to certain government websites and state media, was restored in a couple of months, the Uyghur internet was beyond resurrection. Following the riots, the most popular Uyghur sites – Diyarim.com, Salkin.com, Xabnam.com and others – were permanently closed and their administrators arrested. In Beijing, Ilham Tohti was detained for several months, and Uyghur Online was forced to move its servers overseas. Three months after the riots, authorities in Xinjiang approved a bill making it an offence to use the internet in any way that undermined national security, incited ethnic separatism, or harmed social stability.[62] In July 2010, Diyarim founder Dilshat Perhat and two other prominent Uyghur website administrators – Nureli and Nijat Azat – were jailed for "endangering state security".[63]

The loss of these websites, along with millions of forum posts, articles, photos and videos, was a "cataclysmic event" for the Uyghur internet, one from which it has never truly recovered.[64] According to a report by the Uyghur Human Rights Project, following the restoration of limited internet services in 2010, "a clear divide emerged between those who used the internet before 2009 and those who did not". A repository of knowledge – about art, music, poetry, religion and contemporary politics – was lost. Uyghurs increasingly migrated to national Chinese-language forums, and self-censorship became common, not only of political issues but also of any discussion of identity or religion. Fear of the internet became pervasive, as parents warned their children not to post online, and even experienced digital natives worried about accessing foreign websites or using a VPN to bypass the Firewall, lest they be tracked and prosecuted.

Only Ilham Tohti – released from detention along with two other activists ahead of a state visit by US President Barack Obama[65] – remained to fly the flag for a uniquely Uyghur Chinese identity. Shaken by his experience and distraught at the rapidly worsening situation in Xinjiang, he would have been justified in keeping his head down. But even as his darkest predictions were coming true, and relations between Han and Uyghur reached the worst point they had been in years, he couldn't bring himself to stop speaking out. Ilham called for a 'National Reconciliation Day' to be held annually on 5 July, the date of the Urumqi riots, in order to "build interethnic emotional ties and friendship".[66] In his writing, he continued to emphasise the importance of working towards a system of "multi-ethnic, multicultural" governance, while forever stressing his "national pride" and opposition to separatism. But like his father before him, Ilham would find himself at the mercy of a vicious strain of Chinese politics over which he had no control, and that would ultimately end in his destruction.

Chapter 13

Ghosts in the machine

Chinese hackers expand the Firewall's reach

In the same year the censors took the entire population of Xinjiang offline, they were also working to extend their reach to communities beyond China's borders, building up the capabilities of the Great Firewall to attack its critics wherever they are.

Some of these capabilities were discovered by chance on a day in January 2009. In the attic of a grand old red-brick building on the middle of the University of Toronto campus, just north of the city centre, Nart Villeneuve stared at his computer screen in disbelief. He had been tracking a sophisticated cyberespionage group that was infiltrating computers, email accounts and servers around the world, and spying on their users and contents. The attackers had carefully tailored so-called 'spear-phishing' emails to appear to be from targets' friends and colleagues, convincing people to download malware onto their machines and unknowingly open themselves up for surveillance. The campaign was incredibly advanced, but its creators also appeared to have done something really, really stupid. Villeneuve was thirty-four, tall and broad, with his dark hair shaved as short as possible. Still slightly staggered by his discovery, he picked up his phone and rang Ron Deibert, his supervisor and the founder of Citizen Lab, a pioneering research group and internet security watchdog.

"I'm in," Villeneuve whispered into the handset. "I just Googled it."[1] He was looking at a command and control server, used to send instructions to the malware its creators were spreading around the internet. Those creators had obviously never expected anyone to stumble across it, because they had not thrown up any security. By finding the URL, Villeneuve, Deibert and other researchers were able to see exactly what the hackers saw, and the scope of the operation they had uncovered astounded them.

Their investigation had begun months earlier in Dharamsala. Greg Walton, a Citizen Lab field researcher, had been visiting the Tibetan settlement there for years, another computer expert pulled into a community desperate for them. In the late 1990s and early 2000s, Walton helped expand on the work done by the two previous Tibetan internet pioneers, Dan Haig and Thubten Samdup. He built websites for various NGOs and government departments, taught computer classes, and helped people set up email accounts.[2] Looking back, he realised that they were all too caught up in the benefits of the internet, and its ability to connect and unite the increasingly spread-out Tibetan diaspora, to think of the downsides. Although the early days were tough and the technology rickety, when the internet took off in Dharamsala, it took off fast. Little concern was given to security as more and more Tibetans started opening email accounts and joining listservs.

The downsides of this quickly became apparent. Foreign leaders trying to set up meetings with the Dalai Lama would receive angry missives from Beijing before any summits were even announced publicly, warning them not to have any association with 'separatists'. Tibetans crossing into Chinese-controlled territory were detained at the border and interrogated, with their own emails presented to them as proof of their nefarious activities. And computer after computer was disabled by aggressive malware designed not to spy but to sabotage and destroy. Clearly someone was targeting Tibetans, and all signs pointed to China, but the scale of the operation was unclear. Were the Tibetans being targeted by the security services, the military, so-called 'patriotic hackers', or a combination of all three?

In the beginning, the attacks were fairly unsophisticated: emails in broken English encouraging users to run executable files that any security expert could tell them was akin to committing computer suicide. But this was the early days of the internet, and the Tibetans were by no means the only ones lacking in security know-how. In May 2000, the love bug struck worldwide, as an email with the subject line 'ILOVEYOU' began spreading, first in the Philippines and then elsewhere,[3] along with an attachment that to today's eyes looks suspicious but nevertheless succeeded in infecting millions of computers: 'LOVE-LETTER-FOR-YOU.txt.vbs'.[4] When opened, the love bug spread through computers like a cancer, replacing files with copies of itself, before emailing every person in the target's address book to spread even further. By the time it was finally brought under control, the virus had done millions of dollars' worth of damage[5] and had forced major organisations including the Pentagon and the CIA to temporarily shut down their computer networks to avoid being infected.

Working with the Tibetan Computer Resource Centre and other local security experts, Walton began collecting samples of sketchy emails and malware that were sent to him by Tibetans on a weekly basis. Through these, they could see that the campaign against the Tibetans was not particularly sophisticated, utilising fairly common malware and techniques, but it was broad and near constant, targeting the entire community even though most would have been of little interest to hackers. The attackers were also clearly monitoring the success of their operation closely, as well as the attempts to ameliorate it. When a major educational campaign was launched to encourage Tibetans not to open attachments and to rely only on cloud-based services such as Google Drive to share documents, new malware quickly appeared targeting those services.

Those compromised by the attack included figures at the top of the Tibetan government in exile. Years into the campaign, when Walton and Cambridge University researcher Shishir Nagaraja were asked to investigate the computers in the Dalai Lama's office, they discovered that hackers had access to all the data. They could operate microphones and video cameras on laptops to spy on and record those around them, and they had penetrated a database of refugees who had fled from Tibet to India, putting thousands of people and their families at risk of potential reprisals. Nagaraja remembered being "just gobsmacked" by their findings: this was the first time he had ever investigated a case where the data being hoovered up put people in mortal danger.[6] There was also the almost absurd contrast between the amount of physical security around the Dalai Lama – Indian border guards, police officers and an elite Tibetan commando force – and the ease with which the hackers had breached the digital perimeter.

Before Villeneuve's discovery of the command and control server, the team had been able to track only the targets of the malware campaign. Now they could see exactly what the attackers were doing on the computers they accessed. Once an infected machine connected to it, the server could order it to delete files, copy and share them, spread malware to other devices, or simply sit in the background, spying on and logging all the user's activity.

The primary weapon in the hackers' toolkit was a single piece of malware, originally developed by Chinese programmers and later ported into English, the Gh0st Remote Administration Tool, or Gh0st Rat.[7] Once the malware was delivered to the target computer, it quickly created several files and executables in the Windows system folder, allowing it to be launched and run whenever the computer was restarted, and creating a secret backdoor through which it could connect to the internet and communicate with the command and control server.[8] Gh0st Rat gave the hacker a god-like view of the user's machine: able to see every key press and track every file created or modified. If more specialised malware was needed, for example to break in to an encrypted folder, it could be quietly downloaded and installed without the user's knowledge. These capabilities were contained within simple commands that could be sent from the server to be executed on the infected machine, with names such as 'COMMAND_DELETE_FILE' and 'COMMAND_WEBCAM'.[9]

The version of Gh0st Rat that Villeneuve, Walton and others were tracking was spread through carefully crafted emails that appeared to come from legitimate sources carrying relevant attachments. One they discovered was sent from campaigns@freetibet.org with an attached Microsoft Word document titled 'Translation of Freedom Movement ID Book for Tibetans in Exile'. At first glance, the email appeared legitimate: it carried the emblem of the Tibetan government in exile and spoke of people making a "voluntary contribution into common fund for Tibetan Freedom Movement". Once the target opened the attached document, however, it would exploit a vulnerability in Word to install the Gh0st Rat malware, giving the hackers full control of the target computer.

Through their investigations in Dharamsala, the Citizen Lab team were able to see that the malware targeting Tibetans was calling back to servers based in Hainan, an island province in southern China, near Vietnam. Usually, this would be the limit of what they could learn from examining the malware on the target computers: what was being stolen, and where it was being sent. But thanks to Villeneuve's discovery of the command and control server, after some considerable internet sleuthing and lots of trial and error with URLs, he was able to see a list of all computers infected by the hackers. It was stunning: over the course of two years, the hacking operation – which the Citizen Lab team dubbed GhostNet – had compromised almost 1,300 computers across more than a hundred countries. Of those, the team estimated, about 400 were high-value political, economic and media targets. Most computers were infected for around 145 days, with more than a hundred infected for over 400 days, before a virus checker or some other kind of protection kicked in and stopped the malware, or the hackers simply stopped connecting.[10]

This went way beyond Tibetan dissidents in a remote part of India: diplomats, military officials, legislators, journalists and hundreds of others had been targeted, and their activity surveilled by the GhostNet hackers. "Almost certainly," the team wrote in their report, "documents are being removed without the targets' knowledge, keystrokes logged, web cameras are being silently triggered, and audio inputs surreptitiously activated." While they could not say definitively who was behind the hack, the Citizen Lab report concluded that "the most obvious explanation, and certainly the one in which the circumstantial evidence tilts the strongest, would be that this set of high profile targets has been exploited by the Chinese state for military and strategic-intelligence purposes".[11]

This was not simply because the attackers were using Chinese malware and calling back to Chinese servers, but also because of the precise location of the servers within the country. At the time, Hainan hosted the Lingshui signals intelligence facility and a division of the Third Technical Department of the People's Liberation Army, China's equivalent to the National Security Agency.[12] While the actions of the department were little known at the time, they would soon become headline news around the world.

Chapter 14

NoGuGe

The ignominious end of Google China

The US Embassy to China sits in Beijing's swanky Chaoyang district, north of the imposing headquarters of the Ministry of Foreign Affairs, and the pricey, always in development Sanlitun shopping area. The eight-storey, 46,500-square-metre glass complex is surrounded by security gates, and guarded on the outside by Chinese soldiers, to prevent any potential defectors making a run for the protection of the embassy.[1] In 2009, it was headed by chargé d'affaires Dan Piccuta, a decades-long veteran of the diplomatic service with short-cropped, receding black hair and a salt-and-pepper goatee.[2] A bureaucrat rather than a political appointee, Piccuta was running the embassy while recently inaugurated President Barack Obama vetted candidates for ambassador.

On 14 May 2009, Kaifu Lee requested a call with Piccuta. He was almost four years into his time as head of Google China, and had seen significant successes. Google was easily the number two search engine in China, behind only Baidu, and was number one in maps, translation and mobile search.[3] But far from getting easier, as Google made gains in the market it was facing more pressure from the government. Lee blamed Li Changchun, a fleshy-faced propaganda minister and member of the powerful Politburo Standing Committee.

When Google launched its Chinese search engine, one of the promises it made to Congress was that it would include a link to the uncensored, US-based Google.com on every page. The main Google site was blocked by the Great Firewall, but Li had recently discovered, presumably on a trip abroad, that he could search his own name on Google.com and find unflattering results, including news about a corruption scandal involving him, and other criticism.[4] He demanded Google.cn remove the 'illegal' link. When the company refused – the first time it had actively resisted a direct government request – Li ordered state-owned telecoms firms to stop doing business with Google, threatening its hard-won mobile search success.

Google, Lee told Piccuta, had tried to explain to the government that the .com link was a key part of the company's agreement with Congress, and senior management were adamant that it could not be removed: they would rather exit the market than do so. But Li would not budge; he saw Google as a "tool" of the US government, being used to "foment peaceful revolution in China". The company had already lost several key contracts because of the spat, and Lee begged the US government to intervene on its behalf. As Piccuta later wrote in a report to his superiors in the State Department, Lee "suggested [a] letter could urge further dialogue toward a mutually acceptable resolution and suggest diplomatic or commercial consequences in the event of rash or disruptive action".[5] A tense standoff began as the China team negotiated with the censors to keep the link. Although Google eventually prevailed, the battle did little to improve morale within the company, or the standing of Google in the eyes of the Chinese authorities.[6]

The year 2009 did not turn out to be a good one for Google China. It saw both the twentieth anniversary of the Tiananmen Square massacre, and the sixtieth anniversary of the founding of the People's Republic of China, and the censors were on high alert. In January, they launched an effort to "purify the internet's cultural environment" and blasted Google and other companies for failing to block "vulgar, pornographic sites". In March, YouTube, which had long been subject to intermittent blocks and throttling, was banned completely, after activists shared videos of police beating protesters during ethnic unrest in Tibet.[7] In June, after the argument over the .com link had barely died down, the censors again complained that Google's filters weren't stringent enough, with the Foreign Ministry singling the search engine out for spreading "large amounts of vulgar content that is lascivious and pornographic, seriously violating China's relevant laws and regulations". Complaints that Chinese search engines and web portals were just as lousy with porn went unheeded. The authorities announced 'punitive measures' – a temporary block of the site.[8] Even when access was restored, Google often loaded far slower than Baidu, driving more users to its Chinese rival.

In September, Kaifu Lee, Google China's biggest evangelist, the man who had become indelibly linked to its image and brand for many Chinese users, announced his resignation. In his autobiography, Lee wrote that he felt unsuited to running such a large team: "What I truly enjoyed doing was pioneer work, to explore uncharted territories and create something out of nothing."[9] He gave little clue as to his feelings or the difficulties he faced, and only the slightest of hints when he wrote "it takes a lot of commitment and patience to run an international company in China". Many felt that he had run out of that patience, sick of being a punching bag for the authorities and the Western press, which held Google to a far higher standard than its Chinese competitors.

Lee had borne the brunt of the fights with the government, often dragged into meetings to be berated by high-ranking officials and subjected to a highly publicised and intrusive personal tax audit.[10] At the same time, he felt a lack of support from company headquarters in Mountain View, where executives, especially co-founder Sergey Brin, were growing sceptical of the many compromises Google was making to stay in China. In 2008, activist shareholders put forward two proposals critical of censorship and Google's collaboration with repressive regimes. These were easily defeated, but Brin abstained from the votes, and said afterwards that he agreed "with the spirit of both of these, particularly in human rights, freedom of expression, and freedom to receive information".[11] During a personal trip to Asia in mid-2009, just as the Google China team needed the most support, Brin and fellow co-founder Larry Page dropped in on the company's Tokyo offices, but stayed well clear of Beijing.

Following a trip to Mountain View, where he briefed board members on the company's progress in China, Lee told chief executive Eric Schmidt that he had decided to leave. Google.cn staff threw him a tearful farewell party at the company's Beijing head-quarters. Then the man who many thought of as their general, who had hired and mentored all of them, left for good. It was a huge blow to morale, but not yet the end of the team's *annus horribilis*.

*

In December 2009, as Google's terrible year was coming to a close, the company's security team made a startling discovery: hackers had compromised some of Google's most important systems, and, what's more, they had been inside for months, operating undetected and siphoning off terabytes of data.

The attackers had been deliberate in their approach, esca-lating from a single compromised computer to the entire company network. Patient zero was an employee in the Beijing office. The hackers had built up a profile of the target based on information they gleaned via Facebook, LinkedIn and other social networks, then, appearing to be someone the employee trusted, they sent them a link via instant message.[12] When clicked, the link took the employee to a website poisoned with malware capable of enacting a 'zero-day' exploit, a never before seen vulnerability, in the Internet Explorer browser.[13] The zero-day was used to download more malware onto the employee's computer, and with that the attackers were inside the Google network.[14]

With the China team employee's credentials in their possession, the attackers had access to Moma, the Google intranet, which contained detailed breakdowns of teams, employee contact information, and progress reports for various projects. This was intended to foster internal transparency, and employees were encouraged to know what others were working on and share updates and advice.[15] It was also a hacker's gold mine, providing key information on who to target, and how to go about doing so.

From Moma, the attackers targeted the team responsible for Google's password management system, Gaia. This system unified all of Google's various services, giving users just one login and keeping everything in sync. By compromising it, the hackers would have access to potentially millions of accounts worldwide, able to read users' emails and documents, and see files they had shared. Using a variety of methods, including spear phishing, targeted emails containing malware, toolkits designed to extract passwords from computer memory and keyloggers to capture employee logins, the attackers managed to get administrator credentials for Gaia.[16] They also broke into the file repositories where the software's source code was stored, enabling them to scan it for extra vulnerabilities.

The Google security team, led by director Heather Adkins, who had been with the company since 2002, was among the best in the world. They had experienced countless attacks and, wearing T-shirts with 'Do know evil' on the back, spent hours every day scouring the company's code for bugs and exploits.[17] But when they discovered the 2009 hack, the attackers had been inside the company's servers for at least a year.[18] At the Google headquarters in Mountain View, the company set up the "most elaborate war room in its history" and even invited the National Security Agency to help analyse the attack, in a move that outraged privacy advocates.

Adkins' security team began a forensic analysis of the breach, a digital dusting for fingerprints. Using logs that showed where the attackers sent information from within Google's servers, they were able to build a picture of who was behind the attack and what they were targeting. They were horrified to discover that the attackers had not just compromised the company's core systems, but had also broken into the individual Gmail accounts of Chinese and Tibetan dissidents, including artist Ai Weiwei and Tenzin Seldon, a twenty-year-old regional coordinator of Students for a Free Tibet.[19] This and other clues pointed to the attack coming from China, while the sophistication of it, as well as the resources poured in to keep it going for months on end, suggested it was the work of a state-sponsored group.[20]

Security researchers at Symantec later dubbed the group 'Elderwood' and revealed that it had targeted dozens of other US companies, including Yahoo, Adobe, weapons manufacturer Northrop Grumman, and Dow Chemical.[21] Some reports suggested the victims could have numbered over a hundred.[22] As a Symantec report recounted:

> In most cases, Elderwood uses a convincing 'spear-phishing' fake email to fool an employee into clicking an infected emailed link or into opening a Trojan software-infected attachment that creates a digital backdoor for the cyberspies. In many cases, these attacks have utilised costly 'zero-day' malware that takes advantage of a previously unknown flaw against which no defence exists. Such technology would sell for at least six figures on the cyber black market, leading many to conclude the group is exceedingly well funded.[23]

Although they apparently did not share this information with Google, leaked State Department cables show that US diplomats had also concluded the attack was linked to the Chinese government. Chen Jieren, an editor of the Communist Youth League website and nephew of Party Standing Committee member He Guoqiang, told US Embassy officials that the attack had been directed by the State Council Information Office, the country's top censorship body. Chen said it had been directed by Li Changchun, Kaifu Lee's old nemesis, and security minister Zhou Yongkang, without the knowledge of the wider Politburo.[24] While Chen said the attack was '100 per cent' political, Kaifu Lee separately told diplomats that he suspected Li was working actively with Baidu "against Google's interests in China".

Long the most prominent critic of Google's China approach within the company, Sergey Brin was especially appalled at how the attackers had targeted dissidents' Gmail accounts. Born to Russian Jews, Brin's family had emigrated from the Soviet Union in 1979 when he was six, his astrophysicist father fleeing the tight controls of the Kremlin.[25] In interviews, as he directed Google's response to the hack, Brin drew a direct link to his family history, saying that he saw "the same earmarks of totalitarianism, and I find that personally quite troubling".[26]

Brin had been advocating quietly within Google to stop censoring in China since 2008, but now his voice came to the fore. He won fellow co-founder Larry Page over, and the two outvoted chief executive Eric Schmidt, still a supporter of the China strategy.[27] The following day, on 12 January 2010, Drummond published the blog post outlining the company's new approach: Google would stop censoring its China search. "One of the reasons I am glad we are making this move in China is that the China situation was really emboldening other countries to try and implement their own firewalls," Brin said afterwards.

Kaifu Lee, who by this time had founded his own Beijing-based venture capital firm, thought Google was making a mistake. Like many in China's tech elite, he believed in the promise of the internet as a liberalising force, and was happy to sit back and make money in the process. "The next generation [of leaders] will come up in less than two years," he said in 2010. "They're younger, more progressive, many American-trained, and many have worked in businesses and run banks – they're going to be more open."[28]

That this turned out to be completely untrue did not hurt venture capitalists like Lee, who did not respond to multiple requests to be interviewed for this book. The fund he started in 2009 ballooned from $115 million to more than $1 billion in under a decade,[29] and Lee's prominence as a visionary tech thinker only grew, buoyed by a largely false perception of him as an anti-censorship hero. Lee's old Chinese rival, Robin Li of Baidu, also thrived in the wake of Google's exit. Baidu grew to completely dominate Chinese search, controlling around 80 per cent of the market,[30] and its success made Li a billionaire many times over.

Following the announcement that it would no longer censor its Chinese search engine, Google came in for intense attack from state media. *Global Times*, an ultranationalist tabloid, said the company was a "convenient tool for promoting the US government's political will and values abroad".[31]

"In their hearts, when Google is in trouble that means that western culture is in trouble," another Party newspaper, *China Youth Daily*, said in a commentary. "Using Google to propagate American-style freedom of speech ... is the real reason that Google chose not to address its problems in the market but through politics." In an editorial published in the *People's Daily*, entitled 'Google, do not take Chinese netizens hostage', the author complained that the debate had become hopelessly politicised.[32]

"Such politicisation was not provoked by China, but imposed by the US and the west onto China," the editorial said. "Gorbachev was once widely praised by the west and his political reform even won much admiration in China. But, it was Gorbachev that finally ruined the Soviet Union. Therefore, China must not follow the western world's practice on crucial issues such as internet control and supervision."

As if on cue, US Secretary of State Hillary Clinton gave a poorly timed speech on internet freedom in which she called out China specifically, saying that the US would not "stand by while people are separated from the human family by walls of censorship" and promising to help "make these technologies a force for real progress the world over".[33] An escalation in criticism of Google and the US soon followed. In a response to Clinton's speech, Chinese Ministry of Foreign Affairs spokesperson Ma Zhaoxu said: "[W]e firmly oppose such words and deeds, which are against the facts and harmful to US–China relations."[34] A commentary in Shanghai's *Wenhui Daily* said that Clinton's remarks were "arrogant, illogical, and full of political shows and calculations", and accused her of having a "Cold War mentality".

According to a leaked US State Department cable, the issue of internet freedom was discussed within the Politburo, which viewed it as a new 'battleground' between the US and China, supplanting traditional human rights issues. While some on the Chinese internet praised Clinton's speech, and were swiftly censored, other advocates of online freedom were sceptical, even demoralised. In the same cable, Yu Wanli, an expert on US–China relations, patiently explained to US diplomats that rhetoric like Clinton's empowered the censors, "who could now plausibly argue that the United States was explicitly using the internet as a tool for regime change".

"The internet belongs to every country, we all can go there, we all can add to it, we all can learn from it. We Chinese were free there," Yu said. "Now the United States has claimed it for itself and so it will become an ideological battlefield."

That ideological battlefield was only extending, but before the censors could renew their fight against opponents overseas, they would face one final challenge at home. The rise of a new type of social network would present unique challenges and give an opening to Chinese dissidents and free thinkers to push the boundaries of their increasingly controlled internet.

Chapter 15

The social network

Weibo and the last free-speech platform

It was late summer 2009, and the dorm room was cramped. Four loft beds were squeezed into the tiny space, topped with thin mattresses and bamboo sleeping matts, above small desks overflowing with books, laptops, cables, clothes and other detritus. Several of the beds had small fans clipped to the side and mosquito nets draped over them. The sliding doors that opened to the small balcony, itself bursting with a drying rack and plastic tubs of belongings, were often left open at night to give some respite from the sweltering Shanghai summer heat.

Living on top of one another in this fashion can be a shortcut to intimacy and friendship, or can end in disaster. Luckily, for Chinese dissident political cartoonist Badiucao, it was the former. The roommates stayed up late discussing films, girls, video games and politics. While much about recent Chinese history went unmentioned in their classes, either unknown or studiously avoided, they were able to talk among themselves more freely. As students at an elite Shanghai university with a strong history of free thought, they were exposed to subjects others weren't, and encouraged by professors, sometimes with just a wink and a nod, to seek out information for themselves.

One topic that was never mentioned in school, openly or obliquely, was the 1989 Tiananmen massacre. Twenty years after the government ordered a bloody crackdown on student protesters across the country, the incident had almost been erased from history. So it was with great shock that the four roommates booted up a pirated Hollywood film one of them had downloaded only to find a Chinese subtitled version of the 1995 documentary by Richard Gordon and Carma Hinton, *The Gate of Heavenly Peace*. They watched enraptured for three hours as the film recounted the incidents of the May Fourth Movement, the Cultural Revolution, and finally the 1989 massacre itself. Several of them had tears in their eyes as they saw students their own age brimming with hope and defiance, only to be crushed and scattered as the tanks rolled in.[1]

Afterwards, as they discussed the film, they pieced together bits of family history – grandparents purged as rightists, parents who took part in student protests – filling in gaps in their own knowledge they hadn't even realised were there until hours before. Badiucao felt a great rush of solidarity with his roommates, united in sadness and outrage, determined that their generation would achieve what previous ones had not.

"The guy who downloaded the documentary is now a public security officer," Badiucao told me years later, referring to the secret police dedicated to stamping out dissent and maintaining the one-party system. "There's no room for that kind of thought outside of university. China makes it just hard enough to achieve that people have to censor and watch themselves to get ahead."

*

At the start of the 2010s, few things better symbolised China's changing fortunes and new prosperity than the country's high-speed rail system. Beginning in 2007, Chinese trains, previously a "symbol of backwardness",[2] were replaced by sleek, gleaming white carriages capable of travelling upwards of 200 kilometres an hour. In the decade that followed, the government spent hundreds of billions of dollars to criss-cross the country with high-speed lines, building the largest such network globally. In 2017, more than 20,000 kilometres of track was in service, more than the rest of the world's high-speed rail systems combined.[3] Coming from the West, the *gaotie* can seem like something close to miraculous. Cheap, fast, efficient and clean, China's high-speed rail network is everything the clunky, underfunded train lines of Britain and the United States are not. A train from Shanghai to Nanjing, the capital of neighbouring Jiangsu province, some 300 kilometres away, takes just over seventy-five minutes and can cost as little as $20.

On 23 July 2011, this symbol of the new China received a devastating blow. At 8.30pm on a Saturday, driver Pan Yiheng was guiding a train full of tourists headed from Beijing to the southern coastal city of Fuzhou. As the train pulled onto tracks spanning a slender viaduct near the city of Wenzhou, in Zhejiang province, a dispatcher suddenly screamed in Pan's ear: "Be careful! There's a train in your zone. D3115 is ahead of you!"

Although the line cut out, it did not take Pan long to see what the problem was. In front of him, practically stationary, was another train: D3115. He hauled on the emergency brake, but it was too late. Pan's train hit D3115 at almost 100 kilometres an hour, impaling the driver on his brake, derailing both engines, and sending four train cars plummeting into fields some 30 metres below.[4] Forty people were killed in the accident, with almost 200 more injured. It was the third deadliest high-speed rail disaster in history, and the first fatal crash to befall China's *gaotie* network. And yet, within twenty-four hours, the line was back in service. Several of the carriages were buried in the fields where they fell, and the incident did not make the front pages of the following day's national newspapers.

It did make the internet. Within hours, posts about the crash flooded Weibo, a Twitter-style microblogging site. At first, people mostly posted messages of shock and grief, hope for those trapped in the crippled trains, and sympathy for their families. This soon turned to anger when word got out that officials had ordered several of the downed train cars to be broken up and buried in the fields where they lay, just hours into the rescue operation. When a reporter confronted Ministry of Railways spokesperson Wang Yongping about the absurd official justification for this, that the cars were hampering rescue work, Wang responded: "Whether you believe it or not, I do."[5]

This led to howls of outrage and disgust online that were only amplified when a two-year-old girl was found alive in the wreckage hours after the official search had stopped (Wang said it was "a miracle").[6] Unwilling any longer to trust the official story, internet sleuths began trying to establish a timeline of the accident, and search for causes. They dug up damning press reports and video from prior to the accident, including one clip of the Ministry of Railway's chief engineer boasting that "modern technologies" meant China's high-speed trains could never rear-end each other. Another piece widely circulated was a 2008 *People's Daily* article valorising driver Li Dongxiao, who had begun training on the "world's most complex" engine just ten days before the Beijing high-speed line's opening (to the horror of his far more experienced German instructors).[7]

"This is a country where a thunderstorm can cause a train to crash, a car can make a bridge collapse, and drinking milk can lead to kidney stones," one Weibo user wrote. "Today's China is a bullet train racing through a thunderstorm – and we're all passengers onboard."

Badiucao was one of the many young Chinese invigorated by this sudden outpouring of anger and independent thought. He was amazed at the openness and forthrightness with which people took officials to task online. "I was on Weibo and suddenly everything was happening," he said. "Everyone was very keen to spread information about this incident and express their ideas. At that moment I thought, 'Yes! I will make my voice heard as well.'"

He wasn't much of a writer, so he began drawing, posting cartoons showing the destroyed trains and grieving relatives as well as the officials in charge of the investigation, which many said had become a cover-up. While some previous scandals had been discussed online, this was something else entirely. The Wenzhou train crash was the Weibo generation's coming-out party to the world, showing how, far from being cowed and brainwashed by years of Communist propaganda, young Chinese were sick of corruption and bureaucratic ineptitude, and clamouring for change. "In baring facts of train crash, blogs erode China censorship," hailed a *New York Times* headline, typical of the coverage at the time:

> While the blogs have exposed wrongdoers and broken news before, this week's performance may signal the arrival of Weibo as a social force to be reckoned with, even in the face of government efforts to rein in the internet's influence.[8]

Badiucao felt this too. As he became increasingly engaged in the online debate, he saw Weibo posters upping the ante, visiting the site of the crash themselves to document what was going on, and posting line-by-line takedowns of state media reports. "I felt this deepening of free expression, as everyone began to use the internet in a new way. I wanted to join in and be part of it."

*

When I first began covering China, as an overworked blogger living in my boss's apartment, international media was still enthralled by Weibo. It's hard to remember now, as social media has completely reframed how we interact with the web, but Weibo once seemed poised to have a revolutionary effect on both the Chinese internet and, potentially, society at large. The novelty of having access to anything that might reasonably be called Chinese public opinion was invigorating. Never mind that the average Weibo user was better off and better educated than the norm, or that a majority of users were male, and that even in the early days, censorship of certain topics was rife. Like many other reporters, I filed pieces liberally quoting microbloggers as commentators, or claiming to distil a 'Weibo reaction' on any given topic.

During Weibo's brief period as a genuine platform for discussion and dissent, microbloggers did actually achieve real change. They helped rescue kidnapped children and reunite them with their families;[9] they helped expose corruption and abuses of power;[10] and, most importantly of all, they helped force China to begin to confront the country's endemic air pollution.

A small coterie of influential Weibo bloggers – including real-estate tycoon Pan Shiyi and venture capitalist Charles Xue, known as the Big Vs for the 'verified account' labels by their names – began posting air-quality data published daily by the US Embassy in Beijing. They were joined by hundreds of thousands of other users, and the small act of transparency and defiance quickly snowballed into a national issue, shaming the government into issuing its own reports on air quality.[11] Pan polled his followers on whether they wanted a Chinese version of the Clean Air Act and promised to use his position as a member of the Beijing People's Congress to lobby for local legislation.[12]

While the effectiveness of the Big Vs in calling for action on air quality should not be minimised, the problem was also one that could not be denied. No one living in Beijing, Shanghai or most other major Chinese cities was unaware of the appalling levels of pollution. Nor could residents help but notice that during major events such as the 2008 Olympics, or the 2010 Shanghai Expo, the government was able to take action to ensure blue skies.[13] When the same Big Vs attempted to use their platforms to lobby for other change, they quickly discovered the limits of their status.

The man the authorities turned to to rein in the Big Vs was Lu Wei, the former Xinhua vice president. From the news agency, Lu's star had continued to rise, and he became the vice mayor of Beijing in 2011, where his duties included overseeing the capital's propaganda units and an anti-pornography and illegal publication task force.[14] This promotion came as Xi Jinping was smoothing his transition to power. Despite Lu's loose connection to former premier Wen Jiabao, his relative independence was reportedly seen as an asset, allowing him to leapfrog other officials whose loyalty to Xi was in doubt. In early 2013, Lu was given responsibility for internet policy, first at the State Council, then as head of the newly created Cyberspace Administration of China.[15]

Soon after becoming internet tsar, Lu met with the Big Vs and laid out 'seven bottom lines' for them to follow online.[16] In particular, they had a responsibility to tell the truth, uphold the law and socialist ideals, and protect state interests and social order. The Big Vs were obliged to post public affirmations of the bottom lines, with one, Pan Shiyi, creating a video in which he described the new strictures as like traffic rules that had to be obeyed.[17] For those who could not be brought to heel so easily, other methods were available.

On 23 August 2013, the sixty-year-old Charles Xue was arrested in Beijing along with a twenty-two-year-old woman and charged with soliciting prostitution.[18] Weeks later, he appeared on China Central Television (CCTV) looking shell-shocked and exhausted.[19] In a hoarse voice, he confessed to being addicted to Weibo and not checking his facts. "I didn't raise constructive suggestions to solve the problem. Instead, I just simply spread these ideas emotionally," he said. His arrest came after he had criticised the government and advocated for more liberal economic policies on Weibo, where he had more than 12 million followers. Another prominent online government critic, Qin Zhihui, was arrested and charged with spreading more than 3,000 false rumours over three years to advance his business interests.[20] Pan, too, was dragged into a CCTV studio to discuss how microbloggers should exercise 'social responsibility' and to warn of the potential for harm if they shared 'false' reports.[21]

The failure of Weibo as a free-speech platform is instructive in a number of ways. It spelled out once and for all the Party's inability to tolerate even constructive criticism, and exposed a host of new, previously invisible red lines of public debate. Weibo was a major last stand for China's inventive and obstreperous online dissidents, who threw everything they could at the censors, coming up with ingenious ways to get round the blocks and filters, but were still ultimately forced off it, taking refuge on platforms outside the Great Firewall or in digital spaces shut off not only from the censors but also from the public at large.

Launched in 2009 under the imprimatur of Cao Guowei, chief executive of Sina, China's largest and most successful web portal, Weibo was not the first Chinese social network or microblogging platform.[22] Tencent's Qzone, a Myspace-style offshoot of its hugely successful desktop messaging app QQ, Facebook clone RenRen, and earlier microblogging service Fanfou were all competing to master the space. Two years after Weibo's founding, however, Fanfou was dead, RenRen was haemorrhaging users, and even Tencent was struggling to compete as Weibo grew to more than 25 million daily active users. By 2014, when the company went public on the New York stock exchange, it had more than 60 million.[23] In the stock prospectus, the company boasted of Weibo's "profound social impact in China".

"Getting heard by thousands or even millions of people and reaching people one might not have otherwise is a life-changing experience for ordinary people in China," it said.

None of this success was inevitable, and the summer of 2009 was a spectacularly risky time to launch a social network in China. In July of that year, as a giant police crackdown was launched in the wake of the Urumqi riots, the censors went into action as well. Facebook and Twitter, which had previously been subject to temporary blocks, were banned outright. YouTube had been blocked earlier that summer after videos were posted showing Chinese security forces beating Tibetan protesters during similar unrest the year before. Domestic social media and news websites were also subject to widespread censorship and pressure from the authorities.

A profile of Cao from around this time described the former journalist and accountant as being "willing to gamble on a crowd-based information-sharing service in a society where both crowds and information are sensitive".[24] That Weibo proved so successful was thanks to the skill with which Cao and Sina walked the delicate and often invisible line of acceptable public speech. In its 2014 prospectus, the company warned that "regulation and censorship of information disseminated over the internet in China may adversely affect our business and subject us to liability for information displayed on our platform".[25] To that end, the company "adopted internal procedures to monitor content displayed on our platform, including a team of employees dedicated to screening and monitoring content uploaded".[26]

This army of in-house censors numbered in the hundreds, keeping a careful watch for speech that transcended the bounds of acceptability. Insulting a corrupt official whose downfall had been publicised by state media was OK, but suggesting that a still serving cadre was on the take, or even giving examples of graft, definitely wasn't.[27] Especially verboten was any discussion that veered towards collective action, such as protests or strikes.[28] In his indispensable guide to censorship on the platform, *Blocked on Weibo*, researcher Jason Q. Ng documented hundreds of sensitive keywords and topics that are automatically blocked by filters or get posts flagged for deletion. These include everything from 'foot fetish' to the names of prominent Chinese officials such as Jiang Zemin or Hu Jintao, and seemingly nonsense terms like 'hair preserved meat'. The latter was a play on the Chinese characters for Mao Zedong, and a reference to the continued gruesome display of the Great Helmsman's embalmed body on Tiananmen Square.[29]

For those, like Badiucao, who had come of age on Weibo, the social network that once appeared to give them so much freedom was being reined in before their eyes. But they weren't about to give it up without a fight.

Chapter 16

Gorillas in the mist

Exposing China's hackers to the world

"I have pwned them!"[1]

Aaron Barr was ecstatic. In emails to colleagues in February 2011, the chief executive of cybersecurity firm HBGary Federal bragged about how he had infiltrated (or, in his adopted hacker slang, 'pwned') the hacker collective Anonymous, matching members' online handles to real-life identities and locations.

"I want to start a verbal braul [sic] between us and keep it going because that will bring more media and more attention to a very important topic," he said, thinking he was on the verge of exposing a team of hackers who had become infamous for targeting Master-Card and Visa after those firms cut off whistleblower website WikiLeaks in the wake of it publishing tens of thousands of confidential US government cables.[2] Instead, Barr was days away from his whole world coming crashing down, his reputation and that of his company being destroyed, and the effective end of his career as a security researcher.[3]

Barr had indeed got close to Anonymous, but just as he told colleagues that the hackers had underestimated him, so he misjudged his opponents. The day after Barr's 'pwned' email, his entire server was compromised. Hackers stole more than 40,000 emails and put them on The Pirate Bay file-sharing website. They also said they had deleted more than a terabyte of the company's backups and remotely wiped Barr's iPad. Things got so bad that HBGary Federal's parent company, also called HBGary, sent its president Penny Leavy into a public chat room to beg with the hackers to leave her company alone. "We are kind of pissed at him right now," Leavy told the exuberant hackers, according to a chat log posted online.[4] They told her to fire Barr and transfer HBGary's stake in his company to a defence fund for WikiLeaks source Chelsea Manning, along with Barr's salary. Barr resigned as CEO of HBGary Federal, and within a year both companies were bought by another cybersecurity firm, their reputations destroyed.[5]

According to the leaked emails, Barr's intention in going after Anonymous was to get the attention of the FBI and drum up more government business. Ironically, thanks to work Barr apparently didn't even realise was important, he succeeded in assisting the Feds far more than identifying a few hacktivists ever would.

When Anonymous attacked HBGary, they moved quickly within the company's servers, gaining access to several key email accounts, including that of Greg Hoglund, Leavy's husband and one of HBGary's top researchers. Masquerading as Hoglund, the hackers succeeded in convincing the administrator of an HBGary server to reset its password to 'changeme123'.[6] On the server was the source code for rootkit.com, a project of Hoglund's dedicated to the tools that allow hackers secret access to computers. The site hosted forums for users to discuss various rootkit technology and share code.[7] Once inside the server, the Anonymous hackers unencrypted the site's username and password database and dumped them online.

Within that database was a username intimately familiar to another team of security researchers. Mandiant, a Virginia-based cybersecurity firm, had been tracking a group of sophisticated Chinese hackers it had given the designation APT1, for 'advanced persistent threat', a label typically used in the cybersecurity community to refer to government-sponsored cyberspies. The group, also called the Comment Crew, had targeted major US companies, including Coca-Cola, Lockheed Martin, and nuclear power company Westinghouse.[8] They also broke into the networks of companies with responsibility for critical American infrastructure, including oil and gas pipelines, power grids and waterworks. One of the group's most successful and wide-reaching hacks was of the computer security firm RSA, which sells encryption and multi-factor authentication technology, potentially giving the hackers back doors into thousands of companies around the world.[9]

While the Comment Crew included experienced hackers and coders, capable of writing their own malware and customising the tools they used to attack targets, the avenue of attack was no different to that used against the Tibetan diaspora from the early 2000s onwards, or the Google attack of 2009. Members of APT1 would research companies, drawing up a list of potential targets within them, then begin sending carefully crafted spear-phishing emails with innocent-looking attachments that, when opened, allowed the hackers full access to the target's computer or network. The group was well established and confident, even arrogant, using the same malware, domains, IP addresses and tools for years, crafting an effective playbook that could be brought to bear on pretty much any target.

Nor did the hackers operate in complete secrecy. One member of the team, who went by the handle UglyGorilla, was an established figure on Chinese military and hacking forums. In 2004, during an online question-and-answer session hosted by the *People's Liberation Army Daily*, he referenced reports about US hacking capabilities and asked if China had its own "cyber army".[10] Whether this was a planted question by an already established member of this cyber army or if UglyGorilla was recruited in the coming years is unclear, but his hacking credentials were not. Mandiant was able to track him across the internet, linking him to, among other things, the first recorded version of the Manitsme family of malware, which allowed hackers to easily upload and download files from compromised computers. There's no reason for malware to identify its author: the fact that UglyGorilla did so shows the sense of security, even comfort, under which he was operating. Nor did his signature on Manitsme leave any doubt: in broken English he left embedded in the code, he wrote "v.10 No Doubt to Hack You, Writed by UglyGorilla, 06/29/2007".

Linking UglyGorilla's forum posts and malware had been as far as the Mandiant researchers had been able to get, until the HBGary hack. When the rootkit.com database was dumped online, it included not only the Chinese hacker's username, but also an email address: uglygorilla@163.com. Using this new information, Mandiant was able to link UglyGorilla to several domains he had registered, and more accounts on forums and hacker websites. Also contained in the leak was the IP address used when UglyGorilla registered the rootkit.com account: 58.246.255.28. That corresponded to a rundown neighbourhood in Shanghai's Pudong New Area, a sprawling mess of recent development built on what used to be swamp.

The leak of his IP address was sloppy, but the result of circumstances UglyGorilla could never have controlled for. How could he have predicted that someone connected to rootkit.com would go on an ill-judged rampage against Anonymous, resulting in the site being hacked and its databases dumped online? But like Barr, Ugly-Gorilla misjudged his opponents and made some severe security missteps. On several of the accounts Mandiant linked to his email address, he had used the name Jack Wang. They initially assumed this to be an alias, a Sinicised version of Jack Smith, but on one account UglyGorilla had given a Chinese name: Wang Dong.[11]

Wang Dong was not an alias. Almost a year after Mandiant's report was released, in 2014, a grand jury in the Western District of Pennsylvania indicted five members of People's Liberation Army (PLA) Unit 61398 on thirty-one criminal counts, including conspiring to commit computer fraud, economic espionage, and theft of trade secrets.[12] Included with a press release describing their crimes was a series of photographs under a banner headline, white text on a red background, reading 'WANTED BY THE FBI'. One of the photos showed a pudgy-faced man with a shaved head, prominent ears, and rimless spectacles that looked too small for his face. The text underneath read: "Wang Dong, aka Jack Wang, aka UglyGorilla."

"This is a case alleging economic espionage by members of the Chinese military and represents the first ever charges against a state actor for this type of hacking," US Attorney General Eric Holder said as the indictment was announced, to worldwide shock.

> The range of trade secrets and other sensitive business information stolen in this case is significant and demands an aggressive response. Success in the global market place should be based solely on a company's ability to innovate and compete, not on a sponsor government's ability to spy and steal business secrets. This Administration will not tolerate actions by any nation that seeks to illegally sabotage American companies and undermine the integrity of fair competition in the operation of the free market.

The indictment of Unit 61398 was a major shot across the bows of China's cyberespionage operation, and the fact that Washington would risk relations with its most important trading partner demonstrated the severity of harm being experienced by US companies. The US, of course, had long hacked other countries. Within months of Mandiant's first report on Unit 61398, former National Security Agency contractor, Edward Snowden, flew to Hong Kong, from where he began making dramatic revelations about the extent of US government surveillance and spying. The US had also allegedly built and deployed – along with Israeli intelligence – the Stuxnet virus, a carefully designed cyber-weapon that wreaked havoc on Iran's nuclear energy programme. But to the Americans, this type of espionage was wholly different to the Chinese hacking, which often targeted private companies and appeared to be done for the benefit of Chinese businesses. It was one thing to steal plans for a fighter jet in order to better defend against it, and quite another to hack a company to uncover information about civil suits against a Chinese competitor, or steal files relating to a merger to undermine negotiations, as Unit 61398 was accused of doing. "For too long, the Chinese government has blatantly sought to use cyberespionage to obtain economic advantage for its state-owned industries," then FBI director James Comey said at the time of the indictments. But even as the FBI was exposing Unit 61398, Chinese hackers were allegedly staging one of their most audacious hacks yet.

The crisis began to unfold in April 2015, when a security engineer at the Office of Personnel Management (OPM), the vast federal human resources department, noticed that the agency's network was communicating with a site called opmsecurity.org.[13] This immediately raised alarms with the engineer, Brendan Saulsbury, who knew OPM didn't own any such domain, suggesting it had been created to fool anyone casually looking at the outbound traffic. When he dug into the signal, he found even more deception. The file communicating with opmsecurity.org was called mcutil.dll, and purported to be part of the McAfee antivirus platform. But OPM didn't use McAfee, and Saulsbury and his team soon realised the file was in fact a virus, one that had opened a secret back door from within the OPM servers, exposing deeply sensitive information to the wider world.

Just how sensitive soon became apparent. In a closed-door briefing to US senators about the hack, FBI director Comey estimated that the personal data of 18 million current, former and prospective federal employees had been compromised.[14] The data included fingerprints, health records, security clearance files, background checks, and a host of personal and potentially compromising information about employees and their families. The hackers had penetrated almost the entire OPM network, one of the most sensitive federal systems, which should have been a digital fortress. A scathing congressional report said the breach had jeopardised national security "for more than a generation", adding that the "intelligence and counterintelligence value of the stolen background investigation information for a foreign nation cannot be overstated".[15] A contractor brought in to help investigate the breach summarised it in an email he wrote to his boss: "They are fucked btw."

Soon after the hack was made public, multiple reports linked it to Chinese state-sponsored groups, and likely the PLA. Law enforcement officials said the purpose may have been to build up a giant database of federal employees who could be targeted at a later time for blackmail or identity theft, potentially compromising dozens of government agencies.[16] China, just like in previous cases, strenuously denied the allegations, but in mid-2017 the FBI arrested a Chinese national in connection with the case as he entered the US for a security conference.[17]

In the wake of the Unit 61398 indictments and the OPM hack, President Barack Obama hosted Chinese leader Xi Jinping at the White House, where the two men signed a major bilateral agreement promising "that neither country's government will conduct or knowingly support cyber-enabled theft of intellectual property, including trade secrets or other confidential information".[18] The deal was a big diplomatic win for Obama as he neared the end of his second term, one of the few concessions he scored from an increasingly assertive China despite his much vaunted 'pivot to Asia' and attempts to contain Chinese ambitions in the South China Sea. The Rand Corporation, a US think tank closely linked to the government and defence industry, described the agreement as a "good first step", but many were sceptical about how closely China would stick to the letter of the deal.[19]

Initial signs were good. Security agency FireEye said in a 2016 report that there had been a "notable decline" in the number of Chinese intrusions against companies in the US and twenty-five other countries. FireEye highlighted the FBI indictment and increased public scrutiny of Chinese hacking as major causes behind this shift, although the report also pointed to ongoing reform of the PLA and anti-corruption efforts as potential reasons why hacking might have become more closely supervised and directed.[20] There were also indications that the hackers may have simply been told to leave off the US and find other targets: around the time of the FireEye report, Moscow-based Kaspersky Labs recorded a threefold increase in the number of instances of Chinese hackers targeting Russian companies and state entities.[21] Proper scrutiny of the deal was also undercut by the 2016 US election and the ensuing furore over alleged Russian hacking of the Democratic National Committee and other groups. As the image of shadowy hackers undermining American institutions shifted from Beijing to Moscow, less attention was paid to the role of the Chinese government in future attacks, especially compared with the endless coverage of the actions of Kremlin-linked or Putin-adjacent figures in the run-up to Donald Trump's election.

For those who continued to be targeted by China's elite hackers, other solutions would have to be found.

Part 4: War

Chapter 17
Caught

The death of the Uyghur internet

"So, do you ever want to go to America again?" Ilham Tohti asked his daughter Jewher, one day in January 2013. She had visited four years before on a trip with her dance troupe.[1]

Her father looked tired and stressed, but then he always did in those days. He bore the weight of his own expectations, and the sting of his failures. The situation in Xinjiang had only got worse since the 2009 riots, and there were regular reports of clashes between alleged militants and police. Ilham's moderate voice was being drowned out on both sides: by the Islamists, who saw the atheist Chinese regime as an existential enemy; and by the government itself, which refused to distinguish between legitimate protests and terrorist activity.

He showed her a letter from Indiana University, inviting him to move to Bloomington for a year and work as a visiting scholar. It said he could bring one family member with him for a month, to help him get settled. Jewher's stepmother, Guzelnur Ali, didn't speak any English, and her brothers were both too young, so she was the obvious choice. But the winter break had just begun, and Bloomington was hardly New York or Los Angeles. "I want to stay with my friends," Jewher said. "We've been making plans."

"Too bad. You're coming."

On 2 February, they woke early. The weather in Beijing was dry and achingly cold, the streets outside the apartment still dark and quiet. Neither spoke much as they packed a few last things and triple-checked their flight tickets, bought well in advance. Ilham was under greater pressure from the authorities than ever before, and he worried they would not be allowed to leave the country.

Bleary-eyed from lack of sleep, but with her heart pounding in her chest, Jewher got in the back seat of the taxi with her father. Throughout the journey to the airport, she kept glancing out of the rear window, sure they must be being followed. But they reached the terminal unmolested, and checked in with relative ease, after shuffling some clothes between their bags to get them under the weight limit. "I thought it would be harder for us," Ilham said. The trouble started soon afterwards.

Jewher stood in the long queue for the immigration counters, a step ahead of her father. When it was her turn, she walked up to the tall desk, only her head visible to the officer in a dark blue uniform on the other side. She handed over her passport, its dark red cover embossed with the seal of the People's Republic of China, along with a copy of the letter from Indiana University. The officer scanned her passport, glanced between the computer and her face, and waved her through. As she stood waiting on the other side, a stream of people passing her, she heard her father's raised voice.

"Why should I come with you? I have done everything legally. I have all the documents. Why do you want me to come with you?" Ilham was arguing with the immigration officer, pointing through the barrier towards where Jewher stood, explaining that their flight was due to leave soon, that if they did not go they might miss it. The officer tried to reassure Ilham. Don't worry, he said – he would personally make sure they would still catch their flight, if Ilham was allowed to board it.

"Where are you taking my dad?" Jewher asked, as he was led away from the immigration counter. Ilham told her to take his suitcase and wait for him while he cleared things up. But she refused to be separated, not knowing his fate, and so followed him to the interrogation room, where Ilham immediately began questioning the officers: "Why are you doing this to me? I have everything organised."

One responded that they were only following the legal steps.

"I already have followed the full legal steps. I have everything legal. I have every legal document," Ilham looked like he was going to burst.

They told him to be patient, as they waited in the room for almost two hours. Ilham's intermittent demands for an explanation were just met with more commands to be patient. When he asked who would pay for their replacement tickets if they missed their flight, he was just ignored. Eventually, a young officer entered the room. Their plane was about to depart, she said. Jewher could board it if she wanted to, but Ilham had to stay, for now.

"She's my daughter. She has to go with me. According to her visa, she has to be with me." But the woman ignored him, speaking only to Jewher.

Do you want to go?

Eventually Ilham asked the same question. "Get out of this place," he told her when she tried to refuse. "Please, just go. Do you still want to stay here, when they treat us like this? Just go."

She hugged her father. "Go, go, go," he said. It was the last time she would ever see him in person.

*

Over a year after that day in the Beijing airport, Jewher sat by her computer in Bloomington, where she had been living in de facto exile, refreshing her browser for news on her father's trial. She had talked to Ilham on Skype every day between her leaving China and his arrest in January 2014. She still had the suitcase he'd packed for his move to the US.

Accused of separatism and inciting ethnic hatred, few among Ilham's supporters doubted that he would be found guilty. Chinese courts have a conviction rate of nearly 100 per cent.[2] Five years earlier, Ilham had predicted in an interview that he would be imprisoned, maybe even executed. "That just might be the price our people have to pay," he said. "Though I may have to go, perhaps that will draw more attention to the plight of our people. People will think more about it and perhaps more people will know about me."

Even so, when it came, the verdict was shocking, including to Ilham. "It's not just! It's not just!" he shouted, as the judges sentenced him to life in prison, and police officers dragged him from the court. In the gallery, Guzelnur wailed and fell into the arms of her husband's brothers, who had to carry her out of the building.[3] On the other side of the world, Jewher sobbed and clutched her father's clothes, desperate for any connection to him.

Since her father's arrest, Jewher has been tireless in campaigning for his release, even though Ilham's fate has not received anywhere near the attention given to other Chinese dissidents, such as the late Nobel Peace Prize laureate Liu Xiaobo. When we spoke, years later, she was still energised by this mission, and told their story well. Being separated from her father had given Jewher a greater understanding of Ilham, and her admiration for him had grown massively. "I always thought that my dad was a very intelligent man," she said. "But I used to blame him a lot, and complain 'Why don't you stay?', 'Why do you spend so much time on other people's problems?', but he really cared about Uyghur people, he didn't want them to keep suffering."

By the time Ilham was sentenced to life in prison, the Uyghur internet was long dead. The websites and forums that had served as a link between communities across Xinjiang, on which Uyghurs had discussed art, music, love, religion and politics, building friendships and strengthening communal ties, were gone. The other Uyghur internet pioneers were all in prison or in exile. Users were forced to download software to circumvent the Great Firewall so they could read banned overseas sites, risking arrest and detention for seeking out 'extremist' material. Or they were left with the Chinese internet, censored and controlled, and as Han-dominated as China itself.

None of this had the effect the authorities claimed to be seeking. Ethnic tension in Xinjiang has only become worse as moderate voices like that of Ilham Tohti have been silenced. Young Uyghurs unhappy with Beijing's policies are left with few legitimate avenues for their complaints, making them vulnerable to radicalisation. Both Al Qaeda and the Islamic State have featured Xinjiang in their propaganda in recent years, and Uyghur fighters have been spotted in Syria and Iraq.[4] At the same time, China has militarised Xinjiang more than ever before, and discussion of its repressive policies in the region has become taboo even for foreign journalists. In 2015, French reporter Ursula Gauthier was expelled from China after she accused Beijing of capitalising on the Paris terror attacks to justify yet another crackdown in Xinjiang.[5] In mid-2018, the authorities refused to renew BuzzFeed News reporter Megha Rajagopalan's journalist visa to remain in China, a move many connected to her reporting on Xinjiang.

Jewher recognised the bitter irony that the situation required a figure like her father more than ever before. "He was the exact person that China needs," she said. "Well educated, Muslim, but very moderate, not an extremist. He was good at communicating with people, he knew what was going on, he didn't just bullshit. He could have been a bridge."

Instead, the gap between the Chinese authorities and Uyghurs has grown, even as the Party has attempted to pull them in closer than ever before, seemingly controlling every aspect of their daily lives. Just as Xinjiang was once used as a testing ground by the imperial authorities before they implemented policies in China proper,[6] the region is being used to experiment new policies of control – this time an incredibly advanced, intrusive surveillance and security state that would make Big Brother blush. Uyghurs attempting to practise their religion, by wearing a beard or going veiled, by reading the Qur'an, or by naming their child Muhammed, are viewed with suspicion and hostility. At checkpoints across Xinjiang, police search residents' phones for banned apps such as Facebook or Twitter, and check text messages to see if they are discussing religion or other suspicious topics.[7] Artificial intelligence software is used with the web of CCTV cameras that criss-crosses every major Chinese city to recognise faces and car number plates, and to track people as they go about their daily lives, alerting police when targets stray more than 300 metres from their home or workplace.[8]

Crafting such technology doesn't come cheap, and the Chinese tech firms behind it have seen their profits boom as lucrative security contracts come in. Urumqi-based Leo Technology saw its earnings grow by 260 per cent in the first quarter of 2017, while SenseTime, a Hong Kong- and Beijing-based company, was valued at more than $4.5 billion after attracting investment from Alibaba, among others.[9] SenseTime is based in the government-subsidised Hong Kong Science Park, where it maintains a showroom with working examples of the types of 'smart surveillance' and face recognition technology it sells to public security bureaus across China. But while the company was keen to talk about its status as a 'unicorn' – a start-up valued at over $1 billion – it was less willing to discuss the more negative ramifications of its business. When I attempted to set up an interview and site visit, SenseTime representatives demanded examples of my previous reporting, and, learning that I focus on censorship and human rights, became suspicious, requesting I send a detailed list of questions and reveal what my story angle would be. Finally, after weeks of negotiations ended in a promise to arrange an interview, representatives cut off contact. I was never formally denied access, but it was clear that new roadblocks would go up whenever I tried to get closer to the company's operations.

Since 2009, the internet shutdown and crackdown on the Uyghur web have also become a model for Beijing's censors. Following unrest in Xinjiang's Shanshan county in 2013, local internet access was cut off for three days. In the same year, protests against forced demolitions in Urumqi saw the entire city blacked out. County- and town-level internet shutdowns have also been reported in Tibetan regions of Sichuan province,[10] and in parts of Guangdong where residents have long protested against government land policies.[11] In November 2016, the government passed a sweeping new cyber-security law massively expanding the right of officials to cut off internet access at will in the name of 'national security', including a potential countrywide shutdown. A similar pattern appears to be playing out again, with the mass surveillance and intrusive security checks to which residents in China's far west are subjected poised to become a regular feature of daily life for the rest of the country. Nor have such oppressive policies remained confined to China: Beijing's censorship tactics and internet shutdowns have spread well beyond the country's borders, gleefully adopted by autocratic regimes the world over, as Chinese companies, able to make huge profits thanks to the voracious demands of the domestic security state, have moved further afield in search of clients.

Chapter 18

Key opinion leader

How Chinese trolls go after dissidents overseas

Mount Lofty rises gradually to overlook the southern Australian city of Adelaide, a few kilometres south of the city centre. Lined with gum trees, many scarred by forest fires both historic and recent, in September 2016 its hiking paths were busy. Several excessively fit, cheerful people ran past dressed in bright workout clothes as Badiucao, the Chinese political cartoonist and Weibo blogger, and I puffed our way up the hill.

We had met in person two days earlier. After an eight-hour flight from Hong Kong, I had arrived in Adelaide amid a torrential downpour. Bleary-eyed and damp, I made my way from the poky business hotel where I was staying to a small art gallery nearby. Inside, the showroom was newly painted white, and empty but for a DJ in the process of setting up in the corner. I was painfully early. On the walls hung eight black and white portraits of Australian politicians, including then prime minister Malcolm Turnbull and his predecessor Tony Abbott. Opposite them were five brightly coloured campaign posters, of the type hung on utility poles throughout the country in the run-up to the recent general election. Instead of local politicians, they depicted Chinese president Xi Jinping, his face painted in thick, blotchy oils, emerging from and dominating the plastic canvas behind it.

Slogans including 'China's Reds for the chairman' and 'We'll put Party first' were written underneath.

On the floor, a black tarp was topped with mounds of baby formula shaped to form the faces of six children killed in 2008 by a batch of milk powder contaminated with melamine, an industrial chemical used for making plastic tableware. While Badiucao made his name with aggressive, often profane cartoons in bold colours and thick lines, critiquing and damning the daily outrages of contemporary Chinese politics, the baby formula piece was far more subtle and emotional. Over the course of the two-month installation, the powder would react with the moisture in the air and dissolve. The delicately stencilled faces of the dead babies would blur and disappear, just as their fate and that of the 300,000 other children affected by the scandal were forgotten, as media coverage shifted to terrified Chinese parents mass-buying milk powder overseas, including in Australia.

Opposite the powder, in a small glass case, lay the catalyst for this show, and Badiucao's desire to push beyond his previous work. A passport, its dark red cover embossed with the emblem of the People's Republic of China, with the top right corner sliced off. After years of living in exile, Badiucao was no longer a Chinese citizen.

During the show, to heavy, angry beats, Badiucao graffitied the portraits with thick red Chinese characters, and then stood impassively, in a prison jumpsuit with a bag over his head, as the audience walked around the gallery. In person, he was short and stocky, with his dark hair tied into a short ponytail high on his head, and a wispy goatee. He spoke in a soft, lilting voice, his accent bearing the mark of both Australia and China. Quick to laugh, he was open and honest, the anger and intensity of his art replaced by a wry, sardonic humour and deep introspection.

Badiucao was born in Shanghai in the late 1980s (he asked that I not reveal his exact age), a member of the *balinghou*, or 'post-80s generation', the first to come of age completely detached from the Mao era. Often stereotyped as spoiled and sheltered, *balinghou* were a product of the new China, a country that had always been on the rise and where the Party had always been firmly in control. The generation gap between them and their parents could sometimes be extreme, as people "who spent their own twenties labouring on remote farms have children who measure their world in malls, iPhones, and casual dates".[1]

"The young generation only believes official pronouncements; some even think contradicting the official line is heretical. They do not bother to check the details," novelist Murong Xuecun complained in 2013, adding that that Chinese millennials are "fattened to the point of obesity with Coca-Cola and hamburgers".[2]

Colonised in the nineteenth century by the United States, Britain and France – which forced the Qing Empire to sign treaties granting the foreign powers self-governed 'concessions' – Shanghai was always a different kind of Chinese city. A haven for European Jews during the Second World War, and a hideout for Chinese republicans in the last days of empire, it was also the setting of some of the most violent Communist revolts and purges. The city's bourgeois, outward-looking populace suffered greatly under Mao, as he launched the Anti-Rightist campaigns, and later the Cultural Revolution, in which hundreds of thousands were killed and millions displaced across the country. Badiucao's paternal grandparents were among those swept up in this censorious madness. They were filmmakers, but their work "did not satisfy the officials", he told me, and they were sent to a re-education through labour camp.

While Badiucao's grandparents remembered a China before Mao, and the *balinghou* experienced both opening up and the internet, his parents' generation knew only the Party. Coming of age during the Cultural Revolution, religion, culture and history were replaced by Mao. After the ideology that dominated their lives wreaked havoc on the country, plunging it into starvation, murder and civil war, they were left with nothing. "My parents' generation cared only about money, that's all they had to cling to," Badiucao said. "Money became the most important thing in their lives, the thing that kept you safe."

Staying safe, which meant staying clear of politics, became a point of conflict between parents and son. Clever, creative and outspoken, Badiucao wanted to help change China for the better. His father encouraged him instead to become a dentist or a hair-dresser, reasoning that such professions rarely have problems with the authorities. Instead, Badiucao applied to law school, dreaming of joining the ranks of China's much abused and incredibly brave human rights lawyers, even as he fobbed off his parents with talk of commercial litigation.

He left China partly on the insistence of his father, who saw in his son's talent and rebelliousness a great danger. "It was a constant struggle as I was growing up. There were a lot of fights," he said. His father had once considered moving to Australia, and he encouraged Badiucao to look into it. With the ruthless pragmatism of true Shanghaiers, they chose Adelaide, where, because of South Australia's low birth rate, a young immigrant like Badiucao was worth more in the country's points-based visa system.

From his new sanctuary, Badiucao began posting to Weibo more and more. But as his work grew in popularity, with more shares and comments for every artwork, the more likely it was to be taken down by the site's censors. After a time, anything remotely controversial he posted was immediately removed, as if someone was watching over his shoulder. One day he went to log in and saw an error message: his account had been deleted.

Badiucao became a member of the 'Reincarnation Party',[3] a group of popular Weibo users engaged in a game of cat and mouse with the censors. "We were doing the same thing as the Dalai Lama, rebirth again and again," he said. @Badiucao2 became @Badiucao3 and 4, as he registered scores of accounts at the same time, ready to switch to a new one as soon as its predecessor was deleted. But the censors weren't deterred, and the tactic soon became ineffective. As Xi Jinping and his chief censor Lu Wei spelled out a zero tolerance approach to dissent, Weibo's time as a platform for even partially free debate was coming to an end. Real-name identification requirements were put in place, tying accounts to mobile phone numbers or government IDs, making registration more time consuming and difficult. "I couldn't do it anymore. It wasn't effective," he said. "Every drawing was deleted. If I wanted to register new accounts I would have to give my personal ID, or have someone else take the risk."

WeChat, another popular Chinese social network, wasn't an option. At the time, the messaging app was built for private chats, and what public sharing features it did have were just as censored as Weibo. At around @Badiucao33, he gave up and decamped to Twitter, which was inaccessible to most Chinese but at least gave him a safe platform from which his cartoons, in theory, could then make it back across the Great Firewall.

Years later, as we reached the top of Mount Lofty, joining a coterie of other hikers in a small café looking out over the city, this online exile was clearly playing on his mind. Badiucao had left his phone in the car, over an hour's walk behind us, and was visibly uncomfortable without it. He peppered me with questions about Twitter, which was then struggling financially and rumoured to be seeking a buyer. After losing Weibo and WeChat, he was worried his final sanctuary was going to disappear. He fretted, too, about losing touch with the country of his birth, as he became more and more ensconced in Australian life. Unlike Twitter, Weibo is difficult to browse without an account, and Badiucao worried that, separated from online discussion and grassroots politics, his cartoons would

207

become stale and hackneyed, and he would transform into another irrelevant overseas dissident, fighting yesterday's battles.

*

One of the most inspiring things about covering censorship in China is the ingenuity with which bloggers and dissidents come up with ways to bypass the censors, at least temporarily. On Weibo, posters attempted to sidestep filters and blocks by using codes or homonyms to discuss sensitive topics. These included using '64' or 'May 35' to refer to the 4 June Tiananmen massacre; and 'river crab', a homonym of the Chinese word for 'harmonised', itself a euphemism for the act of censorship. Ironically, Chinese is a language perfectly suited to getting around keyword filters. Whereas English would soon descend into nonsense by trying to replace words with homonyms, there are thousands of potential Chinese characters to choose from that obscure meaning but preserve the sounds of a word. However, these tactics often kept users only a short step ahead of the authorities. Today, the number of censored terms related to Tiananmen runs into the hundreds.[4] Compared with their targets, the censors also have practically unlimited amounts of time and resources, and it can be difficult for even the most committed online dissident not to get worn down.

Images, on the other hand, present a host of extra challenges for the censor. While algorithms can be written to detect certain types of undesirable content, such as pornography (by searching for large quantities of skin-coloured pixels[5]), it is far more difficult to come up with code that can reliably detect political art and flag it for review, let alone censor it from the get-go, as keyword filters are able to do. The difficulty in blocking images is compounded by the ease with which they are disseminated and shared. While Badiucao and other cartoonists may have been driven off Weibo, from outside the Firewall their work could still occasionally make it back onto the Chinese web, attracting dozens or hundreds of shares before a human censor spotted the offending post and manually deleted it. While their message may sometimes be simplistic, cartoons can also be understood by far more people, and far quicker than a homonym-heavy tweet or an 800-word article, increasing their effectiveness prior to censorship.

Autocrats and ideologues of all stripes are averse to satire, and cartoons seem to have a unique ability to get under their skin. This was evident in the 2015 attack in Paris on the satirical weekly *Charlie Hebdo*. Europe, and particularly France, has no shortage of anti-Islamic and Islamophobic invective, some of it far more influential and insulting to the Prophet Muhammed than his depictions in *Charlie*, but words do not go viral in the same way as images and cannot be understood in so many languages. (Indeed, the power of images is the primary reason why depictions of Muhammed were forbidden by early Islamic scholars; they wanted to avoid idol worship.[6]) Other cartoonists have also come under attack. In 2011, armed thugs attacked Syrian cartoonist Ali Ferzat and broke his hands as a warning to stop satirising President Bashar al-Assad.[7] He later went into exile. In Malaysia, Zulkiflee Anwar Ulhaque, better known as Zunar, faced more than four decades in prison for his work criticising then Prime Minister Najib Razak.[8]

"In many quarters, cartoons are reaching people now more than ever with the advent of social media," Aseem Trivedi, an Indian cartoonist who was threatened with life in prison, said in 2015. "If there's a message that speaks to something greater, its chances of going viral and spreading to the masses are high."[9]

Badiucao was not the only Chinese artist forced into exile. Wang Liming, better known as Rebel Pepper, was another cartoonist who emerged on Weibo during its heyday in the early 2010s.[10] He became a particularly active member of the Reincarnation Party, with more than a hundred accounts deleted. "At the height of this suppression, my accounts could be shut as frequently as four to five times a day," he told me. "Usually before I even had a chance to publish anything, it was not accessible." Unlike Badiucao, who was safe overseas, Wang felt the personal risks of pushing boundaries online. In 2008, he was threatened with arrest after he shared an article about Xinjiang and Tibet from an overseas Chinese newspaper in a messaging group. "That was the first time I experienced the terror of censorship," he said. A few years later, he spent a night in police detention over a similar issue.

In 2014, Wang was travelling in Japan with his wife when the censors struck again, wiping out all his social media accounts and a page about him on Baidu Baike, a censored Wikipedia clone.[11] State media accused him of being a "Japan worshipping traitor",[12] and his store on Alibaba's online marketplace Taobao was shut down and other forms of income also cut off, forcing him to beg the public for donations.[13] Several people who had re-posted or shared Wang's cartoons were detained or questioned by police.

Scared of what would happen if they went home, the couple was "forced to stay in Japan", Wang told me. While fortunately they were on a long trip, so had packed heavily; however, they had not prepared to move countries, and only had summer clothes, while the majority of their belongings were back in China. "Many Japanese friends sympathised with me and gave me lots of support," Wang said. "As the Japanese government was reluctant to accept political asylum seekers from China, my friends helped me find ways to stay in Japan." At first, this was through a university fellowship, before Wang and his wife were able to apply for work visas.

Moving to Japan did not stop Wang from drawing, nor did it free him from the attention of the censors. He faced constant harassment from Chinese pro-government trolls, including multiple death threats. As he became more famous, Badiucao, too, attracted this kind of attention. Since he was already off Weibo and based in

Australia, he couldn't easily be muzzled, so his critics attempted to scare him into silence.

"When I illustrated the 'Free The Five' feminists, they launched a campaign to attack me on Twitter," he told me, referring to a group of young women arrested in early 2015 in the run-up to International Women's Day. After he drew portraits of them to call for their release, the images were widely shared and used to illustrate coverage of the snowballing story (both then US Secretary of State Hillary Clinton and the editorial board of *The New York Times* publicly criticised the arrests).[14] Badiucao's Twitter account was flooded with messages, clogging up his timeline and making normal use of the app almost impossible. "They would just write horrible things, calling me a pervert or a traitor, a running dog of the Americans," he said.

When this failed to shut him up, the trolls decided to smear him instead, sharing articles and posts with fake accounts of his life and motivations, some purporting to have been written by him. "Their stories were very specific, as if they were my own diary, imagining what I was like in China, what were my reasons for leaving China," he said. The strangest turn came when he discovered that someone had set up a website – Badiucao.net – interspersing his cartoons with pornography and speculations over his true identity.

"Reading Badiucao's cartoons, you can easily see his naive point of view," one early post read. "Its content is nothing more than Western thought, he talks about Chinese politics only to flatter the West. But the Chinese people understand, far better than Badiucao, and the reason they ignore him is because they know that the path China is currently walking is the correct one." Other posts called him an "Australian clown" who advocated for Tibetan separatism and promoted pornography and "sick", "vulgar" art. One upside was that the campaign encouraged him to open his own website ("Luckily, I already owned badiucao.com"), to push the fake one out of search rankings. Today, it does not appear on the first page of results for 'badiucao' or '巴丢草' in either Google or Baidu, though it remains online.

Badiucao and Rebel Pepper were among the early victims of this type of overseas harassment by pro-government trolls, but online abuse is a common tactic, said Sophie Beach, editor of *China Digital Times*, the website founded by Xiao Qiang that focuses on censorship and free expression. It shows how far the government is willing to go in stamping out dissent even beyond its borders. "Dissidents and activists have been subjected to very personal attacks," she told me via Skype from California. "The kind of language used in the attacks is the kind of language used in government propaganda." In the years since then, trolls like those who went after Badiucao have become emboldened, launching campaigns on foreign social media against other dissidents, Australian and Taiwanese celebrities, and even the president of Taiwan, after Tsai Ing-wen irritated Beijing by attending an official flag-raising ceremony.[15]

China's online influence effort is sprawling, dwarfing even those of Russia and the US. This is achieved both through paid commentators, known as *'wumao'* for the fifty cents they were reportedly paid per post in the early days, and by volunteer trolls, who are encouraged and led by state media, and usually go after overseas targets.[16] *Wumao* are bogeymen of the Chinese web, and the term is used loosely – anyone who takes a pro-government line is cast as an agent of the Party – but their existence has been widely documented. These 'opinion leaders' have their origins in the university bulletin boards that dominated the early Chinese internet, as researcher David Bandurski has documented:

In March 2005, a bold new tactic emerged in the wake of a nationwide purge by the Ministry of Education of college bulletin-board systems. As Nanjing University, one of the country's leading academic institutions, readied itself for the launch of a new campus forum after the forced closure of its popular "Little Lily" BBS, school officials recruited a team of zealous students to work part time as "Web commentators." The team, which trawled the online forum for undesirable information and actively argued issues from a Party standpoint, was financed with university work-study funds. In the months that followed, party leaders across Jiangsu Province began recruiting their own teams of Web commentators. Rumours travelled quickly across the Internet that these Party-backed monitors received 50 *mao*, or roughly seven cents, for each positive post they made. The term Fifty Cent Party, or *wumaodang*, was born.[17]

According to most accounts, contrary to a caricature of *wumao* as constantly arguing with enemies of the Party, they generally focus on positive news, drowning out controversial topics with government-approved posts. After all, attacks on a *baizuo*, or 'white leftist', as some liberals and progressives are called on the Chinese web, can give them oxygen and attention the censors would rather they not enjoy. A 2016 study estimated that internet commenters employed by the government created around 448 million fake social media posts every year, focusing on "cheerleading" for the government rather than tussling with its critics.[18]

The researchers wrote:

They do not step up to defend the government, its leaders, and their policies from criticism, no matter how vitriolic; indeed, they seem to avoid controversial issues entirely. Instead, most [*wumao*] posts are about cheerleading and positive discussions of valence issues. We also detect a high level of coordination in the timing and content in these posts. A theory consistent with these patterns is that the strategic objective of the regime is to distract and redirect public attention from discussions or events with collective action potential.

In 2011, dissident artist Ai Weiwei got a self-described *wumao* to agree to an interview with him in return for a new iPad.[19] The anonymous interviewee, a twenty-six-year-old journalism student from Shanghai, had been working as a 'public opinion channeller' for several years.[20]

"Generally, after something happens, and sometimes before new stories even break, we'll receive an e-mail. It will tell you first about the incident, about the news, and then tell you what orientation to take," he said. "So it tells you a general ideological orientation, and you go and channel the ideas of web users toward that orientation, or you go and blur the focus of web users, or you might go and stir the emotions of web users [over some issue]."

While the ham-fisted attempts to smear him were largely ineffective, sometimes even comical, they did make Badiucao worry that his true identity would be exposed and his family in China would suffer because of it. "Sometimes I did receive threats to my personal safety," he said. "At first it was very overwhelming." His parents had joined him in Australia, although they, unlike Badiucao, still hold Chinese citizenship, and he was worried they could be targeted. "As my fame grows my fears grow. But really, if I just give up and stop doing the work I was doing, they'll know that's my weakness and they'll keep doing the same to others," he said. "Comparing my situation to other activists and artists in China, mine is really much better. I keep telling myself not to be afraid, you're thousands of miles away from their control, you should overcome it. I'm in a safe position, I should express myself for those who cannot. It's a process, overcoming the fear, but also a struggle."

The censors were successful in muzzling Weibo, but this did not kill it as a business. Today it is more popular than ever, having pivoted from focusing on news to courting celebrities and China's huge entertainment industry.[21] As a forum for free speech it is a shadow of what it once was, however, and Weibo's failure in this regard shows the power of the censors to stamp out any threat. The platform once seemed impossible to crack down on or truly control, and yet it has been almost completely neutered. In late 2017, Weibo vowed to clean up its act even further, and ensure that content posted did not "disrupt China's socialist core values".[22]

The Weibo crackdown also showed how those who could not or would not be controlled via algorithms, such as the Big Vs, or Badiucao and Rebel Pepper, are targeted by other means. For internet users outside China, the fate of the Weibo generation is a warning: that platforms which appear to be freewheeling and unassailable are far more fragile than they seem, and that governments, should they wish to, can rein almost anyone in.

Chapter 19

Root and stem

The internet is more vulnerable than you think

In September 2017, I drove to the Chinese University of Hong Kong (CUHK), my Uber blasting K-pop and almost getting lost in the maze-like campus. CUHK sits nestled on a tree-covered hilltop in the shadow of Tai Mo Shan, the city's highest peak, overlooking Tolo Harbour and the sprawling Sha Tin New Town, one of a handful of satellite settlements built north of Hong Kong proper to house the city's ever-expanding population. Quiet, spacious, green and pedestrian-friendly, the campus is a world apart from Hong Kong Island or Kowloon. On that day, it was bathed in sunlight, with a cool breeze cutting through the stifling late summer temperature.

CUHK is also home to the Hong Kong Internet Exchange (HKIX), one of hundreds of such institutions around the world that quietly and largely invisibly ensure that the internet functions as it does. As Kenneth Lo, an HKIX systems engineer, explained to me in a sparse conference room inside the company's hillside office, an exchange functions similarly to a home internet router, just on a much larger scale.[1] As your home router allows devices on your network – phones, games consoles, laptops – to communicate with each and connect to the internet, so an internet exchange handles routing requests between various internet service providers (ISPs) and the internet backbone. The shorter the distance requests have to travel, the faster websites will load, so by keeping traffic within a certain geographic area as much as possible, internet exchanges are able to boost speeds and make things more efficient for users. Another HKIX engineer used the example of a highways department: just as local governments look to relieve congestion by building new roads and links to other cities, the internet exchange ensures that users are able to connect to servers as fast and cleanly as possible.

After a crash course in internet exchanges, Lo and his colleagues took me to what I had come to see. A ten-minute drive across campus at another featureless, grey building off a narrow street packed with parked cars, Lo swiped us through a security gate and we walked inside. At a checkpoint, I wrote down my name and phone number, and in return received a temporary pass to clip on my shirt: number 111.

Lo entered another code to unlock the door beyond the security desk and we were met by a blast of cold and the noise of several air-conditioning units working overtime. Long, tall rows of server stacks filled the room, standing atop squares of carpet that looked like a collection of free samples from the most boring textile shop in the world. Above the server stacks, wire baskets hung from the ceiling, filled with wads of yellow and blue cables bound together with tape. Lo led me along a couple of rows of servers before stopping before one that looked identical to the others, opening its door, and gesturing inside. "There it is," he said.

Several rows of servers sat inside, each a cluster of ventilation ports, sockets and buttons, with a series of blue ethernet and grey fibre-optic wires leading off them into the mess of cables overhead. I gave Lo a helpless look and he pointed at one in the middle, seemingly no different from the rest apart from a slight increase in green LEDs. I had been warned that this would be a let-down, but had assured Lo and his colleagues that I wanted to see this anyway.

Because while internet exchanges are important for the web to operate, this black box was vital. I was looking at the F-Root, one of thirteen servers without which the internet as we know it would break down.

*

Despite the inventors of the internet being spread around the world and of multiple nationalities, in the beginning, the technology was unequivocally American. Many of the technology's founders worked at the US Defense Advanced Research Projects Agency (DARPA) in Arlington, Virginia, and it was there that Arpanet, a precursor to the modern internet, was invented.[2] Even as the internet became a global phenomenon, control over it remained in the US, because while the technology allowed for computers all over the world to talk to each other, it required some kind of system to coordinate all this communication, allocating computers names and numbers so their users knew who they were talking to. In the early days of Arpanet, that system was a man: John Postel, a pony-tailed, bespectacled Californian working out of an office in the small town of Marina del Rey, west of central Los Angeles. Postel maintained the hosts.txt file, a list of all the computers connected to Arpanet and their numerical addresses.[3] As the internet evolved, so did hosts.txt, into the Internet Assigned Numbers Authority (IANA),[4] which Postel was contracted to run by the US government. His new organisation was responsible for assigning all IP numbers – which gave each computer connected to the internet a unique address – and domain names, which made those addresses memorable. A running list of all of these addresses and domains was maintained on the root server, a more advanced form of the hosts.txt file, in Postel's office in Marina del Rey.

This gave Postel a huge amount of power over the early web, as internet historians Tim Wu and Jack Goldsmith explain:

"[T]he root authority is very close to a truly global authority for the internet – the ultimate intermediary on which everyone depends."[5] The root ensures whitehouse.gov points to the same website for everyone in the world, and it's what prevents anyone else from registering that domain. Whoever controls the root also controls which top-level domains – .com, .gov, .edu, etc. – exist, and could, hypothetically, delete them, wiping out all .com domains in one fell swoop. But while Postel acted as a 'benevolent dictator' of the early web, his control over the root was in fact dependent on a contract between the US government and the Stanford Research Institute, which administered the physical computers on which the global domain name system (DNS) relied.[6]

In 1992, that government contract went up for tender, and control over the root passed from Postel to a private company, Network Solutions, which also received a monopoly on selling domain names (which had previously been handed out for free).[7] This monopoly was both highly lucrative – giving the company a market capitalisation of $3.4 billion in 1999[8] – and highly controversial.[9] Internet pioneers such as Postel held the company in especial disdain, seeing it as an unwelcome new player in the space they had helped create, and an aggressive, bullying one at that.[10] But even as Network Solutions flexed its muscles, Postel retained certain powers over naming policy, and he had what the company could never buy, the loyalty of the people who actually administered the internet.

On 28 January 1998, as clouds massed outside the window of his office in the University of Southern California's Information Sciences Institute,[11] Postel decided to test that loyalty.[12] He emailed the administrators of eight of the twelve regional DNS servers – mirrors of the root server maintained by Network Solutions – and asked them to recognise his computer as root instead. With no small amount of trepidation, but a large amount of trust in Postel, the admins, from Sweden to Japan to the US, did so, effectively cleaving the internet in two, with one part run out of Network Solutions in Virginia, and the other from Postel's server in California.[13]

The risks of such a move were huge, as one expert put it at the time: "If we break the root, everything fails."[14] Postel, however, as one of the inventors of much of the technology involved, knew this better than anyone, and had set up his server to mirror that of Network Solutions, meaning that most users did not notice the power grab taking place. The 'test', as Postel would later describe it, was intended as a shot across the bows of the US government, and a protest at Washington's decision months before to block an attempt by Postel and fellow internet pioneer Vint Cerf to create a new public–private partnership that would take over internet governance from Network Solutions.[15] As well as a pointed demonstration of his own power, Postel also exposed a gaping vulnerability in the existing system – after a series of frantic meetings and calls between government officials, network admins, Postel's bosses at USC, and Postel himself, in which the government agreed to endorse the internet pioneer's 'test' explanation, officials also made it clear that future tampering with the root would be treated as a criminal offence.[16]

In the wake of the 'test', the government agreed to transfer some of its authority over the internet to the newly created Internet Corporation for Assigned Names and Numbers (ICANN),[17] a non-profit tasked with promoting "the global public interest in the operational stability of the internet".[18] ICANN was based on a proposal drawn up by Postel, which reflected, in his words, "the consensus judgment of the global internet community".[19] Unfortunately, however, after a career spent working towards this point, Postel would not live to see his goals fully realised – he died of heart complications on 16 October 1998, just a month after ICANN was founded. He was fifty-five.[20]

No sooner had the intra-US battle for control over the root finished, a new international dispute blew up. For ICANN was not what it seemed.[21] While Washington talked a good game, it had not relinquished control over the root, and ICANN operated under contract to the US Commerce Department. ICANN, which had absorbed IANA, essentially replaced Postel as the entity responsible for the day-to-day running of the ever-expanding internet,[22] but the ultimate power to make any changes to the root remained with the US government.

Understandably, this arrangement didn't sit well with many other countries, particularly in Europe, where many internet pioneers were based and key technologies (such as the world wide web, the top layer of the internet and the one with which we interact most on a daily basis) had been invented. Around this time, preparations began for the United Nations World Summit on the Information Society (WSIS), a major international conference intended to help bridge a growing 'digital divide' between rich and poor countries.[23] As the meeting neared, however, it became apparent that it would largely be a referendum on US control over the internet, with developing countries making it clear that "what was good for an internet with one million users would be not good enough for an internet with one billion users".[24]

Washington fuelled this burgeoning resentment by declaring, in the run-up to WSIS, that the US intended to "maintain its historic role in authorising changes or modifications to the authoritative root zone file".[25] While few failed to recognise the historical success of the internet under US oversight, there was a legitimate fear that any country with unilateral control over the root could use it as a political weapon by, for example, deleting entirely the top-level domain for a given country or otherwise hampering its use. For much of the early 2000s, the Iraqi top-level domain .iq was in limbo, after the company licensed to administer it, the Texas-based Infocom, was prosecuted over its founders' dealings with designated terror groups in Libya and Syria.[26] Following the US-led invasion and occupation of Iraq in 2003, as the country struggled to transition into something like democracy, responsibility for .iq was given to a body nominated by Ayad Allawi, the Washington-picked acting president of Iraq.[27] While a truly international ICANN might have dealt with the situation in exactly the same manner, it is not hard to see why some would be uncomfortable with the potential for US foreign policy demands to impact global internet governance.

'Operation Iraqi Freedom' may have played at role in the European Union's decision at WSIS to break with Washington and back a proposal to strip ICANN of its naming responsibilities and give them to a United Nations body. *The New York Times* reported at the time that "political unease with the US approach, symbolised by opposition to the war in Iraq, has spilled over into these technical discussions".[28] That this approach put the EU in alliance with some of the internet's most prolific censors appalled some diplomats. "We really can't have a Europe that is applauded by China and Iran and Saudi Arabia on the future governance of the internet," former Swedish Prime Minister Carl Bildt wrote. "Even those critical of the United States must see where such a position risks taking us."[29]

The debate that played out at WSIS set the stage for a fight over internet governance that continues to this day. On one side, proponents of intergovernmental control over the internet argue that this would stabilise the network, giving all countries an equal say and ensuring that no one government could use control over the web for political purposes. Opponents of this view argue that more government involvement is precisely what would politicise the process, adding needless bureaucracy, and turning technical questions into referenda on geopolitics. As ICANN delegate Wolfgang Kleinwächter explained:

One look into the debates of the United Nations Security Council or into the complicated discussion around United Nations reform demonstrate that one unwanted result of such an internationalisation could be the blocking of decisions, which could lead to a slowdown of the further innovative development of the internet with all its political and economic consequences ... If a root zone file change for the TLD of India would need the approval by the Government of Pakistan, then the current simple system could become rather complex and could provoke unneeded but complicated 'Internet wars'. Another risk could be that sooner or later a substantial majority of Governments could have the idea, to create an artificial scarcity on Internet resources – domain names and IP addresses – with the aim to justify global or local domain name taxes or IP address license fees.[30]

In the end, despite near universal opposition, the US won out at WSIS, demonstrating the power that root control still provided. ICANN would retain control over internet naming, but Washington agreed to the establishment of the new Internet Governance Forum in which governments could influence, though not control, internet policy going forward.[31]

While arguments against US hegemony over the internet are valid, there is no small amount of cynicism and self-interest from some government proponents of UN or other multinational governance of the internet. Such a system would empower them, putting them on an equal footing with the US, and enable them to pass internet policy beneficial to their needs. For the censors, this would mean an endorsement of concepts like cyber-sovereignty and the banning of programmes such as those run by the US and others which seek to undermine internet controls and promote free speech in closed societies. It would also mean the stripping of any existing international protections for online expression, giving countries an even freer rein to digitally punish political opponents and dissidents and restrict their ability to use the internet. China and Russia, along with a rotating cast of various autocratic governments from around the world, have been the leading proponents of a multilateral – state-led – internet governance system, while the US and the EU have backed a multi-stakeholder approach, in which civil society groups and private industry are also given a seat at the table and largely act as a pro-free speech counterweight to the censors.

This debate often boils down to support for one of two bodies as a chosen venue for internet governance: the multi-stakeholder ICANN, or the UN's International Telecommunication Union (ITU).[32] Founded in Paris in 1865 to manage international telegraph networks,[33] the ITU has expanded over the years to add radio, television and telecoms to its remit. In 1988, now under the auspices of the UN, it established the International Telecommunication Regulations (ITRs), creating a regulatory framework for "global interconnection and interoperability".[34] While the original ITRs did not cover the internet, still then in its infancy, in the years that followed the ITU made it clear that it felt its jurisdiction should extend to the new technology. In 2012, as the ITRs were due to be renegotiated for the first time, the censors spotted an opportunity for a power grab.

Chapter 20

The censor at the UN

China's undermining of global internet freedoms

Dubai is a city of concrete, cranes, air conditioning, and ludicrous water features that have no right to exist in the desert. In the middle of the city, surrounded by skyscrapers and highways, sits the blocky white building of the Dubai World Trade Centre. In December 2012, as temperatures dipped to the comparatively balmy high twenties, preparations began for the World Conference on International Telecommunications (WCIT). Inside an artificially lit meeting hall, long tables were draped in dark grey cloth and blue, low-backed chairs clustered behind them. Atop each table, white signs with thick black lettering spelled out the names of each delegation in French, one of the official languages of the International Telecommunication Union (ITU).

Like many UN bodies, the ITU has a weird relationship with democracy and transparency. Its members are nominated and appointed by (for the most part) democratically elected governments, and are in theory accountable to those voters, but meetings often take place behind closed doors and receive little press attention. All this changed as WCIT (pronounced 'wicket') approached. Amid rumblings that the ITU would use the meeting as an opportunity to take control of the internet, civil society groups and internet pioneers began to sound the alarm.

In May, Vint Cerf, one of the inventors of TCP/IP and a long-time collaborator of Jon Postel, wrote in *The New York Times* that "a new front in the battle for the internet is opening at the International Telecommunications Union". Cerf and others feared the ITU would attempt to replace ICANN as the main authority for internet naming and numbering, or pass onerous restrictions on online speech, such as requiring real-name identification for all internet users.[1] While the ITU denied it was planning a power grab, many of its proponents did not help its case. In a meeting with ITU secretary general Hamadoun Touré in Geneva, Vladimir Putin, then in his brief interregnum as Russian prime minister, praised the ITU boss for proposing the establishment of "international control over the internet".[2] According to a transcript of the meeting released by the Kremlin, Touré, who studied in St Petersburg and was elected to his position with Moscow's support,[3] said he considered himself a "representative of the Russian Federation at the ITU".

As battle lines were drawn up, Washington was adamant that the conference "should not be dealing with the internet sector". The US ambassador to the conference, Terry Kramer, a former telecommunications executive appointed by Barack Obama, warned that "what are seemingly harmless proposals can open the door to censorship, because people can then say, listen, as part of internet security, we see traffic and content that we don't like".[4]

If Putin and Touré were representative of the bureaucrats and petty tyrants Cerf feared would gain control of the internet, Eli Dourado was a perfect example of the type of civil society involvement seen as vital to ensuring that the technology remained open and free. A blond, bespectacled thirty-two-year-old, Dourado had stumbled into a pivotal role at WCIT almost by accident.[5] As a researcher at George Mason University in Arlington, Virginia, just across the river from Washington DC, Dourado had begun looking into internet governance and the coming ITU conference.

Like many others in his field, he became frustrated that nothing about what was to be discussed was public. But speaking to US officials, he discovered that, while ITU meetings were anything but transparent, they were not officially classified, meaning the documents involved could be shared without legal consequences. Hundreds of people had access to these documents, but no one wanted to publish them for the public to see, because they were either government officials who didn't wish to risk diplomatic fallout, or industry members not willing to anger an organisation that could soon be regulating them.

What was missing, Dourado and his colleague Jerry Brito realised, was a service through which the documents could be made public anonymously. Its name was obvious: the year before WCIT, Chelsea Manning had leaked a classified US military video showing an Apache helicopter firing on civilians and journalists in Iraq, sparking international outrage and making the service to which she gave the video famous around the world. Thus WCITLeaks was born.

The pair came up with the idea on a Tuesday morning, and spent all afternoon coding a basic website that could accept anonymous uploads and convert documents to PDFs to conceal their origin. They launched it the following day and got their first major WCIT document within an hour. Dourado and Brito had tapped into a vast well of frustration within the ITU process, and the documents quickly began pouring in. At a conference in London a few days after the service launched, a woman excitedly asked Dourado, 'Have you heard of WCITLeaks?' They had become a brand name.

Having opened the door a crack, Dourado decided to push through it. After a one-on-one meeting with Ambassador Kramer, in which the diplomat appeared to be trying to work out whether Dourado would be more trouble to the delegation inside or from without, he got the nod to go to Dubai.

The first few days of WCIT were a whirlwind of confusing bureaucracy, as meetings stretched on for hours, with any contentious issues knocked down to working groups for further discussion, and then to ad hoc groups, and then back up to the main plenary session when there was still no agreement. The phrase 'spirit of consensus and compromise' was repeated over and over, with the assumption that everyone was going to leave equally unhappy – and that was good.

In the end, it didn't really work out like that. About a week into the conference, host country United Arab Emirates (UAE) dropped a bombshell, announcing that it was putting forward a new 'multi-regional common proposal' that would completely rewrite the proposed treaty delegates had just spent the last few days hashing out.[6] Ominously, this as yet unrevealed proposal was backed by some of the most prolific censors of the internet – Russia, China, Saudi Arabia, the UAE, Algeria, Sudan, and Egypt. Even more worryingly, the plan was not made available for viewing on the WCIT system, despite promises from the UAE that delegations would be allowed to review it before the vote. The following afternoon, a Saturday, Dourado managed to get his hands on a draft Word document that was being passed around, replete with amendments, deletions and suggested additions.[7] He immediately uploaded it to WCITLeaks, sparking a flurry of press attention and widespread outrage even from some supporters of the ITU. Despite repeated assurances WCIT was not an ITU power grab over the internet, the leaked document proposed just that.[8] It would expand the ITU's remit beyond traditional telecoms to all providers of internet and voice services, and give the organisation a leading role in cybersecurity regulation. Worse, it would nationalise key aspects of internet governance currently handled by ICANN and legitimise state censorship and surveillance, by giving countries "the sovereign right to establish and implement public policy, including international policy, on matters of internet governance, and to regulate the national internet segment, as well as the activities within their territory of operating agencies providing internet access or carrying internet traffic".

The document showed how China and Russia, then the two leading proponents of nationalised internets and widespread censorship, were working together to advance their interests at the UN, a partnership that could have devastating results for worldwide internet freedoms. As the WCITLeaks version began to circulate more widely and attract more and more criticism, support for the proposal seemed to evaporate. Egypt protested that it had never agreed to back the plan, and on Sunday afternoon the ITU announced that the proposal had been withdrawn. The following morning, in an apparent death blow, Egypt issued a strong statement in favour of internet freedom and said it would never support expanding the ITU's scope to include "content regulation and censorship".[9] According to one report, Touré himself intervened to get Russia to withdraw the proposal, fearing that failure to do so could lead to a breakdown of the entire conference.[10]

This looked like a win for the 'spirit of consensus and compromise', but soon afterwards everything was thrown into disarray again. Conference chair Mohamed Nasser Al-Ghanim announced that, given the continued deep divides on a number of issues, a closed-door meeting of member states would be called to hammer out a compromise treaty text all could agree upon. Soon after Al-Ghanim's announcement, Dourado received an urgent email: "US DEL Meet in Ajman Suite now." Shaking with adrenaline and nerves, he made an impassioned case that the US could not compromise on key demands like internet naming and cybersecurity. He had little standing to make such demands, but was backed up by representatives of civil society groups and several large internet firms, none of whom wanted UN oversight of their businesses. But the delegation also included many members from the telecoms and radio communications sector, who were already governed by the ITU and had no interest in rocking the boat and reducing US leverage over issues that mattered to them.

The worst fears of Dourado's clique seemed to have come true when the 'Chairman's draft' of the treaty was released the following evening. It would greatly expand the ITU's power over the internet, with provisions on internet naming and numbering, cybersecurity, anti-spam rules many feared could leave the door open for censorship, and a non-binding resolution stating that the ITU should "play an active and constructive role" in internet governance.[11]

On the last day of the conference, as the US delegation – with White House backing – was preparing to refuse to sign the treaty, but with little certainty its allies would follow suit, Nigeria threw an assist. The West African nation introduced a last-minute amendment to the treaty that would guarantee the 'human right' of all member states to access international telecommunications services.[12] The right would be granted to the state, rather than its individual citizens, and was based on a Cuban and Sudanese proposal aimed at undermining US and other sanctions against those countries.[13] It could also have left the door open to legitimising state control over the internet.[14]

This forced the matter for the US and many of its allies, who might have been willing to compromise on some internet governance issues, but were not willing to do anything that might undermine sanctions, or recognise the ITU – a technical body dominated by unelected bureaucrats – as a new arbiter of international human rights. "It's with a heavy heart and a sense of missed opportunities that the US must communicate that it's not able to sign the agreement in the current form," Kramer said.

The UK, Sweden and Canada all quickly followed suit, saying that they could not vote for the treaty in its current form and calling on the ITU to recognise the existing multi-stakeholder model, which, in Kramer's words, ensured internet policy was driven not by states "but by citizens, communities, and broader society". Overnight, as the treaty was prepared for an official signing ceremony, opposition to it grew, with the EU coming out against it and many private industry groups lobbying their delegations not to sign. In the end, eighty-nine countries signed the new ITRs while fifty-five abstained, meaning that they stuck to the 1988 rules. While, in theory, those countries that adopted the new regulations should have taken steps to implement what they had agreed to, without broad support from much of the world's major economies, the effectiveness of the treaty was undermined. The censors were, for now, on the back foot.

*

While WCIT ended in embarrassment and acrimony, the stage was set. No longer could the ITU or the UN pretend not to have designs on internet governance, and the role of countries such as Russia and China in pushing to weaken protection for free speech and open access to the web was clear, as were their potential allies in such an endeavour. In the wake of WCIT, Beijing has only played a more active role in these matters, focusing on shoring up the Great Firewall's international flank as internal dissent has been stamped out. This was in line with China's transition from a state largely ambivalent about international institutions to one keen to take full advantage of them and work to shape their goals in line with Beijing's own. As historian David Shambaugh has shown, in recent decades China has "become one of the world's strongest advocates of the UN, as it is founded on the basis of both of China's most cherished diplomatic principles: state sovereignty and universal equal representation".[15]

Since 2008, China has worked to "selectively alter rules, actors, and the 'balance of influence' largely from within existing institutions – while simultaneously trying to establish alternative institutions and norms of global governance," Shambaugh writes.

This work takes place both in the open and behind the scenes, as one diplomat remarked to Human Rights Watch in 2017: "China does not want to be in a position of voting against a resolution on internet freedom. It doesn't want to be in a position to vote against freedom of expression or freedom of association ... and so it does a few things ... it works through proxies who have less to lose."[16]

It makes sense, therefore, that China, as it cements ever greater control over the internet at home, would seek to have its policies reflected at the UN level. The doctrine of cyber-sovereignty, which also emerged during the 2010s, not only serves to legitimise China's actions to a domestic audience and put a sheen of political theory on self-interested censorship, but also to expound Chinese-style internet governance overseas, reducing threats to the Great Firewall and preventing criticism or official international censure.

Nor are China's efforts in this regard confined to the UN and other multilateral bodies. Despite Beijing's disdain for the multi-stakeholder model, it has been quietly increasing its influence at ICANN and other governance forums, and in technical bodies that set standards for everything from internet browsers to the wifi spectrum. Since 2013, for example, the World Wide Web Consortium (W3C), the main international standards organisation for the web, has actively courted Chinese web developers and tech firms, opening a new centre at Beihang University in Beijing.[17] In a press release announcing the move, Huai Jinping, the university's president, hailed the fact that "many Chinese organisations are starting to play an important role in noted international standards bodies such as W3C". Another major standards body, the Internet Engineering Task Force (IETF), has also expanded its footprint in China.[18]

Also in 2013, ICANN opened its Beijing Engagement Centre to increase its links with the country.[19] The development was hailed by Hu Qiheng, president of the Internet Society of China, a supposedly non-governmental organisation with strong ties to the Ministry of Industry and Information Technology (MIIT), China's top censor. The Internet Society of China also issues the 'Public pledge of self-regulation and professional ethics for China internet industry', a basically mandatory agreement all tech firms in the country sign that puts them in line with Beijing's censorship policies. In March 2017, Song Zheng, the original head of ICANN China, was replaced by Zhang Jianchuan, who began his career in the China Internet Network Information Centre, a division of MIIT.[20]

While Chinese organisations obviously deserve a seat at the multi-stakeholder table, the context in which they do so is important. Since Xi Jinping came to power, he has launched a concerted crackdown not just on the internet, but also on civil society at large; this means that any NGOs allowed to function in this field are those, like the Internet Society of China, whose policies fully line up with those of Beijing. Private firms, too, have no bandwidth to stray from state policies on internet governance and cybersecurity. Companies such as Huawei, with its deep ties to the Chinese military, Baidu, Tencent and Alibaba, all of whom have histories of complying with and supporting internet censorship, are growing in influence in international standards bodies and other forums.

Since 2016, Beijing has ramped up its push for "ideological security" within these key tech firms, urging them to strengthen their "Party-building" efforts.[21] Nominally private companies have been encouraged to set up Party committees in the manner of state-owned enterprises, and to increase their genuflection to the Party line on key issues. The number of Party members in these firms has increased to over 5,000, with Baidu alone having 3,600 registered members. "The Party branch and committee within companies need to play a surveillance role to guarantee the healthy development of China's internet environment," a Party school professor told state media in late 2016.[22]

According to Peter Micek, general counsel for Access Now, a New York-based advocacy group that lobbies for open internet policies, standards bodies have traditionally "been flooded with and really directed by Cisco engineers and others from the West. But now, more and more Chinese engineers, and engineers from Chinese companies, are proposing and developing and adopting standards."[23] Sometimes these debates come down to which company's pet standard gets adopted as a general one, but often the issues discussed and fought over are 'universal values' about free speech, internet access and surveillance. "This is one place where quietly there is a more concerted effort to take control of what the internet actually is," Micek said.

As researcher Shanthi Kalathil writes, "now that Chinese internet companies have benefited from the absence of foreign competition in the domestic market, they are ready to head overseas, having internalised China's norms around internet sovereignty, censorship and surveillance".[24]

The cycles of global governance are frequent, and for those willing to play the long game, there are plenty of opportunities. The censors could afford an occasional tactical retreat, as in 2012, safe in the knowledge that a new battlefield would soon open up, with new avenues and allies for success. Two years after the Dubai debacle, Touré's replacement, Zhao Houlin, was elected unopposed as the new head of the ITU.[25] Zhao, a sixty-four-year-old telecoms engineer, was nominated for the position by China's MIIT.[26] In the run-up to WCIT, Zhao had advocated for a greater government role in internet naming and numbering.[27] Speaking after his election, he was clear in his belief that the ITU had a role in internet governance,[28] but prevaricated over how important it was to protect freedom of speech online, saying that member states "don't have a common interpretation of what censorship means".[29] If Touré was Moscow's man at the ITU,[30] Zhao was now Beijing's.

His appointment could not have come at a better time for Beijing, which was just ramping up its promotion of a new doctrine: cyber-sovereignty. A month after Zhao began his job, Chinese censorship tsar Lu Wei wrote in an op-ed for the *Huffington Post* that "cyber sovereignty must rule [the] global internet".[31] The debate that had raged between advocates of the multi-stakeholder model and those who favoured a multilateral system was a largely meaningless one, Lu wrote, a "friction" to be overcome through diplomacy, rather than two completely different, contradictory visions for how the internet is to be governed.

In 2015, Beijing came out swinging in the run-up to the Ten-Year Review of the World Summit on the Information Society (WSIS+10), which was intended to evaluate the 2005 Tunis agreement, where Washington had been forced to offer compromises to critics of US control of the internet. China argued for the establishment of a "multilateral, democratic, and transparent international internet governance system that ensures equal participation of all, reasonable allocation of internet resources, and joint management of key internet infrastructure". While the Chinese proposal paid lip service to the multi-stakeholder approach, it warned that the model "should not be lopsided, and any tendency to place sole emphasis on the role of businesses and non-governmental organisations while marginalising governments should be avoided". ICANN should be further internationalised, Beijing said, and the UN given a primary role in setting internet policy.[32]

China was supported in this endeavour by Russia, Cuba and the Group of 77, a confusingly named collection of 134 developing nations. While much of the worst language was negotiated out of the eventual agreement, with the US and others threatening at times to pull out entirely, Beijing succeeded in inserting the term 'multilateral' into the eventual agreement and establishing a greater role for the ITU in internet governance.[33] Days after the UN meetings wrapped up, Xi Jinping stepped on stage at an internet conference in China to call for a "reform of global internet governance" in line with the principles of cyber-sovereignty.[34]

Chapter 21

Sovereignty

When Xi Jinping came for the internet

The crowd sat in white, cotton-covered chairs atop an ugly, yellow-patterned carpet of the type inexplicably favoured by conference venues across China. At the front of the room, VIPs sat in wide, beige leather armchairs before the stage. Behind a white podium, between two giant screens showing the empty stage, hung a heavily photoshopped image of Wuzhen, the sleepy river town in Zhejiang province where the event was taking place in December 2015.

There was applause as Chinese President Xi Jinping walked out, dressed in his trademark dark suit and red tie, his hair the boot-polish black of all Chinese politicians, regardless of age. At sixty-two, his once good looks were now slightly puffed out and jowly; throughout his speech, the only time he would crack a smile was as he spoke of visiting Wuzhen many years ago as provincial Party secretary, at the start of his long climb to the summit of Chinese politics.

"Welcome to the beautiful town of Wuzhen for this important discussion on the development of the internet in the world," Xi said, after welcoming the various world leaders and autocrats seated before him.[1] His spoke in a deep monotone, with the occasional rolling syllable betraying his Beijing upbringing. While his presentation was conservative, often dull, the message was truly radical. Over the next twenty-five minutes, he called for a "reform of internet governance" and expounded a vision of the web completely at odds with its more than thirty-year history, one that would upend and reinvent the internet as we know it. "Cyberspace is not a domain beyond the rule of law," Xi said. "Greater effort should be made to strengthen ethical standards and promote civilised behaviour."

That Xi would seek to take greater control of the web than even his predecessors – who oversaw the creation and expansion of the Great Firewall – should come as no surprise. As he spoke in Wuzhen, Xi had been Party general secretary for just over three years. As the "chairman of everything",[2] he had consolidated more power than any Chinese leader since Mao Zedong. Unlike his predecessors, who deliberately cultivated consensus politics to avoid the horrors of Mao's cult of personality, Xi quickly established himself as supreme, unassailable. Once seen as a potential liberal reformer,[3] he wrested control over the economy from Li Keqiang, the country's premier and nominal head of government; cemented his authority over the People's Liberation Army (PLA); and moved to wipe out any threat to his position as 'core leader' through a far-reaching anti-corruption campaign and extensive crackdown on civil society.[4] In 2014, newly installed as the head of the "central leading group for cybersecurity and informatisation", Xi came for the internet.

*

Wuzhen does not look like the type of place where world-changing proclamations are made. Tiny by Chinese standards, with a population of less than 60,000,[5] the centuries-old town lies a two-hour drive from Shanghai. Picturesque and peaceful, tourists take wedding photos and selfies on its ancient stone bridges and in front of its pavilions and canal houses. In recent years, Wuzhen has attracted a different sort of crowd. Wearing suits and travelling business class, politicians and technologists from across China have flocked to the town for the annual World Internet Conference, the first of which was dubbed China's "online coming-out party".[6]

The irony of such an event being hosted by the world's most prolific internet censor was not lost on ordinary Chinese, who nicknamed the Wuzhen meeting the Local Area Network Conference,[7] in reference to the LAN protocols that allow computers to connect to each other, but not the outside world. Rights groups denounced the inaugural event and called for a boycott. With very little of the world in attendance, and several Western media outlets barred from covering it, the conference – under the subtitle 'an interconnected world shared and governed by all' – ended in embarrassing scandal after attendees refused to endorse a draft declaration meant to represent the consensus of all conference participants, forcing its withdrawal. Slipped under hotel-room doors in the middle of the night,[8] the declaration affirmed countries' right to enforce their 'cyber-sovereignty' and vowed, among other things, to wipe out online pornography. Conference participants were given a mere eight hours to suggest amendments, during which time most were asleep, before it was supposed to be announced and endorsed the following morning. Fearing an open revolt from furious attendees, however, the organisers never introduced it.

The 2014 draft declaration and its surrounding controversy was the first time many observers outside China heard the phrase 'cyber-sovereignty'. The concept has been around for several years, digested and regurgitated through several layers of Party think tanks and journals before eventually reaching top-level policymakers. Today, it is the driving policy behind Chinese internet strategy, and represents a major threat to the existing global web order.

First mentioned in a 2010 State Council information office white paper,[9] the doctrine goes "way beyond the rules of any other country" in spelling out the government's right to control the web, according to Tim Wu, Columbia Law School professor and coiner of the phrase 'net neutrality'.[10] One of the first Party journals to pick up on the concept was *China Information Society*, which is closely linked to the People's Liberation Army. "Cyber-sovereignty directly impacts national security and stability," the article said, calling on Chinese officials to do everything they can to "raise awareness" of it.[11] It continued:

> If a country loses its cyber-sovereignty, it will result in the loss of control over the systems governing lifeline economic sectors such as national industry, transportation, finance and resources, and result in untold economic damage. It will result in the loss of control over the guidance of online public opinion, sparking serious unrest and upheaval in society, directly challenging state power. It will result in the loss of control over military information networks, leading to command failures in the case of war ... resulting in a nation defeated and broken.[12]

That the PLA would take an interest in internet governance shows the true character of the doctrine. Cyber-sovereignty seeks to establish an international, as opposed to global, internet. Instead of the world wide web as we know it, countries would each maintain their own national internet, by force if necessary, with the border controls and immigration standards they see fit.[13] The doctrine risks turning the entire world into China, where people use a mirror image of the internet, resembling that outside the Great Firewall, but skewed and misshapen. Within the Firewall, buttressed by legions of censors and protectionist laws, Chinese internet users search on Baidu rather than Google, they share news and photos on WeChat, not Facebook, and shop with Alibaba, not Amazon. As Lu Wei, then the head of China's state information office and the country's top censor, told guests at a Lunar New Year banquet in 2015, "Only through my own proper management of my own internet, [and] your own proper management of your own internet ... can the online space be truly safe, more orderly and more beautiful."[14]

Such a vision of the internet – bordered and tightly controlled by government – would be antithetical to the techno-libertarians active in the early days of the web. The internet was not built with physical geography in mind,[15] nor did its early boosters have much time for states or borders. Speaking in February 1996, Nicholas Negroponte, co-founder of the MIT Media Lab and an early investor in *Wired* magazine, echoed a widely held consensus when he said the internet "cannot be regulated".

"It's not that laws aren't relevant, it's that the nation state is not relevant," he told a conference in Bonn, Germany. "Cyberlaw is, by nature, global and we're not very good at global law."[16] For a long time, the internet was thought of as a thing apart – people talked sincerely about things taking place in 'meatspace' as opposed to cyberspace, or clarified that an activity had occurred IRL (in real life). As academics Tim Wu and Jack Goldsmith write, in the 1990s, "[I]t was widely believed that cyberspace might challenge the authority of nation-states and move the world to a new post-territorial system."[17] That system would be governed not by law, but by code.

*

One of the leading advocates of a cyber utopia free from nation states and their laws was John Perry Barlow, perhaps the weirdest and most unlikely of the many eccentrics and free thinkers active in the early days of the internet.

Barlow was born in Wyoming in 1947 to a well-off family of devout Mormons; when he was growing up, the only TV he was allowed to watch was religious programming, and even that wasn't until he turned eleven.[18] John's father, Norman Barlow, was a Republican state legislator, and John himself later ran Dick Cheney's first congressional campaign,[19] before eventually breaking with the Republican Party after it was taken over by Cheney's very own brand of foreign interventionism and neoconservatism.

In high school, Barlow met Bob Weir, one of the founding members of the Grateful Dead – the legendary California rock band. The pair separated at graduation, when Barlow went to study comparative religion at Wesleyan University on the US east coast, but they remained close, and Barlow contributed lyrics to dozens of Grateful Dead tracks.[20] After university, Barlow might have been expected to join the Dead in San Francisco, or continue to Harvard Law, where he'd been offered a place, but instead he returned to Wyoming and took over his parents' cattle ranch.

Barlow was thoroughly settled into farm life by 1987, when he signed up to an early online bulletin board founded by fellow Dead Head and influential internet thinker Stewart Brand: the Whole Earth 'Lectronic Link (WELL).[21] What Barlow saw in WELL, and in the internet as a whole, was a brand-new form of community, separate from the rest of the world and unspoiled by its greed and neuroses. "Digital technology is ... erasing the legal jurisdictions of the physical world and replacing them with the unbounded and perhaps permanently lawless waves of cyberspace," he wrote in *Wired*, going on to endorse a concept he credited to Brand that would become the battle cry for their fellow techno-libertarians: "information wants to be free".[22]

Just as he evangelised the freedom enabled by the internet, Barlow attacked the forces that sought to rein it in, like the US National Security Agency, which, he presciently argued, "meticulously observes almost every activity undertaken and continuously prevents most who inhabit its domain from drawing any blinds against such observation".[23] In 1990, Barlow recruited Mitch Kapor and John Gilmore, two tech moguls who got rich in the first Silicon Valley boom, and founded the Electronic Frontier Foundation (EFF),[24] an organisation dedicated to "defending civil liberties in the digital world".[25] The three were soon joined by a host of Valley luminaries, and major corporate players, including Microsoft and HP, became donors. EFF lawyers went on to fight and win several key early court cases involving the internet, including a suit filed by Steve Jackson Games against the Secret Service in which the judge found that "electronic mail deserves at least as much protection as telephone calls", establishing the right for people to encrypt their communications.

In 1996, furious at the Communications Decency Act (CDA), an attempt to criminalise the publication of 'indecent' materials online where children under the age of eighteen could see them (i.e. nearly everywhere), Barlow wrote his landmark work: "A declaration of the independence of cyberspace".[26] It was an absurdly self-important document, but one reflective of the utopian thought of the time. Ironically, despite Barlow's assertion that "legal concepts ... do not apply to us", it was in court that EFF had its greatest impact, joining the American Civil Liberties Union in a successful suit to overturn parts of the CDA. In a major win for internet freedom, Supreme Court Justice John Paul Stevens, writing for the majority, ruled in favour of extremely broad speech protections with regard to the internet, "a unique medium ... located in no particular geographical location but available to anyone, anywhere in the world".[27]

Writing years later, EFF senior counsel David Sobel said the case "established the fundamental principles that govern free speech issues in the electronic age".[28] But while the win did much to establish the US as a world leader in internet freedom, the prediction by Barlow and others that the internet would be a place without borders, without nations, was proven to be wildly incorrect. As the internet has evolved from its American and English-language origins, and as the do-it-yourself, communal culture of the early web has been replaced by corporate walled gardens and self-censoring social networks, the protections of US law for online speech have become less and less relevant. Today, the internet looks much less like

Barlow's dreamed-of utopia and more like his nightmare.

While Barlow has long been an easy punching bag for two decades of internet sceptics, many things he predicted have indeed come to pass – "I said this whole notion of property is going to get hammered," he remarked in 2016. "It has been hammered."[29] – and the enduring impact of the declaration and, most of all, the creation of EFF on internet freedom is substantial. The most perverse thing to happen in the more than two decades since Barlow began typing his call to arms is not just that governments have proven themselves more than able to exercise power over the internet, but that they have adopted the language of techno-utopianism as they do so.

Successive US presidents, from Clinton to Bush to Obama, hailed the internet as a tool for spreading economic and political liberalisation around the world.[30] This is the internet as Tom Friedman's "nutcracker to open societies", and it is far more naive and at odds with reality than anything Barlow put forward. Often it has proved to be counterproductive to the very goals its proponents put forward. This utopianism reached a height in 2009, during the election protests in Iran. An apparent intervention by the US government to keep Twitter online during the unrest confirmed the worst fears of the censors in Tehran and Beijing. "Behind what America calls free speech is naked political scheming. How did the unrest after the Iranian elections come about?" an editorial in the *People's Daily* sneered. "It was because online warfare launched by America, via YouTube video and Twitter microblogging, spread rumours, created splits, stirred up, and sowed discord between the followers of conservative and reformist factions."[31]

Just as Yu Wanli, the expert who warned US diplomats against overreacting after the Google China fiasco, had predicted, the internet was turning into an 'ideological battlefield'. Moreover, from the view of the censors, American forces were already far ahead of their rivals. To win this fight, China would need allies.

Chapter 22

Friends in Moscow

The Great Firewall goes west

The headquarters of *Rossiya Segodnya* looked more like a multi-storey car park or a prison than an office complex. Boxy and grey-brown, the buildings stretched across almost two blocks on the southern edge of the Garden Ring, which encircles and delineates central Moscow. Large pillars loomed over guests as they arrived in April 2016, passing a security building at the main entrance emblazoned with the news agency's logo, a white and blue map of the world with Russia highlighted in red.

Formed by an executive order signed by President Vladimir Putin in December 2013, *Rossiya Segodnya* was the crown jewel of the Kremlin's overseas propaganda efforts, combining the former *RIA Novosti* news service and Voice of Russia radio into a new outlet tasked with providing "information on Russian state policy and Russian life and society for audiences abroad".[1] Putin tapped a long-time ally of his, Dmitry Kiselyov, a former TV presenter with a long history of homophobic and nationalist outbursts, to run the new super-agency.[2] Kiselyov soon launched *Sputnik*, an online news service published in more than three dozen languages. *Sputnik*, like its sister television station RT, which was also placed under Kiselyov's control, was slick and sexy in a way that Chinese state media has never managed to be. Both Russian outlets were more like Radio Free Asia or Voice of America, amping up dissenting voices in the US and Western European countries, rather than the turgid, bland rehashing of propaganda talking points seen on Chinese state television.

While Russia's propagandists were outstripping their Chinese counterparts overseas, their control of the message at home was nowhere near as tight as Beijing's, so in 2016 the *Rossiya Segodnya* headquarters hosted the cream of the Chinese censorship community for the Safe Internet Forum, sponsored by the Russian Ministry of Communications and Mass Media.[3] The forum, which billed itself as "the industry's prime conference on online child and adult safety", was the brainchild of Konstantin Malofeev. Large and bearded, with a round, cheerful face and bulbous nose, Malofeev was a billionaire former investment banker and conservative activist. He first came to prominence in 2014, when he was accused of funnelling hundreds of thousands of dollars to pro-Russian rebel groups in eastern Ukraine, earning him a place on several international sanctions lists.[4]

Malofeev was one of several conservative religious figures who rose swiftly up the ranks of Putin's inner circle as the president sought to shore up domestic support by burnishing his Orthodox credentials, taking a hard line on culture war issues such as gay rights and abortion.[5] The forty-four-year-old Malofeev, nicknamed "God's oligarch",[6] helped lead, along with long-time Putin ally Igor Shchyogolev, a resurgence of Orthodox thought among Russia's elite, similar to how the religious right in the US allied with and partially co-opted that country's ultra-rich. Malofeev, like Putin, tried to paint Russia as a safe harbour from the pro-gay, pro-Islam decadence of Western democracies, saying in 2014 that "just as Christians in the west in Ronald Reagan's time helped us against the evil of communism, we now have to return our debt to Christians who are suffering under totalitarianism in the west. This so-called liberalism, tolerance, and freedom, these are just words, but behind them you can see the totalitarianism."

Beyond his conservative religious beliefs, Malofeev was also that rarest of things: a twenty-first-century monarchist. "Monarchies have been alive in history for thousands of years," he argued. "Republics, just for several centuries, yet we assume that monarchies belong to the past and republics to the future." As a young man, he maintained a friendly correspondence with Grand Duke Vladimir Kirillovich, heir to the Russian imperial throne, the abolishment of which in 1917 Malofeev greatly regretted. After the Grand Duke's death, he turned his support to Putin, suggesting that the Russian president could one day make himself tsar.[7]

Following protests that marred Putin's third inauguration as president, Malofeev turned his attention to internet censorship, forming the Safe Internet League to lobby for a blacklist of websites disseminating child pornography and other illegal material. Russia's internet, he warned, was the "most dirty in any developed country" and needed cleaning up.[8] He saw China, with its zero-tolerance approach to porn, drugs and dissent, as an ideal model, and sought to learn from it.

In a swanky conference room filled with the Russian and Chinese internet elite, foreign journalists and concerned businesspeople, Malofeev sat on stage in front of a blue, *Matrix*-style map of the world. He was joined by Lu Wei, China's jovial, smooth-talking head censor; and Fang Binxing, widely acknowledged (and loathed) as the architect of the Great Firewall.[9] In a statement ahead of the forum, the Safe Internet League promised that Lu and Fang would offer their wisdom on cybersecurity, ensuring the "quality of internet content", cybercrime, and "countering new religious movements' online activities".[10]

"Freedom is not a right, but a responsibility," Lu told the forum. "Complete freedom can bring not only the threat of terrorism, but also threats to the life and freedom of citizens. Our countries are facing a robust campaign of information propaganda. That is why we must give serious attention to checking and filtering incoming information. Without regulation there can be no standing up against online scams and terrorist propaganda."[11] In their speeches, the Russian and Chinese censors promoted their shared vision of cyber-sovereignty. Igor Shchyogolev, the Russian minister of tele-communications, praised Chinese companies for moving their data onto Russian servers, a key plank of the doctrine, allowing security services the same influence over and access to foreign companies' data as they have for domestic firms.[12]

While both Russia and China had long complained of US dominance of key internet infrastructure and had worked together at the United Nations and elsewhere, the forum was remarkable for the open framing by censors from both sides of the internet as a battleground, where Washington sought to undermine and disrupt its enemies. "The US government directly controls American internet companies," Fang said. "Other countries have no right to interfere in internal affairs." Malofeev compared the dispute to the space race. The Soviet Union was the first country to launch a satellite into orbit, but it did not attempt to govern the cosmos, so why should the US continue to rule over the internet just because it was invented on American soil? He accused the US of having a "cowboy", finders keepers attitude to the internet.[13] Following the conference, the Safe Internet League published a glowing statement praising China's internet as "the most advanced in the world".[14] Chinese censors, the League said, had successfully solved one of the "most pressing problems of the modern internet industry": how to block malicious traffic.

The Ukraine crisis, with its ensuing sanctions and denunciations of Russia by the West, pushed the Kremlin closer to Beijing than it had been in decades. Initially this involved just economic support, with China happily buying up billions of dollars of Russian gas, but Malofeev's forum showed how other exchanges were also taking place behind the scenes. Since the 2012 election protests, the Kremlin had realised how lacking its own censorship apparatus was, and sought to learn from the Chinese how to rein in the internet. Much of the initial exchanges were through the Shanghai Cooperation Organisation (SCO), a shadowy coalition of China, Russia and four former Soviet republics. For almost a decade, the SCO has made 'information war' a key focus, and has lobbied for international restrictions on disseminating information "harmful to the spiritual, moral, and cultural spheres of other states", which it deems a "security threat".[15]

In 2015, Russia and China signed a cyber 'non-aggression' pact, promising not to hack each other and joining forces to advance the cause of cyber-sovereignty. The Kremlin's urgency in establishing a Russian firewall was compounded by the publication, the following April, of the Panama Papers, which linked cellist Sergei Roldugin, one of Putin's closest friends, to billions of dollars stored in offshore accounts.[16] Putin denounced the revelations as a US plot, and Alexander Bastrykin, head of the Russian anti-corruption agency, said the country needed to follow China's lead in fighting "unprecedented informational pressure" from the West.[17]

This went beyond just Chinese government support. Corporations such as Huawei, the telecoms giant founded by former People's Liberation Army engineer Ren Zhengfei, were invited to sell the censorship technology needed to turn Russia's internet into a mirror of China's.[18] Russian IT experts knew when they had been outclassed, with one telling reporters that, despite hopes domestic manufacturers would fulfil the demand created by sanctions, "We are in fact actively switching to Chinese [technologies]."[19] With the tools in place, Russia's parliament provided the legal basis for a new Great Firewall.[20] Legislation was introduced to force internet service providers (ISPs) to store communications records, give security services back doors into encrypted messages and chat apps, and transfer control of all internet exchanges to the Kremlin, creating a tight border around the Russian internet that could be easily policed and monitored.[21] This was a stunning transformation, in a matter of decades, of an internet once as free and open as any other country's – a transformation that had long been a dream of the Kremlin's, but was achieved only with Chinese assistance and encouragement.

*

The Soviet Union took its first steps onto the internet in 1990, a year before conservatives in the Communist Party attempted to remove reformist General Secretary Mikhail Gorbachev in a coup.[22] At the start of the decade, the country was lagging far behind the West, which had imposed tight import restrictions on computer equipment, leaving Soviet engineers with only poor imitations of the latest hardware and a rapidly widening technology gap.[23]

Just as CERN, the European nuclear research organisation, became a key hub for Western technology pioneers, eventually resulting in Tim Berners-Lee inventing the world wide web, Soviet researchers at the Kurchatov Institute of Atomic Energy in Moscow were instrumental in linking the Union to the nascent global internet.[24] In the early 1980s, the Institute had acquired a copy of the Unix operating system, and set a team of programmers to adapting it for Russian-speaking users. In 1988, they won a prize – the existence of which was kept highly secret – from the Soviet Council of Ministers, for the creation of the 'dialogue united mobile operating system', or Demos.[25]

In 1990, the Kurchatov Institute launched its first computer network, dubbed Relcom for 'reliable communications', and connected several other research organisations across the Union, including the newly formed Demos academic collective, dedicated to improving the operating system. Relcom was a pretty shoddy network, forced to use ordinary telephone lines with negligible bandwidth and worse speeds, but it was a start. In its first year, around thirty organisations were connected to the network. By 1991, this number had grown to over 400, and the network had its first foreign connection, with a computer at the University of Helsinki in Finland.[26]

Unlike in China, where Party officials quickly grasped the potential of the internet both as an economic driver and as a source of political unrest, and moved to take control of it for their own ends, their Soviet counterparts do not seem to have realised what was taking place under their noses. Valery Bardin, one of the co-founders of Demos, said that the early technology was introduced to the Union without any assistance or oversight from state institutions, which were too busy dealing with ongoing economic crises and the turmoil unleashed by perestroika.[27] When the August coup was launched, the putschists – even KGB chairman Vladimir Kryuchkov – were largely unaware of the new communications platform and did nothing to try to cut it off. On the morning of 19 August 1991, Bardin was awoken by a phone call from a journalist friend, who told him the coup was taking place. In Crimea, where he had been holidaying, Gorbachev had been detained by KGB agents, and his deputy, Gennady Yanayev, declared acting leader of the Soviet Union by the State Committee on the State of Emergency, as the plotters called themselves. Bardin hurried to Demos's offices, where he was joined by programmer Dmitry Burkov and several other members of staff. At the same time, around 7am, the tanks began rolling into Moscow.[28]

As Yanayev was being declared leader, the young scientists and programmers connected via Relcom began discussing the coup on the UseNet forum talk.politics.soviet. At 5pm on the first day, Vadim Antonov, a long-haired, skinny, bespectacled Relcom staffer, posted: "I've seen the tanks with my own eyes. I hope we'll be able to communicate during the next few days. Communists cannot rape Mother Russia once again!"[29]

Antonov and his wife, Polina, who also worked at Relcom, began sending regular emails to Larry Press, a university professor and computer scientist based in California. "Don't worry, we're ok, though frightened and angry," Polina wrote to Press early on during the coup. "Moscow is full of tanks and military machines – I hate them. They try to close all mass media, they stopped CNN an hour ago, and Soviet TV transmits opera and old movies ... Now we transmit information enough to put us in prison for the rest of our life."

While the Antonovs and those around them were freaking out, imagining a return to Stalinism, the coup was already unravelling. For reasons that remain unclear, the plotters failed to detain Russian president Boris Yeltsin as he returned to Moscow from a trip to Kazakhstan on the morning of 19 August. An order for his arrest was signed and KGB agents surrounded his residence, but they never followed through, allowing him to slip away.[30] Yeltsin quickly became the nexus of resistance to the Gang of Eight, barricading himself and his supporters inside the White House, the home of the Russian parliament in central Moscow, from where he issued a declaration that a reactionary coup had taken place and urged the military to play no part in it. "The country is in mortal danger," Yeltsin's hastily printed statement said.

A group of Communist criminals has carried out a coup d'état. If today citizens of Russia do not counter the activities of the putschists with conscience, determination, and courage, then the dark days of Stalinism will return!

If you do not resist the state criminals you betray freedom! You betray Russia! You betray yourself![31]

Yeltsin and his supporters called for a general strike, to continue until Gorbachev was permitted to address the people. With all mass media under the control of the Gang of Eight, they were forced to disseminate their statements by hand, photocopying the declarations and handing them out in squares and pasting them on walls. Members of Yeltsin's team began scouring the city for more photocopiers, and this brought one of them to the Demos/Relcom offices. Bardin answered the door and told the young aide not only did the building have a Xerox machine, it had something much better: an unfiltered connection to the outside world.[32]

"The first piece of paper we got was the decree by Yeltsin," Vadim Antonov said later. "We simply typed it in, sent it to the network and made the copies they wanted. When we got quite a lot of requests for more information from people on the net, we contacted Yeltsin's people and asked them to provide us regular information."[33]

A two-way information exchange was quickly set up, with Yeltsin's team providing details about the progress of the resistance within Moscow, and Press and other supporters outside Russia transcribing censored media reports and sending them back in. Panic and disillusionment can spread quickly during protests and street movements, as solidarity breaks down and people worry that they will be left alone to bear the blame if everything goes wrong. The importance of a connection to the outside world, bringing with it both encouragement and the potential of international scrutiny and support, cannot be overstated. During the 2014 Umbrella Movement pro-democracy protests in Hong Kong, I witnessed this for myself, as young protesters, wearing goggles and masks to protect themselves from tear gas, clapped reporters on the backs and beamed at us, so grateful for even the thin shield foreign media coverage might provide them from official retribution. "You can't imagine how grateful we are for your help and support in this terrible time," Polina wrote to Press. "The best thing is to know we aren't alone."

The Demos/Relcom team's connection to the outside world was gossamer thin, however, reliant on shoddy phone lines, badly built routers and the continued inattention of the KGB. Alexey Soldatov, head of the Kurchatov Institute, understood this better than most. Keep the connection going no matter what, he urged Bardin, even if it means we go to jail.[34] By this point, that was looking increasingly like a possibility. All information exchange with the West had been banned, and radio and television broadcasts "not conducive to the process of stabilising the situation in the country" had been blocked or shut off. The Demos/Relcom team was already in too deep – its only option was to keep going, and hope the coup unravelled.

By the morning of 21 August, that unravelling was already well under way. Yeltsin was still shored up in the White House, surrounded by troops loyal to him and cranking out denunciations of the Gang of Eight. At 8am, the communication block on Gorbachev's dacha was lifted, as his guards recognised which way the wind was blowing, and he swiftly declared the plotters' actions illegal and dismissed them from office. As one joke went at the time, you knew Communism was finished in Russia when the Bolsheviks couldn't even mount a proper coup.[35] The failed putsch was the final nail in the coffin of the Soviet Union, which was officially dissolved before the year was out.

Yeltsin was the hero of the coup, including to many of the tech pioneers who helped him get his message out. The early years of the new independent Russian Federation were good ones for the internet. Following the Soviet Union's collapse, both Relcom and Demos, established under the auspices – but not the attention – of the government at the Kurchatov Institute, quickly went private. They became ISPs, catering to a rapidly ballooning customer base.[36]

Much like Beijing at the same time, Moscow in the mid-1990s was internet mad. In 1994, ICANN created the domain extension .ru, and two years later Russia got its first dedicated search engine and its first blog, the '*Evening Internet*', written by activist Anton Nossik.[37] In 1997, *The New York Times* wrote that "the internet is a rapidly growing force here", describing a flourishing of private ISPs, websites and email providers, and a city covered in advertisements for all types of online services. Fees for connecting to the internet were extortionate, with some providers charging as much as $3 per minute, or $50 a month, in a country where the average monthly salary was just $200. But this didn't dissuade people: there was money to be made on Runet, and everyone wanted in.[38]

As internet usage surged and people revelled in their new freedoms online, the censors, too, were adapting. In 1995, the KGB became the FSB and established the Federal Agency for Government Communications and Information, or FAPSI.[39] Any hardware or software used for encryption had to get a FAPSI seal of approval, and since the agency also produced its own products, few were given out to any potential competitors. ISPs were forced to install a black box – the System of Operative Search Measures (SORM) – on their servers, which would allow FAPSI and the FSB to spy on users' communications.[40]

SORM was the brainchild of a new FSB director and key Yeltsin ally, a hard-faced, balding former KGB agent who had spent most of the last years of the Soviet Union ensconced within East Germany: Vladimir Putin.[41]

Chapter 23

Plane crash

China helps Russia bring Telegram to heel

It was January 2012. Dressed all in black, with a hooded vest over a turtleneck, Pavel Durov looked like a cross between Steve Jobs and the playboy son of a Moscow oligarch. Handsome, with a pale, clean-shaven face and dark, short hair swept neatly to one side, he spoke English fluently, though with a thick Russian accent. Except for the occasional stammer, as he struggled to elucidate a complicated point in a foreign language, he looked suave and confident.

"We are one of the reasons why Facebook is not doing so well in Russia," he told the crowd of technologists in Munich, Germany.[1] Durov was riding high, the most famous and most successful of Russia's new tech pioneers. He had reason to be pleased with himself. On a map of social media usage worldwide, much of the globe is coloured Facebook blue, with two notable gaps: China – where the Great Firewall has blocked Facebook for years – and Russia, where Durov's company, VKontakte, reigned supreme.[2]

Unlike in China, where internet companies succeeded only by collaborating with the censors, and were repaid by being able to take advantage of an environment almost completely absent of foreign competition, the relationship between Russia's internet entrepreneurs and the authorities was far more combative. No one better exemplified this than Durov, whose downfall mirrors the transition of Russia's internet from a freewheeling, capitalist network to one of tight controls, largely cut off from the outside world. Durov's story shows how the Kremlin evolved from its classic model of surveillance and intimidation, which had proved to be ill-suited to the internet, to one of filters and blacklists, intentionally modelled on the Great Firewall and helped along by its creators.

Like Facebook, VKontakte was the product of a tech prodigy studying at an elite college. Durov, like Mark Zuckerberg, was born in 1984, and got his start developing apps and websites for his fellow students at Saint Petersburg State University. A friend who was studying in the US at the time, Vyacheslav Mirilashvili, showed Durov Facebook, and the two quickly realised the potential for a Russian copycat service. With funding provided by Mirilashvili's father, a Georgian-Israeli tycoon with interests in gambling, real estate and energy, they began work on VK.[3] Durov almost missed his chance. He founded VK in late 2006, just as Facebook was branching out from its initial focus on students and allowing anyone to sign up.[4]

From the beginning, VK was shameless in aping Facebook, right down to its blue-tinted website design. To this day, both sites' login pages look almost identical. While MySpace, Friendster and Snapchat would be quick to point out Zuckerberg's own lack of qualms in this regard, VK's willingness to run roughshod over intellectual property would quickly turn out to be one of its greatest selling points. Like Baidu, which overtook Google in China in part by helping users search for illegal MP3s, VK was a hub for finding and sharing copyrighted materials, becoming one of the largest violators of intellectual property in the world.[5] This didn't win it any favours with the motion picture or recording industries, but it gave it an edge with users that Facebook simply couldn't match. By July 2007, there were more than 1 million VK accounts.[6]

As VK's userbase ballooned, Durov became an internet celebrity, courted by both the foreign press and the Kremlin as 'Russia's Mark Zuckerberg'. Initially press shy, with money and fame came a reputation for cockiness, even arrogance. In the most famous incident, Durov challenged an employee to throw his cash bonus out of a window of the company's swanky St Petersburg headquarters. As pink 5,000 rouble notes (worth around $157 at the time), folded into paper aeroplanes, floated down onto the street below, a large crowd gathered and scuffles broke out.[7] The paper plane throwing was widely covered in the Russian and foreign press, increasing Durov's notoriety. In another widely covered incident, the VK founder responded to an attempt by Uzbek-Russian oligarch Alisher Usmanov, an early investor who owned about 40 per cent of VK, to buy the company outright by posting a photo of his middle finger on Twitter, captioned "my official answer".

*

Days before Boris Yeltsin resigned and made him president, in December 1999, Putin called a meeting of internet pioneers, both the Demos/Relcom old guard and a handful of the country's new internet entrepreneurs and journalists.

Putin was the first high-ranking Russian official to pay real attention to the internet, and to grasp its power to help both himself and his enemies. At the meeting, a proposal was put forward that the government take over allocation of .ru domains from the semi-autonomous Kurchatov Institute, effectively giving the Kremlin the right to decide who got a website and who didn't. Soldatov and many others in the room were outraged, and after a fierce debate, Putin backed down. But many attendees left the meeting thinking that their victory had just been for show, designed to burnish Putin's credentials as a forward-looking, liberal reformer, while at the same time sending a warning of his power over them, should he decide to exercise it.[8] As Nossik, Russia's first blogger, recounted later:

> In his brief but passionate speech that day, Putin made special mention of Chinese and Vietnamese models of internet regulation, stating that he viewed them as unacceptable. "Whenever we'll have to choose between excessive regulation and protection of online freedom, we'll definitely opt for freedom," he concluded to the puzzlement and disbelief of everyone in the room. We all knew of his record as a KGB operative in charge of hunting down dissidents in Leningrad during the 1980s. Frankly, many of us thought that Putin's words were more of a smokescreen than proof of serious intent. We were wary of the government, and expecting the worst.[9]

For years, however, Putin largely honoured his "solemn oath to protect the Russian internet", even as he moved swiftly to neutralise the country's traditional media. Throughout the 2000s, oligarchs who owned radio and TV stations were co-opted or pushed out, and only a handful of opposition newspapers, mostly small circulation, were left outside the Kremlin's control.[10] Journalists who refused to play ball with the new reality were marginalised, forced out of the country, or showed up dead. Throughout this time, the internet "became Russia's only territory of unlimited free speech".[11] As Durov described it: "The best thing about Russia at that time was the internet sphere was completely not regulated. In some ways, it was more liberal than the United States."[12]

Putin's media strategy was the brainchild of his 'puppet master', Vladislav Surkov, who launched youth groups and tame opposition parties to burnish his patron's power and sow chaos among his enemies.[13] According to some reports, Surkov also sought to bring Durov under his wing, seeing in the VK founder an ideal adviser on internet policy and online social engineering. Whether because of his own right-wing, libertarian politics, or because he was wary of being seen as too close to the Kremlin, Durov kept Surkov at a distance.

This came back to haunt the young tech mogul when Putin finally did turn his attention to the internet. In May 2008, after serving two terms, Putin turned over the presidency to his closest adviser, Dmitry Medvedev. This was widely seen as a charade to allow him to run again in future, but during Medvedev's time in the top job, the pair feuded publicly, and Medvedev proved far more liberal and reformist than his mentor, leading some to think that Putin's gamble may have failed. So it was to many Russians' disappointment and disgust when, at a rally of their United Russia party in September 2011, Medvedev stood aside and endorsed Putin to stand in the presidential election the following year.

This crass job swapping between the country's two most powerful men outraged the type of urban bourgeoisie who had previously been happy to stay away from politics if it meant they could continue to make money.[14] Resistance coalesced around the December parliamentary elections, with thousands of people volunteering to be polling station observers, while multiple websites sprang up to monitor the voting process and report irregularities. One of the biggest voices online was that of Alexei Navalny, a xenophobic, right-wing populist turned anti-corruption blogger and fierce critic of Putin's party, United Russia.[15]

Protests broke out in Moscow, where election observers told crowds about the blatant fraud they had witnessed in polling stations.[16] Police cracked down, detaining Navalny and other protest leaders, but the demonstrations continued. On 10 December, more than 50,000 people attended a rally in Moscow's Bolotnaya Square, right outside the Kremlin. On the same day, protests were held in ninety-nine cities across the country and in front of more than forty Russian embassies and consulates around the world.[17]

It was a huge display of solidarity in defiance of Putin and, just as in 1991, many participants were stunned to discover that so many people felt the same as they did.[18]

Russia's rulers had had a bad year, with the Arab Spring having toppled or destabilised several of their allies in North Africa and the Middle East, often with the open involvement of the US and NATO. Western media, while joyously boosting the uprisings in Egypt and Tunisia, repeatedly emphasised the role of Twitter and Facebook in the protests, further confirming to Kremlin minds the danger of these Western technologies to its own control.[19] As if to underline this, Alec Ross, an adviser to US Secretary of State Hillary Clinton, praised the internet in a speech in London as a catalyst for the Arab Spring, saying: "Dictatorships are now more vulnerable than they have ever been before." Displaying an obliviousness to how his words would be received in Moscow or Beijing that was characteristic of Clinton's internet freedom policy, Ross added: "The Che Guevara of the 21st century is the network."[20]

Putin wasn't about to become the twenty-first-century's Batista. LiveJournal, the main blogging platform in Russia, was hit with a massive distributed denial of service (DDoS) attack, as were several opposition websites and newspapers.[21] As a spokesperson for the Federal Investigative Committee told reporters: "The opinion of the blogosphere is having a growing influence over the most serious political, economic, and social processes ... there are information wars being waged here aimed at undermining people's trust in the state."[22]

Most of the largest protest groups were hosted on Facebook, thanks to its popularity with the type of pro-Western liberals who made up the base of the anti-Putin movement, but organising also took place on VK, including in a massive group started by Navalny that had more than 100,000 subscribers.[23] Edward Kot was one of the group's moderators, and he was shocked to discover, logging in one day, that he couldn't create any new posts. Fearing that the group had been censored, he complained to VK's customer support, and soon received a personal reply from Durov, who explained that the hyperactive group had hit a secret limit of 1,634 posts per day. Twenty minutes later, on Durov's order, the group was unlocked.[24]

"For the sake of our group, VKontakte changed their algorithms," Navalny wrote on his blog. Kot was effusive in his thanks in an email to Durov. "All's fine," the VK founder responded. "In the last few days, the FSB has been asking us to block protest groups, including yours. We didn't comply. I don't know how it will all end for us, but we are up and running."[25] Durov uploaded a scan of an FSB letter sent to VK, asking it to "cease the activities" of seven protest groups, including Navalny's.[26] He accompanied it with a photograph of a dog wearing a hoodie with its tongue sticking out, captioned "an official response to the intelligence services on the request to block groups".

The young libertarian tried to frame his decision as a business one, writing online that "if foreign sites continue to exist in a free state, and Russian ones begin to be censored, the [Russian-language internet] can await only its slow death". VK, he said, was an "apolitical company which does not support either those in power, the opposition, or one of the parties".[27] This time, however, he wasn't just thumbing his nose at some oligarch investor, but at the Kremlin and Putin himself. He may have believed he was maintaining neutrality, but in aiding Navalny, he had effectively thrown in his lot with the protesters.

The cost of doing so quickly became apparent. FSB agents, wearing camouflage uniforms and carrying automatic rifles, knocked violently on the door of Durov's St Petersburg apartment. Pretending not to be home, he crept to the window, from where he could see more security agents waiting outside the building. The men in the corridor began shouting through the door to open up, as his phone rang over and over again with calls from unfamiliar numbers. Frustrated by Durov's refusal to let them in, and unable to get a warrant in time to knock the door down, the agents left after an hour, but Durov's problems were only just beginning.[28]

The failure of the security services to control both the protests and the internet enraged the Kremlin. FSB deputy director Sergei Smirnov complained that "new technologies [are being] used by Western special services to create and maintain a level of continual tension in society with serious intentions extending even to regime change ... Our elections, especially the presidential election and the situation in the preceding period, revealed the potential of the blogosphere."[29] He called for the development of new ways to tackle these threats, and a month after Putin began his third term as president, the State Duma provided them. Four members of the lower house introduced legislation, modelled on the Great Firewall, to create a "common register [of sites] which contain information that is prohibited for distribution in the Russian Federation" – an internet blacklist.[30] Ostensibly for the protection of children, the blacklist allowed the Federal Service for Supervision of Communications, Information Technology and Mass Media, known as Roskomnadzor, to take sites offline without trial if they were deemed to be hosting unlawful content.[31] Websites or pages that could not be taken down were to be blocked at the national level by ISPs.

Limited blacklists and website bans had been in place for years, but the one launched in 2012 took effect nationwide.[32] The country's internet providers caved to Kremlin demands to allow deep packet inspection (DPI) of all internet traffic, a key technology of the Great Firewall, which enabled prohibited sites and content to be blocked with ease. By the end of 2012, Russia's censors had the legal and technical tools to force protests groups and unwanted criticism offline, whether hosted in Russia or overseas. Durov's defiance the previous year would now be impossible. But it hadn't been forgotten. On 5 April, a white Mercedes registered to a senior VK employee was filmed fleeing a traffic stop, running over a police officer's foot in the process. Investigators said that Durov was at the wheel, and despite VK arguing that this was impossible since he didn't drive, the police soon turned up at the company's headquarters, demanding internal documents and files. Seeing the writing on the wall, Durov fled the country.

Around the same time, a private investment fund close to the Kremlin announced that it had bought 48 per cent of VK from Durov's co-founders, Mirilashvili and Lev Leviev. Although the traffic violation was later downgraded to a simple administrative fine, allowing Durov to return to Russia, his days at the helm of his company were numbered. In early 2014, Durov sold his remaining stake in VK to an ally of Usmanov, the oligarch he had once so publicly rebuffed.[33] In April, following protests against Putin ally Viktor Yanukovych in Ukraine and the Russian invasion of Crimea, Durov resigned as CEO, telling a tech blog, "I'm out of Russia and have no plans to go back … unfortunately the country is incompatible with internet business at the moment."[34] In September, Usmanov's Mail.ru, the country's largest email provider, acquired the remaining shares of VK for $1.47 billion. Russia's Facebook was neutered.[35]

*

Durov was not in Russia to see the final days of the free internet for which he had been such a keen evangelist. He left the country for good in April 2014, fleeing with several hundred million dollars he had banked from the sale of his final VK shares.[36] With a $250,000 'investment' in the country's Sugar Industry Diversification Foundation, he acquired a passport from the Caribbean island nation of St Kitts and Nevis, and began flitting around the world's financial hubs – London, Paris, Singapore – before finally settling in Dubai.

While the Russian government had been successful in reining in VK, internet usage was changing as people became more and more attached to their smartphones. Just as China's censors, comfortable in their conquest of Weibo, faced a new challenge with the emergence of WeChat, a messaging app that quickly became the most popular in the country, Russia's, too, faced a changing internet. But while WeChat users were swiftly controlled by the app itself, in cooperation with the censors, Durov was about to challenge the Kremlin again. He used his millions to launch and support Telegram, an encrypted messaging app developed during his paranoid last days at the helm of VK. Like Durov himself, the app was protean, registered as a company in multiple countries to avoid regulations.[37] On Telegram, user data is spread across servers around the world, making it harder to subpoena, and chats can be set to self-destruct after a certain amount of time.[38] Its logo was a white paper plane, flying through the air.

The launch of the app was well timed, coming on the back of not only an uptick in censorship in Russia, but also the revelations, courtesy of Edward Snowden, of the breadth and scale of US spying overseas. Telegram gave users a way (at least in theory) to avoid NSA and FSB snooping, and to communicate securely and secretly. It's difficult to recall, post-Snowden, how rare encryption once was, even among some in the cybersecurity community. Glenn Greenwald, who helped break the NSA spying story, almost missed out on it due to his lack of a secure email account and initial unwillingness to use the clunky PGP encryption method to communicate with Snowden.[39] Telegram, along with a similar app, Signal, which was endorsed by Snowden himself, helped make encrypted communications easy and straightforward.[40] Increased competition from these apps in turn forced larger tech companies to adopt similar security protocols, with Facebook-owned WhatsApp and Microsoft-owned Skype both adopting end-to-end encryption for fear of losing market share.

Encryption doesn't only hamper spies; it can also help bypass filtering, making DPI impossible and forcing censors to either block all traffic from the app or allow it through. China swiftly banned Telegram, with an editorial in the *People's Daily* saying it had been used by human rights lawyers to coordinate "attacks on the party and government".[41]

Chinese dissidents weren't the only ones using the platform, however, and if the timing of the Snowden revelations helped Telegram, another geopolitical development proved almost fatal. After members of the Islamic State attacked locations across Paris in December 2015 with assault rifles and explosives, leaving 130 people dead and scores more injured, it was revealed that the group had been using Telegram to recruit and communicate with fighters across the world.[42] Telegram purged a swath of Islamic State-linked accounts, but the damage was done, and questions about terrorism continued to dog Durov. He didn't help matters by admitting in public that it was probably technically impossible to scrub the group from the app.[43] Despite this, Telegram user numbers boomed, especially in Russia, where the app was hugely popular and seen as something of an icon of internet freedom thanks to Durov's own celebrity and well-publicised battles with the censors.

In April 2017, a briefcase bomb exploded on the St Petersburg metro, killing sixteen people including the perpetrator. Police said the attack was coordinated on Telegram, which had been used by the plotters "to conceal their criminal intentions".[44] That announcement followed criticism of Durov by the head of Roskomnadzor, Russia's top censor, who accused the Telegram founder of being "neutral with respect to terrorism and crime", and said that Telegram had failed to respond to the authorities' demand to store metadata in Russia and allow the security services access to it.[45]

The language was clear. Durov may have been an inadvertent ally of dissident liberals when he defied the FSB's demands to shut down VK groups, but now he was something far worse: an enabler of terrorism. In early 2018, Roskomnadzor officially informed Telegram that it was in violation of the data storage law and warned it could order ISPs to block the service. The app's days in Russia were numbered.[46] Just as VK's hobbling was symbolic of the Kremlin's turn against the free and open internet, the downfall of Durov's second company showed how much further the country had headed down the trail first blazed by China. When the founders of Runet first connected their country to the world, it would have been nigh impossible to block a service like Telegram. Now, thanks to the expertise of Chinese censors and Chinese equipment guarding the borders to Russia's internet, such a block was as simple as pressing a button.

*

Blue, black and white, the paper aeroplanes flew over the heads of the crowd gathered in central Moscow on Prospekt Sakharova in April 2018.[47] Thousands thronged the wide boulevard, named after the Soviet nuclear physicist, dissident and peace campaigner Andrei Sakharov, folding more projectiles and holding signs reading "Big Brother is watching you" and "Even the introverts are protesting." Others carried red and white flags emblazoned with the logo of Roskomnadzor in black, made to look like the Nazi standard. They were protesting the decision by the state censor, two weeks earlier, to finally ban Telegram. After a court ruled against the app due to Durov's refusal to turn over encryption keys to the authorities, ISPs around the country were ordered to block its servers and prevent users from accessing it.[48]

Watching the protests from exile in Dubai, Durov was overjoyed. The paper plane, which had once been a symbol of the arrogant excess enjoyed by him and his fellow tech millionaires, had become an emblem of freedom. He had urged people to fly the planes in protest against the censor's decision, but never expected to attract so much support. "If you live in Russia and support free internet, fly a paper plane from your window at 7pm local time today," he wrote on 22 April 2018. "Please collect the aeroplanes in your neighbourhood an hour later – remember, today is Earth Day."[49] Hundreds turned up to the first protest. A week later, an estimated 12,000 people gathered on Prospekt Sakharova, and filled the sky with floating, darting paper projectiles.

If the reaction of Telegram users to the ban was a surprise, so was the forcefulness with which Roskomnadzor enacted it. As Durov and others urged their followers to install VPNs and other censorship circumvention tools, the authorities began a scorched earth approach. They blocked hundreds of thousands of IP addresses associated with Amazon and Google, after the two companies' cloud servers were used to get around the Telegram ban.[50] Hundreds of other websites and businesses using the servers in Russia were affected, with users unable to load them or carry out transactions. "The fact that Roskomnadzor affected others is not a mistake on their part," one website administrator told the online magazine *Meduza*. "I think this is how they apply pressure – and not just on Telegram, but on anybody even remotely connected to them." At a regular press conference, Dmitry Peskov, Putin's press secretary, was forced to deny, despite evidence to the contrary, that the Kremlin was seeking to build a Chinese-style Great Firewall of Russia.[51]

Within days, tens of thousands of Microsoft IP addresses joined the now millions of Google and Amazon nodes that had been blocked. Dozens of VPN apps and proxy services were also banned.[52] Popular Google services, including Gmail, YouTube, Google Drive and the reCAPTCHA security tool, reported disruptions.[53] One business owner estimated that he was losing over $32,000 a day due to the disruptions, while others predicted total losses to the economy could quickly reach $1 billion.[54] Smart TVs, airline ticket sales, bike rentals, Bitcoin mining, online gaming and mobile wifi were among the many services reportedly affected by the mass IP blocking.[55]

Soon enough, there were signs the pressure was working. Early on in Telegram's fight against the ban, Durov publicly thanked "Apple, Google, Amazon, Microsoft – for not taking part in political censorship". However, although neither company linked their actions to Telegram, around the time Roskomnadzor began mass blocking their IP addresses, Google and Amazon announced that they would move to prevent domain fronting, where developers forward their traffic through the companies' servers to get around state-level blocks.[56] By using domain fronting, those attempting to bypass censorship made it so that, in order to completely block them, the authorities would have to block Google and Amazon too, generally too big a step for most countries to take. The encrypted messaging app Signal, which had used domain fronting to get around blocks in Egypt, Oman, Qatar and the UAE, said after Google's announcement that "domain fronting as a censorship circumvention technique is now largely non-viable".

"The idea behind domain fronting was that to block a single site, you'd have to block the rest of the internet as well. In the end, the rest of the internet didn't like that plan," the app's developers wrote in a blog post.[57] Reacting to the ban, Leonid Bershidsky, a former editor of *Vedomosti* and Slon.ru, wrote that "Google and Amazon have failed the test of whether they'd sacrifice their commercial interests in Russia (and other authoritarian regimes) to some higher principle".[58] In separate statements, both companies pointed out that they had never approved of or allowed domain fronting, which was previously possible thanks to loopholes they were now closing.

At the protest in Moscow, Alexei Navalny, who had once depended on Durov to help him spread his message on VK, now came out to defend Telegram. "I will not put up with this silently. Will you put up with this?" he asked the crowd from the stage, receiving a resounding "No" and chants of "Down with the tsar!"[59] Representatives of Russia's Libertarian Party, which had organised the rally, also addressed the crowd. "Russia is at a crossroads – full-scale censorship has not yet been introduced," Durov wrote on his Telegram channel. "If action is not taken, Russia will lose Telegram and other popular services." As one protester in Moscow put it to *The New York Times*: "This is not just about Telegram, it is an attempt to isolate the Russian segment of the internet."

Just as China had successfully built an internet apart, tightly controlled, orderly, and brooking no dissent, now Beijing had exported that model to its most powerful ally. But the censors were not done yet.

Chapter 24

One app to rule them all

How WeChat opened up new frontiers
of surveillance and censorship

The upbeat synth pop of MGMT's 'Electric Feel' plays in the back-ground as the man, dressed in a white button-down shirt, his wallet in a breast pocket, welcomes guests to the party.[1]

"Hey, Email is here! Come on in," he says in Tibetan, as he warmly greets a bespectacled man in a T-shirt and shakes his hand. Just behind the first guest, a bald man in a jumper sidles in and reaches out his own hand: "I am Attachment, Email's friend."

"Oh Email's friend? Welcome, welcome!" the host says. As the bald man walks past him, he quietly lifts the host's wallet out of his breast pocket. Seconds later, the host slaps his breast and looks dumbfounded, vamping it up for the camera as a voiceover intones, "You could lose your wallet or your personal information if you allow random attachments into your house; they could be infected with viruses. You will end up losing your head one of these days. Remember this for next time: never open attachments unless you are expecting them."

The video was low budget and painfully earnest, but it had an effect, viewed thousands of times on YouTube by members of the Tibetan diaspora. It was created by the Tibet Action Institute, a Dharamsala-based organisation created to improve cybersecurity

275

education for members of one of the most hacked communities around the world. In the video and others like it, users are taught to use Google Docs and Dropbox to share documents, rather than downloading email attachments, and how to run virus checks on files they were sent. Similar videos explained the dangers of sharing USB drives, gave a masterclass in creating strong passwords, and provided tips on how to browse the internet securely.

The Tibetan diaspora was one of the first communities to be targeted by China's army of hackers, and it has become among the most effective in battling the cyberspies. In classrooms and meeting halls across Dharamsala, security experts like Lobsang Gyatso Sither conduct workshops on email encryption, secure messaging apps, and other ways to stay safe online.

Broad-shouldered, with a square face and narrow, heavily creased eyes, Sither was born in Dharamsala in 1982, one of a generation of exiles who have never lived in Tibet.[2] He studied computer science at universities in India and the UK, before returning to the Himalayas in 2009. Back in Dharamsala, he worked alongside Greg Walton, the Citizen Lab researcher, to help investigate the hacking campaigns targeting the Tibetan community and start to educate people on how to avoid being compromised. After Walton left, Sither continued studying the problem, and in 2011 he joined Tibet Action and began holding educational sessions.

Those he worked with generally fell into two camps with regard to how they viewed the constant cyber threat: ambivalence or paranoia. Both could be frustrating to deal with, such as trying to educate people who were adamant they had 'nothing to hide' that their accounts being compromised could affect those who very much do fear extra scrutiny. At the other end of the spectrum, there were those who were so freaked out by the idea that Chinese spies were watching them all the time that it hampered their work – exactly the kind of chilling effect the censors were hoping to inculcate. "We try to find the balance between security and not getting people too scared," Sither told me. "It's a challenge sometimes."

Another major challenge was the rise of Chinese social media apps, particularly Tencent's WeChat, an uber-popular messaging app that spread through the diaspora via relatives in Chinese-controlled Tibet. As more and more Western social networks and apps were blocked by the Great Firewall, WeChat increasingly became the only software those outside Tibet could use to talk to their families. Sither said there had been a decrease in the number of email hacking campaigns targeting Tibetans as WeChat became more and more popular. "Because WeChat is so embedded in the community in some ways, I don't think they need to hack systems as much as they used to because that information is already being given to them," he said.

Like Weibo before it, WeChat was briefly seen as a potential blow to the censors. Even after they reined it in, the app continued to receive laudatory coverage in the foreign press, which often ignored the ways in which it was even more censored, and far more dangerous, than Weibo or other apps.

*

Just as Apple faltered in the late 1990s, coming close to bankruptcy before the release of the iPod turned the company around, WeChat was the second life of a company that almost became a Chinese also-ran. Tencent first found success in 1999 with QQ, a messaging service based on the popular ICQ protocol. Although it was rudimentary by today's standards, QQ was hugely successful, and an early example of how quality Chinese apps could – with the help of the censors – compete with those of foreign companies. When I first moved to China in 2010, my Chinese colleagues and friends were all still using QQ to such an extent that foreigners had to adopt it or not be able to stay in touch. Tencent's app was so successful that

QZone, its auxiliary blogging platform, was China's leading social network for many years.

Tencent's second foray into social media was less successful. Although it was initially competitive, Tencent Weibo quickly became second to the far more popular Sina Weibo, which today is synonymous with microblogging. While Tencent made lucrative investments in gaming and e-commerce, its core brand was slipping. This all changed in 2011, with the launch of WeChat (Weixin in China), which quickly saw its user numbers balloon as it muscled out Chinese competitors and, with the help of the Great Firewall, most foreign ones as well. Facebook messenger was blocked in 2009, the South Korean app Line in 2015, and finally WhatsApp in 2017, along with several secure messaging apps, leaving WeChat as the only real alternative.[3] Throughout this period, the app attracted staggeringly positive press coverage, in both the Chinese and foreign media, despite its many flaws. These included widespread censorship and surveillance, and performance issues related to its endless growth, as Tencent added more and more services to WeChat, making Apple's notoriously bloated iTunes app look streamlined and focused by comparison. The leg up from the government Tencent had received was ignored in the fawning foreign press coverage, which also largely overlooked the company's failure to build a significant overseas userbase. This included an embarrassing retreat in 2015 after an expensive campaign to attract foreign users with a glitzy ad campaign starring Argentinian footballer Lionel Messi fizzled out.[4]

Just as Facebook increasingly *is* the internet for many people in developing countries where the social media giant has invested aggressively, WeChat is the primary – if not the only – app many Chinese users interact with. WeChat is used for messaging, paying bills, booking appointments, playing games, hailing taxis, and dozens of other services that are spread across numerous individual apps outside China. As Connie Chan, a partner at the Silicon Valley venture capital firm Andreessen Horowitz, wrote in a review of WeChat's business model:

> Philosophically, while Facebook and WhatsApp measure growth by the number of daily and monthly active users on their networks, WeChat cares more about how relevant and central WeChat is in addressing the daily, even hourly needs of its users. Instead of focusing on building the largest social network in the world, WeChat has focused on building a *mobile lifestyle* – its goal is to address every aspect of its users' lives, including non-social ones.[5]

The cornerstone of this model is WeChat's payments system, which has utterly transformed the way in which many Chinese cities and even smaller towns operate. Along with Alibaba's similar, competing service, WeChat Pay took mobile payments from a niche and often annoying practice to absolute dominance in a matter of years. Such is the popularity of mobile payments in China that foreigners often find it difficult to pay with cash, and even buskers print QR codes to allow people to donate money electronically. While not enough credit is given to Chinese consumers and merchants for being faster in adopting and propagating mobile payments than their counterparts in many other countries, Tencent still deserves a huge amount of recognition, creating not only a platform for this growth, but also subsidising it at times to encourage the use of mobile payments.

This, of course, was not done for benevolent purposes. As Chan writes, mobile payments were "the Trojan horse that allows WeChat to quickly onboard user payment credentials that then unlock new monetisation opportunities for the *entire* ecosystem". Tencent has gobbled up restaurant recommendation apps, ride-sharing services and numerous other popular distractions to make sure that people never need to leave its app or the wider WeChat Pay system. In doing so, it has also created a privacy nightmare for Chinese users, with one app having access to everything from their selfies and status updates to their utility bills and hair salon appointments. While the alarm has been raised in the US and elsewhere over the amount of data on users Facebook has hoovered up, Tencent may have even more, and is more willing to share that data with the Chinese government.

In a report on privacy protections in messaging apps, Amnesty International gave Tencent a score of zero out of 100, highlighting its privacy policy, which states that WeChat is permitted to "retain, preserve, or disclose your personal information … in response to a request by a government authority, law enforcement agency, or similar body (whether situated in your jurisdiction or elsewhere)".[6] In early 2018, WeChat was forced to deny storing users' chat logs after a prominent Chinese executive accused Tencent founder Pony Ma of "watching all our WeChat every day". While Ma may not have had access to users' messages, the authorities most likely did. Under a Chinese cybersecurity law passed the previous year, all internet companies were required to store logs and relevant data for at least six months, and provide them to law enforcement when requested.[7]

China's law enforcement agencies have also undermined Tencent's claims to care about user privacy. Discussing an anti-corruption case in Hefei, in eastern Anhui province, officials revealed that they had been able to retrieve "a series of deleted WeChat conversations from a suspect" in order to punish several Party members accused of graft-related offences.[8] Non-Party members, too, have been arrested over matters supposedly conducted in private over WeChat. In Xinjiang, a forty-nine-year-old Muslim man, Huang Shike, was arrested after forming a group on the app to discuss the Qur'an. He was later jailed for two years for having violated laws about using the internet to discuss religion.[9] Users have also been charged with insulting Xi Jinping and other top officials in private WeChat messages.[10]

This would be worrying enough for a social media platform, but Tencent (along with Alibaba) has also partnered with the government on a new social credit system, a technology that has moved from a plot point in the Netflix dystopian science fiction show *Black Mirror* to reality in staggering speed. An extreme version of a credit score, China's social credit system uses a variety of data, gleaned from apps including WeChat and Alibaba's Alipay, to build a trustworthiness profile of the user, and this affects how likely that person is to receive a loan or be able to rent a car or even use a bike-sharing service.[11] The system derives from a plan announced by the State Council in 2014 to establish a nationwide tracking and credit system, combining financial and other data with people's fingerprints and biometrics. In the words of journalist Mara Hvistendahl:

> For the Chinese Communist Party, social credit is an attempt at a softer, more invisible authoritarianism. The goal is to nudge people toward behaviors ranging from energy conservation to obedience to the Party.

For those with good credit, the benefits can be tangible: they can rent rooms without a deposit, get upgraded on flights, or receive free gifts when they apply for loans. For those at the opposite end of the scale, things are far more difficult: prices go up, they are often denied services, and they can even be prevented from travelling. In mid-2018, it was announced that airlines and train companies would be adopting the social credit system to bar certain passengers under the principle 'once untrustworthy, always restricted'.[12] Scores are not only affected by users' own behaviour, but also by that of their friends and family – too much hanging out with untrustworthy people can send a person's score plummeting.

Other actions that can cause deductions include missing a restaurant reservation, cheating in an online game and jaywalking; while good deeds such as donating blood or recycling can boost a user's score.[13] More perniciously, scores also go up or down based on how much a user conforms to political goals, significantly raising the cost of dissent, not only for the person in question but also for their family and friends.[14]

This can have an effect beyond China's borders, as the tendrils of the social credit system, and the apps that fuel it, become harder to avoid. Concerns over surveillance on WeChat, as well as the app's well-documented censorship of sensitive topics, even in chats conducted by users outside China, have led to calls to boycott it. But within China this is essentially impossible: WeChat is just too important. It would be like asking someone in North America to give up Facebook, email and their credit card. This often leaves people who know they may be targeted by government surveillance in a somewhat hopeless position. I have spoken to many journalists in China who are deeply suspicious of Tencent, but still have to use WeChat because, if they didn't, they simply could not get in touch with sources. In my own experience, I have tried to convince sources to switch to a different app to discuss sensitive topics, only to face pushback because doing so can be very difficult: most secure messaging apps are not available on Chinese app stores, and using them requires jumping the Great Firewall. This attitude is helped by the widespread belief, among sources and fellow journalists, that they are likely to already be compromised by Chinese government hackers, or could easily be were they to be targeted. For those using Chinese-made phones and non-Apple operating systems, this is probably true. A UN employee who works on internet policy, talking to me anonymously, said that his unit was instructed not to use Android devices, so great was the risk of being compromised by Chinese apps.

The addition of the social credit system to this melange of privacy and censorship concerns could make things even more difficult for those attempting to change China from within. Dissidents could find their scores lowered for engaging in 'antisocial behaviour', or blacklisted entirely, making them a dangerous person to associate with. Journalists, too, could be used by the algorithm to assess people's trustworthiness: if a Chinese citizen is associating with too many foreign reporters, their score could drop, or their movement around the country could be restricted. Getting out of this system may prove almost impossible. Lobsang Sither, the Tibetan cybersecurity expert, admitted that he was fighting a losing battle simply trying to get members of the diaspora not to use WeChat for messaging, and they faced none of the extra incentives or downsides encountered by users within China. "When WeChat came out and everyone in Tibet was using it, that permeated into the diaspora," he said. "Then it became really hard to combat it. We talked about security on WeChat, best practices, but to actually get people to stop using it has been a huge challenge, because that might be the only app their family in Tibet knows how to use. How can you tell them not to talk to their family when they haven't for a decade?"

Chapter 25

Buttocks

Uganda's internet blackouts follow China's lead

On 26 January 2017, Yoweri Museveni waved from a black, open-top truck as a military band played and lines of green-uniformed troops carrying long rifles marched for his inspection in Masindi, a small town in Uganda's north-west, near Lake Albert and the Congolese border. At seventy-two, Museveni's face was deeply lined, his features scrunched together around a hooked nose and sparse moustache, giving him the appearance of perpetual mild annoyance. The Ugandan president and former rebel leader had been in power for over three decades. He was one of a crop of old African revolutionaries, like Zimbabwe's Robert Mugabe, who took office promising democratic reforms and fair governance, but then clung on well beyond their time, backed by vast security states modelled on the very colonial controls they once fought against. Surrounded by the troops of the Uganda People's Defence Force, Museveni was marking thirty-one years since he had overthrown the regime of Milton Obote.

Wearing a dark suit and a wide, flat-brimmed farmer's hat, Museveni walked to a podium where he stood flanked by red, black and yellow banners, the colours of the Ugandan flag. Gesturing out to the crowd, he said in a deep, gravelly voice, "I hear some people are saying I am their servant, I am not a servant of anybody."[1]

"I am a freedom fighter, that's why I do what I do," he added, to hesitant, sparse applause, which died down as quickly as it had started. "I don't do it because I am your servant. I am not your servant. I am just a freedom fighter; I am fighting for myself, for my beliefs. That's how I come in; I'm not an 'employee'."

It was a bizarre speech, a slap in the face to those who had sought in repeated, less than fair elections to oust Museveni or at least pressure him to enact reforms and fulfil the promises made in 1986 when he first took power.[2] Urban, young, middle-class Ugandans made up the bulk of opposition support, and 200 kilometres south in Kampala, Uganda's capital and largest city, many were outraged by Museveni's comments. Twice as many Kampalans had voted for alternative candidates rather than cast their lot for Museveni in a general election the previous year,[3] dodging tight security and other restrictions in order to do so,[4] and now here was the country's seemingly eternal president saying he was only out for himself, not the people.

Stella Nyanzi, a forty-two-year-old academic with an easy, gleeful smile and short braids she wrapped in bright, wildly patterned headbands, was sitting at her computer in her home in Kampala when she saw the news about Museveni's speech.[5] A long-time critic of the president, Nyanzi had sparred with him and his wife, Janet, also the country's education minister, after she backed out of an election promise to provide free sanitary pads to all schoolgirls.[6] After Janet Museveni said the government couldn't afford the programme, Nyanzi launched her own crowdfunding page, organising around the hashtag #Pads4GirlsUG. The success of Nyanzi's campaign embarrassed the government and put a target on her head, made larger by her open disdain for the Museveni administration, which she expressed in frequent caustic, satirical diatribes against him she posted on Facebook.

As she read the outraged reactions to Museveni's speech in Masindi, Nyanzi rolled her eyes at those of her compatriots who still expected anything better from the man who ruled their country. Museveni, she wrote on Facebook, is just "a pair of buttocks".

"This is what buttocks do. They shake, jiggle, shit, and fart," Nyanzi said. "Rather than being shocked by what the *matako* said in Masindi, Ugandans should be shocked that we allowed these buttocks to continue leading our country."[7]

It would be the final straw that brought down the entire weight of the Ugandan security state upon her, exposing a web of surveillance and censorship that had been quietly tightening around the country's dissidents and opposition activists as Museveni and his allies sought, with Chinese assistance, to import the Great Firewall to East Africa.

*

China is pervasive in Africa. Across the continent, Chinese entrepreneurs have opened shops and businesses, Chinese companies are building hotels, hospitals and roads, and Chinese products are for sale.[8] Chinese state media, first under the banner of CCTV International and then the Voice of China, invested heavily in programming for African audiences, spreading Chinese soft power and lauding Beijing's commitment to the continent and 'win-win solutions'. Documentaries on African businesspeople succeeding with Chinese assistance and investment, or mega-projects such as the colossal Tan–Zam railway line, which connects Tanzania and Zambia via 300 bridges and more than 10 kilometres of tunnels, sell a vision of China as a different kind of foreign power, one interested in helping lift the continent up, rather than exploit it.[9]

This presence has visibly changed parts of some countries. In capital cities across the continent, small Chinatowns have sprung up around embassies and consulates, catering to diplomats and other government workers, and to the employees of Chinese firms such as Huawei, ZTE and Eximbank, and 'soft power' institutions such as the Confucius Institute, which provides subsidised language and culture classes. Driving from Jomo Kenyatta International Airport along a busy highway into Nairobi a few years ago, I was reminded of travelling between cities in China, such was the frequency of Chinese-language signs on building sites at the side of the road and the familiar logos of massive state-owned enterprises and Chinese banks.

There are many misconceptions and half-truths about China's role in Africa. The impression a casual reader can get from a lot of coverage in the West is that Beijing suddenly became interested in the continent and began ramping up investment and aid in the last decade or so, muscling aside traditional donors and former colonial powers to take a seat at the African table. This ignores a long connection between the Chinese Communist Party and African revolutionary and anti-colonial movements, and the millions of dollars that have been flowing from China to the continent since the early 1960s.[10] While it is true that Chinese commercial interest in Africa has increased in recent years, the continent has always been a key diplomatic battleground. Since the end of the Chinese civil war in 1949, dozens of African countries have received millions in aid and investment to switch their allegiance from the Taiwan-based Republic of China (ROC) to Beijing. After Burkina Faso spurned Taipei in 2018, only the tiny, landlocked Kingdom of eSwatini still recognised Taiwan.[11] During the Cold War, in the wake of the Sino-Soviet split, China also worked its diplomatic and financial muscles to win allies from Moscow as well. In 1964, these investments paid off, with a successful push by Beijing to usurp Taipei's seat at the United Nations. The vote was led in part by Tanzania and supported by many other African nations.[12]

After the 2008 global financial crash, as Europe and the US pulled back, China doubled down on Africa. While the Chinese official aid budget is highly secretive, experts estimate that in the period from 2000 to 2014, Beijing spent the same as Washington, and that it is on track to overtake the total US aid budget before the end of the decade.[13] The majority of Chinese aid spending during that period was in Africa, with Angola and Ethiopia combined receiving almost $32 billion. Official assistance was bolstered by lucrative loans to Chinese and African businesses to fund infrastructure projects and other spending. At the same time, Beijing also ramped up its military footprint on the continent, expanding a naval base in Djibouti, on the strategically important Gulf of Aden, and committing thousands of troops to United Nations peace-keeping missions across Africa.[14] In the hit action film *Wolf Warrior II* – tagline: "Whoever attacks China will be killed no matter how far the target is" – Chinese soldiers, arriving in a fictional African nation wracked with war, mock US military impotence on the continent, while their enemies stop shooting at them for fear of incurring Beijing's wrath.[15]

China has brought huge benefits to Africa, but it has also brought problems. Chinese firms, not known for fair dealing and treating workers well at home, have exported these attitudes to African nations, accentuating existing problems of corruption and exploitation. Many Chinese-funded infrastructure projects have largely been built by workers imported from China, who sent the money back home, stopping it from benefiting local communities. This also prevented a transfer of knowledge and technology that would enable the creation of native industries to compete with the Chinese companies, even in terms of maintaining and running the projects supposedly built for the benefit of the host country, although new research suggests that the use of African workers is increasing as Chinese workers become more and more costly.[16] By focusing on the principle of 'non-interference in internal affairs', established as a key tenet of Chinese outward investment since the 1950s, Beijing has also been accused of propping up some of Africa's worst dictators and enabling human rights abuses by lending money to so-called rogue regimes.[17]

It is important to critique China's role in Africa, highlighting Beijing's missteps and the negative effects of its policies on the continent, particularly as China evolves into a true superpower. However, criticism of Chinese policies should not be misconstrued as an implicit endorsement of the policies sought by Western nations, nor should democratic governments have their failures overlooked or be held to a lower standard than Beijing. As Deborah Brautigam, an expert on China's role in Africa, writes:

> Many of the fears about Chinese aid and engagement are misinformed, the alarm out of proportion ... China's rise in Africa is cause for some concern, but it need not evoke the level of fear and alarm raised by some who have condemned China's aid and engagement as destabilising, bad for governance, and unlikely to help Africa to end poverty.[18]

Much of the criticism levelled at China in this regard comes from Western countries that have themselves failed to achieve many of the goals they advocate in Africa, or to meet the standards to which they seek to hold Beijing. In particular, those complaining that Beijing is propping up pariah regimes like those of Zimbabwe or Sudan often ignore the massive damage done by US, British or French support for dictators and autocrats across Africa, not to mention active military engagement on the continent. For every Robert Mugabe helped along by Beijing, there is a Muammar Gaddafi, who was held up as an important ally in the 'War on Terror' before Washington and London intervened militarily to enable his overthrow, plunging Libya into chaos. Beijing's support during President Omar al-Bashir's genocide in Darfur was reprehensible, but so was France's aid for the Hutu majority government in Rwanda as tens of thousands of Tutsis were being murdered in the street.[19] Blaming China for propping up African dictators ignores the millions those leaders have received from international – primarily Western – corporations for mining rights, oil drilling and other natural resources.[20] Few companies have clean hands; Chinese firms are no better, but they are also not particularly worse.

The internet in Africa is a key example. Western tech firms have invested heavily on the continent, with lofty rhetoric about empowering the 'next billion' users and spreading the benefits of the internet to every corner of the globe. By and large, however, such investment has been self-serving, such as Facebook's Internet.org, which allows users to get online for free, but only within Facebook's walled garden, locking them in as customers and pushing a version of the internet that is all Facebook and nothing else. A completely corporate-controlled, private internet is just as dangerous to online freedoms as one policed by government censors – just ask breastfeeding mothers, cartoonists, trans activists, and anyone else who has fallen foul of Facebook's prudish in-house censors. Other Western companies have happily sold tools to autocratic regimes to help them surveil and spy on their populations, running roughshod over their rights and enabling political repression.

African internet users are under attack from two sides: from monopolistic tech giants, and from their own governments, who are looking not to Silicon Valley but to Beijing for their cues on how to handle online dissent. The key danger of the Great Firewall is that, by its very existence, it acts as a daily proof of concept for authoritarians and dictators the world over: proof that the internet can be regulated and brought to heel. This risk has been accentuated in recent years by China's active role in exporting both the tools of censorship and the political rhetoric for justifying it. Support for Beijing's doctrine of cyber-sovereignty has been cultivated in capitals across Africa, furthering China's goals at the United Nations and in other bodies, and chipping away at the online freedoms of African internet users in the name of propping up the Great Firewall.

*

With deep-set, slightly bulbous eyes, a large nose, and a heavily lined face, Kizza Besigye is an unlikely icon. And yet, for decades, he was the face of Uganda's opposition, staring out from blue posters plastered across the country's major cities, above the slogan 'Together for change'. Besigye dedicated almost twenty years to challenging Museveni's grip on power, losing election after election, and failing twice to get dubious results overturned by the country's Supreme Court. The two started as allies, fighting together in the bush against the increasingly dictatorial regime of Milton Obote in 1982, where the then twenty-six-year-old Besigye served as Museveni's personal physician.[21]

In 2011, after a third attempt at wresting the presidency from Museveni, Besigye organised 'walk to work' protests over the high price of food and fuel. They were inspired by a typically tactless Museveni comment on the rising cost of fuel, which he responded to by urging the public not to "drive to bars". He also said high food prices were good for farmers, and that he deserved a Nobel Peace Price "for managing the country, especially the army, very well".[22] As people began walking to work as a peaceful form of dissent against the government, Museveni approved plans for a $1.3 million inauguration ceremony to mark his fourth term as president. He also ordered his security services to crack down hard on the protests.[23] Besigye was arrested on 28 April and beaten so badly by police that he suffered temporary blindness and multiple other injuries.[24] In subsequent protests, at least two people were killed and more than 100 injured.[25] On 12 May 2011, Museveni was sworn in for a fourth term, as police fired tear gas and water cannon at protesters in Kampala.[26] They had flocked to the streets near the airport to welcome Besigye back to the country from Kenya, where he had been seeking medical treatment. A year later, he would be arrested for a fifth time, after slipping a police cordon around his house to address an opposition rally in the capital.[27]

While Museveni's security services succeeded in cracking down on the protests, they faced criticism behind closed doors for failing to prevent them in the first place. On 13 January 2012, the Chieftaincy of Military Intelligence (CMI) launched operation *Fungua Macho* – 'Open your eyes' in Swahili.[28] A week later, in a secret memo to the president that was leaked to the media, his spies boasted that they had begun vacuuming up "hordes of data" on matters seen "as a threat to national interests".

"Operation Fungua Macho is an offensive against the rising defiance from both within and outside the government apparatus," the memo said. "Due to leaks in intelligence and the rising defiance from the opposition, the NRM [National Resistance Movement] government has been facing a challenge of cracking down on the rising influence of the opposition both in and out of the country."

The initiative, which dramatically ramped up domestic surveillance of Ugandan opposition activists, journalists, and even allies of the government, showed how the powers once only available to sprawling surveillance monoliths like the US National Security Agency can increasingly be bought out of the box from Chinese, European and American firms. According to the leaked memo to Museveni, the CMI bought a "Complete IT Intrusion Portfolio" from a British-German company, Gamma Group, which manufactures "turnkey surveillance projects" for government agencies and security services.[29] One of Gamma's primary tools was FinFisher, a "leading offensive IT intrusion program",[30] which activists say

293

has been used to spy on dissidents and opposition politicians in dozens of countries, including Bahrain, Kazakhstan, Mongolia and Ethiopia.[31]

In Uganda, the security services set up fake wireless hotspots and networks running FinFisher surveillance tools in estates and neighbourhoods where targets lived, government institutions, hotels, and even the country's parliament. Select individuals were also targeted with Trojan horse viruses, which, according to leaked FinFisher promotional materials, were capable of remote monitoring of target computers, logging keystrokes, accessing files and recording audio.[32] While Museveni's spies warned that their efforts could be in vain if targets protected themselves with encryption and virtual private networks, they said the chances of most being tech savvy enough to do so were low.

"Given the calibre of our negative minded politicians, we stand a very high chance of easily crushing them by being a step ahead," the CMI memo said. "This can be testified by the success rate we have had especially in curtailing the 'Walk to Work' demos that started this week. With our implants and imbeds, we have been able to get hordes of information revealing secret plans, especially of FDC [Forum for Democratic Change], even before they act upon them." The memo explicitly mentioned blackmail as a potential use of the information gleaned from surveillance, saying that it could be used to "manage and control the media houses and opposition politicians".

"We are also looking for people to use from within their own circles so as to access their gadgets," the memo said. "Infection and extraction takes not less than [five] minutes, hence such an operation doesn't necessarily require a very highly trained person. In the short run, priority for infection has been given to all MPs and influential people involved in the 'Walk to Work' demos."

A foreign reporter who has written extensively on Ugandan politics told me that her computer was infected with malware after she signed on to a hotel wifi network, and on two occasions she returned to her accommodation to find that her devices had been tampered with. In one case, the operating system command line interface was open, suggesting the intruder had been installing something while she was away from the machine; another time, a hotel staffer was screwing the hard disk back into the computer, presumably after having copied its contents. The clumsiness of both of these incidents could suggest an attempt to intimidate as well as spy on her, or could be a result of hiring cheap proxies to conduct basic surveillance operations. Multiple other people I spoke to in Uganda also told me they were sure they were being spied on, and would not use non-encrypted phone lines or messaging apps.

Just as the Ugandan security services were adopting the worst practices of their Western counterparts, with the ready assistance of European surveillance companies, they also looked east for guidance, embracing internet control strategies from China's extensive playbook.

*

On the morning of 18 February 2016, Samson Tusiime woke early.[33] It was still an hour before sunrise, and outside his home in a suburb of Kampala it was quiet, the night chill slowly giving way to balmy equatorial spring temperatures. A handsome thirty-year-old with a thin, long face, shaved head and a carefully manicured goatee, Tusiime had grown up in Fort Portal, 300 kilometres west of Kampala in the shadow of Mount Stanley, on the border with Congo. He had moved to the capital to study law at Makerere University, Besigye's alma mater, and it was here, as a twenty-year-old, he joined the Forum for Democratic Change (FDC). Leaving school, Tusiime did not go into law, as many had expected, but took a job doing marketing for a private security firm. He eventually transitioned into Uganda's burgeoning tech sector, becoming a sought-after consultant for start-ups and small businesses. At the same time, he attracted thousands of followers on Twitter, where he was an active critic of the government and booster for Besigye and the FDC.[34]

For the 2016 election, which saw Besigye go up against Museveni for a fourth time, Tusiime had volunteered to be an FDC election observer. Ugandan polling stations are required by law to produce final vote tallies known as Declaration of Results forms.[35] In previous years, multiple reports had said that these forms showed a clear victory for Besigye, but when the official figures were released by the supposedly independent Election Commission, they revealed that Museveni had made suspiciously massive gains. FDC supporters were determined to bring some transparency to the process, posting observers at as many of the 30,000 or so polling stations around the country as possible, with the plan that they would photograph the preliminary tallies and post them online, making it harder for the government to fix the vote later. Despite three failed attempts at unseating Museveni, Besigye was still hugely popular with opposition supporters, and his official nomination as FDC candidate brought Kampala "to a standstill".[36] In a country where politicians typically handed out cash and gifts to voters to ensure their support, Besigye's fans turned out in droves to give him money, livestock, food and furniture.

Tusiime had planned to get to his local polling station early to fill out his ballot for Besigye, so he could then focus on his work. Checking WhatsApp at 5am, he was greeted with the message 'Unable to connect. Please try again later.' When he loaded Facebook and Twitter, he had similar problems. Across Uganda, other FDC volunteers were making the same discovery: the social networks they had depended on to get the message out had been blocked. "If we couldn't get that data from the field, it made it very easy for the state to tinker with the results," Tusiime told me. "With the internet being off, there was a total blackout of news."

In theory, the Ugandan authorities had to have a court order to force telecoms companies to take sites offline, but according to multiple people with knowledge of the situation, these were not provided until after the fact. Police simply turned up at the companies' offices and told the technicians what to block.

Phone lines were still open, and news soon started trickling in of egregious vote tampering around the country. In Museveni's home town of Ntungamo, voters were reportedly given ballot papers already filled out for him. If they refused, they were told, "We know your family." At one polling station, according to a report journalist Helen Epstein received at an independent election-monitoring station, Museveni received 760 votes to just two for Buseveni, in a parish with 437 registered voters.[37]

A small number of tech-savvy activists had been prepared for a potential blackout or slowdown,[38] and they quickly began sharing links to VPN apps and proxy servers that allowed people to access Facebook and Twitter. This was made more difficult as the Google Play store, the main source of downloads for Android users, was also blocked. Activists shared install files via email and text, running up their minutes explaining to friends how to get a VPN working. The social media ban lasted four days; in that time, according to some estimates,[39] 1.5 million people downloaded VPN software, a dramatic radicalisation of a populace previously unaware of the need for censorship circumvention. One new online dissident described the experience of dodging the censors as being like a "ninja". "There is a feeling you get that I cannot even describe. You feel more powerful than the mighty state. You feel like you have broken the chains that have been holding you captive," he told a Western reporter.[40] In a television interview, Museveni suggested that those getting around the block to post on Twitter – where the hashtag #UgandaDecides continued to be a strong trend despite the ban – could be committing "treason", and he tut-tutted at internet users for abusing their freedoms: "You know how they misuse them – telling lies. If you want a right, then use it properly."

While the ban was successful in disrupting the opposition's plans for greater transparency, it did not put a lid on dissent, and may have even outraged many otherwise ambivalent voters. Most pernicious, however, was the financial effect the four-day ban had on many Ugandans. Election day was a bank holiday, and so many Ugandans had topped up their mobile money accounts in order to keep making payments. Millions of Ugandans used mobile money to pay for everything from utilities and school fees to groceries. When the internet shutdown kicked in, it also blocked mobile payments, cutting off many Ugandans from their money and leaving them unable to pay for basic services for several days.[41] Even worse off were small business owners, who relied on mobile money to receive payments and operated on whisper-thin margins. "It's like shutting down a banking system," one observer said at the time. "My *boda boda* man is starving and so is the woman who he buys groceries from. That is irresponsible of the government. What happened to securing the livelihood of the citizens?"[42]

Days later, as smoke from burning tyres still drifted over Kampala and the smell of tear gas lingered in areas where it had been used to clear angry crowds, Museveni was declared the winner, with 62 per cent of the vote compared with 34 per cent for Besigye, who had been placed under 'preventative arrest' along with six other high-ranking FDC officials.[43] Besigye denounced the results as blatantly fraudulent and called for an independent audit. Even Washington, Museveni's long-time sponsor, was clearly tired of his game, with a State Department spokesperson saying that the election appeared to be "deeply inconsistent with international standards", while rattling off a list of reported ballot stuffing, vote buying and official intimidation, before saying: "The Ugandan people deserve better."

As Museveni's swearing-in approached on 12 May, the security state went into high gear. Hundreds of police were deployed to the streets of major cities, which were bereft of the type of celebrations that had once accompanied his election victories. Another social media blockade was launched, although the proliferation of VPN software during the election and since made it considerably less effective. Besigye was still under house arrest, but the day before his rival was due to be sworn in, he slipped his guard and made it to a rally in Kampala, where, dressed in a dark suit and blue tie and flanked by the Ugandan flag and the banner of the FDC, he took an oath of office "to the public of Uganda". To great cheers from the crowd, he was declared the "people's legitimately elected president".[44] Hours later, as he paraded through the streets of the capital surrounded by supporters, police violently broke up the crowd and arrested the new 'president'.[45] He was flown to a police station in Karamoja, in Uganda's far north-east, and charged with treason. Protests broke out in support of Besigye even there, in what had traditionally been a Museveni stronghold, and the army had to be called in to control the crowds. Besigye was flown back to Kampala in handcuffs and jailed for two months before eventually being released on de facto house arrest again.[46]

Museveni's swearing-in was hugely dull affair, his statements greeted by half-hearted applause and uncertain laughter, as he ridiculed critics as "those stupid ones" and attacked the International Criminal Court as a "bunch of useless people", causing the US ambassador to storm out along with diplomats from other Western nations. Full internet access was not restored until several days later.[47] Unlike the previous outage, which had united tech-savvy Ugandans in solidarity against Museveni's censorship, this second demonstration of his power to cut off social media on a whim was demoralising. As one activist told me: "We felt totally helpless against this big powerful monster who can just switch off the entire internet in the whole of the country."

Two weeks later, as Tusiime was cleaning his shoes at home, preparing to go out for the evening, a van carrying nine police officers pulled up and bundled him into the vehicle. He was taken to a Special Investigations Unit facility in Kireka, east of the city, where he would spend the next five days.[48] What got Tusiime in trouble was not his organising around the election, or his heckling of Museveni on Twitter, but a T-shirt. Shortly after Besigye's alternative inauguration, Tusiime had a custom shirt made with the FDC leader's face on it. He posted a photo on Facebook along with the number of the man who had made the shirt, who soon received an influx of orders. Tusiime was accused of "mobilising to destabilise the state" and interrogated about his links to the FDC. Eventually, after widespread outrage online, which caused the hashtag #Free Samwyri to trend on Ugandan Twitter, a lawyer friend of Tusiime's succeeded in getting him released on bail and the charges reduced to a less serious offence.

*

Stella Nyanzi's trouble began almost immediately after the 'buttocks' post. Armed men began trailing her sister's car, and police searched her home, scaring her children. When she attempted to board a plane to go to a conference in Amsterdam, she discovered that she was subject to a travel ban; two weeks after that she was suspended from her job at Makerere University.[49] Almost two months after the original post, in March 2017, she was stopped by plain-clothes police while driving and taken to the Directorate of Criminal Investigation and Crime Intelligence, where she was interrogated about her criticism of the president and his wife. The timing of her arrest seemed to her very suspicious; #Pads4GirlsUG had just begun to seriously take off, embarrassing the government, which had refused to follow through on its own promise of providing sanitary pads. At a hearing days later, she was charged under the Computer Misuse Act

2011 for engaging in "cyber harassment" and "offensive communication".[50] In court to hear the charges read out, Nyanzi grinned at the ridiculousness of it all and waved to her supporters. After pleading not guilty, she was denied bail and sent to a maximum-security prison. Prosecutors attempted to extend her stay behind bars by insisting on a full psychiatric evaluation before the next hearing, a move usually confined to violent or sexual crimes.

While Nyanzi's case demonstrated the increasing power of the Ugandan state to crack down on online dissidents, it also provided a pertinent example of the power of the internet and why it so scared autocrats such as Museveni. Nyanzi was in prison for thirty-three days, during which time the authorities discovered that she was far more troublesome behind bars than outside them. Her case became a cause célèbre online, with comments she made to friends and supporters quickly shared and amplified. "The demeanour and response of the prison warders to me changed because they realised even though I was in prison, everything I told my visitors would go on Facebook," Nyanzi told me. "It was like they were being policed by having a big-mouthed woman in jail." One of her first successes was in improving the toilet situation in her cell, which she shared with many other women. The toilet was frequently clogged up and rarely cleaned, and Nyanzi refused to eat so she did not have to use it. After this news spread online, the prison sent workers to fix the problem. "People ask the question of whether the internet has power, I saw its power," she said. "It is a small example, but for me it was like 'Wow.' For that short time, I was in the belly of the ugly state, but I saw that I was protected and my conditions were changing."

If the state had made a mistake in jailing Nyanzi, it had also erred in what it chose to charge her with. When we spoke, Nyanzi was still irked that the authorities had chosen the 'buttocks' post. Out of all the writing she had done criticising Museveni, she said, they chose "one of the most polite I'd written ... a short, empty, bored rant". Nyanzi specialised in vulgar, deliberately profane critiques, delighting in tweaking the noses of those in power and outraging the sensibilities of conservative, Christian Uganda. In choosing a post where she had used a relatively benign term, the authorities inadvertently made it much easier for it to be shared and quoted. "The usage of that post backfired against them," she said. "In terms of circulation it's perhaps a lot easier to circulate buttocks than sexual acts." It was also funnier, more inherently ridiculous, that this forty-two-year-old mother of three was being jailed over 'buttocks'. The case attracted media attention that it might not have otherwise done. *The Washington Post* ran a headline "This professor called her president 'a pair of buttocks.' Now she's in a maximum security prison", while on *The Daily Show*, South African-born host Trevor Noah suggested Museveni should have taken it as a compliment, "because butts are sort of in right now".

While much of her arrest and incarceration still seemed patently absurd to Nyanzi, one thing that did throw her for a loop was the insight she got into the state's surveillance capabilities. "I didn't think Museveni's intelligence were necessarily interested or had the ability to monitor everyday critics such as myself," Nyanzi said. She was quickly disabused of this notion when the plain-clothes police who detained her boasted how they had been able to track her phone signal right to the car she was driving. During interrogations, she was presented with transcripts of phone and text conversations she had had with other women organising the pads campaign, and with her family and friends. "Some of it was the most mundane sort of things," she said. "Even conversations that I had been having on my mother's phone, not in my name, some of those were also transcribed." Thankfully, the authorities had not been able to get into Nyanzi's email – "That would have been damaging for me" – but her phone was obviously thoroughly compromised, likely with some kind of malware that captured all her communications, as she was shown messages sent via secure platforms such as WhatsApp, which would have been seriously difficult to intercept.

"What was scary for me, maybe also very empowering, was to discover how fragile his power is," Nyanzi told me after we had talked for some time, our secure phone connection occasionally dropping out. "If a few Facebook posts from a loud-mouthed, obnoxious, irreverent woman could shake him so much, what does that reveal about the hollowness of the dictatorship's power."

*

Museveni's power grew even as his credibility waned and his most stalwart defenders in the West began to edge away from him. Just as they had looked to Western companies for their expertise in surveillance and cyberespionage, the Ugandan security services turned to China to learn how to filter and control the country's internet. In July 2017, Evelyn Anite, a former journalist turned government minister who complains about "selfish opposition hooligans" on social media, travelled to Beijing to meet with officials from the China National Electronics Import & Export Corporation (CEIEC), a state-owned defence company that has previously been sanctioned by the US government for selling embargoed weapons.[51] Anite signed a preliminary agreement for CEIEC to supply a "comprehensive cyber-security solution", enabling the Uganda Communications Commission (UCC), the telecom industry's chief regulator, the police and the Ministry of Internal Affairs "to guard against cyber criminals". Uganda, Anite told her hosts in Beijing, was "helpless" in guarding against criminals "using social media platforms such as WhatsApp, Facebook, YouTube and Twitter to commit crimes with impunity".[52]

The following month, the Ugandan government, following a pattern set by every censorious regime from China to Russia to

Australia, set up a committee dedicated to tackling online pornography, which Simon Lokodo, the minister for ethics and integrity, said had "encompassed the entire nation".[53] In September, the UCC issued a statement noting "the increasing use of social and electronic media to perpetrate illegalities like sectarianism, hate speech, inciting public violence and prejudice, pornographic content among others, which is not only exposing the unsuspecting public to financial, social and emotional distress but also posing serious national security concerns". Users were warned to "restrain themselves" from authoring, posting or sharing "any forms of electronic communications containing and/ or referring to illegal and/or offensive content".[54]

Other Chinese companies cashed in on the Museveni government's desire for greater censorship. Huawei – which has deep ties to the People's Liberation Army and the Chinese state – had previously landed a lucrative contract to build a national fibre-optic backbone,[55] and was also consulted by the government to provide surveillance and telecommunications monitoring tools.[56] Just as Huawei replaced Cisco and other US firms in providing internet-filtering technology at home, it has slowly muscled out Western competitors in Africa.[57] Huawei's government connections are such that when it launched its 'going global' initiatives, it received a $10 billion line of credit from the China Development Bank, controlled by the State Council.[58] In 2017, Huawei earned 15 per cent of its global revenue in Africa, according to the *Financial Times*.[59] Huawei has also provided monitoring and censorship tools to the governments of Zambia, Ethiopia and Zimbabwe, among others.[60]

"Huawei has been here for some time," Tusiime told me. "They built a national platform which connects every government ministry and department, and provided infrastructure for Uganda Telecom. Their footprint is very pronounced around here." Like all Ugandans I talked to, he was concerned that the trend was towards greater censorship, perhaps even a Chinese-style firewall.

"They're just becoming bolder and bolder," said Lydia Namubiru, a journalist and media educator. "There's no reason to think they won't become even bolder, because there's no real check on their power." She pointed to a wider tendency in East Africa towards increased government control, and a trend by which one leader ups the ante and the others follow suit. "[Museveni's] government is really powerful, largely unchecked, has a majority in parliament, has a very pro-regime police force, and is ruling over a young, poor population which is largely unemployed and more concerned about earning some income than over political rights."

In many ways, Chinese assistance in internet filtering and censorship is a fulfilment of the worst fears about Beijing's involvement in Africa. "China is giving countries such as mine alternative sources of wealth and power and affiliation," Nyanzi told me. "But it also has those dangerous, repressive, autocratic tendencies. It's a shame that Museveni chooses to copy some of the bad policies that China has." Uganda has benefited enormously from Chinese investment, as have many other African countries. But when citizens cannot choose their rulers, they cannot ensure that the imports are wholly positive. Just as many more African government officials have benefited from deals made for Chinese money than ordinary people, governments on the continent are importing the one thing from China their people would rather they not: a culture of repressive authoritarianism and complete control. As Nyanzi put it to me: "China is a poisonous knife that we have to peel our food with."

Epilogue

Silicon Valley won't save you

The Marriott Global Reservations Sales and Customer Care Center in Omaha, Nebraska, is a boxy, tan, two-storey building opposite a Walgreens pharmacy and a Lutheran church. Its large car park is bordered by carefully manicured grass and spruce trees. Inside, employees answer customers' calls and queries from all over the world – reservations, complaints, requests for refunds, and just general abuse.

In January 2018, Roy Jones, a forty-nine-year-old native Omahan, was working the night shift. Bald and heavily built, with a gingery blond goatee and thin-rimmed glasses, Jones was fond of vaping and hip-hop.[1] He made $14 an hour answering questions from Marriott customers via the hotel chain's Twitter accounts, sitting at his computer for eight-hour stints while most of the city around him was asleep.[2] Customer service can be a soul-destroying job, answering the same inane queries again and again from frustrated, impatient people, who often fail to recognise or care that they're speaking to another human being, especially if it's through an app like Twitter. But Jones liked the work: he had had some run-ins with the law as a younger man, and issues with both drugs and alcohol that made holding down a job difficult. In the year and a half he had been working for

Marriott, however, he had been promoted and given a raise, and he was valued by his superiors.

One day in early January, as Jones arrived at the Marriott call centre, a storm was brewing for the company on the other side of the world. An email sent to customers of Marriott's customer loyalty programme in China included the seemingly innocuous question "What is your country of residence?" Respondents could select from a dropdown menu that included China, Tibet, Taiwan and Hong Kong as separate potential answers, appearing, in the eyes of Chinese nationalist trolls seeking to take offence, to endorse those territories' independence from China.[3] As outrage built on Chinese social media platforms, egged on by state media, the Shanghai Cyberspace Administration ordered the hotel chain to shut down its Chinese-language website and app for a week in order to "thoroughly clear all erroneous information", and executives were dragged in for a meeting with tourism officials.

When Jones started his shift, he was vaguely aware that there was some problem in China, but he had not been briefed on how to deal with it, or whether extra sensitivities might be required to avoid further offending Chinese users. He was also busy dealing with another Marriott own goal: an NFL promotion in which users were rewarded with hotel reward points for answering sports trivia questions was being spammed by bots that were scooping up all the points and selling them. The deluge of bot messages was soon joined by hundreds of tweets about the China issue. As Jones reviewed them, trying to see what, if any, of the stream of information on his screen was a legitimate customer service request, he inadvertently hit 'like' on one of the messages, instead of dismissing it.[4] The tweet in question was from the India-based Friends of Tibet, a pro-independence lobby group, and it congratulated Marriott for listing the territory "as a country along with Hong Kong and Taiwan".[5] Jones was not aware of what he had done; later, he had no explanation "other than being overworked" and hitting 'like' by accident. Within hours, however, a top Marriott human resources officer was on a flight to Omaha, and Craig Smith, president of the hotel chain's Asia Pacific office, gave a grovelling apology to the state-run *China Daily*, in which he begged forgiveness for the company's actions which "appeared to undermine Marriott's long held respect for China's sovereignty and territorial integrity".[6]

"This is a huge mistake, probably one of the biggest in my career," he told the newspaper, while announcing an "eight point rectification plan". This included expanding "employee education" globally, and creating a special complaint channel for Chinese customers. Marriott also froze its social media accounts, and fired Jones. At almost fifty, having finally found a career that stuck after years of uncertainty, he was devastated. He saw himself as an easy scapegoat for the hotel chain to avoid upsetting China, and he began reading up on Chinese censorship and Beijing's efforts to spread its influence around the world, sharing links on a personal Twitter account and retweeting criticisms of Marriott; internally, however, he was worried about what would happen next, and afraid he had disappointed his elderly parents. "This job was all I had," Jones told *The Wall Street Journal*. "I'm at the age now where I don't have many opportunities."

Fresh from their victory over Marriott, nationalist trolls looked around for other examples of companies hurting the feelings of the Chinese people. Users began checking dropdown menus on dozens of websites. Delta Air Lines and Spanish fashion brand Zara were rapped for listing Taiwan as a country, while Mercedes-Benz had to apologise for a 'Monday motivation' post on Instagram quoting the Dalai Lama: "Look at the situations from all angles, and you will become more open."[7] Shawn Zhang, a Chinese law student at the University of British Columbia, said that after he posted an image of the Tibetan flag on Twitter, his parents were visited at their home in Wuyi, Zhejiang province, by security agents, who urged them to pressure Zhang to delete the post. (He didn't.[8]) On 25 April, the Chinese Civil Aviation Administration (CAAA) sent a letter to thirty-six foreign air carriers demanding they identify Hong Kong, Macau and Taiwan as parts of China, in a move that was later denounced by the White House as "Orwellian nonsense" but largely followed by companies terrified of alienating customers in the world's second-largest aviation market.[9]

The attack on Github that opened this book was a pivotal moment, when the architects of the Great Firewall turned their attention to the rest of the world, unwilling to tolerate challenges to their dominance wherever they came from. In some ways, however, the attack was more like a traditional counterespionage operation: the tools targeted were being used to undermine Chinese law and challenge the jurisdiction of China's authorities over their domestic internet. While disturbing, the Github attack was no worse than other activities states take in the name of security, and less egregious or illegal than others one could list, including by democracies and self-declared defenders of the free internet. In the years since the Github attack, a new, far more alarming trend has developed: the exporting of Chinese internet censorship itself. The technologies behind the Great Firewall have spread to Russia and other Chinese allies, and countries in Africa, South America and Asia have adopted internet control policies expounded by Beijing, often with the active assistance of Chinese officials and corporations. The space for criticism of China's actions and policies, always limited within the country itself, has begun shrinking overseas, as Beijing attacks anyone who would offer a dissenting view to its territorial ambitions or Communist Party political hegemony.

In its statement about the CAAA order, the White House promised to resist "China's efforts to export its censorship and political correctness to Americans and the rest of the free world".[10]

But as this book has shown, more often than not, US policy on internet freedom serves to embolden censors and justify controls on social media and other platforms. By making the internet a battleground for imperial powers, all those who end up on the same side as Washington are cast as its agents, and their integrity and their ability to operate freely overseas suffer. This was seen in Iran, Russia and China during the Green Revolution and the Arab Spring, when both conservatives and liberals in the US clumsily attempted to adopt online revolutionaries as their own, and so made them into potential CIA agents in the eyes of the very populations they were trying to convince. Away from censorship, I have seen it myself in Hong Kong, where pro-democracy groups, desperate for funding and legitimacy, turn to politicians whose criticism of China is driven by an ideological hatred of socialism more than anything else. While this enables them to attract support in the US, it often hurts them back at home, and assists Beijing's efforts to depict the opposition movement within Hong Kong as a creation of foreign meddlers. Too often, as well, those who would promote dissident thought abroad are far less tolerant of similar efforts at home. In the panic over so-called 'fake news' and allegations of Russian interference in US politics, complaints about broadcaster RT's and other state media's efforts to boost critics of US domestic and foreign policy mirror those made against Radio Free Asia and Voice of America when they make an effort to interview and profile Chinese or Russian dissidents.

Hypocrisy is to be expected in politics, but nowhere has it been more starkly pronounced than among the tech firms that have been the biggest winners of the most recent internet bubble. At a stultifyingly dull tech conference in Shanghai in 2015, I sat in a glitzy ballroom as an executive from Twitter attempted to pitch the platform to Chinese businesses and boasted about its global reach, even as the Great Firewall prevented all of us in the audience from using the app. The following year, Twitter hired its first ever managing director for China, Kathy Chen, a former employee of the People's Liberation Army and China's Ministry of Public Security, who in her first act as company executive posted a public message to Chinese state media saying: "Let's work together to tell great China [sic] story to the world!"[11] Chen left the company eight months later after Twitter struggled to make any headway and moved its China ad sales team to Singapore.[12]

No company has been more shameless in its attempts to woo Beijing than Facebook. Founder Mark Zuckerberg has posed for photos running in the Beijing smog, given employees copies of Xi Jinping's *On the Governance of China*, and even reportedly asked Xi to name his first child (Xi declined). According to *The New York Times*, Facebook also developed a confidential internal tool to suppress posts from appearing in users' news feeds in specific countries, which employees who spoke to the paper said was designed to help Facebook get into China.[13] Asked to respond to the news, Facebook would only say: "We have long said that we are interested in China, and are spending time understanding and learning more about the country."

Zuckerberg's efforts to find a compromise that would allow Chinese censors to filter content on Facebook while giving the company access to the only major market it hasn't yet penetrated may have only been stymied by the vagaries of Communist Party internal politics. In early 2018, Lu Wei, the gregarious former internet tsar and top censor with whom Zuckerberg (and other US tech leaders) had cultivated a particularly close relationship, was expelled from the Party and denounced in state media. Lu, who more than anyone except Xi Jinping himself was responsible for the transformation of China's internet controls in the past five years, was accused of trading power for sex, building personal cliques, and embezzling money. In a statement, China's corruption watchdog said that Lu "did whatever he wanted, commenting on central government policies with bias and distortion, obstructing central government investigations, with his growing ambition he used public tools for personal interests and did whatever it took for personal fame".[14]

Lu's downfall was only the beginning of Facebook's problems in 2018, as the company was also buffeted by revelations that Cambridge Analytica, a political consulting firm, had harvested the data of millions of users, helped by the social platform's woeful privacy protections.[15] That scandal came on the back of continuing concerns over fake news, of which Facebook users were among the biggest consumers and spreaders, further damaging the company's public image and users' confidence in the tech giants to protect them.

Such new-found scepticism about our tech overlords is to be welcomed. Time and again, Silicon Valley has shown that it cannot be trusted to put users' rights and privacy above profit. As far back as 2013, the Snowden revelations showed how many firms were willingly passing on user data to the US National Security Agency and other state security services; the same companies only introduced encryption and greater privacy protections afterwards due to concerns that users could decamp en masse for other platforms. As this book has shown, few major companies have a good record on dealing with China and other enemies of the open internet, regardless of the firms' pro-freedom rhetoric. Even when they do push back, such as when Google and other tech giants fought efforts by China and others to expand United Nations oversight of the web, it is largely for the purpose of protecting revenue, not users. This goes back to the founding days of the internet and the libertarian ethos that motivated many of its creators. 'Information wants to be free' was always more about the freedom of companies to make money than the ability of users to share information without fear or restriction. Companies that warn of government censorship should they be more stringently regulated often tightly restrict how their own users can express themselves. Facebook has censored LGBTQ people, Black Lives Matter activists, and breast-feeding mothers.[16] YouTube has long been accused of overzealously enforcing copyright, taking down legitimate parodies or videos that fall under 'fair use' protections.[17] There are already worrying signs that the fallout from the great fake news panic of 2016 will be the increased censorship and marginalisation of minority voices, partic-ularly those on the political fringes, as platforms such as Facebook and Google attempt to litigate which sites constitute a legitimate news source.[18]

As this book went to print, news emerged that Google had been developing a secret app for the Chinese market, codenamed Dragonfly.[19] According to journalist Ryan Gallagher, who broke the story, the Android search tool would automatically identify and filter websites blocked by the Great Firewall, and it had been demonstrated to officials within the Chinese government. Drag-onfly's existence was a closely guarded secret, even within Google itself, and Gallagher's reporting sparked outrage among employees, some of whom saw it as the final betrayal of Google's 'don't be evil' ethos. In an open letter to their bosses, hundreds of Googlers complained of a lack of transparency within the company and warned that Dragonfly and a return to China "raise urgent moral and ethical issues" that were not being addressed.[20]

Those who had lived through the original China experiment were less than impressed. Brandon Downey, a former Google engineer, summarised the argument for Dragonfly thus: "Look, China is already censoring the internet. So why don't we at least give people what information we can, because some is better than none?"[21]

"Whatever you think about this as an argument, there is one key fact you should know, and it's this: Google has already done this once, and it ended in disaster," he said. "So why do it? The answer is that

Google is acting like a traditional company; one that squeezes every dime out of the marketplace, heedless of intangibles like principle, ethical cost, and even at the risk of the safety of its users."

When Google originally exited China, Sergey Brin was presented as the main driver of that move. The son of Soviet refugees, he was held up as the moral weathervane of the company. Yet, in a staff meeting after the Dragonfly report, Brin, now head of Google parent Alphabet, claimed not to know about the project. This seemed unbelievable to many observers,[22] not least to Downey, who wrote: "It was Sergey Brin who boldly drove the withdrawal from China; yet now Google is using Sergey's yacht's name as code for its secret project to build AI-based censorship into Google search. Google has changed."

The behaviour of Google and Facebook with regard to China should be more than enough evidence that tech giants will not protect users from censorship. Unfortunately, many elected politicians are no better. As they attempt to score easy wins in a media environment obsessed with the dangers of the internet, some are already tilting towards restricting speech, even if they do not express it openly. In many countries, fears over fake news or terrorists organising online have already been used to justify greater controls of all internet activity. Beijing has been only too happy to assist countries that wish to move towards the Chinese model, and its companies are ready and willing to provide the tools to do so. While outright state control is less of a threat in most developed democracies, history shows the risks of complacency. In the late 2000s, Australian politicians attempted to introduce a blacklist of sites associated with child pornography. ISPs in the country would have been mandated to block all sites on the list, the contents of which were kept secret, making effective democratic oversight incredibly difficult. While few people would argue against blocking child porn, when WikiLeaks published a copy of the proposed blacklist in 2009, it was revealed to have included gambling services, YouTube videos, regular porn, a dog boarding kennel, and WikiLeaks itself.[23] The Australian politicians behind the policy may have been acting in good faith to protect children, even if they obstinately ignored much of the criticism that finally sank the bill, but democratic leaders aren't immune from controlling the internet to protect their own power. During a 2017 referendum in Catalonia on whether to declare independence from Spain, held despite the objections of Madrid, websites associated with the vote were seized, software was deleted from app stores, and users were blocked from sharing pro-independence information.[24]

This isn't to say that the internet should be completely unfiltered, or that users should be able to publish and share any content they please, no matter how vile, destructive or illegal. But measures taken to make the internet a safer place must be implemented in a way that empowers and protects users, not those doing the filtering, be they working for private corporations or the state.

The easiest way to do this is by introducing greater democracy across the board. Users should be empowered to effect change within the services they use. This does not mean simply the freedom to choose within a market: the idea that anyone upset with Facebook or Google can simply not use those services has not been feasible for years. Both companies, along with a host of other Silicon Valley firms, are too enmeshed within our daily lives and their products too important to be simply boycotted. You may be able to give up Facebook, but can you live without Instagram and WhatsApp as well? Many people who switch to an alternative search engine to avoid Google tracking still use Gmail or YouTube. Even those who have been censored by these platforms admit to still using them, as the costs and difficulties of not doing so are so great.[25] This is even more the case in much of the developing world, where Facebook, for many users, is the internet. "If you pulled the plug on Facebook, there would literally be riots in the streets," Antonio García Martínez, a former Facebook advertising executive told *New York Magazine* in the wake of the Cambridge Analytica scandal. "So in the back of Facebook's mind, they know that they're stepping on people's toes. But in the end, people are happy to have the product, so why not step on toes?"[26] As journalist Mark Scott has written, "tough calls will have to be made between free speech and online safety, and elected officials, not opaque tech companies, must be the ones to judge what content crosses the line. If you're going to censor the web, you better make sure those doing so are accountable to voters."[27]

Giving users a voice and power over platforms will not be easy; it will almost certainly require government intervention, which brings with it another set of risks. Facebook, Google and other firms are unlikely to volunteer to undergo this type of disruption, which would fundamentally change how they operate. Most likely, a new, user-focused, democratic and transparent internet will have to be built from the ground up. As technologists Ben Tarnoff and Moira Weigel have argued, "this means developing publicly and co-operatively owned alternatives that empower workers, users and citizens to determine how they are run. These democratic digital structures can focus on serving personal and social needs rather than piling up profits for investors."[28]

We are at a pivotal moment in internet history. There are currently two major visions for how the technology should work: the libertarian, 'information wants to be free' fantasy, which enabled the growth of huge tech monopolies that abuse our data, control our expression and endanger our privacy; and the hyper-controlled Chinese model, where the state acts as the ultimate arbiter of what can and should be said, for our own good and its perpetual power. True change will only come when we develop an alternative vision, one of a user-controlled, transparent and democratic internet built around the technology's original promises – of freedom, education and international solidarity – not the pursuit of profit or top-down control.

James Griffiths, Hong Kong, September 2018

Acknowledgements

All journalism is done standing on the shoulders of those who went before, and I am eternally grateful for the work of my colleagues cited in this book for helping me understand and pointing the way. I would be remiss not to mention several works in particular without which this book would not exist: *Bad Elements* by Ian Buruma; *Who Controls the Internet?* by Jack Goldsmith and Tim Wu; *Consent of the Networked* by Rebecca MacKinnon; *The Red Web* by Andrei Soldatov and Irina Borogan; and *The Net Delusion* by Evgeny Morozov; as well as the reporting of David Bandurski, Gady Epstein and Paul Mozur.

That anyone is willing to speak to a journalist, let alone for extended periods of time, sometimes at potential risk to themselves, is a constant surprise and encouragement. Huge thanks to everyone who agreed to be interviewed for this book: in particular, Badiucao, Li Hongkuan, Dan Haig, Jewher Ilham, Stella Nyanzi and others who shared their stories and lives with me. Thanks too to those not directly mentioned in the text who spoke to me on background or to help me better understand a particular topic.

I am also grateful, in no particular order, to:

My parents, Catherine and Paul, my sister, Emma, and the rest of my family

My friend Erik Crouch, who not only served as my best man but also offered detailed feedback throughout the writing process and suggested a new structure that opened the book up and made it far better than it would have been without his input

Current and former colleagues at CNN, especially Hilary Whiteman, Marc Lourdes, Steve George, Rick Davis, Paul Armstrong and Andrew Demaria, for their support of this book

Kenneth Tan, for taking a chance on me and changing my life by moving me to Shanghai

Joyce Murdoch, Sarah Graham and other former colleagues at the *South China Morning Post*

My agent, Marysia Juszczakiewicz

My editor, Kim Walker

Dominic Fagan, Rik Ubhi and others at Zed Books; Judith Forshaw for her expert copyediting, and production manager Linda Auld

Mike Jones, Patrick Lozada, Catherine Griffiths, Paul Griffiths, Joyce Murdoch and Steve George for reading early versions of this book and offering feedback

Caroline Malone, Jeff Wasserstrom, Lydia Namiburu, Nick Marro, Lily Kuo, Lokman Tsui, Sarah Cook, Andrei Soldatov, Alec Ash, Antony Dapiran, Charlie Smith and Tom Phillips for advice and guidance at key moments

Ryan Kilpatrick for researching Lu Wei's background and reading far too many paeans to cyber-sovereignty

Shen Lu, Serenitie Wang and Nanlin Fang for their assistance with my CNN reporting, which I also drew on in writing this book

Ben Westcott, Josh Berlinger, Kati Bornholdt, Erik Crouch, Bridget O'Donnell, Patrick Lozada, Joshua Newlan, Juliet Perry, Adam White, Andrea Lo, Lindsey Ford, Sofia Mitra Thakur, Jerome Taylor, Huw Lloyd, Eric Shapiro, Pamela Boykoff, Alan Yu, Bryan Harris, Sarah Karacs, Zahra Jamshed, Elaine Yu, Steve George, Nash Jenkins, Isabella Steger, Ravi Hiranand, Wilfred Chan, Sam Green, Rohan Pinto, Sam Pickard, Thaddeus Cheung, and many more I have forgotten to mention, for their continued friendship, instant messages, sofas and spare bedrooms

Chelsea Manning and Wikileaks

The makers of the Ulysses and Simplenote apps

The Hong Kong public library system and the staff at the Tiu Keng Leng branch

Finally, thank you to Ella Wong, for everything.

Notes

In writing this book, I have endeavoured as much as possible to rely on first-hand sources, in both Chinese and English, and interviews with the principals or their own writings. When drawing on others' reporting or research, I have attempted to be overzealous in my citations. Any errors introduced are my own.

Introduction

1 'Github status report', Github, 29 March 2015, https://status.github.com/messages/2015-03-29

2 'Google's Eiffel doodle bug', The Connexion, 31 March 2015, https://www.connexionfrance.com/French-news/UPDATE-Google-s-Eiffel-doodle-bug

3 J. Newland, 'Large scale DDoS attack on github.com', The Github Blog, 27 March 2015, https://blog.github.com/2015-03-27-large-scale-ddos-attack-on-github-com/

4 'Github status report', Github, 5 April 2015, https://status.github.com/messages/2015-04-05

5 'Baidu's traffic hijacked to DDoS Github.com', Insight-labs, 27 March 2015, http://web.archive.org/web/20160304020144/http://insight-labs.org/?p=1682; E. Hjelmvik, 'China's man-on-the-side attack on GitHub', Netresec, 31 March 2015, http://www.netresec.com/?page=Blog&month=2015-03&post=China%27s-Man-on-the-Side-Attack-on-GitHub

6 '国家网信办发言人："Outlook受中国攻击"的说法纯属污蔑', Office of the Central Cyberspace Affairs Commission, 22 January 2015, http://www.cac.gov.cn/2015-01/22/c_1114097853.htm

7 C. Smith, 'We are under attack', GreatFire.org, 19 March 2015, https://en.greatfire.org/blog/2015/mar/we-are-under-attack

8 The developer spoke to me on condition that I identify him only by a pseudonym.

9 D. O'Brien, 'Speech that enables speech: China takes aim at its coders', Electronic Frontier Foundation, 28 August 2015, https://www.eff.org/deeplinks/2015/08/speech-enables-speech-china-takes-aim-its-coders

10 J. Barlow, 'A declaration of the independence of cyberspace', Electronic Frontier Foundation, 8 February 1996, https://www.eff.org/cyberspace-independence

11 B. Schneier, 'Someone is learning how to take down the internet', Schneier on Security, 13 September 2016, https://www.schneier.com/blog/archives/2016/09/someone_is_lear.html

Part 1
Chapter 1

1 'How Civic Square has become less than friendly', The Standard, 29 September 2014, http://www.thestandard.com.hk/section-news.php?id=149919&story _id=43069145&d_str=20140929&sid=11

2 R. Iyengar, 'One month after tear gas, Hong Kong protesters ponder their next step', Time, 29 October 2014, http://time.com/3545081/tear-gas-hong-kong-occupy-central-umbrella-revolution-month/

3 Cantonese is good for this: there's no combination of numbers a dedicated Hong Konger can't turn into a dirty joke.

4 J. Griffiths and V. Kam, 'Hong Kongers "thumb their noses at Beijing" with pro-independence votes', CNN, 6 September 2016, https://edition.cnn.com/ 2016/09/04/asia/hong-kong-legco-election/index.html

5 J. Griffiths, 'Hong Kong protesters pop champagne after leader says he'll step down', CNN, 10 December 2016, https://edition.cnn.com/2016/12/10/asia/hong-kong-cy-leung-regina-ip/index.html

6 P. Boehler, 'Voices from Tiananmen', South China Morning Post, 2014, http:// multimedia.scmp.com/tiananmen/

Chapter 2

1 F. Dikotter, The Cultural Revolution: a people's history, 1962–1976, London: Bloomsbury, 2016.

2 M. Hassan, 'Beijing 1987: China's coming-out party', Nature 455 (2008), pp. 598–9.

3 P. Greenberg, 'Beijing from ground level', The Washington Post, 11 October 1987, https://www.washingtonpost.com/archive/lifestyle/travel/1987/10/11/ beijing-from-ground-levelinto-the-bicycle-fray/5259f362-cd7e-487e-9018-14c1b90527a9/

4 A. Faruqui and M. Hassan, The Future of Science in China and the Third World: proceedings of the Second General Conference, Beijing, PR China, 14–18 September, 1987, Singapore: World Scientific, 1989, p. 4.

5 W. Zorn, J. Hauben and A. Plubell, How the Lost E-mail Message 'Across the Great Wall...' Brought People Together, Karlsruhe: Karlsruhe Institute of Technology, 2014, https://www.informatik.kit.edu/downloads/HQarticle-08Feb2014-final-version-engl.pdf

6 World Bank, China: University Development Project, Washington DC: World Bank, 1981, http://documents.worldbank.org/curated/en/669881468240345 194/China-University-Development-Project

7 J. Hauben, 'Across the Great Wall': the China–Germany email connection 1987–1994', paper presented at Columbia University, 2010.

8 W. Zorn, China's CSNET Connection 1987: origin of the China Academic Network CANET, speech to the Hasso-Plattner-Institute at Potsdam University, 2012.

9 '中国互联网：从第一封邮件走向世界', ScienceNet.cn, 22 August 2014, http:// news.sciencenet.cn/htmlnews/2014/8/301669.shtm

10 X. Wu, *Chinese Cyber Nationalism: evolution, characteristics and implications*, Lanham MD: Lexington Books, 2005, p. 17.

11 '*Wolf smoke signals war*', *China Heritage Quarterly*, June 2006, http://web. archive.org/web/20120318174504/http://www.chinaheritagequarterly.org/ articles.php?searchterm=006_wolf.inc&issue=006

12 Wu, *Chinese Cyber Nationalism*, p. 18.

13 E. Harwit and D. Clark, '*Shaping the internet in China: evolution of political control over network infrastructure and content*', *Asian Survey* 41, no. 3 (2001), pp. 377–408.

14 M. Farley, '"*Cyberdissident*" *in China on trial for subversion*', *Los Angeles Times*, 5 December 1998, http://articles.latimes.com/1998/dec/05/news/mn-50740

15 G. Barme and S. Ye, '*The Great Firewall of China*', *Wired*, 1 June 1997, https:// www.wired.com/1997/06/china-3/

16 *Computer Information Network and Internet Security, Protection and Management Regulations*, State Council, 1997.

17 J. Griffiths, '*VPN down: China goes after Astrill, other anti-censorship apps in run up to WW2 anniversary parade*', *South China Morning Post*, 26 August 2015, http://www.scmp.com/tech/apps-gaming/article/1852658/vpn-down-china-goes-after-astrill-other-anti-censorship-apps-run

18 '*How censorship works in China: a brief overview*' in '*Race to the Bottom*': *corporate complicity in Chinese internet censorship*, New York NY: Human Rights Watch, 2006, https://www.hrw.org/reports/2006/china0806/3.htm

19 G. Walton, *China's Golden Shield: corporations and the development of surveillance technology in the People's Republic of China*, Montreal: International Centre for Human Rights and Democratic Development, 2001, https://web. archive.org/web/20020206170828/http://www.ichrdd.ca/english/commdoc/ publications/globalization/goldenShieldEng.html

20 J. Goldsmith and T. Wu, *Who Controls the Internet?: Illusions of a borderless world*, New York NY: Oxford University Press, 2006, p. 93.

21 Author interview with Michael Robinson, January 2018.

22 D. Sheff, '*Betting on bandwidth*', *Wired*, 1 February 2002, https://www.wired. com/2001/02/tian/

23 *Evolution of Internet in China*, China Education and Research Network, 2001, https://web.archive.org/web/20061125232222/http://www.edu.cn/ introduction_1378/20060323/t20060323_4285.shtml

24 Sheff, '*Betting on bandwidth*'.

Chapter 3

1 I interviewed Li Hongkuan several times from May 2017 to February 2018, both in person and by telephone.

2 M. Laris, '*Internet police on the prowl in China*', *The Washington Post*, 24 October 1998.

3 The correct translation is 'Reference News', but *xiao* sounds like the Mandarin

word for 'small'. F. Blumberg, *When East Meets West: media research and practice in US and China*, Newcastle: Cambridge Scholars Publishing, 2007, pp. 67–8.

4 Q. He, *The Fog of Censorship: media control in China*, New York NY: Human Rights in China, 2008.

5 'Sitrep no. 29: Article justifies martial law; PLA to use any and all means to enforce martial law; Defense minister appears, so does Li Peng; tension on Tiananmen Square', US Embassy cable, 3 June 1989, https://wikileaks.com/plusd/cables/89BEIJING15407_a.html

6 G. Barme and S. Ye, 'The Great Firewall of China', *Wired*, 1 June 1997, https://www.wired.com/1997/06/china-3/

7 L. Hai, 'Statement of Lin Hai, computer scientist, Shanghai, China', Congressional-Executive Commission on China, 4 November 2002, https://www.gpo.gov/fdsys/pkg/CHRG-107hhrg83512/html/CHRG-107hhrg83512.htm

8 G. Epstein, 'Cat and mouse', *The Economist*, 6 April 2013, https://www.economist.com/news/special-report/21574629-how-china-makes-sure-its-internet-abides-rules-cat-and-mouse

9 M. Chase and J. Mulvenon, *You've Got Dissent! Chinese dissident use of the internet and Beijing's counter-strategies*, Santa Monica CA: Rand Corporation, 2002, p. 54, https://www.rand.org/pubs/monograph_reports/MR1543.html

10 K. Platt, 'China hits at e-mail to curb dissent', *The Christian Science Monitor*, 31 December 1998, https://www.csmonitor.com/1998/1231/123198.intl.intl.1.html

11 C. Smith, 'China sentences internet entrepreneur for trading e-mail list with dissidents', *The Wall Street Journal*, 21 January 1999, https://www.wsj.com/articles/SB916818019827637500

12 Smith, 'China sentences internet entrepreneur'.

13 Barme and Ye, 'The Great Firewall of China'.

14 S. Lubman, 'China convicts Tiananmen Spring dissidents', UPI, 5 January 1991, http://www.upi.com/Archives/1991/01/05/China-convicts-Tiananmen-Spring-dissidents/1900663051600/

15 M. Farley, 'China is abuzz over openness', *Los Angeles Times*, 30 June 1998, http://articles.latimes.com/1998/jun/30/news/mn-65084

16 'Wei Jingsheng released', Human Rights Watch, 16 November 1997, https://www.hrw.org/news/1997/11/16/wei-jingsheng-released

17 'UN treaty bodies and China', Human Rights in China, https://www.hrichina.org/en/un-treaty-bodies-and-china

18 J. Goldsmith and T. Wu, *Who Controls the Internet?: Illusions of a borderless world*, New York NY: Oxford University Press, 2006, pp. 90–1.

19 'China dissidents add branches to banned opposition party', *Los Angeles Times*, 5 February 1999, http://articles.latimes.com/1999/feb/05/news/mn-5115

20 Chase and Mulvenon, *You've Got Dissent!*, p. 12.

21 P. Pan, 'Wang Youcai arrives in Rhode Island after stop in San Francisco', *The Washington Post*, 5 March 2004, https://www.sfgate.com/politics/article/China-frees-Tiananmen-dissident-Wang-Youcai-2814286.php

22 *China: nipped in the bud. The suppression of the China Democracy Party*, New York NY: Human Rights Watch, 2000, https://www.hrw.org/report/2000/09/01/china-nipped-bud/suppression-china-democracy-party; J. Gittings, *The Changing Face of China: from Mao to market*, Oxford: Oxford University Press, 2006.

23 'Permanent normal trade relations with China' [video], C-SPAN, 8 March 2000, https://www.c-span.org/video/?155905-1/permanent-normal-trade-relations-china&start=1849

24 J. Green, '*China bashing on the campaign trail*', Bloomberg, 17 November 2011, https://www.bloomberg.com/news/articles/2011-11-17/china-bashing-on-the-campaign-trail

Chapter 4

1 D. Ownby, *Falun Gong and the Future of China*, New York NY: Oxford University Press, 2008, pp. 171–2.

2 I. Johnson, *Wild Grass: three stories of change in modern China*, New York NY: Pantheon Books, 2004, pp. 248–9; T. Crowell and D. Hsieh, '*Tremors of discontent*', *Asiaweek*, 1999, http://edition.cnn.com/ASIANOW/asiaweek/99/0507/nat1.html; author interview with Falun Gong practitioner and demonstration participant Shi Caidong, September 2017.

3 Johnson, *Wild Grass*, pp. 248–9.

4 Ownby, *Falun Gong and the Future of China*, p. 180.

5 J. Zittrain and B. Edelman, '*Empirical analysis of internet filtering in China*', Berkman Center for Internet and Society, 2003, https://cyber.harvard.edu/filtering/china/; '*Freedom on the net: China*', Freedom House, 2012, https://freedomhouse.org/report/freedom-net/2012/china

6 D. Bamman, B. O'Connor and N. Smith, '*Censorship and deletion practices in Chinese social media*', *First Monday* 17, no. 3–5 (2012), http://firstmonday.org/ojs/index.php/fm/article/view/3943/3169; N. Kristof, '*Banned in Beijing!*', *The New York Times*, 22 January 2011, https://www.nytimes.com/2011/01/23/opinion/23kristof.html

7 My history of Falun Gong draws heavily on Ownby, *Falun Gong and the Future of China* and D. Palmer, *Qigong Fever: body, science and utopia in China*, New York NY: Columbia University Press.

8 Ownby, *Falun Gong and the Future of China*, p. 10.

9 Palmer, *Qigong Fever*, p. 1.

10 Chinese sources give Li's birthdate as 27 July 1952, which he disputes, arguing it was input on his household registration documents in error during the Cultural Revolution and the correct date is 13 May 1951. However, as David Ownby recounts, 13 May is the date traditionally celebrated in China as Buddha's birthday, suggesting that Li's claim should be taken with more than a grain of salt. Ownby, *Falun Gong and the Future of China*, p. 81.

11 B. Penny, '*The life and times of Li Hongzhi: "Falun Gong" and religious biography*', *The China Quarterly* 175 (2003), pp. 643–61. '*A short biography of*

Mr. Li Hongzhi founder of Falun Xiulian Dafa, president of the Research Society of Falun Buddha Science' was originally published as an appendix to an early edition of *Zhuan Fala*, but is no longer distributed by the group (a Falun Gong translation remains online at an archived website: https://web.archive.org/web/20010109225900/http://www.compapp.dcu.ie:80//~dongxue/biography.html); *'Brief biography of Li Hongzhi: founder of Falun Gong and president of the Falun Gong Research Society'*, *Chinese Law and Government* 32, no. 6 (1999), pp. 14–23, https://web.archive.org/web/20040920074809/http://www.trinity.edu/rnadeau/Chinese%20Religions/Li%20Hongzhi.htm

12 *'True face of Li Hongzhi'*, Embassy of the People's Republic of China to the United States of America, http://www.china-embassy.org/eng/zt/ppflg/t36564.htm

13 Also translated as the China Qigong Research Association.

14 Ownby, *Falun Gong and the Future of China*, p. 87.

15 '张震寰', CPC Encyclopaedia, http://dangshi.people.com.cn/GB/165617/165618/166491/167909/12285608.html

16 Ownby, *Falun Gong and the Future of China*, p. 64, 166.

17 D. Mainfort, *'Sima Nan: fighting qigong pseudoscience in China'*, *Skeptical Briefs* 9.1 (1999), https://www.csicop.org/sb/show/sima_nan_fighting_ qigong_pseudoscience_in_china

18 C. Hitchens, *'For whom the Gong tolls'*, *The Nation*, 20 November 2000, https://www.thenation.com/article/whom-gong-tolls/. Today, Sima Nan is much better known as a staunch Chinese nationalist, defender of the government and critic of the Western liberal values that Hitchens became a chauvinistic defender of later in life.

19 Ownby, *Falun Gong and the Future of China*, p. 166.

20 Palmer, *Qigong Fever*, p. 219.

21 H. Li, *'Zhuan Falun'*, FalunDafa.org, 2014, http://falundafa.org/eng/eng/zfl2014/ZFL2014-004.htm

22 Ownby, *Falun Gong and the Future of China*, p. 167.

23 Ownby, *Falun Gong and the Future of China*, p. 169.

24 Based on an author interview with Shi Caidong in September 2017, and a written account of Shi's experiences provided by him to the author.

25 Zhu's words as remembered by Shi Caidong. Multiple reports from the time attest to Zhu meeting with the protesters, as do several books on Falun Gong, including those of Ian Johnson, Maria Hsia Chang and David Palmer. Kang Xiaoguang, a Chinese academic, does not mention Zhu in his account of the protest, but agrees that protesters went inside Zhongnanhai to meet with senior officials from the petitions office.

26 Palmer, *Qigong Fever*, pp. 268–9.

27 X. Kang, 法輪功事件全透視, Hong Kong: Ming Pao Publishing, 2000, p. 120.

28 Falun Gong representatives contest this account.

29 Crowell and Hsieh, *'Tremors of discontent'*.

30 Kang, 法輪功事件全透視, p. 122.

31 Ownby, *Falun Gong and the Future of China*, p. 3.

32 S. Cook, *The Battle for China's Spirit: religious revival, repression, and resistance under Xi Jinping*, Washington DC: Freedom House, 2017, p. 11, https://freedomhouse.org/sites/default/files/FH_ChinasSprit2016_FULL_FINAL_140pages_compressed.pdf

33 Ownby, *Falun Gong and the Future of China*, p. 145.

34 C. Smith, '*Banned Chinese sect is spurred on by exiled leader*', The New York Times, 5 January 2001, https://www.nytimes.com/2001/01/05/world/banned-chinese-sect-is-spurred-on-by-exiled-leader.html. Experts agree that Li was not advocating violence or making a call to arms, and a supplementary essay was published by the group clarifying that no action would ever be taken against Jiang Zemin, the architect of the crackdown, because karma would catch up with him in the end.

35 '*Five people set themselves afire in China; Beijing attributes Tiananmen Square protest to Falun Gong, which disavows it*', The Washington Post, 2001.

36 R. MacKinnon, '*Falun Gong denies tie to self-immolation attempts*', CNN, 24 January 2001, http://edition.cnn.com/2001/ASIANOW/east/01/23/china.falungong.03/index.html

37 Ownby, *Falun Gong and the Future of China*, p. 127.

38 E. Rosenthal, '*5 linked to banned sect in China set themselves on fire in protest*', The New York Times, 24 January 2001, https://www.nytimes.com/2001/01/24/world/5-linked-to-banned-sect-in-china-set-themselves-on-fire-in-protest.html

39 While extinguishers have become a far more common sight at sensitive locations since Tibetan monks began setting themselves on fire in mass numbers in recent years, they were not at the time.

40 Ownby, *Falun Gong and the Future of China*, p. 127.

41 P. Pan, '*China may charge foreign reporters over Tiananmen burning*', The Washington Post, 9 February 2001, https://www.washingtonpost.com/archive/politics/2001/02/09/china-may-charge-foreign-reporters-over-tiananmen-burning/c0bfa602-912f-40ee-ab3e-efdea0deea49

42 P. Pan, '*Human fire ignites Chinese mystery; motive for public burning intensifies fight over Falun Gong*', The Washington Post, 2001.

43 Ownby, *Falun Gong and the Future of China*, p. 218.

44 '*Self-immolation hoax on Tiananmen Square*', Minghui, http://en.minghui.org/cc/88/

45 Here is a perfect example of a likely exaggerated claim getting in the way of the truth. A great deal of objective documentation shows that there are far more organs in the Chinese donor system than there are donors, with the obvious explanation being that, despite claims to have ended the practice in recent years, Chinese authorities are still using executed prisoners for transplants. Far less evidence is available that organs are harvested while the prisoners are alive. By focusing on this claim, rather than the sufficiently horrifying non-consensual harvesting of organs from executed prisoners of conscience, Falun Gong risk undermining their own credibility and losing support.

Chapter 5

1   J. Ye and J. Areddy, 'Flowers for Google in China', The Wall Street Journal, 13 January2010,https://blogs.wsj.com/chinarealtime/2010/01/13/flowers-for-google-in-china/; N. Carlson, 'Chinese build a shrine to Google in Beijing', Business Insider,14January2010,http://www.businessinsider.com/the-shrine-the-cameras-the-gawkers-the-scene-outside-google-china-2010-1?op=1

2   S. Levy, In The Plex: how Google thinks, works, and shapes our lives, New York NY: Simon and Schuster, 2011, p. 312.

3   D. Drummond, 'A new approach to China', Google Blog, 12 January 2010, https://googleblog.blogspot.hk/2010/01/new-approach-to-china.html

4   L. Chao, 'Google China employees in limbo', The Wall Street Journal, 13 January 2010, https://blogs.wsj.com/digits/2010/01/13/google-china-employees-in-limbo/

5   Levy, In The Plex, p. 312.

6   Levy, In The Plex, p. 267.

7   My account of Google's travails in China owes a huge debt to Stephen Levy's In The Plex.

8   J. Lau, 'A history of Google in China', Financial Times, 9 July 2010, http:// ig-legacy.ft.com/content/faf86fbc-0009-11df-8626-00144feabdc0

9   C. Thompson, 'Google's China problem (and China's Google problem)', The New York Times Magazine, 23 April 2006, http://www.nytimes.com/2006/04/23/magazine/23google.html?pagewanted=all

10 S. So and J. Westland, Red Wired: China's internet revolution, London: Marshall Cavendish Business, 2010, p. 54.

11 Thompson, 'Google's China problem'.

12 Google disposed of its Baidu stake in mid-2006, a few months after it launched the censored Google.cn. A. Yeh, 'Google disposes of Baidu stake', Financial Times, 22 June 2006, https://www.ft.com/content/6756285a-026d-11db-a141-0000779e2340

13 'Yahoo! introduces Yahoo! China', Yahoo Press Room, 24 September 1999, https://web.archive.org/web/20080331032042/http://yhoo.client.shareholder.com:80/press/ReleaseDetail.cfm?ReleaseID=173569

14 'China's internet industry wants self-discipline', People's Daily, 27 March 2002, http://en.people.cn/200203/26/eng20020326_92885.shtml

15 J. Goldsmith and T. Wu, Who Controls the Internet?: Illusions of a borderless world, New York NY: Oxford University Press, 2006, p. 9.

16 'Public pledge of self-regulation and professional ethics for China internet industry', Internet Society of China, 9 August 2011, http://www.isc.org.cn/english/Specails/Self-regulation/listinfo-15321.html

17 Goldsmith and Wu, Who Controls the Internet?, p. 9.

18 'Xiaoning et al. v. Yahoo! Inc, et al., 4:2007cv02151', California Northern District Court.

19 198964, 'Excerpts from Document Eleven issued by the General Offices of the Communist Party of China and the State Council', Democracy Forum, 20 April

2004, as cited by the Committee to Protect Journalists, https://cpj.org/awards/2005/shi-tao.php

20 X. Liu, 'An open letter to Jerry Yang, chairman of Yahoo! Inc. regarding the arrest of Shi Tao' in 'Race to the Bottom': corporate complicity in Chinese internet censorship, New York NY: Human Rights Watch, 2006, https://www.hrw.org/reports/2006/china0806/14.htm

21 L. Rao, 'The most expensive sake that Alibaba's Jack Ma ever had', Fortune, 25 September 2015, http://fortune.com/2015/09/25/yahoo-alibaba-investment-jack-ma/

Part 2
Chapter 6

1 'How censorship works in China: a brief overview' in 'Race to the Bottom': corporate complicity in Chinese internet censorship, New York NY: Human Rights Watch, 2006, https://www.hrw.org/reports/2006/china0806/3.htm

2 R. Faris, J. Palfrey, E. Zuckerman, H. Roberts and J. York, '2010 circumvention tool usage report', Berkman Klein Center for Internet and Society at Harvard University, 14 October 2010, https://cyber.harvard.edu/publications/2010/Circumvention_Tool_Usage

3 R. MacKinnon, Consent of the Networked: the world-wide struggle for internet freedom, New York NY: Basic Books, 2012, p. 36.

4 'How censorship works in China'.

5 'Provisions on the Administration of Internet News Information Services', translation via the Congressional Executive Commission on China, 25 September 2005, https://www.cecc.gov/resources/legal-provisions/provisions-on-the-administration-of-internet-news-information-services

6 G. King, J. Pan and M. Roberts, 'How censorship in China allows government criticism but silences collective expression', American Political Science Review 107, no. 2 (2013), p. 1.

7 King, Pan and Roberts, 'How censorship in China allows government criticism', p. 5.

8 X. Qiang, 'Image of internet police: JingJing and Chacha online – Hong Yan', China Digital Times, 22 January 2006, https://chinadigitaltimes.net/2006/01/image-of-internet-police-jingjing-and-chacha-online-hong-yan-o°ae¥™aaio°a/

9 P. Link, 'The anaconda in the chandelier', New York Review of Books, 11 April 2002, http://www.chinafile.com/library/nyrb-china-archive/china-anaconda-chandelier

10 King, Pan and Roberts, 'How censorship in China allows government criticism', p. 5.

11 R. Zhong, P. Mozur and I. Zhao, 'Horns honk, and censors in China get a headache', The New York Times, 12 April 2018, https://www.nytimes.com/2018/04/12/business/china-bytedance-duanzi-censor.html

12 She was ridiculing ongoing anti-Japanese protests over a territorial dispute between Beijing and Tokyo, in which young protesters had targeted Japanese

businesses and smashed Japanese products. Cheng retweeted a mocking suggestion that they instead target a government-run pavilion at the Shanghai Expo, adding the three words that landed her with a charge of "disrupting public order". D. Grammaticas, 'Chinese woman jailed over Twitter post', BBC News, 18 November 2010, http://www.bbc.com/news/world-asia-pacific-11784603

13 A. Greer Meisels, 'What China learned from the Soviet Union's fall', The Diplomat, 27 July 2012, http://thediplomat.com/2012/07/what-china-learned-from-the-soviet-unions-fall/

14 J. Palmer, 'What China didn't learn from the collapse of the Soviet Union', Foreign Policy, 24 December 2016, https://foreignpolicy.com/2016/12/24/what-china-didnt-learn-from-the-collapse-of-the-soviet-union/

15 G. Epstein, 'Cat and mouse', The Economist, 6 April 2013, https://www.economist.com/news/special-report/21574629-how-china-makes-sure-its-internet-abides-rules-cat-and-mouse

16 Epstein, 'Cat and mouse'.

17 Interview with Xiao Qiang [video], Radio Free Asia, 28 February 2017, https://www.youtube.com/watch?v=M73jzwJbjhI

18 S. Leavenworth, 'Website chronicles China's massive effort to control internet content', McClatchy, 9 April 2015, http://www.mcclatchydc.com/news/nation-world/world/article24782851.html

19 'Xiao Qiang', MacArthur Fellows Program, 2001, https://www.macfound.org/fellows/671/

20 S. Wade, 'Minitrue: delete reports on call to ease internet control', China Digital Times, 7 March 2017, https://chinadigitaltimes.net/2017/03/minitrue-delete-reports-call-limit-internet-censorship/

21 A. Ramzy, 'KFC targeted in protests over South China Sea', The New York Times, 19 July 2016, https://www.nytimes.com/2016/07/20/world/asia/south-china-sea-protests-kfc.html

22 S. Wade, 'Minitrue: do not hype illegal demonstrations', China Digital Times, 19 July 2016, https://chinadigitaltimes.net/2016/07/minitrue-not-hype-illegal-demonstrations/

23 '新华网评"抵制肯德基"：自己折腾自己不是爱国', Xinhua, 19 July 2016, http://military.china.com/important/11132797/20160719/23092151_all.html

24 Q. He, The Fog of Censorship: media control in China, New York NY: Human Rights in China, 2008, pp. 71–2.

25 J. Areddy, 'The architect of China's Great Firewall caught in anti-corruption net', The Wall Street Journal, 21 November 2017, https://www.wsj.com/articles/lu-wei-chinas-former-internet-czar-comes-under-investigation-for-corruption-1511290607

26 L. Lim, 'The curious case of the vanishing Chinese city', NPR, 21 September 2011, https://www.npr.org/2011/09/21/140633602/the-curious-case-of-the-vanishing-chinese-city

27 C. Bartholomew, Report to Congress of the U.S.–China Economic and Security Review Commission, Collingdale PA: Diane Publishing, 2010, p. 153.

28 Xinhua, '*Jiang Enzhu on renaming Xinhua Hong Kong branch*', *People's Daily*, 17 January 2000, http://en.people.cn/english/200001/17/eng20000117N126.html

29 He, *The Fog of Censorship*, p. 69.

30 He, *The Fog of Censorship*, pp. 71–2.

31 J. Gao, '观察站：揭示中共网络总管鲁炜的仕途之路', *Duowei News*, 12 May 2013, http://news.dwnews.com/china/news/2013-05-12/59173432-all.html

32 '*Lu Wei*', World Economic Forum, https://www.weforum.org/people/lu-wei

33 Gao, '观察站：揭示中共网络总管鲁炜的仕途之路'.

34 Associated Press, '*China's "Grandpa Wen" widely admired for work to rally victims in hard-hit earthquake areas*', *International Herald Tribune*, 16 May 2008, https://archive.li/hAebK#selection-421.1-426.0

35 P. Foster, '*Book by Chinese dissident brands Wen Jiabao a "fraud"*', *The Telegraph*, 17 August 2010, https://www.telegraph.co.uk/news/worldnews/asia/china/7949426/Book-by-Chinese-dissident-brands-Wen-Jiabao-a-fraud.html

36 T. Fuller, '*New Chinese rules could redirect profits in financial news sector*', *International Herald Tribune*, 12 September 2006, https://www.nytimes.com/2006/09/12/technology/12iht-rules.2781524.html

37 X. Xin, *How the Market Is Changing China's News: the case of Xinhua news agency*, Lanham MD: Lexington Books, 2012, p. 128.

38 D. Sedney, '*Austr Stratford discusses Xinhua regulations with Xinhua News Vp Lu Wei*', WikiLeaks, 23 March 2007, https://wikileaks.org/plusd/cables/07BEIJING2009_a.html

Chapter 7

1 Author interview with Dan Haig, September 2017.

2 J. Cool, '*Communities of innovation: cyborganic and the birth of networked social media*', PhD thesis, University of Southern California, 2008, p.166.

3 Author interview with Thubten Samdup, September 2017.

4 W. Li et al., '*The agreement of the Central People's Government and the Local Government of Tibet on measures for the peaceful liberation of Tibet*', China Internet Information Center, 23 May 1951, http://www.china.org.cn/english/zhuanti/tibet%20facts/163877.htm

5 DIIR, '"*The 17-point agreement": the full story as revealed by the Tibetans and Chinese who were involved*', Tibet.net, 2001, https://web.archive.org/web/20080606090544/http://www.tibet.net:80/en/diir/pubs/phri/17point/data/17ptsfs.html

6 J. Mirsky, '*Tibet: the CIA's cancelled war*', *New York Review of Books*, 9 April 2013, http://www.nybooks.com/daily/2013/04/09/cias-cancelled-war-tibet/; J. Chen, '*The Tibetan rebellion of 1959 and China's changing relations with India and the Soviet Union*', *Journal of Cold War Studies* 8, no. 3 (2006), p. 54.

7 T. Shakya, *The Dragon in the Land of Snows: a history of modern Tibet since 1947*, London: Pimlico, 1999, p. 200; P. Jackson, '*Witness: reporting on the Dalai Lama's escape to India*', Reuters, 27 February 2009, https://www.reuters.

com/article/us-witness-jackson-dalailama/witness-reporting-on-the-dalai-lamas-escape-to-india-idUSTRE51Q4OB20090227

8 A. Ghosh, *'Internet bandwidth: India needs a backbone'*, IS ComputerWorld, January 1995, https://www.academia.edu/2012661/Internet_bandwidth_-_India_needs_a_backbone_-_January_1995

Chapter 8

1 E. Rosenthal, *'China's leaders: the meeting site; at one resort in China, two distinct worlds'*, The New York Times, 10 August 2001, https://www.nytimes.com/2001/08/10/world/china-s-leaders-the-meeting-site-at-one-resort-in-china-two-distinct-worlds.html

2 A. Sulzberger, *'China's leaders; in Jiang's words: "I hope the Western world can understand China better"'*, The New York Times, 10 August 2001, https://www.nytimes.com/2001/08/10/world/china-s-leaders-jiang-s-words-hope-western-world-can-understand-china-better.html

3 *'Jiang renews warning against "pernicious" internet'*, Agence France-Presse, 11 July 2001.

4 *'How censorship works in China: a brief overview'* in *'Race to the Bottom': corporate complicity in Chinese internet censorship*, New York NY: Human Rights Watch, 2006, https://www.hrw.org/reports/2006/china0806/3.htm

5 *'Golden Shield project'*, Guangdong Hongan Group, 2012, https://web.archive.org/web/20150416093636/http://www.gdhongan.com:80/industroy.asp?ChannelID=7#

6 J. Kahn, *'China has world's tightest internet censorship, study finds'*, The New York Times, 4 December 2002, https://www.nytimes.com/2002/12/04/world/china-has-world-s-tightest-internet-censorship-study-finds.html

7 *Wengui v Li* [2018] 8:2018cv00259 (Maryland District Court), https://dockets.justia.com/docket/maryland/mddce/8:2018cv00259/412429

8 J. Berlau, *'Asia Minor'*, The New Republic, 25 March 2002, https://newrepublic.com/article/66182/china-national-endowment-for-democracy-dissident

Chapter 9

1 *'Li Yuanlong criminal indictment'*, Guizhou Province People's Procuratorate, Bijie Branch, 2006.

2 A. Li, *'China's censorship of the internet and social media: the human toll and trade impact'*, Congressional Executive Commission on China, 17 November 2011, https://chinacommission.gov/pages/hearings/general/hearing1/index.php

3 G. Jiao, *'讨伐中宣部'*, Radio Free Asia, 25 March 2004, https://www.rfa.org/cantonese/features/hottopic/china_media-20040325.html

4 *'焦国标: 我为我的《致美国兵》自豪八百辈子'*, New Century Net, 3 April 005, https://web.archive.org/web/20050514124645/http://www.ncn.org/asp/zwginfo/da-KAY.asp?ID=63193&ad=4/3/2005

5 R. Soong, *'The counterattack against Jiao Guobiao'*, Zona Europa, 2 April 2005, http://www.zonaeuropa.com/20050402_1.htm

6   Y. Li, '在思想上加入美国国籍', *Epoch Times*, 13 May 2005, http://www. epochtimes.com/gb/5/5/13/n920342.htm

7   Li, '*China's censorship of the internet and social media*'.

8   '*Internet essays bring subversion charge*', Agence France-Presse, 28 February 2006, https://chinadigitaltimes.net/2006/02/internet-essays-bring-subversion-charge-afp/

9   'Journalist Li Yuanlong indicted for subversion for e-mailing essays abroad', Congressional Executive Commission on China, 31 March 2006, https://www.cecc.gov/publications/commission-analysis/journalist-li-yuanlong-indicted-for-subversion-for-e-mailing-essays

10 '*Falun Gong practice sites*', FalunDafa.org, 2018, http://en.falundafa.org/contacts/country/united-states.html#Region_New-York

11 'Minghui.org', DNS Trails, 2018, https://dnstrails.com/domain/minghui.org; 'Practice schedule for the Tri-State area', FalunDafa.org, 1999, https://web.archive.org/web/19990128145614/http://www.falundafa.org:80/tri_e.htm

12 '*Eastern US Buddhas Study Falun Dafa Association*: exempt organizations select check', US Internal Revenue Service (IRS), https://apps.irs.gov/app/eos/displayAll.do?dispatchMethod=displayAllInfo&Id=67573&ein=134021152&country=US&deductibility=all&dispatchMethod=searchAll&isDescending=false&city=&ein1=&postDateFrom=&exemptTypeCode=al&submitName=Search&sortColumn=orgName&totalResults=1&names=Eastern+Buddhas&resultsPerPage=25&indexOfFirstRow=0&postDateTo=&state=NY

13 '*Eastern US Buddhas Study Falun Dafa Association*: return of organization exempt from income tax', 2014, http://990s.foundationcenter.org/990_pdf_archive/134/134021152/134021152_201505_990EZ.pdf

14 'Falun Gong trademark', United States Patent and Trademark Office.

15 *China and Falun Gong*, Congressional Research Service Report RL33437, 2006, p. 1.

16 D. Ownby, *Falun Gong and the Future of China*, New York NY: Oxford University Press, 2008, p. 138.

17 '*A technical analysis of the Chinese "Green Dam Youth-Escort" censorship software*', WikiLeaks, 10 June 2009, https://wikileaks.org/wiki/A_technical_analysis_of_the_Chinese_%27Green_Dam_Youth-Escort%27_censorship_software

18 J. Ng, *Blocked on Weibo: what gets suppressed on China's version of Twitter (and why)*, New York NY: The New Press, 2013, p. 42.

19 Author interview with Bill Xia, September 2017.

20 V. Beiser, '*Digital weapons help dissidents punch holes in China's Great Firewall*', *Wired*, 1 November 2010, https://www.wired.com/2010/11/ff_firewallfighters/

21 I. Clarke, '*A distributed decentralised information storage and retrieval system*', master's thesis, University of Edinburgh, 1999, https://freenetproject.org/papers/ddisrs.pdf

22 R. Sandvik, '*The New York Times is now available as a Tor Onion service*', *The*

New York Times, 27 October 2017, https://open.nytimes.com/https-open-nytimes-com-the-new-york-times-as-a-tor-onion-service-e0d0b67b7482

23 J. Biggs, '*Daily Stormer has officially retreated to the dark web*', TechCrunch, 24 August 2017, https://techcrunch.com/2017/08/24/daily-stormer-has-officially-retreated-to-the-dark-web/

24 J. Damm and S. Thomas, *Chinese Cyberspaces: technological changes and political effects*, Abingdon: Routledge, 2006, p. 70.

25 '*About UltraSurf and UltraReach*', UltraSurf, 2018, https://ultrasurf.us/about/

26 C. Callanan, H. Dries-Ziekenheiner, A. Escudero-Pascual and R. Guerra, *Leaping Over the Firewall: a review of censorship circumvention tools*, Washington DC: Freedom House, 2011, https://freedomhouse.org/sites/default/files/inline_images/Censorship.pdf

27 J. Applebaum, *Technical Analysis of the Ultrasurf Proxying Software*, Cambridge MA: Tor Project, 2012, p. 1, https://media.torproject.org/misc/2012-04-16-ultrasurf-analysis.pdf

28 UltraSurf now encourages users to verify their install file's digital signature against a list on its website, making this attack vector more difficult. See https://ultrasurf.us/verify/

29 '*Tor's critique of Ultrasurf: a reply from the Ultrasurf developers*', UltraSurf, 16 April 2012, https://web.archive.org/web/20170515185101/https://ultrasurf.us/Ultrasurf-response-to-Tor-definitive-review.pdf

30 Beiser, '*Digital weapons help dissidents punch holes in China's Great Firewall*'.

31 '*Global Internet Freedom Inc. articles of incorporation*', State of North Carolina, 2001.

32 J. Hudson, '*US repeals propaganda ban, spreads government-made news to Americans*', Foreign Policy, 14 July 2013, http://foreignpolicy.com/2013/07/14/u-s-repeals-propaganda-ban-spreads-government-made-news-to-americans/

33 'Mission', *Broadcasting Board of Governors*, https://www.bbg.gov/who-we-are/mission/

34 *Radio Free Asia*, Congressional Report, 24 October 1997, https://web.archive.org/web/20070927001620/http://opencrs.cdt.org/rpts/97-52_19971024.pdf

35 Mandarin is uniquely suited to this type of censorship-dodging because the tonal language has so few separate phonemes. So, in the most famous instance, 肏你妈, 'fuck your mother', becomes 草泥马, 'grass mud horse', but both are pronounced roughly the same: *cao ni ma*.

36 J. Ramirez, '*Internet freedom group helps dissidents abroad*', *Newsweek*, 25 January 2010, http://www.newsweek.com/internet-freedom-group-helps-dissidents-abroad-71155

37 Broadcasting Board of Governors, 'Dynamic Internet Technology Inc. in Secaucus, NJ, Mailing and Distribution Services (R604)', 28 August 2007.

38 S. Rimensnyder, '*Triangle Boy howdy*', *Reason*, March 2002, https://reason.com/archives/2002/03/01/triangle-boy-howdy; M. Johnson, '*CIA-backed venture eyes anonymity software*', CNN, 15 February 2001, http://edition.cnn.com/2001/TECH/internet/02/15/anonymity.software.idg/index.html

39 S. Hsu, 'Triangle Boy white paper', SafeWeb, 2001, http://www.webrant.com/safeweb_site/html/www/tboy_whitepaper.html

40 P. Roberts, 'Symantec purchases SSL VPN maker SafeWeb', Computer World, 20 October 2003, https://www.computerworld.com/article/2572939/security0/symantec-purchases-ssl-vpn-maker-safeweb.html

41 S. Zhou, 'Global internet freedom: corporate responsibility and the rule of law', US Senate Subcommittee on Human Rights and the Law, 20 May 2008, https://www.judiciary.senate.gov/meetings/global-internet-freedom-corporate-responsibility-and-the-rule-of-law

42 'H.R.2764: Consolidated Appropriations Act', US Congress, 2008, https://www.congress.gov/bill/110th-congress/house-bill/2764/text

43 J. Pomfret, 'US risks China's ire with decision to fund software maker tied to Falun Gong', The Washington Post, 11 May 2010, http://www.washingtonpost.com/wp-dyn/content/article/2010/05/11/AR2010051105154.html

44 Pomfret, 'US risks China's ire with decision to fund software maker tied to Falun Gong'.

45 A. Sullivan, 'Twitter maintenance?', The Atlantic, 15 June 2009, https://www.theatlantic.com/daily-dish/archive/2009/06/twitter-i-maintenance-i/200310/

46 J. Last, 'Tweeting while Tehran burns', Weekly Standard, 17 August 2009, http://www.weeklystandard.com/tweeting-while-tehran-burns/article/240739

47 M. Pfeifle, 'A Nobel Peace Prize for Twitter?', Christian Science Monitor, 6 July 2009, https://www.csmonitor.com/Commentary/Opinion/2009/0706/p09s02-coop.html

48 E. Morozov, The Net Delusion: the dark side of internet freedom, London: Hachette UK, 2012, p. 15–18.

49 'The Clinton internet doctrine', The Wall Street Journal, 23 January 2010, https://www.wsj.com/articles/SB10001424052748704320104575014560882205670

50 M. Lander and B. Stelter, 'Washington taps into a potent new force in diplomacy', The New York Times, 16 June 2009, http://www.nytimes.com/2009/06/17/world/middleeast/17media.html

51 Though considering the award eventually went to Barack Obama, then less than a year into his presidency, perhaps it wouldn't have been so ridiculous.

Chapter 10

1 C. Smith et al., The Internet in China: a tool for freedom or suppression? Washington DC: Committee on International Relations, US House of Representatives, SN109-157, 2006, p. 1; 'Internet in China' [video], C-Span, 26 February 2006, https://www.c-span.org/video/?191220-1/internet-china

2 J. Goldsmith and T. Wu, Who Controls the Internet?: Illusions of a borderless world, New York NY: Oxford University Press, 2006, p. 10.

3 Committee to Protect Journalists, 'Blogger's website deleted by Microsoft following government's request', IFEX, 9 January 2006, https://ifex.org/china/2006/01/09/blogger_s_website_deleted_by_microsoft/

4   S. Levy, *In the Plex: how Google thinks, works, and shapes our lives*, New York NY: Simon and Schuster, 2011, pp. 278–80.

5   C. Thompson, 'Google's China problem (and China's Google problem)', *The New York Times Magazine*, 23 April 2006, http://www.nytimes.com/2006/04/23/magazine/23google.html?pagewanted=all

6   Levy, *In the Plex*, p. 281.

7   K. Lee, '*Google* 和中国', Kai-fu's Student Network, 2005, https://web.archive.org/web/20050812012559/http://www.kaifulee.com:80/Articles/googleandchina.htm

8   A. McLaughlin, 'Google in China', Google Blog, 27 January 2006, https://googleblog.blogspot.hk/2006/01/google-in-china.html

9   K. Lee, *Making a World of Difference*, self-published by Kai-Fu Lee, 2011.

10 Levy, *In the Plex*, p. 283.

11 Smith et al., *The Internet in China*, p. 2.

12 Smith et al., *The Internet in China*, p. 56.

13 Smith et al., *The Internet in China*, pp. 66–7.

14 Smith et al., *The Internet in China*, p. 96.

15 Smith et al., *The Internet in China*, p. 97.

16 Lee, *Making a World of Difference*.

17 Levy, *In the Plex*, p. 295.

18 '*Baidu vs Google*' [video], YouTube, 24 May 2006, https://www.youtube.com/watch?v=EPnmsFl__nU

19 HKTDC, '*Baidu's Robin Li on Google's "mistakes" in China*' [video], YouTube, 20 January 2014, https://www.youtube.com/watch?v=OTQ8S7dNYZc

20 Levy, *In the Plex*, p. 288.

21 Lee, *Making a World of Difference*.

22 Levy, *In the Plex*, p. 288.

23 '*Google*, 我们爱你，但我们不爱"谷歌"', NoGuGe.com, 2007, https://web.archive.org/web/20070408185725/http://www.noguge.com:80/

24 Thompson, '*Google's China problem (and China's Google problem)*'.

25 Levy, *In the Plex*, p. 298.

26 Lee, *Making a World of Difference*.

27 Levy, *In the Plex*, p. 288.

Part 3
Chapter 11

1   Uyghur names are patronymic. For example, in Ilham Tohti's case, the second name is that of his father. While Ilham is often erroneously referred to as Tohti in media reports, I use his first name for the sake of clarity and consistency with the naming of other Uyghurs in this book.

2   '伊力哈木·土赫提分裂国家案庭审纪实', Xinhua, 24 September 2014, https://web.archive.org/web/20140928053741/http://news.xinhuanet.com/legal/2014-09/24/c_1112614703.htm

3   P. Wen and S. Liu, 'Uighur scholar Ilham Tohti sentenced to life in jail by Chinese

court, *The Sydney Morning Herald*, 23 September 2014, https://www.smh.com. au/world/uighur-scholar-ilham-tohti-sentenced-to-life-in-jail-by-chinese-court-20140923-10kxgp.html

4 Sixth National Population Census of the People's Republic of China.

5 N. Baranovitch, 'From the margins to the centre: the Uyghur challenge in Beijing', *The China Quarterly* 175 (2003), p. 731.

6 Baranovitch, ' From the margins to the centre', p. 732.

7 A stereotype that is reinforced by the annual Spring Festival gala, a nationally televised event in which Uyghur song and dance groups are trooped out dressed in traditional clothes to perform songs about ethnic harmony and their love for China.

8 Baranovitch, ' From the margins to the centre', p. 734; K. Kan, *'Pride and prejudice: Yoyng, Uighur and in Beijing'*, *That's Beijing*, 15 July 2014, https:// uhrp.org/featured-articles/pride-and-prejudice-young-uighur-and-beijing

9 S. Toops, 'Where Inner Asia meets Outer China: the Xinjiang Uyghur Autonomous Region of China' in S. M. Walcott and C. Johnson (eds), *Eurasian Corridors of Interconnection: from the South China to the Caspian Sea*, New York NY: Routledge, 2013, p. 64.

10 My account of Ilham Tohti's early life is drawn largely from a short autobiography he published online in 2011, his daughter's account, and those of friends of his.

11 J. Millward, *Eurasian Crossroads: a history of Xinjiang*, New York NY: Columbia University Press, 2007, p. 267.

12 F. Dikötter, *The Cultural Revolution: a people's history*, London: Bloomsbury, 2016, pp. 157–61, 190–1.

13 Millward, *Eurasian Crossroads*, p. 275.

14 Millward, *Eurasian Crossroads*, p. 274.

15 N. Holdstock, *China's Forgotten People: Xinjiang, terror and the Chinese state*, London: I. B. Tauris, 2015, p. 45.

16 I. Tohti, 'My ideals and the career path I have chosen', Uyghur Online, 2011.

17 I. Tohti, 'Present-day ethnic problems in Xinjiang Uighur Autonomous Region: overview and recommendations', Daxiong Gonghui, 2014, as translated by China Change.

18 What to call Xinjiang is a sensitive topic. Many Uyghur groups refer to it as East Turkestan, which was also the name of two short-lived independent republics in the region. To refer to it as such, however, is seen by many in China as a tacit endorsement of independence for the region. Equally, some Uyghurs view the name Xinjiang as inextricably linked to Chinese colonisation. For the sake of clarity, I will use the names most commonly used, which means Xinjiang for the province, but Urumqi and Kashgar over their Putonghua names, Wulumuqi and Kashi.

19 BBC Monitoring, 'Xinjiang territory profile', BBC News, 17 August 2018, http:// www.bbc.com/news/world-asia-pacific-16860974

20 State Council Population Census Office, *Department of Employment Statistics'*, Beijing: National Bureau of Statistics of China, 2012.

21 Holdstock, *China's Forgotten People*, p. 13.

22 P. Perdue, *China Marches West*, Cambridge MA: Harvard University Press, 2005, p. 33.

23 Holdstock, *China's Forgotten People*, p. 13.

24 Holdstock, *China's Forgotten People*, p. 15.

25 Millward, *Eurasian Crossroads*, p. 124.

26 Historian James Millward has recorded references to Xinjiang supplanting 'western regions' in Qing parlance earlier to 1884, but the latter date is generally accepted as the point at which Xinjiang became the formal name for a province or region of the empire.

27 Holdstock, *China's Forgotten People*, p. 16.

28 J. Jacobs, *Xinjiang and the Modern Chinese State*, Seattle WA: University of Washington Press, 2016, p. 83, 168.

29 S. Starr, *Xinjiang: China's Muslim borderland*, New York NY: M. E. Sharpe, 2004, p. 6.

30 Holdstock, *China's Forgotten People*, p. 16.

31 I. Tharoor, 'A brief history of the Uighurs', *Time*, 9 July 2009, http://content.time.com/time/world/article/0,8599,1909416,00.html; '*The Uyghur ethnic minority*', China.org.cn, http://www.china.org.cn/e-groups/shaoshu/shao-2-uygur.htm

32 Starr, *Xinjiang*, p. 359.

33 Holdstock, *China's Forgotten People*, p. 20.

34 Millward, *Eurasian Crossroads*, p. 97.

35 Jacobs, *Xinjiang and the Modern Chinese State*, p. 6.

36 Y. Zengxin, *Buguozhai wendu*, vol. 1, pp. 186–90, 194–202, as cited in Jacobs, *Xinjiang and the Modern Chinese State*.

37 Holdstock, *China's Forgotten People*, p. 66.

38 T. Cliff, *Oil and Water: being Han in Xinjiang*, Chicago IL: University of Chicago Press, 2016, p. 105.

39 D. McMillen, 'Xinjiang and the production and construction corps: a Han organisation in a non-Han region', *Australian Journal of Chinese Affairs* 6 (1981), p. 77.

40 Cliff, *Oil and Water*, p. 205.

41 Author interview with 'Gu Li', May 2017.

42 Author interview with Jewher Ilham, March 2017.

43 J. Ilham, *Jewher Ilham: a Uyghur's fight to free her father*, New Orleans LA: University of New Orleans Press, 2015, p. 28.

Chapter 12

1 'Shaoguan', *People's Government Gazette*, 2016.

2 '*Chinese GDP by region 2000–2010*', National Bureau of Statistics.

3 A. Jacobs, '*At a factory, the spark of China's violence*', *The New York Times*, 15 July 2009, https://www.nytimes.com/2009/07/16/world/asia/16china.html; Staff reporters, '*Guangdong police detain 13 suspects over factory brawl*', *South China Morning Post*, 2009.

4 '*Better care to make Xinjiang workers feel at home: south China city official*', Xinhua, 22 July 2009, https://web.archive.org/web/20090723180831/http:// news.xinhuanet.com/english/2009-07/22/content_11754297.htm

5 K. McLaughlin, '*Fear grips Shaoguan's Uyghurs*', *Far Eastern Economic Review*, 17 July 2009, https://web.archive.org/web/20090721012546/http://www.feer. com/politics/2009/july58/Fear-Grips-Shaoguans-Uighurs

6 '*Better care to make Xinjiang workers feel at home*'.

7 Staff reporters, '*Guangdong police detain 13 suspects over factory brawl*'.

8 L. Lam, Q. Tang and M. Juma, '"*No rapes*" *in riot town*', Radio Free Asia, 29 June 2009, https://www.rfa.org/english/news/uyghur/ethnic-clash-06292009 102144.html

9 Staff reporter, '港資廠爆漢維兩族衝突　女工被姦觸發300人群毆　2死118傷', Apple Daily, 27 June 2009, https://hk.news.appledaily.com/international/daily/ article/20090627/12924858

10 '*Up to 70 percent of women factory workers in Guangzhou sexually harassed*', *China Labor Bulletin*, 6 December 2013, http://www.clb.org.hk/en/content/ 70-percent-women-factory-workers-guangzhou-sexually-harassed

11 '*Rumormonger held over south China toy factory brawl*', *Global Times*, 29 June 2009, http://www.globaltimes.cn/content/440821.shtml

12 Y. Zhou, P. Wang and Y. Pan, '"*Unintentional scream*" *triggered Xinjiang riot*', Xinhua, 8 July 2009, http://english.cctv.com/20090708/110231.shtml

13 M. Juma, '*Armed assailants stormed dorms*', Radio Free Asia, 5 July 2009, https://www.rfa.org/english/news/uyghur/armedchinese-07042009104353.html

14 Jacobs, '*At a factory, the spark of China's violence*'.

15 '*Death penalty sustained to man in south China's fatal factory brawl*', Xinhua, 28 October 2009, http://english.cctv.com/20091028/103366.shtml

16 I. Zhai, '*Two killed in ethnic clash at toy plant: Han, Uygur workers in night of violence*', *South China Morning Post*, 2009.

17 Staff reporters, '*Guangdong police detain 13 suspects over factory brawl*'.

18 My account of the events of 5 July is based on official reports by the Xinhua news agency, declassified US government cables, reports by Human Rights Watch and Amnesty International, and the work of historians Tom Cliff and Nick Holdstock.

19 N. Holdstock, *China's Forgotten People: Xinjiang, terror and the Chinese state*, London: I. B. Tauris, 2015, p. 187; R. Goldberg, '*The Urumqi riots: what contacts say happened*', US Embassy cable, 31 July 2009, WikiLeaks, https:// wikileaks.com/plusd/cables/09BEIJING2183_a.html

20 This is reflective of the uneasy balance between China's nominally independent government and the ruling Communist Party. Xi Jinping might be the president of the People's Republic of China, but his most important title is that of General Secretary of the Communist Party.

21 Holdstock, *China's Forgotten People*, p. 186.

22 Human Rights Watch, '*We Are Afraid to Even Look for Them*': *enforced disappearances in the wake of Xinjiang's protests*, New York NY: Human Rights Watch, 2009, p. 11.

23 M. Juma, S. Hoshur, Mehriban and L. Qiao, '*Urumqi tense, quiet after violence*', Radio Free Asia, 5 July 2009, https://www.rfa.org/english/news/uyghur/riots-07052009153209.html

24 E. Wong, '*Riots in western China amid ethnic tension*', *The New York Times*, 5 July 2009, https://www.nytimes.com/2009/07/06/world/asia/06china.html; Holdstock, *China's Forgotten People*, p. 187.

25 Goldberg, '*The Urumqi riots*'.

26 Human Rights Watch, '*We Are Afraid to Even Look for Them*', p. 12.

27 Goldberg, '*The Urumqi riots*'.

28 '*129 killed, 816 injured in China's Xinjiang violence*', Xinhua, 6 July 2009, https://www.chinadaily.com.cn/china/2009-07/06/content_8382866.htm

29 Zhou, Wang and Pan, '"*Unintentional scream*" triggered Xinjiang riot'.

30 '*Number of injured in Urumqi riot increases to 1,680*', Xinhua, 13 July 2009, http://en.people.cn/90001/90776/90882/6698698.html

31 Q. Xiao, '*The current situation in Urumqi*', *China Digital Times*, 7 July 2009, https://chinadigitaltimes.net/2009/07/bbs-posts-the-current-situation-in-urumqi/

32 R. Goldberg, '*140 dead in Urumqi riots, death toll may go higher, state media says order restored*', US Embassy cable, 5 July 2009, WikiLeaks, https://wikileaks.com/plusd/cables/09BEIJING1868_a.html

33 '*Official: internet cut in Xinjiang to prevent riot from spreading*', Xinhua, 7 July 2009, https://web.archive.org/web/20090710013813/http://news.xinhuanet.com/english/2009-07/07/content_11666802.htm

34 Human Rights Watch, '*We Are Afraid to Even Look for Them*', p. 12.

35 Holdstock, *China's Forgotten People*, p. 190.

36 Goldberg, '*The Urumqi riots*'.

37 D. Martin, '*Mobs vow revenge in China's Urumqi city*', *The Sydney Morning Herald*, 7 July 2009, https://www.smh.com.au/world/mobs-vow-revenge-in-chinas-urumqi-city-20090707-daoc.html

38 C. Choi, W. Clem and J. Shi, 'Fresh unrest rocks Xinjiang: police fire tear gas as thousands of Han march', *South China Morning Post*, 2009.

39 R. Harris and A. Isa, '"*Invitation to a mourning ceremony*": perspectives on the Uyghur internet', *Inner Asia* 13 (2011), p. 30.

40 M. Amir-Ebrahimi, '*Performance in everyday life and the rediscovery of the "self" in Iranian weblogs*', *Bad Jens*, 2004.

41 C. Larson, '*How China wins and loses Xinjiang*', *Foreign Policy*, 10 July 2009, http://foreignpolicy.com/2009/07/10/how-china-wins-and-loses-xinjiang/

42 Harris and Isa, '"*Invitation to a mourning ceremony*"', p. 28.

43 Anonymous poster, '*Shaoguan incident, tragedy and opportunity*', Uyghur Online, 2009, condensed and translated from Chinese.

44 Holdstock, *China's Forgotten People*, p. 121.

45 R. Kadeer, '*The real Uyghur story*', *The Wall Street Journal*, 8 July 2009, https://www.wsj.com/articles/SB124698273174806523

46 Holdstock, *China's Forgotten People*, p. 197.

47 T. Ng, 'Warning over Twitter, YouTube "subversion": hostile forces exploiting web tools, article says', South China Morning Post, 2009.

48 H. Szadziewski and G. Fay, 'Trapped in a virtual cage: Chinese state repression of Uyghurs online', Uyghur Human Rights Project, 2014, p. 2.

49 A pseudonym. Jesse still travels to Xinjiang, and for his own security and that of his family requested that he not be identified.

50 My description of the functioning of the internet is largely drawn from Res Shuler's 2002 Stanford white paper 'How does the internet work' and from TeleGeography's maps of the physical internet.

51 Submarine cable map at http://www.submarinecablemap.com/#/submarine-cable/asia-america-gateway-aag-cable-system

52 See http://visitslo.com/

53 H. Timmons, 'Ruptures call safety of internet cables into question', International Herald Tribune, 4 February 2008, https://web.archive.org/web/20080206083645/http://www.iht.com/articles/2008/02/04/technology/cables.php

54 D. Herold, Online Society in China: creating, celebrating, and instrumentalising the online carnival, London: Routledge, 2011, p. 1.

55 China Unicom network map at http://www.chinaunicom.com.sg/network-map

56 China Telecom network maps at http://web.archive.org/web/20170330101644/http://www.chinatelecom.com.hk/www/other/global and http://ipms.chinatelecomglobal.com/resources/images/continents/APAC.jpg

57 Author interviews with internet infrastructure researcher Doug Madory and academic Lokman Tsui, March 2017.

58 For example, IP addresses provided by Hong Kong Broadband begin with the numbers 59.149.207, while those beginning 202.160.0 are provided by Brunei-based ISP TelBru.

59 D. Wang, 'After July 5th, there are no netizens in Xinjiang', China Digital Times, 24 October 2009, https://chinadigitaltimes.net/2009/10/wang-dahao-%E7%8E%8B%E5%A4%A7%E8%B1%AA-after-july-5th-there-are-no-netizens-in-xinjiang/

60 D. Grammaticas, 'Trekking 1,000km in China for e-mail', BBC News, 11 February 2010, http://news.bbc.co.uk/2/hi/asia-pacific/8506601.stm

61 B. Cao, 'A year without internet in Xinjiang', Xinhua, 20 April 2014, https://web.archive.org/web/20140430043736/http://news.xinhuanet.com/english/indepth/2014-04/20/c_133276600.htm

62 Harris and Isa, '"Invitation to a mourning ceremony"', p. 29.

63 M. Abdilim, 'Uyghur webmasters sentenced', Radio Free Asia, 28 July 2010, https://www.rfa.org/english/news/uyghur/webmasters-07282010170425.html

64 Szadziewski and Fay, 'Trapped in a virtual cage', p. 78.

65 J. Garnaut, 'Obama behind release of Chinese activists', The Age, 25 August 2009, https://www.theage.com.au/world/obama-behind-release-of-chinese-activists-20090824-ewhi.html

66 I. Tohti, 'My ideals and the career path I have chosen', Uyghur Online, 2011.

Chapter 13

1   R. Deibert, *Black Code: inside the battle for cyberspace*, Toronto: McClelland & Stewart, 2013, p. 21.
2   Author interview with Greg Walton, September 2017.
3   M. Kane, '"*ILOVEYOU*" e-mail worm invades PCs', ZDNet, 4 May 2000, https://web.archive.org/web/20081227123742/http://news.zdnet.com/2100-9595_22-107318.html?legacy=zdnn
4   E. Chien, '*VBS.LoveLetter.Var*', Symantec, 5 May 2002, https://www.symantec.com/security_response/writeup.jsp?docid=2000-121815-2258-99
5   P. Hayes, 'No "sorry" from Love Bug author', *The Register*, 11 May 2005, https://www.theregister.co.uk/2005/05/11/love_bug_author/
6   'File on 4: Cyber spies', BBC Radio 4, 25 September 2011, https://www.bbc.co.uk/programmes/b014q04r
7   G. Walton et al., '*Tracking Ghostnet: investigating a cyber espionage network*', *Information Warfare Monitor*, 29 March 2009, p. 34.
8   'Threat encyclopedia: *Ghostrat*', Trend Micro, 21 September 2012, https://www.trendmicro.com/vinfo/us/threat-encyclopedia/malware/ghostrat
9   Security Ninja, '*Gh0st RAT part 2: packet structure and defense measures*', InfoSec Institute, http://resources.infosecinstitute.com/gh0st-rat-part-2-packet-structure-defense-measures/
10 Walton et al., '*Tracking Ghostnet*', pp. 40–4.
11 Walton et al., '*Tracking Ghostnet*', p. 48.
12 M. Stokes, '*The Chinese People's Liberation Army signals intelligence and cyber reconnaissance infrastructure*', Project 2049, 2011, p. 10, https://web.archive.org/web/20180209020355/http://project2049.net/documents/pla_third_department_sigint_cyber_stokes_lin_hsiao.pdf

Chapter 14

1   Associated Press, 'New US Embassy in Beijing dedicated', *Los Angeles Times*, 8 August 2008, http://articles.latimes.com/2008/aug/08/world/fg-embassy8
2   H. Stauffer, 'New Castle native Dan Piccuta's gets new appointment to second-highest diplomatic post in US embassy in China', NC News Online, 2007, http://www.ncnewsonline.com/archives/diplomat-new-castle-native-dan-piccuta-s-gets-new-appointment/article_2928cbc0-8c65-5ebd-a80b-0795ca730e22.html
3   K. Lee, *Making a World of Difference*, self-published, 2011.
4   A. Nathan and B. Gilley, *China's New Rulers: the secret files*, New York NY: New York Review of Books, 2002, p. 112.
5   D. Piccuta, 'Google China paying price for resisting censorship', US Embassy cable, 18 May 2009, WikiLeaks, https://wikileaks.com/plusd/cables/09BEIJING1336_a.html
6   S. Levy, *In the Plex: how Google thinks, works, and shapes our lives*, New York NY: Simon and Schuster, 2011, p. 306.
7   E. Chang, 'YouTube blocked in China', CNN, 26 March 2009, http://edition.cnn.com/2009/TECH/ptech/03/25/youtube.china/

8   L. Donnelly, P. Foster and A. Andrews, '*China Google boss departure reignites debate over censorship*', *The Telegraph*, 5 September 2009, http://www.telegraph.co.uk/news/worldnews/asia/china/6143553/China-Google-boss-departure-reignites-debate-over-censorship.html

9   Lee, *Making a World of Difference*.

10 '*Google claims harassment by Chinese government*', US Embassy cable, 12 July 2009, WikiLeaks, https://wikileaks.com/plusd/cables/09BEIJING1957_a.html

11 Levy, *In the Plex*, p. 309.

12 R. Westervelt, '*For Google, DNS log analysis essential in Aurora attack investigation*', Search Security, 15 June 2010, http://searchsecurity.techtarget.com/news/1514965/For-Google-DNS-log-analysis-essential-in-Aurora-attack-investigation

13 G. Curtz, '*Operation "Aurora" hit Google, others*', McAfee, 14 January 2010, https://web.archive.org/web/20120911141122/http://blogs.mcafee.com/corporate/cto/operation-aurora-hit-google-others

14 J. Markoff, '*Cyberattack on Google said to hit password system*', *The New York Times*, 19 April 2010, https://www.nytimes.com/2010/04/20/technology/20google.html

15 B. Girard, *The Google Way: how one company is revolutionizing management as we know it*, San Francisco CA: No Starch Press, 2009, p. 114.

16 Westervelt, '*For Google, DNS log analysis essential in Aurora attack investigation*'.

17 Levy, *In the Plex*, p. 267.

18 'Chinese hackers who breached Google gained access to sensitive data, U.S. officials say', *The Washington Post*, 20 May 2013 https://www.washingtonpost.com/world/national-security/chinese-hackers-who-breached-google-gained-access-to-sensitive-data-us-officials-say/2013/05/20/51330428-be34-11e2-89c9-3be8095fe767_story.html?utm_term=.bb62af33dd6a

19 J. Anderlini, '*The Chinese dissident's "unknown visitors"*', *Financial Times*, 15 January 2010, https://www.ft.com/content/c590cdd0-016a-11df-8c54-00144feabdc0; D. Sherne, '*China hacks student e-mails*', *The Stanford Daily*, 31 January 2010, https://www.stanforddaily.com/2010/01/21/china-hacks-student-e-mails/

20 Levy, *In the Plex*, p. 308.

21 A. Cha and E. Nakashima, 'Google attack part of vast campaign', *The Washington Post*, 14 January 2010, http://www.washingtonpost.com/wp-dyn/content/article/2010/01/13/AR2010011300359.html

22 B. Worthen, '*Researcher says up to 100 victims in Google attack*', *The Wall Street Journal*, 26 February 2010, https://www.wsj.com/articles/SB10001424052748704625004575090111817090670

23 G. O'Gorman and G. McDonald, *The Elderwood Project*, Mountain View CA: Symantec, 2010, http://www.symantec.com/content/en/us/enterprise/media/security_response/whitepapers/the-elderwood-project.pdf

24 J. Huntsman, '*Google update: PRC role in attacks and response strategy*', US Embassy cable, 26 January 2010, WikiLeaks, https://wikileaks.com/plusd/cables/10BEIJING207_a.html

25 M. Malseed, 'The story of Sergey Brin', Moment, February 2007, https://web. archive.org/web/20130121055147/http://www.oldsite.momentmag.net/ moment/issues/2007/02/200702-BrinFeature.html

26 S. Lohr, 'Sergey Brin on Google's China move', The New York Times, 22 March 2010,https://bits.blogs.nytimes.com/2010/03/22/interview-sergey-brin-on-googles-china-gambit/; J. Vascellaro, 'Brin drove Google to pull back in China', The Wall Street Journal, 24 March 2010, https://www.wsj.com/articles/SB100014240527 48704266504575141064259998090

27 Levy, In The Plex, p. 311.

28 Levy, In The Plex, p. 313.

29 Sinovation Ventures at http://www.sinovationventures.com/

30 'China search engine landscape 2017', Emerging Communications, 22 December 2017, http://www.emergingcomms.com/china-search-engine-landscape

31 K. Hille, 'Chinese media hit at "White House's Google"', Financial Times, 2010, https://www.ft.com/content/e6022fe0-05c6-11df-88ee-00144feabdc0

32 J. Zhang, 'Google, do not take Chinese netizens hostage', People's Daily, 19 January 2010, http://en.people.cn/90001/90780/91344/6873383.html

33 H. Clinton, 'Remarks on internet freedom', State Department, 2010.

34 J. Huntsman, 'Secretary's internet freedom speech: China reaction', US Embassy cable, 25 January 2010, WikiLeaks, https://wikileaks.com/plusd/cables/ 10BEIJING183_a.html

Chapter 15

1   Author interview with Badiucao.

2   E. Osnos, 'Boss rail', The New Yorker, 22 October 2012, https://www.newyorker. com/magazine/2012/10/22/boss-rail

3   'Chinese high speed network to double in latest master plan', Railway Gazette, 21 July 2016, http://www.railwaygazette.com/news/infrastructure/single-view/ view/chinese-high-speed-network-to-double-in-latest-master-plan.html

4   Safety Supervision Bureau, '"7·23"甬温线特别重大铁路交通事故调查报告', State Administration of Work Safety, 2011, http://www.chinasafety.gov.cn/ zjnsjg/ajes/sgxx_405/dcbg/201112/t20111228_206865.shtml

5   A. Henochowicz, 'Whether you believe it or not, I do', China Digital Times, 25 July 2012, https://chinadigitaltimes.net/2012/07/word-week-believe-it-not-i-do/

6   S. Jiang, 'Chinese netizens outraged over response to fatal bullet train crash', CNN, 26 July 2011, http://edition.cnn.com/2011/WORLD/asiapcf/07/25/china. train.accident.outrage/

7   D. Bandurski, 'History of high-speed propaganda tells all', China Media Project, 25 July 2011, http://chinamediaproject.org/2011/07/25/history-of-high-speed-propaganda-tells-all/

8   M. Wines and S. LaFraniere, 'In baring facts of train crash, blogs erode China censorship', The New York Times, 28 July 2011, https://www.nytimes. com/2011/07/29/world/asia/29china.html

9   J. DeLisle, A. Goldstein and G. Yang, *The Internet, Social Media, and a Changing China*, Philadelphia PA: University of Pennsylvania Press, 2016, p. 62.

10 Xinhua, '*New media major outlet for exposing corruption*', People's Daily, 25 June 2013, http://en.people.cn/90882/8298919.html

11 J. Van de Ven, '*Air pollution policy making and social media in Beijing 2011– 2013*', Danwei, 24 April 2014, https://web.archive.org/web/20160913184837/ http://www.danwei.com/beijing-fog-investigating-air-pollution-policy-making-in-beijing-between-2011-and-2013/

12 J. Chin, '*Chinese internet users scream for Clean Air Act*', The Wall Street Journal, 29 January 2013, https://blogs.wsj.com/chinarealtime/2013/01/29/ chinese-internet-users-scream-for-clean-air-act/

13 In 2014, one of the 'hottest terms' online according to *China Daily* was 'APEC Blue', reflecting the "longing of people for clean air instead of smog" as they experienced during the international economic meeting in Beijing that year. '*Top 10 new expressions of the year*', China Daily, 23 December 2014, https://web. archive.org/web/20150402161930/http://africa.chinadaily.com.cn/china/2014-12/23/content_19210404.htm/

14 '*Vice mayor: Lu Wei*', City of Beijing, 26 December 2012, http://www.chinadaily. com.cn/beijing/2012-12/26/content_16055912.htm

15 J. Areddy, '*The architect of China's Great Firewall caught in anti-corruption net*', The Wall Street Journal, 21 November 2017, https://www.wsj.com/articles/ lu-wei-chinas-former-internet-czar-comes-under-investigation-for-corruption-1511290607

16 Y. Su et al., '网管: 释放由堵到疏信号', People's Daily, 13 August 2013, http:// paper.people.com.cn/rmrbhwb/html/2013-08/13/content_1282485.htm

17 '*Big Vs and bottom lines*', The Economist, 31 August 2013, https://www. economist.com/china/2013/08/31/big-vs-and-bottom-lines

18 D. Barboza, '*Chinese-American commentator and investor is arrested in Beijing*', The New York Times, 25 August 2013, https://www.nytimes.com/2013/08/26/ world/asia/chinese-american-commentator-and-investor-is-arrested-in-beijing.html

19 Xinhua, '薛蛮子被刑事拘留 警方正调查其网上违法行为', Netease, 15 September 2013, http://news.163.com/13/0915/00/98P8QHIO00014JB5.html

20 C. Buckley, '*Crackdown on bloggers is mounted by China*', The New York Times, 10 September 2013, https://www.nytimes.com/2013/09/11/world/asia/ china-cracks-down-on-online-opinion-makers.html?pagewanted=1

21 Agence France-Presse, '*Top blogger Pan Shiyi appears on TV amid internet crackdown*', South China Morning Post, 11 September 2013, http://www.scmp. com/news/china/article/1308505/top-blogger-pan-shiyi-appears-tv-amid-internet-crackdown

22 Nor even was it the only service known as 'weibo'. The term, meaning microblog, was also used by Tencent Weibo, which has since slid into irrelevance. For the purposes of this book, Weibo refers to Sina Weibo.

23 Weibo Corporation, '*Form 1 registration statement*', Securities and Exchange Commission, 2014, p. 1.

24 G. Epstein, 'Sina Weibo', *Forbes*, 3 March 2011, https://www.forbes.com/global/2011/0314/features-charles-chao-twitter-fanfou-china-sina-weibo.html#7a2e72fd36d6

25 Weibo Corporation, '*Form 1 registration statement*', p. 44.

26 Weibo Corporation, '*Form 1 registration statement*', p. 138.

27 G. King, J. Pan and M. Roberts, '*How censorship in China allows government criticism but silences collective expression*', American Political Science Review, 2013.

28 P. Marolt and D. Herold, *Online Society in China: creating, celebrating and instrumentalising the online carnival*, London: Routledge, 2011, pp. 53–68.

29 J. Ng, *Blocked on Weibo*, New York NY: The New Press, 2013, p. 186.

Chapter 16

1 A. Barr, '*Email to Karen Burke*', HBGary emails, 5 February 2011, WikiLeaks, https://wikileaks.org/hbgary-emails/emailid/39192

2 '*Anonymous hacktivists say WikiLeaks war to continue*', BBC News, 9 December 2010, http://www.bbc.com/news/technology-11935539

3 N. Anderson, '*How one man tracked down Anonymous – and paid a heavy price*', Ars Technica, 10 February 2011, https://arstechnica.com/tech-policy/2011/02/how-one-security-firm-tracked-anonymousand-paid-a-heavy-price/

4 Untitled, '*Anonymous IRC chat log*', Pastebin, 7 February 2011, https://pastebin.com/x69Akp5L

5 J. Leyden, '*US gov IT services vendor swallows HBGary*', The Register, 29 February 2012, https://www.theregister.co.uk/2012/02/29/hbgary_mantech/

6 N. Anderson, '*How Anonymous accidentally helped expose two Chinese hackers*', Ars Technica, 20 February 2013, https://arstechnica.com/information-technology/2013/02/how-anonymous-accidentally-helped-expose-two-chinese-hackers/

7 Rootkit.com archive at https://web.archive.org/web/20110113042750/http://www.rootkit.com/

8 Department of Justice, '*US charges five Chinese military hackers for cyber espionage against US corporations and a labor organization for commercial advantage*', US Department of Justice, 19 May 2014, https://www.justice.gov/usao-wdpa/pr/us-charges-five-chinese-military-hackers-cyber-espionage-against-us-corporations-and; D. Sanger et al., '*Chinese army unit is seen as tied to hacking against US*, The New York Times, 18 February 2013, http://www.nytimes.com/2013/02/19/technology/chinas-army-is-seen-as-tied-to-hacking-against-us.html; M. Clayton, 'Stealing US business secrets: experts ID two huge cyber "gangs" in China', The Christian Science Monitor, 14 September 2012, https://www.csmonitor.com/USA/2012/0914/Stealing-US-business-secrets-Experts-ID-two-huge-cyber-gangs-in-China

9 J. Markoff, '*SecurID company suffers a breach of data security*', The New York Times, 17 March 2011, https://www.nytimes.com/2011/03/18/technology/18secure.html

10 Mandiant, *APT1: exposing one of China's cyber espionage units*, Milpitas CA: Mandiant, 2013, p. 52.

11 Mandiant, *APT1*, p. 55.

12 Department of Justice, '*US charges five Chinese military hackers*'.

13 B. Koerner, '*Inside the cyberattack that shocked the US government*', Wired, 23 October 2016, https://www.wired.com/2016/10/inside-cyberattack-shocked-us-government/

14 E. Perez and S. Prokupecz, '*US data hack may be 4 times larger than the government originally said*', CNN, 24 June 2015, http://edition.cnn.com/2015/06/22/politics/opm-hack-18-milliion/index.html

15 *The OPM Data Breach: how the government jeopardised our national security for more than a generation*, Congressional Report, Washington DC: Committee on Oversight and Government Reform, 2016.

16 K. Liptak et al., '*China might be building vast database of federal worker info, experts say*', CNN, 6 June 2015, http://edition.cnn.com/2015/06/04/politics/federal-agency-hacked-personnel-management/

17 E. Perez, 'FBI arrests Chinese national connected to malware used in OPM data breach', CNN, 24 August 2017, http://edition.cnn.com/2017/08/24/politics/fbi-arrests-chinese-national-in-opm-data-breach/index.html

18 'President Xi Jinping's state visit to the United States', Office of the Press Secretary, White House, 25 September 2015, https://obamawhitehouse.archives.gov/the-press-office/2015/09/25/fact-sheet-president-xi-jinpings-state-visit-united-states

19 S. Harold, '*The US–China cyber agreement: a good first step*', Rand Corporation, 1 August 2016, https://www.rand.org/blog/2016/08/the-us-china-cyber-agreement-a-good-first-step.html

20 FireEye, *Red Line Drawn: Chinese recalculates its use of cyberespionage*, Milpitas CA: FireEye, 2016, https://www.fireeye.com/content/dam/fireeye-www/current-threats/pdfs/rpt-china-espionage.pdf

21 S. Kravchenko, '*Russia more prey than predator to cyber firm wary of China*', Bloomberg, 25 August 2016, https://www.bloomberg.com/news/articles/2016-08-25/russia-more-prey-than-predator-to-cyber-firm-wary-of-china

Part 4
Chapter 17

1 My account of Ilham and Jewher's attempted flight from China is based on interviews with Jewher, and the account she gives in her book *Jewher Ilham: a Uyghur's fight to free her father*.

2 T. Chen, '*China convicts almost everyone it accuses; one group is fighting back*', *The Wall Street Journal*, 1 July 2016, https://www.wsj.com/articles/the-fight-to-free-the-innocent-from-chinas-99-9-conviction-rate-1467384598

3 E. Wong, 'China sentences Uighur scholar to life', *The New York Times*, 23 September 2014, https://www.nytimes.com/2014/09/24/world/asia/china-court-sentences-uighur-scholar-to-life-in-separatism-case.html

4   J. Griffiths, 'Al-Qaeda magazine calls for Xinjiang to be "recovered by the Islamic Caliphate"', *South China Morning Post*, 21 October 2014, http://www.scmp.com/news/china/article/1621190/new-al-qaeda-magazine-calls-xinjiang-be-recovered-islamic-caliphate; S. Osborne, 'Isis threatens China and vows to "shed blood like rivers"', *The Independent*, 1 March 2017, https://www.independent.co.uk/news/world/middle-east/isis-china-threaten-terror-attack-muslim-islamist-group-islamic-state-a7606211.html

5   *'China "expels" French journalist over Uighur article'*, BBC News, 26 December 2015, http://www.bbc.com/news/world-asia-china-35181299

6   J. Jacobs, *Xinjiang and the Modern Chinese State*, Seattle WA: University of Washington Press, 2016, p. 3.

7   M. Rajagopalan, *'This is what a 21st-century police state really looks like'*, BuzzFeed, 17 October 2017, https://www.buzzfeed.com/meghara/the-police-state-of-the-future-is-already-here?utm_term=.jiJKNDzG2#.mnPM42wem

8   T. Phillips, 'China testing facial-recognition surveillance system in Xinjiang – report, *The Guardian*, 18 January 2018, https://www.theguardian.com/world/2018/jan/18/china-testing-facial-recognition-surveillance-system-in-xinjiang-report

9   S. Pham, 'Chinese AI startup dwarfs global rivals with $4.5 billion valuation', CNNMoney, 9 April 2018, http://money.cnn.com/2018/04/09/technology/china-ai-sensetime-startup/index.html

10 C. Beam, 'Behind China's cyber curtain', *The New Republic*, 6 December 2013, https://newrepublic.com/article/115709/chinas-aba-county-where-government-shut-internet

11 *'China police block access to protest village'*, The Telegraph, 12 December 2011, https://www.telegraph.co.uk/news/worldnews/asia/china/8951275/China-police-block-access-to-protest-village.html

Chapter 18

1   J. Palmer, *'China's generation gap has never yawned wider'*, Aeon, 7 March 2013, https://aeon.co/essays/china-s-generation-gap-has-never-yawned-wider

2   M. Xuecun, *'Let them eat grass'*, Foreign Policy, 2 January 2013, http://foreignpolicy.com/2013/01/02/let-them-eat-grass/

3   转世党, or zhuǎnshì dǎng.

4   K. Kuang, *'How China has censored words relating to the Tiananmen Square anniversary'*, PRI, 4 June 2016, https://www.pri.org/stories/2016-06-03/how-china-has-censored-words-relating-tiananmen-square-anniversary

5   S. Robinson, *'Filtering inappropriate content with the Cloud Vision API'*, Google Cloud Big Data and Machine Learning blog, 17 August 2016, https://cloud.google.com/blog/big-data/2016/08/filtering-inappropriate-content-with-the-cloud-vision-api

6   D. Burke, *'Why images of Mohammed offend Muslims'*, CNN, 4 May 2015, https://edition.cnn.com/2015/05/04/living/islam-prophet-images/

7   *'Syria unrest: famed cartoonist Ali Ferzat "beaten"'*, BBC News, 25 August 2011, http://www.bbc.com/news/world-middle-east-14665113

8   H. Blackstone, 'Thrown in prison for drawing cartoons', The Independent, 27 October 2015, https://www.independent.co.uk/voices/campaigns/voicesin danger/thrown-in-prison-for-drawing-cartoons-a6709841.html

9   S. Crispin, 'Drawing the line: cartoonists under threat', Committee to Protect Journalists, 19 May 2015, https://cpj.org/reports/2015/05/drawing-the-line-cartoonists-under-threat-free-expression-zunar-charlie-hebdo.php

10 Author interview with Rebel Pepper, April 2017.

11 I. Fish, 'Rebel without a country', Foreign Policy, 31 August 2015, http://foreignpolicy.com/2015/08/31/chinas-most-infamous-political-cartoonist-dissident-tokyo-japan-exile-rebel-pepper/

12 'China's rebel cartoonist', The Wall Street Journal, 17 May 2015, https://www.wsj.com/articles/chinas-rebel-cartoonist-1431901472

13 A. Henochowicz, 'Still in Japan, cartoonist Rebel Pepper seeks help', China Digital Times, 12 May 2015, https://chinadigitaltimes.net/2015/05/still-in-japan-cartoonist-rebel-pepper-seeks-help/

14 S. Jiang, 'Released Chinese feminists: out of jail but not free', CNN, 14 April 2015, https://edition.cnn.com/2015/04/14/asia/china-feminists-release-jiang/

15 Z. Huang, 'Chinese trolls jumped the Firewall to attack Taiwan's president and military on Facebook', Quartz, 3 January 2017, https://qz.com/876614/chinese-trolls-jumped-the-firewall-to-attack-taiwans-military-and-president-tsai-ing-wen-on-facebook/

16 R. Han, 'The "voluntary fifty-cent army" in Chinese cyberspace', China Policy Institute, 29 February 2016, http://blogs.nottingham.ac.uk/chinapolicy institute/2016/02/29/the-voluntary-fifty-cent-army-in-chinese-cyberspace/

17 D. Bandurski, 'China's guerrilla war for the web', Far Eastern Economic Review, 2008.

18 G. King et al., 'How the Chinese government fabricates social media posts for strategic distraction, not engaged argument', American Political Science Review 111, no. 3 (2017), pp. 484–501, http://gking.harvard.edu/files/gking/files/50c.pdf?m=1463683069

19 W. Ai, 'China's paid trolls: meet the 50 Cent party', New Statesman, 17 October 2012, https://www.newstatesman.com/politics/politics/2012/10/china%E2%80%99s-paid-trolls-meet-50-cent-party

20 D. Bandurski, 'Ai Weiwei chat with opinion manipulator surfaces', China Media Project, 9 May 2011, http://chinamediaproject.org/2011/05/09/ai-weiwei-chat-with-opinion-manipulator-surfaces/

21 L. Tao, 'China's Weibo leverages star power to profit from huge youth following as oldies lose interest', South China Morning Post, 9 October 2017, http://www.scmp.com/tech/china-tech/article/2114545/chinas-weibo-leverages-star-power-profit-huge-youth-following-oldies

22 C. Chen and I. Deng 'Weibo, Tencent volunteer to clean up content as China intensifies crackdown', South China Morning Post, 12 April 2018, http://www.scmp.com/tech/china-tech/article/2141375/chinese-social-media-platforms-volunteer-clean-content-crackdown

Chapter 19

1   Author interview with Kenneth Lo, September 2017.

2   B. Leiner, V. Cerf, D. Clark, R. Kahn, L. Kleinrock, D. Lynch, J. Postel, L. Roberts and S. Wolff, *'Brief history of the internet'*, Internet Society, 1997, https://www.internetsociety.org/internet/history-internet/brief-history-internet/

3   J. Klensin, 'Role of the domain name system (DNS)', Request for Comments: 3467, February 2003, https://tools.ietf.org/html/rfc3467

4   J. Postel, 'IAB official protocol standards', Request for Comments: 1083, December 1988, https://tools.ietf.org/html/rfc1083; J. Snyder, K. Komaitis and A. Robachevsky, *'The IANA timeline: an extended timeline with citations and commentary'*, The Internet Society, 9 May 2016, https://www.internetsociety.org/ianatimeline/

5   J. Goldsmith and T. Wu, *Who Controls the Internet?: illusions of a borderless world*, Oxford and New York NY: Oxford University Press, 2006, p. 168.

6   Goldsmith and Wu, *Who Controls the Internet?*, pp. 34–5.

7   Snyder et al., *'The IANA timeline'*.

8   D. Sparks, 'Network solutions: by any other name, a monopoly.com', Bloomberg, 19 April 1999, https://www.bloomberg.com/news/articles/1999-04-18/commentary-network-solutions-by-any-other-name-a-monopoly-dot-com

9   *'Network Solutions flourishes'*, Wired, 10 February 1999, https://www.wired.com/1999/02/network-solutions-flourishes/; M. Mueller, M. (2009) *Ruling the Root: internet governance and the taming of cyberspace*, Cambridge MA: MIT Press, 2009, pp. 151–2.

10 Goldsmith and Wu, *Who Controls the Internet?*, p. 36.

11 Historical weather data from Weather Underground.

12 Goldsmith and Wu, *Who Controls the Internet?*, p. 29; V. Cerf, *'I remember IANA'*, Request for Comments: 2468, October 1998, https://tools.ietf.org/html/rfc2468

13 R. Chandrasekaran, 'Internet reconfiguration concerns federal officials', *The Washington Post*, 31 January 1998, https://www.washingtonpost.com/archive/business/1998/01/31/internet-reconfiguration-concerns-federal-officials/c98b71a0-8e4a-4aab-96f6-1868c81fe60c/; Mueller, *Ruling the Root*, p. 162.

14 Goldsmith and Wu, *Who Controls the Internet?*, p. 30.

15 W. Kleinwächter, 'De-mystification of the internet root: do we need governmental oversight?' in *Reforming Internet Governance: perspectives from the Working Group on Internet Governance*, New York NY: United Nations Publications, 2005, p. 214.

16 Goldsmith and Wu, *Who Controls the Internet?*, p. 46.

17 D. Dougherty and M. Roberts, *'USC/ICANN transition agreement'*, Internet Corporation for Assigned Names and Numbers, 2012, https://www.icann.org/resources/unthemed-pages/usc-icann-transition-2012-02-25-en

18 Kleinwächter, 'De-mystification of the internet root', p. 215.

19 Goldsmith and Wu, *Who Controls the Internet?*, p. 168.

20 J. Lytle, 'Jon Postel, internet pioneer, dies at 55', USC News, 26 October 1998, https://news.usc.edu/9865/Jon-Postel-Internet-Pioneer-Dies-at-55/

21 Goldsmith and Wu, *Who Controls the Internet?*, p. 169.

22 Snyder et al., '*The IANA timeline*'.

23 'Why a summit on the information society', World Summit on the Information Society, 2005, https://www.itu.int/net/wsis/basic/why.html

24 Kleinwächter, 'De-mystification of the internet root', p. 215.

25 'US principles on the internet's domain name and addressing system', *National Telecommunications and Information Administration,* United States Department of Commerce, 30 June 2005, https://www.ntia.doc.gov/other-publication/2005/us-principles-internets-domain-name-and-addressing-system

26 United States Attorney Northern District of Texas, '*Infocom corporation and its operators sentenced in federal court*', US Department of Justice, 13 October 2006, https://www.justice.gov/archive/usao/txn/PressRel06/elashi_bayan_ghassan_basman_infocom_sent_pr.html

27 '*Request of NCMC for redelegation of .IQ top-level domain*', IANA Report, July 2005, https://www.iana.org/reports/2005/iq-report-05aug2005.pdf

28 T. Wright, 'EU tries to unblock internet impasse', *International Herald Tribune,* 30 September 2005, https://archive.nytimes.com/www.nytimes.com/iht/2005/09/30/business/IHT-30net.html

29 C. Bildt, '*European Union, Iran, Saudi Arabia, Cuba*', Bildt Comments, 3 October 2005, https://bildt.blogspot.hk/2005/10/european-union-iran-saudi-arabia-cuba.html

30 Kleinwächter, 'De-mystification of the internet root', p. 221.

31 Goldsmith and Wu, *Who Controls the Internet?*, p. 171.

32 Neither organisation quite lives up to its stereotype. Governments have a huge amount of power and influence at ICANN, while the ITU has always included some input from civil society, and has made efforts to increase this in recent years.

33 '*Discover ITU's history*', International Telecommunication Union, 2018, https://www.itu.int/en/history/Pages/DiscoverITUsHistory.aspx

34 J. Goldsmith, 'WCIT-12: an opinionated primer and hysteria-debunker', LawFare, 30 November 2012, https://www.lawfareblog.com/wcit-12-opinionated-primer-and-hysteria-debunker

Chapter 20

1 V. Cerf, 'Keep the internet open', *The New York Times*, 24 May 2012, https://www.nytimes.com/2012/05/25/opinion/keep-the-internet-open.html

2 '*Prime Minister Vladimir Putin meets with secretary general of the International Telecommunication Union Hamadoun Toure*', Russian Government Archive, 2012, http://archive.government.ru/eng/docs/15601/print/

3 A. Soldatov and I. Borogan, *The Red Web: the struggle between Russia's digital dictators and the new online revolutionaries*, New York NY: PublicAffairs, 2015, p. 231.

4 T. Kramer, '*Development and progress of the World Conference on International Telecommunications currently being held in Dubai, United Arab Emirates until*

December 14, 2012', US Department of State, 6 December 2012, https://web. archive.org/web/20121208055049/https://www.state.gov/e/eb/rls/ rm/2012/201637.htm

5 Author interview with Eli Dourado, August 2017.

6 E. Dourado, 'Behind closed doors at the UN's attempted "takeover of the internet"', *Ars Technica*, 20 December 2012, https://arstechnica.com/tech-policy/2012/12/behind-closed-doors-at-the-uns-attempted-takeover-of-the-internet/

7 Russia, UAE, China, Saudi Arabia, Algeria, Sudan and Egypt, *'Proposals for the work of the conference'*, WCITLeaks, 5 December 2012, http://files.wcitleaks. org/public/Merged%20UAE%20081212.pdf

8 K. McCarthy, *'Leaked document confirms fears of UN Internet powergrab'*, .nxt, 8 December 2012, https://web.archive.org/web/20130218124106/http:// news.dot-nxt.com/2012/12/14/leaked-document-confirms-fears

9 E. Dourado, 'Behind closed doors at the UN's attempted "takeover of the internet"'.

10 D. Burstein and G. Lynch, 'WCIT bombshell: Russia withdraws internet regulation push, apparently under ITU pressure', Commsday, 10 December 2012, https://web.archive.org/web/20170519042116/https://www.commsday. com/russia-combines-with-china-arab-states-on-dramatic-internet-regulatory-push/

11 M. Smith and J. Menn, 'Opposing camps dig in on internet treaty talks', Reuters, 13 December 2012, https://www.reuters.com/article/us-telecom-treaty-itu/ opposing-camps-dig-in-on-internet-treaty-talks-idUSBRE8BB1KS20121213

12 Plenary 14, *'Finished transcript'*, WCIT, 2012.

13 R. Pepper and C. Sharp, 'Summary report of the ITU-T World Conference on International Telecommunications', *Internet Protocol Journal* 16, no. 1 (2013), https://www.cisco.com/c/en/us/about/press/internet-protocol-journal/back-issues/table-contents-59/161-wcit.html; K. Salaets, 'A blow to internet freedom', Information Technology Industry Council, 2012, https://web.archive.org/ web/20170805165237/https://www.itic.org/news-events/techwonk-blog/a-blow-to-internet-freedom

14 G. Guillemin, 'WCIT: what happened and what it means for the internet', European Digital Rights, 2012, https://edri.org/edrigramnumber10-24wcit-what-happend/

15 D. Shambaugh, *China Goes Global: the partial power*, New York NY: Oxford University Press, 2013, p. 137.

16 Human Rights Watch, *The Costs of International Advocacy: China's interference in United Nations human rights mechanisms*, Washington DC: Human Rights Watch, 2017, https://www.hrw.org/report/2017/09/05/costs-international-advocacy/chinas-interference-united-nations-human-rights

17 *'W3C invites Chinese web developers, industry, academia to assume greater role in global web innovation'*, W3C, 20 January 2013, https://www.w3.org/2013/01/ china-host.html.en

18 Internet Society, '*Successful IETF meeting reflects growing contribution of Chinese engineering*', *Internet Society Newsletter* 9, no. 11 (2010), https://web.archive.org/web/20120924171300/http://www.internetsociety.org/articles/successful-ietf-meeting-reflects-growing-contribution-chinese-engineering

19 '*ICANN Engagement Center to open in Beijing*', ICANN, 8 April 2013, https://www.icann.org/en/system/files/press-materials/release-08apr13-en.pdf

20 '*ICANN hires domain name policy expert to head engagement in China*', ICANN, 30 March 2017, https://www.icann.org/resources/press-material/release-2017-03-30-en

21 J. Hu and O. Lam, '*In quest for "ideological security", China pushes to extend Communist Party influence inside tech firms*', Global Voices, 6 September 2017, https://globalvoices.org/2017/09/06/in-quest-for-ideological-security-china-pushes-to-extend-communist-party-influence-inside-tech-firms/

22 Y. Sheng, '*Internet industry a "new ideological battleground": expert*', *Global Times*, 28 October 2016, http://www.globaltimes.cn/content/1014448.shtml

23 Author interview with Peter Micek, July 2017.

24 S. Kalathil, *Beyond the Great Firewall: how China became a global information power*, Washington DC: Center for International Media Assistance, 2017, p. 22, https://www.cima.ned.org/wp-content/uploads/2017/03/CIMA-Beyond-the-Great-Firewall_150ppi-for-web.pdf

25 Xinhua, '*China's Zhao Houlin elected as secretary-general of ITU*', *China Daily*, 23 October 2014, http://www.chinadaily.com.cn/world/2014-10/23/content_18790932.htm

26 H. Touré, '*Candidacy for the post of secretary-general*', International Telecommunications Union, 4 November 2013, http://files.wcitleaks.org/public/S14-PP-C-0010!!MSW-E.pdf

27 S. Oster, '*Whose internet is it anyway? China wields more influence*', Bloomberg, 21 November 2014, https://www.bloomberg.com/news/articles/2014-11-21/whose-internet-is-it-anyway-china-wields-more-influence

28 'Interview with Houlin Zhao, ITU secretary-general elect', International Telecommunications Union, 2014, https://www.itu.int/en/plenipotentiary/2014/Pages/zhao-interview.aspx

29 Y. Kang, 'Internet censorship matter of interpretation: Zhao', Yonhap, 23 October 2014, http://english.yonhapnews.co.kr/full/2014/10/23/50/1200000000AEN20141023005000320F.html

30 A. Soldatov and I. Borogan, *The Red Web: the struggle between Russia's digital dictators and the new online revolutionaries*, New York NY: PublicAffairs, 2015, p. 235.

31 W. Lu, 'Cyber sovereignty must rule global internet', WorldPost, 15 December 2014, https://www.huffingtonpost.com/lu-wei/china-cyber-sovereignty_b_6324060.html

32 '*Position paper of China on the overall review of the implementation of the outcomes of the World Summit on the Information Society (WSIS)*', Permanent

Mission of the People's Republic of China to the UN, 12 August 2015, http://www.china-un.org/eng/gdxw/t1288450.htm

33 D. Levin, '*At UN, China tries to influence fight over internet control*', *The New York Times*, 16 December 2015, https://www.nytimes.com/2015/12/17/technology/china-wins-battle-with-un-over-word-in-internet-control-document.html

34 S. Tian, 'Xi urges internet expansion, int'l cooperation, "order"', Xinhua, 16 December 2015, http://www.xinhuanet.com/english/2015-12/16/c_134923095.htm

Chapter 21

1 '*President Xi Jinping delivers a keynote speech at 2015 World Internet Conference,* [video], CGTN, 15 December 2015, https://www.youtube.com/watch?v=GNR3MV9C2-Q

2 G. Barmé, 'Introduction: under one heaven', The China Story, 2015, https://www.thechinastory.org/yearbooks/yearbook-2014/introduction-under-one-heaven/

3 N. Kristof, 'Looking for a jump-start in China', *The New York Times*, 5 January 2013, https://www.nytimes.com/2013/01/06/opinion/sunday/kristof-looking-for-a-jump-start-in-china.html

4 C. Buckley, '*Xi Jinping assuming new status as China's "core" leader*', *The New York Times*, 4 February 2016, https://www.nytimes.com/2016/02/05/world/asia/china-president-xi-jinping-core.html

5 '*Wuzhen*', World Internet Conference, 8 November 2017, http://www.wuzhenwic.org/2017-11/08/c_46138.htm

6 P. Carsten, '*At China online coming-out party, Beijing spells out internet control ambition*', Reuters, 25 November 2014, https://www.reuters.com/article/china-internet-wuzhen/at-china-online-coming-out-party-beijing-spells-out-internet-control-ambition-idUSL3N0TE02V20141125

7 朝阳群众, 'BBC ｜ 世界互联网大会开幕 习近平谈网络秩序', *China Digital Times*, 19 November 2014, https://chinadigitaltimes.net/chinese/2014/11/bbc-%E4%B8%96%E7%95%8C%E4%BA%92%E8%81%94%E7%BD%91%E5%A4%A7%E4%BC%9A%E5%BC%80%E5%B9%95-%E4%B9%A0%E8%BF%91%E5%B9%B3%E8%B0%88%E7%BD%91%E7%BB%9C%E7%A7%A9%E5%BA%8F/

8 C. Shu, 'China tried to get world internet conference attendees to endorse this ridiculous draft declaration', TechCrunch, 21 November 2014, https://techcrunch.com/2014/11/20/worldinternetconference-declaration/

9 'The internet in China: *protecting internet security*', Information Office of the State Council of the People's Republic of China, 2010, http://www.china.org.cn/government/whitepaper/2010-06/08/content_20207978.htm

10 E. Osnos, 'Can China maintain sovereignty over the internet?', *The New Yorker*, 10 June 2010, https://www.newyorker.com/news/evan-osnos/can-china-maintain-sovereignty-over-the-internet

11 Z. Ye, '对网络主权的思考', 人民网, 20 July 2015, http://theory.people.com.
cn/n/2015/0720/c386965-27332547.html

12 D. Bandurski, '*Thoughts on "internet sovereignty"*', China Media Project, 2
October 2015, https://medium.com/@cmphku/thoughts-on-internet-sovereignty-
ae18a125b89e

13 D. Bandurski, '*Two share a boat*', China Media Project, 29 September 2015,
https://medium.com/@cmphku/two-share-a-boat-a5a22b60744

14 D. Bandurski, '*Lu Wei on the "dream of the web"*', China Media Project, 17
February 2015, http://chinamediaproject.org/2015/02/17/lu-wei-on-the-dream-
of-the-web/

15 J. Goldsmith and T. Wu, *Who Controls the Internet?: illusions of a borderless
world*, Oxford University Press, 2006, p. 6.

16 A. Higgins and A. Azhar, '*China begins to erect second Great Wall in cyberspace*',
The Guardian, 5 February 1996.

17 Goldsmith and Wu, *Who Controls the Internet?*, pp. 13–14.

18 J. Jarnow, *Heads: a biography of psychedelic America*, Cambridge MA: Da
Capo Press, 2016.

19 K. Drum, '*A profile of Dick Cheney*', *Washington Monthly*, 9 November 2003,
https://washingtonmonthly.com/2003/11/09/a-profile-of-dick-cheney/

20 J. Barlow, '*Lyrics by John Perry Barlow*', Electronic Frontier Foundation, 1990,
https://web.archive.org/web/20180208000604/https://w2.eff.org/Misc/
Publications/John_Perry_Barlow/HTML/barlows_lyrics.html

21 Goldsmith and Wu, *Who Controls the Internet?*, p. 17.

22 J. Barlow, '*The economy of ideas*', *Wired*, 1 March 1994, https://www.wired.
com/1994/03/economy-ideas/

23 J. Barlow, 'Decrypting the puzzle palace', *Communications of the ACM*, July
1992, http://groups.csail.mit.edu/mac/classes/6.805/articles/digital-telephony/
Barlow_decrypting_puzzle_palace.html

24 Goldsmith and Wu, *Who Controls the Internet?*, p. 18.

25 '*A history of protecting freedom where law and technology collide*', Electronic
Frontier Foundation, https://www.eff.org/about/history

26 J. Barlow, '*A declaration of the independence of cyberspace*', Electronic Frontier
Foundation, 8 February 1996, https://www.eff.org/cyberspace-independence

27 *Reno v. ACLU* [1997] 96-511 (Supreme Court of the United States), https://
caselaw.findlaw.com/us-supreme-court/521/844.html

28 EFFector, '*Ten years after ACLU v. Reno: free speech still needs defending:
action alert*', Electronic Frontier Foundation, 25 June 2007, https://www.eff.org/
effector/20/25

29 A. Greenberg, '*It's been 20 years since this man declared cyberspace
independence*', *Wired*, 8 February 2016, https://www.wired.com/2016/02/
its-been-20-years-since-this-man-declared-cyberspace-independence/

30 Donald Trump, in typically iconoclastic fashion, is the first US leader in decades
to be openly sceptical of the internet, suggesting it be 'closed up' in some way to
prevent terrorist attacks. D. Goldman, '*Donald Trump wants to "close up" the*

internet', CNN, 8 December 2015, http://money.cnn.com/2015/12/08/
technology/donald-trump-internet/index.html

31 L. Hornby, *'China paper slams US for cyber role in Iran unrest'*, Reuters, 24
January 2010, https://www.reuters.com/article/china-us-internet/rpt-china-
paper-slams-us-for-cyber-role-in-iran-unrest-idUSTOE60N00T20100124

Chapter 22

1 *'Executive order on measures to make state media more effective'*, Kremlin.ru, 9
December 2013, http://en.kremlin.ru/events/president/news/19805

2 S. Ennis, *'Dmitry Kiselyov: Russia's chief spin doctor'*, BBC News, 2 April 2014,
http://www.bbc.com/news/world-europe-26839216

3 *'About the forum'*, Safe Internet Forum, 2016, https://web.archive.org/
web/20170302174356/http://safeinternetforum.ru/en/o-forume/

4 C. Weaver, *'Malofeev: the Russian billionaire linking Moscow to the rebels'*,
Financial Times, 24 July 2014, https://www.ft.com/content/84481538-1103-
11e4-94f3-00144feabdc0

5 G. Ellis and V. Kolchyna, *'Putin and the "triumph of Christianity" in Russia'*, Al
Jazeera, 19 October 2017, https://www.aljazeera.com/blogs/europe/2017/10/
putin-triumph-christianity-russia-171018073916624.html

6 J. Keating, *'God's oligarch'*, Slate, 20 October 2014, http://www.slate.com/
articles/news_and_politics/foreigners/2014/10/konstantin_malofeev_
one_of_vladimir_putin_s_favorite_businessmen_wants_to.html

7 S. Walker, *'"Russia's soul is monarchic": tsarist school wants to reverse 100
years of history'*, *The Guardian*, 6 March 2017, https://www.theguardian.com/
world/2017/mar/06/russia-revolution-tsarist-school-moscow-nicholas-ii

8 Keating, *'God's oligarch'*.

9 M. Seddon, *'Russia's chief internet censor enlists China's know-how'*, *Financial
Times*, 27 April 2016, https://www.ft.com/content/08564d74-0bbf-11e6-9456-
444ab5211a2f

10 *'China's cyberspace administration head Lu Wei to participate in 7th
International Safer Internet Forum'*, Safe Internet Forum, 2016, https://web.
archive.org/web/20170302183945/http://safeinternetforum.ru/en/novosti/
china-s-cyberspace-administration-head-lu-wei-to-participate-in-7th-
international-safer-internet-for.html

11 *'Moscow Safer Internet Forum adopts Russia–China cybersecurity cooperation
roadmap'*, Safe Internet Forum, 2016, https://web.archive.org/web/
20180219224139/http://safeinternetforum.ru/en/novosti/moscow-safer-
internet-forum-adopts-russia-china-cybersecurity-cooperation-roadmap.html

12 A. Soldatov, 'Once a defender of internet freedom, Putin is now bringing China's
Great Firewall to Russia', WorldPost, 3 May 2016, https://www.huffingtonpost.
com/andrei-soldatov/putin-china-internet-firewall-russia_b_9821190.html

13 Seddon, *'Russia's chief internet censor enlists China's know-how'*.

14 'Китайский Интернет опережает мировые разработки', Safe Internet
League, 2016, http://ligainternet.ru/news/news-detail.php?ID=505

15 T. Glelten, *'Seeing the internet as an "information weapon"'*, NPR, 23 September 2010, https://www.npr.org/templates/story/story.php?storyId=130052701

16 L. Harding, *'Revealed: the $2bn offshore trail that leads to Vladimir Putin'*, *The Guardian*, 3 April 2016, https://www.theguardian.com/news/2016/apr/03/panama-papers-money-hidden-offshore

17 T. Parfitt, *'Putin ally calls for China-style censorship'*, *The Sunday Times*, 20 April 2016, https://www.thetimes.co.uk/article/putin-ally-calls-for-china-style-censorship-0x69klqqs

18 *'Russia in talks with China's Huawei on data storage technologies' licensing'*, Sputnik, 24 August 2016, https://sputniknews.com/science/20160824104 4578435-russia-huawei-bulat-data/

19 A. Soldatov and I. Borogan, *'Putin brings China's Great Firewall to Russia in cybersecurity pact'*, *The Guardian*, 29 November 2016, https://www.theguardian.com/world/2016/nov/29/putin-china-internet-great-firewall-russia-cybersecurity-pact

20 A. Luhn, *'Russia passes "Big Brother" anti-terror laws'*, *The Guardian*, 26 June 2016,https://www.theguardian.com/world/2016/jun/26/russia-passes-big-brother-anti-terror-laws

21 *'Russia mulls limitations on internet exchange points over fears of US eavesdropping*, RT, 23 August 2017, https://www.rt.com/politics/400627-russia-mulls-limitations-on-internet/

22 My account of the August coup is largely drawn from *Lenin's Tomb* by David Remnick, *The Man Without a Face* by Masha Gessen, and *The Red Web* by Andrei Soldatov and Irina Borogan, as well as other sources listed in the notes.

23 A. Soldatov and I. Borogan, *The Red Web: the struggle between Russia's digital dictators and the new online revolutionaries*, New York NY: PublicAffairs, 2015, p. 27.

24 M. Gorham et al., *Digital Russia: the language, culture and politics of new media communication*, Abingdon: Routledge, 2014, p. 39.

25 Soldatov and Borogan, *The Red Web*, p. 27.

26 Soldatov and Borogan, *The Red Web*, p. 30; *'History of Relcom'*, Relcom, http://www.relcom.ru/o-nas/history-of-company/

27 Gorham et al., *Digital Russia*, p. 38.

28 Soldatov and Borogan, *The Red Web*, p. 31.

29 L. Press, *'Relcom during the coup'*, *Personal Computing*, 1991, http://som.csudh.edu/fac/lpress/articles/relcom.pdf

30 M. Gessen, *The Man Without a Face: the unlikely rise of Vladimir Putin*, New York NY: Riverhead Books, 2012, p. 110.

31 Soldatov and Borogan, *The Red Web*, p. 34.

32 A. Soldatov and I. Borogan, *'An act of courage on the Soviet internet'*, Slate, 19 August 2016, http://www.slate.com/articles/technology/future_tense/2016/08/the_1991_soviet_internet_helped_stop_a_coup_and_spread_a_message_of_freedom.html

33 Interview with Vadim Antonov on PSB's 'The internet show' [video], 1995, https://www.youtube.com/watch?v=IzqMrhG50q0

34 Soldatov and Borogan, p. 36.

35 V. Sebestyen, 'The KGB's bathhouse plot', *The New York Times*, 20 August 2011,http://www.nytimes.com/2011/08/21/opinion/sunday/the-soviet-coup-that-failed.html

36 Soldatov and Borogan, *The Red Web*, pp. 47–9.

37 A. Nossik, '*Russia's first blogger reacts to Putin's internet crackdown*', *The New Republic*, 15 May 2014, https://newrepublic.com/article/117771/putins-internet-crackdown-russias-first-blogger-reacts

38 M. Lakhman, '*Mother Russia does a slow dance with the net*', *The New York Times*, 7 October 1997, http://partners.nytimes.com/library/cyber/euro/100797 euro.html

39 Soldatov and Borogan, p. 52.

40 Soldatov and Borogan, pp. 65–6.

41 Soldatov and Borogan, p. 89.

Chapter 23

1 'Pavel Durov in conversation with Jimmy Wales' [video], DLD12, 24 January 2012, https://www.youtube.com/watch?v=hEHd4HbOLYM

2 R. Hutt, 'The world's most popular social networks, mapped', World Economic Forum, 20 March 2017, https://www.weforum.org/agenda/2017/03/most-popular-social-networks-mapped/

3 E. Avriel, 'The richest Israelis got NIS 10 billion richer in 2013', *Haaretz*, 5 June 2013, https://www.haaretz.com/israel-news/business/.premium-israel-s-super-rich-really-are-different-1.5273638

4 C. Abram, 'Welcome to Facebook, everyone', Facebook, 26 September 2006, https://www.facebook.com/notes/facebook/welcome-to-facebook-everyone/2210227130/

5 J. Yaffa, '*Is Pavel Durov, Russia's Zuckerberg, a Kremlin target?*', Bloomberg, 7 August 2013, https://www.bloomberg.com/news/articles/2013-08-01/is-pavel-durov-russias-zuckerberg-a-kremlin-target

6 R. Synowitz, 'VKontakte by the numbers', Radio Free Europe/Radio Liberty, 24 April 2014, https://www.rferl.org/a/vkontakte-by-the-numbers/25361419.html

7 K. Cutler, 'VKontakte's Pavel Durov explains bizarre money-throwing incident', TechCrunch, 28 October 2013, https://techcrunch.com/2013/10/28/vkontaktes-pavel-durov-explains-bizarre-money-throwing-incident/

8 A. Soldatov and I. Borogan, *The Red Web: the struggle between Russia's digital dictators and the new online revolutionaries*, New York NY: PublicAffairs, 2015, p. 98.

9 A. Nossik, '*Russia's first blogger reacts to Putin's internet crackdown*', *The New Republic*, 15 May 2014, https://newrepublic.com/article/117771/putins-internet-crackdown-russias-first-blogger-reacts

10 P. Pomerantsev, 'Putin's Rasputin', *London Review of Books* 33, no. 20 (2011), pp. 3–6, https://www.lrb.co.uk/v33/n20/peter-pomerantsev/putins-rasputin

11 Nossik, '*Russia's first blogger reacts to Putin's internet crackdown*'.

12 D. Hakim, '*Once celebrated in Russia, the programmer Pavel Durov chooses exile*', *The New York Times*, 2 December 2014, https://www.nytimes.com/2014/12/03/technology/once-celebrated-in-russia-programmer-pavel-durov-chooses-exile.html

13 G. Faulconbridge, '*Kremlin "puppet master" faces errant oligarch*', Reuters, 16 September 2011, https://www.reuters.com/article/us-russia-prokhorov-surkov/kremlin-puppet-master-faces-errant-oligarch-idUSTRE78F2TB20110916

14 Soldatov and Borogan, *The Red Web*, p. 136.

15 P. Leander and A. Sakhnin, '*Russia's Trump*', *Jacobin*, 11 July 2017, https://jacobinmag.com/2017/07/alexey-navalny-putin-opposition-movement-trump

16 Soldatov and Borogan, *The Red Web*, p. 140.

17 M. Gessen, *The Man Without a Face: the unlikely rise of Vladimir Putin*, New York NY: Riverhead Books, 2012, p. 289.

18 Gessen, *The Man Without a Face*, pp. 287–8.

19 Soldatov and Borogan, *The Red Web*, p. 125.

20 J. Halliday, '*Hillary Clinton adviser compares internet to Che Guevara*', *The Guardian*, 22 June 2011, https://www.theguardian.com/media/2011/jun/22/hillary-clinton-adviser-alec-ross

21 Soldatov and Borogan, *The Red Web*, p. 149.

22 Yaffa, '*Is Pavel Durov, Russia's Zuckerberg, a Kremlin target?*'

23 C. Johnston, '*Crime, punishment, and Russia's original social network*', Motherboard, 12 February 2015, https://motherboard.vice.com/en_us/article/vvbq73/v-for-vkontakte

24 Soldatov and Borogan, *The Red Web*, p. 153.

25 P. Durov, 'Здравый смысл', Lenta.ru, 12 December 2011, https://lenta.ru/articles/2011/12/12/durov/

26 'Глава "ВКонтакте" показал спецслужбам собачий язык', Lenta.ru, 9 December 2011, https://lenta.ru/news/2011/12/08/mrdurov/

27 O. Razumovskaya, '*Russian social network: FSB asked it to block Kremlin protesters*', *The Wall Street Journal*, 8 December 2011, http://blogs.wsj.com/emergingeurope/2011/12/08/russian-social-network-fsb-asked-it-to-block-kremlin-protesters/

28 Johnston, '*Crime, punishment, and Russia's original social network*'.

29 Soldatov and Borogan, *The Red Web*, p. 163.

30 '*On amending Federal Law "On the Protection of Children from Information Harmful to Their Health and Development and Other Legislative Acts of the Russian Federation"*', 2012, 139-FZ.

31 '*Russia internet blacklist law takes effect*', BBC News, 1 November 2012, http://www.bbc.co.uk/news/technology-20096274

32 Soldatov and Borogan, *The Red Web*, p. 166.

33 M. Kiselyova, 'Usmanov tightens hold on Russian social net VKontakte as founder sells stake', Reuters, 24 January 2014, https://www.reuters.com/article/russia-vkontakte/usmanov-tightens-hold-on-russian-social-net-vkontakte-as-founder-sells-stake-idUSL5N0KY3DQ20140124

34 I. Lunden, 'Durov, out for good from VK.com, plans a mobile social network outside Russia', TechCrunch, 22 April 2014, https://techcrunch.com/2014/04/22/durov-out-for-good-from-vk-com-plans-a-mobile-social-network-outside-russia/

35 'Russia's Mail.Ru buys remaining stake in VKontakte for $1.5 bln', Reuters, 16 September 2014, https://www.reuters.com/article/russia-mailru-group-vkontakte/russias-mail-ru-buys-remaining-stake-in-vkontakte-for-1-5-bln-idUSL6N0RH28K20140916

36 Lunden, 'Durov, out for good from VK.com'; N. Kononov, 'The Kremlin's social media takeover', The New York Times, 10 March 2014, https://www.nytimes.com/2014/03/11/opinion/the-kremlins-social-media-takeover.html?_r=0

37 V. Walt, 'With Telegram, a reclusive social media star rises again', Fortune, 23 February 2016, http://fortune.com/telegram-pavel-durov-mobile-world-congress/

38 'FAQ', Telegram, https://telegram.org/faq#q-do-you-process-data-requests

39 G. Greenwald, No Place to Hide: Edward Snowden, the NSA, and the US surveillance state, New York NY: Henry Holt and Company, 2014, p. 7.

40 R. McCormick, 'Edward Snowden's favorite encrypted chat app is now on Android', The Verge, 3 November 2015, https://www.theverge.com/2015/11/3/9662724/signal-encrypted-chat-app-android-edward-snowden

41 R. Kilpatrick, 'China blocks Telegram messenger, blamed for aiding human rights lawyers', Hong Kong Free Press, 13 July 2015, https://www.hongkongfp.com/2015/07/13/china-blocks-telegram-messenger-blamed-for-aiding-human-rights-lawyers/

42 CNN Library, 'Paris attacks fast facts', CNN, 8 December 2015, https://edition.cnn.com/2015/12/08/europe/2015-paris-terror-attacks-fast-facts/index.html; S. Stalinsky et al., 'Germany-based encrypted messaging app Telegram emerges as jihadis' preferred communications platform', Memri, 23 December 2016, https://www.memri.org/reports/encryption-technology-embraced-isis-al-qaeda-other-jihadis-part-v-%E2%80%93-september-2015-0

43 N. Lomas, 'After Paris attacks, Telegram purges ISIS public content', TechCrunch, 19 November 2015, https://techcrunch.com/2015/11/19/telegram-purges-isis-public-channels/

44 'ФСБ: теракт в метро Петербурга подготовили с помощью Telegram', Meduza, 26 June 2017, https://meduza.io/news/2017/06/26/fsb-terakt-v-metro-peterburga-podgotovili-s-pomoschyu-telegram

45 I. Webb, 'Is the end near for Telegram in Russia?', Global Voices, 26 June 2017, https://globalvoices.org/2017/06/26/is-the-end-nigh-for-telegram-in-russia/

46 'Telegram is fighting for its life in Russia, and it's unclear how much longer until it's kaput', Meduza, 20 March 2018, https://meduza.io/en/short/2018/03/20/telegram-is-fighting-for-its-life-in-russia-and-it-s-unclear-how-much-longer-until-it-s-kaput

47 'Here's what happened at the Telegram protest in Moscow', The Moscow Times, 30 April 2018, https://themoscowtimes.com/news/thousands-in-moscow-protest-ban-against-messaging-service-telegram-61307; 'Митинг против блокировки Telegram. Прямая трансляция' [video], Svoboda Radio, 30 April 2018, https://www.youtube.com/watch?v=NG9WvRA5S8k

48 'Russian ISPs finally start blocking Telegram', Meduza, 16 April 2018, https://meduza.io/en/news/2018/04/16/russian-isps-finally-start-blocking-telegram

49 P. Durov, 'Telegram message', Durov's Channel, 2018.

50 I. Kravtsova, '"It's simple negligence": Russian business owners talk about becoming collateral damage in the federal censor's war on Telegram', Meduza, 18 April 2018, https://meduza.io/en/feature/2018/04/18/it-s-simple-negligence

51 'В Кремле не рассматривают создание в РФ файервола против Telegram по примеру Китая', Interfax, 19 April 2018, http://www.interfax.ru/russia/609199

52 'Russia blocks tens of thousands of Microsoft IP addresses', Meduza, 19 April 2018, https://meduza.io/en/news/2018/04/19/russia-blocks-tens-of-thousands-of-microsoft-ip-addresses; 'Роскомнадзор ограничил доступ к 18 VPN и прокси–сервисам для блокировки Telegram', Interfax, 20 April 2018, http://www.interfax.ru/russia/609326

53 'Russia's crackdown on Telegram disrupts Google services across the country', Meduza, 23 April 2018, https://meduza.io/en/news/2018/04/23/russia-s-crackdown-on-telegram-disrupts-google-services-across-the-country

54 'Russia's economy could lose 1 billion dollars by the end of the year, because of the Telegram ban', Meduza, 26 April 2018, https://meduza.io/en/news/2018/04/26/russia-s-economy-could-lose-1-billion-dollars-by-the-end-of-the-year-because-of-the-telegram-ban

55 'Here are some of the dozens of online services disrupted by Russia's scattershot assault on Telegram', Meduza, 26 April 2018, https://meduza.io/en/feature/2018/04/26/the-damage-done

56 R. Brandom, 'A Google update just created a big problem for anti-censorship tools', The Verge, 18 April 2018, https://www.theverge.com/2018/4/18/17253784/google-domain-fronting-discontinued-signal-tor-vpn; C. MacCarthaigh, 'Enhanced domain protections for Amazon CloudFront requests', AWS Security Blog, 27 April 2018, https://aws.amazon.com/blogs/security/enhanced-domain-protections-for-amazon-cloudfront-requests/

57 M. Rosenfield, 'Amazon threatens to suspend Signal's AWS account over censorship circumvention', Signal, 1 May 2018, https://signal.org/blog/looking-back-on-the-front/

58 L. Bershidsky, 'Russian censor gets help from Amazon and Google', Bloomberg, 2 May 2018, https://www.bloomberg.com/view/articles/2018-05-02/eu-data-privacy-regulations-could-give-google-more-power

59 N. Vasilyeva, 'Thousands rally in Moscow for internet freedom', The Seattle Times, 30 April 2018, https://www.seattletimes.com/business/thousands-rally-in-moscow-for-internet-freedom/

Chapter 24

1 'Detach from attachments!' [video], Tibet Action Institute, 2 December 2011, https://www.youtube.com/watch?v=v4E1SRDmtZE

2 Author interview with Lobsang Gyatso Sither, September 2017.

3 S. Liao, 'How WeChat came to rule China', The Verge, 1 February 2018, https://www.theverge.com/2018/2/1/16721230/wechat-china-app-mini-programs-messaging-electronic-id-system

4 B. Perez, *'Tencent scraps WeChat global expansion plans despite strong profits'*, *South China Morning Post*, 19 March 2015, http://www.scmp.com/lifestyle/article/1741792/tencent-scraps-wechat-global-expansion-plans-despite-strong-profits; E. Lukman, *'This could get Messi: WeChat hires world's best footballer as TV ad star'*, Tech in Asia, 2 July 2013, https://www.techinasia.com/wechat-lionel-messi-ad

5 C. Chan, *'When one app rules them all: the case of WeChat and mobile in China'*, Andreessen Horowitz, 6 August 2015, https://a16z.com/2015/08/06/wechat-china-mobile-first/

6 Amnesty International, *For Your Eyes Only? Ranking 11 technology companies on encryption and human rights*, London: Amnesty International, 2016, https://www.amnesty.org/en/documents/POL40/4985/2016/en/

7 Z. Huang, *'What Tencent left out when it denied spying on you over WeChat'*, Quartz, 3 January 2018, https://qz.com/1170046/tencents-wechat-denies-storing-chat-history-but-its-users-are-monitored-by-the-chinese-government/

8 J. Mai, *'Growing privacy fears in China after cadres punished over "deleted" WeChat messages'*, *South China Morning Post*, 29 April 2018, http://www.scmp.com/news/china/policies-politics/article/2143920/growing-privacy-fears-china-after-cadres-punished-over

9 Associated Press, *'China jails Muslim man for 2 years over Islam WeChat groups'*, *South China Morning Post*, 12 September 2017, http://www.scmp.com/news/china/policies-politics/article/2110823/china-jails-muslim-man-2-years-over-islam-wechat-groups

10 O. Lam, *'Don't call "Xi the Bun": Chinese netizens are being jailed for chatroom jokes'*, *Hong Kong Free Press*, 31 December 2017, https://www.hongkongfp.com/2017/12/31/dont-call-xi-bun-chinese-netizens-jailed-chatroom-jokes/

11 M. Hvistendahl, *'Inside China's vast new experiment in social ranking'*, *Wired*, 14 December 2018, https://www.wired.com/story/age-of-social-credit/

12 *'China to bar people with bad "social credit" from planes, trains'*, Reuters, 16 March 2018, https://www.reuters.com/article/us-china-credit/china-to-bar-people-with-bad-social-credit-from-planes-trains-idUSKCN1GS10S

13 M. Zeng, *'China's social credit system puts its people under pressure to be model citizens'*, The Conversation, 23 January 2018, https://theconversation.com/chinas-social-credit-system-puts-its-people-under-pressure-to-be-model-citizens-89963

14 R. Foyle Hunwick, *'How do you control 1.4 billion people?'*, *The New Republic*, 25 April 2018, https://newrepublic.com/article/148121/control-14-billion-people

Chapter 25

1 'Museveni: I am nobody's employee', NTVUganda, 26 January 2017, https://www.youtube.com/watch?v=BYbqo6DMDKc

2 G. Muzoora, '*I am not anyone's servant, says Museveni*', *Daily Monitor*, 27 January 2017, http://www.monitor.co.ug/News/National/I-am-not-anyone-s-servant--says-Museveni/688334-3789590-whwy85/index.html

3 'Presidential Elections 2016: *district summary report*', Ugandan Electoral Commission, 22 February 2016, p. 1, http://www.ec.or.ug/sites/default/files/docs/02-District_Summary_PRESIDENT_1_Final22Feb2016.pdf

4 T. Hopper, '"*Tweeting from Canada, voting in Uganda*": how Ugandans evaded an election day internet crackdown', *National Post*, 19 February 2016, http://nationalpost.com/news/canada/tweeting-from-canada-voting-in-uganda-how-ugandans-evaded-an-election-day-internet-crackdown

5 Author interview with Stella Nyanzi, April 2018.

6 N. Slawson, '*Fury over arrest of academic who called Uganda president buttocks*', *The Guardian*, 13 April 2017, https://www.theguardian.com/global-development/2017/apr/13/stella-nyanzi-fury-arrest-uganda-president-a-pair-of-buttocks-yoweri-museveni-cyber-harassment

7 *Matako* is the Bugandan word for buttocks. '*Museveni matako nyo!*', S. Nyanzi Facebook post, 27 January 2017, https://www.facebook.com/stella.nyanzi/posts/10154878225000053

8 H. French, *China's Second Continent: how a million migrants are building a new empire in Africa*, New York NY: Alfred A. Knopf, 2014.

9 D. Brautigam, *The Dragon's Gift: the real story of China in Africa*, Oxford: Oxford University Press, 2009. p. 40.

10 Brautigam, *The Dragon's Gift*, p. 32.

11 J. Wu and B. Blanchard, '*Taiwan loses another ally, says won't help China ties*', Reuters, 20 December 2016, https://www.reuters.com/article/us-china-taiwan-saotome/taiwan-loses-another-ally-says-wont-help-china-ties-idUSKBN1492SO

12 Brautigam, *The Dragon's Gift*, p. 34.

13 J. Griffiths, '*Report exposes size of China's secretive aid budget*', CNN, 11 October 2017, https://edition.cnn.com/2017/10/11/asia/china-overseas-aid/index.html

14 S. George and B. Lendon, '"*Weaponizing capital*": US worries over China's expanding role in Africa', CNN, 14 March 2018, https://edition.cnn.com/2018/03/09/asia/djibouti-port-china-us-intl/index.html

15 K. Hsu, '*China finally has its own Rambo*', *Foreign Policy*, 1 September 2017, http://foreignpolicy.com/2017/09/01/china-finally-has-its-own-rambo/

16 French, *China's Second Continent*.

17 Brautigam, *The Dragon's Gift*, p. 12.

18 Brautigam, *The Dragon's Gift*, p. 307.

19 '*Nicolas Sarkozy admits Rwanda genocide "mistakes"*', BBC News, 25 February 2010, http://news.bbc.co.uk/2/hi/africa/8535803.stm

20 Brautigam, *The Dragon's Gift*, p. 285.

21 'Uganda's Kizza Besigye – veteran opposition leader profiled', BBC News, 17 February 2016, http://www.bbc.com/news/world-africa-12431180

22 I. Gatsiounis, 'Deadly crackdown on Uganda's walk-to-work protests', Time, 23 April 2011, https://web.archive.org/web/20140411141002/http://content.time.com/time/world/article/0,8599,2067136,00.html

23 M. Namiti, 'Uganda walk-to-work protests kick up dust', Al Jazeera, 28 April 2011, https://www.aljazeera.com/indepth/features/2011/04/201142831330647345.html

24 'Uganda's Kizza Besigye arrested for fourth time', BBC News, 28 April 2011, http://www.bbc.com/news/world-africa-13222227

25 D. Smith, 'Uganda riots reach capital as anger against President Museveni grows', The Guardian, 29 April 2011, https://www.theguardian.com/world/2011/apr/29/uganda-riots-kampala-museveni

26 D. Smith and S. Boseley, 'Uganda's Museveni sworn in as police fire teargas at protesters', The Guardian, 12 May 2011, https://www.theguardian.com/world/2011/may/12/uganda-museveni-police-teargas

27 E. Biryabarema, 'Uganda police arrest opposition leader, fire teargas at protest', Reuters, 5 October 2012, https://www.reuters.com/article/ozatp-uganda-politics-20121005-idAFJOE89400320121005

28 For God and My President: state surveillance in Uganda, London: Privacy International, 2015.

29 'Company profile', Gamma Group, 2018, https://www.gammagroup.com/GammaTSE.aspx

30 'Gamma Group, Finfisher: governmental IT intrusion and remote monitoring solutions', Surveillance Industry Index, https://sii.transparencytoolkit.org/docs/Gamma-Group_FinFisher_Product-Descriptionsii_documents

31 B. Marczak, J. Scott-Railton, A. Senft, I. Poetrano and S. McKune, 'Pay no attention to the server behind the proxy: mapping FinFisher's continuing proliferation', The Citizen Lab, 15 October 2015, https://citizenlab.ca/2015/10/mapping-finfishers-continuing-proliferation/

32 Elaman, 'FinFisher IT intrusion products', WikiLeaks, https://wikileaks.org/spyfiles/files/0/310_ELAMAN-IT_INTRUSION_FINFISHER_INTRODUCTION_V02-08.pdf

33 Author interview with Samson Tusiime, April 2018.

34 @samwyri, Twitter, https://twitter.com/samwyri

35 H. Epstein, 'The cost of fake democracy', The New York Review of Books, 16 May 2016, http://www.nybooks.com/daily/2016/05/16/uganda-cost-of-fake-democracy/

36 H. Epstein, Another Fine Mess: America, Uganda, and the War on Terror, New York NY: Columbia Global Reports, 2017.

37 Epstein, 'The cost of fake democracy'.

38 P. Nyamishana, 'The power of social media in Uganda's 2016 elections', Global Voices, 10 February 2016, https://globalvoices.org/2016/02/10/the-power-of-social-media-in-ugandas-2016-elections/

39 G. Phillips and G. Atuhaire, '*How Ugandans overturned an election day social media blackout*', Motherboard, 24 February 2016, https://motherboard.vice.com/en_us/article/nz7zv8/uganda-election-day-social-media-blackout-backlash-mobile-payments

40 Hopper, '"*Tweeting from Canada, voting in Uganda*"'.

41 C. Bold and R. Pillai, '*The impact of shutting down mobile money in Uganda*', Consultative Group to Assist the Poor, 7 March 2016, http://www.cgap.org/blog/impact-shutting-down-mobile-money-uganda

42 Phillips and Atuhaire, '*How Ugandans overturned an election day social media blackout*'.

43 F. Karimi, S. Ntale and G. Botelho, '*Uganda leader Museveni declared winner – despite issues, tensions*', CNN, 21 February 2016, https://edition.cnn.com/2016/02/20/africa/uganda-election/

44 'Tension in Kampala after Ugandan opposition leader Kizza Besigye swore himself in as the president' [video], KTN News Kenya, 11 May 2016, https://www.youtube.com/watch?v=TeXgcw29rl8

45 'Police arrests Besigye ahead of Museveni swearing-in' [video], NTVUganda, 11 May 2016, https://www.youtube.com/watch?v=UskRVm3KbVc

46 Epstein, *Another Fine Mess*.

47 J. Propa, '*Ugandans are finally back on social media after days-long blackout*', Global Voices, 17 May 2016, https://globalvoices.org/2016/05/17/ugandans-are-finally-back-on-social-media-after-days-long-blackout/

48 G. Muhame, '*How Besigye portrait tee-shirt landed Tusiime in trouble*', Chimp Reports, 4 June 2016, http://chimpreports.com/exclusive-interview-how-besigye-portrait-tee-shirt-landed-tusiime-in-trouble/; P. Nyamishana, '*Ugandan man arrested over T-shirt featuring opposition leader*', Global Voices, 1 June 2016, https://globalvoices.org/2016/06/01/ugandan-man-arrested-over-t-shirt-featuring-opposition-leader/

49 B. Mwesigire, '*Uganda: Stella Nyanzi charged for calling President Museveni a "pair of buttocks"*', African Arguments, 10 April 2017, http://africanarguments.org/2017/04/10/uganda-stella-nyanzi-charged-calling-president-museveni-pair-buttocks/

50 Slawson, '*Fury over arrest of academic who called Uganda president buttocks*'.

51 T. Le, '*Beijing demands Washington lift sanctions against firms*', China Daily, 10 January 2007, http://www.chinadaily.com.cn/china/2007-01/10/content_779108.htm

52 Y. Mugerwa, '*China to help Uganda fight internet abuse*', Daily Monitor, 26 July 2017, http://www.monitor.co.ug/News/National/China-Uganda-Internet-Evelyn-Anite-Africa-Internet-Users/688334-4032626-u1l61r/index.html

53 A. Gitta, '*Uganda: government introduces pornography control committee*', DW, 29 August 2017, http://www.dw.com/en/uganda-government-introduces-pornography-control-committee/a-40286069

54 '*Warning against irresponsible use of social and electronic communication platforms*', Uganda Communications Commission, 2017.

55 E. Kisambira, 'Uganda's backbone is a model for Africa', Network World, 20 May 2008, https://www.networkworld.com/article/2279753/data-center/uganda-s-backbone-is-a-model-for-africa.html

56 A. Toor, 'Uganda government used advanced spyware to "crush" opposition, report says', The Verge, 16 October 2015, https://www.theverge.com/2015/10/16/9549151/uganda-finfisher-surveillance-spyware-privacy-international

57 N. Ahrens, China's Competitiveness: myth, reality, and lessons for the United States and Japan, Washington DC: Center for Strategic and International Studies, 2013, p. 2; R. McGregor, The Party: the secret world of China's Communist rulers, New York NY: Penguin Books, 2012, p. 204.

58 Brautigam, The Dragon's Gift, p. 87.

59 D. Pilling, 'Chinese investment in Africa: Beijing's testing ground', Financial Times, 13 June 2017, https://www.ft.com/content/0f534aa4-4549-11e7-8519-9f94ee97d996

60 J. Reed, 'Africa's Big Brother lives in Beijing', Foreign Policy, 30 July 2013, http://foreignpolicy.com/2013/07/30/africas-big-brother-lives-in-beijing/

Epilogue

1 My description of Roy Jones is based on interviews he gave to the press and his social media presence. He did not respond to multiple requests to be interviewed for this book. To guard his privacy I am not linking to his profiles or revealing information not already public that I was able to glean from them.

2 M. Hansen, 'Omaha man "liked" a tweet, and then he lost his dream job', Omaha World Herald, 21 March 2018, http://www.omaha.com/columnists/hansen/hansen-omaha-man-liked-a-tweet-and-then-he-lost/article_74b9021a-3753-5b33-b096-f0af3c8372d6.html

3 F. Chen, 'Marriott China caught in nationalist groundswell', Asia Times, 11 January 2018, http://www.atimes.com/article/marriott-china-caught-nationalist-groundswell/

4 W. Ma, 'Marriott employee Roy Jones hit "like." Then China got mad', The Wall Street Journal, 3 March 2018, https://www.wsj.com/articles/marriott-employee-roy-jones-hit-like-then-china-got-mad-1520094910

5 'Friends of Tibet congratulate global hotel chain…', @friendsoftibet, Twitter, 9 January 2018, https://twitter.com/friendsoftibet/status/950776498683723777

6 J. Xu, 'Marriott announces "rectification plan" to regain trust', China Daily, 18 January 2018, http://www.chinadaily.com.cn/a/201801/18/WS5a600374a310e4ebf433e9ac.html

7 D. Ren, 'Delta Air Lines, Zara join Marriott in China's bad books over Tibet, Taiwan gaffes', South China Morning Post, 12 January 2018, http://www.scmp.com/news/china/society/article/2128046/delta-air-lines-zara-join-marriott-chinas-bad-books-over-tibet; P. Li and A. Jourdan, 'Mercedes-Benz apologizes to Chinese for quoting Dalai Lama', Reuters, 6 February 2018, https://www.reuters.com/article/us-mercedes-benz-china-gaffe/mercedes-benz-apologizes-to-chinese-for-quoting-dalai-lama-idUSKBN1FQ1FJ

8   T. Glavin, '*As China pushes censorship on B.C. students, democracy falls back*', *National Post*, 17 January 2018, http://nationalpost.com/opinion/terry-glavin-as-china-pushes-censorship-on-b-c-students-democracy-falls-back

9   D. Shane, '*White House calls China's warning to airlines "Orwellian nonsense"*', CNN Money, 6 May 2018, http://money.cnn.com/2018/05/05/news/companies/white-house-response-china-warning-taiwan/index.html

10   S. Sanders, '*Statement from the press secretary on China's political correctness*', White House, 5 May 2018, https://www.whitehouse.gov/briefings-statements/statement-press-secretary-chinas-political-correctness/

11   J. Horwitz, '*Twitter's new China head was a People's Liberation Army engineer who worked on military security*', Quartz, 18 April 2016, https://qz.com/664004/twitters-new-china-head-is-a-communist-party-ex-engineer-who-worked-on-military-security/

12   D. Randall, '*Twitter's China boss Kathy Chen quits after eight months*', Reuters, 2 January 2017, https://www.reuters.com/article/us-twitter-chen-idUSKB N14M17P

13   M. Isaac, '*Facebook said to create censorship tool to get back into China*', *The New York Times*, 22 November 2016, https://www.nytimes.com/2016/11/22/technology/facebook-censorship-tool-china.html

14   G. Wu, '*Former cybersecurity head who sought "personal fame" expelled from Party*', Caixin, 13 February 2018, https://www.caixinglobal.com/2018-02-13/former-cybersecurity-head-who-sought-personal-fame-expelled-from-party-101211314.html

15   C. Cadwalladr and E. Graham-Harrison, '*Revealed: 50 million Facebook profiles harvested for Cambridge Analytica in major data breach*', *The Guardian*, 17 March 2018, https://www.theguardian.com/news/2018/mar/17/cambridge-analytica-facebook-influence-us-election

16   D. Lux, '*Facebook's hate speech policies censor marginalized users*', Wired, 14 August 2017, https://www.wired.com/story/facebooks-hate-speech-policies-censor-marginalized-users/; J. Angwin and H. Grassegger, '*Facebook's secret censorship rules protect white men from hate speech but not black children*', Pro Publica, 28 June 2017, https://www.propublica.org/article/facebook-hate-speech-censorship-internal-documents-algorithms; C. McGoogan, '*Breastfeeding, statues and plus-sized models: 10 things Facebook's moderators censored*', *The Telegraph*, 22 May 2017, https://www.telegraph.co.uk/technology/2017/05/22/breastfeeding-statues-plus-sized-models-10-things-facebooks/

17   S. Thielman, '*Google offers legal support to some YouTube users in copyright battles*', *The Guardian*, 19 November 2015, https://www.theguardian.com/technology/2015/nov/19/google-youtube-copyright-lawsuits-fair-use-dmca

18   M. Sheffield, '*"Fake news" or free speech: is Google cracking down on left media?*', Salon, 18 October 2017, https://www.salon.com/2017/10/18/fake-news-or-free-speech-is-google-cracking-down-on-left-media/

19   R. Gallagher, '*Google plans to launch censored search engine in China, leaked documents reveal*', The Intercept, 1 August 2018, https://theintercept.com/2018/08/01/google-china-search-engine-censorship/

20 Letter from Google employees to Sundar Pichai and others, August 2018.

21 B. Downey, 'An old approach to China', Google Docs, 2018, https://docs.google.com/document/d/1ZlQAG7qJXglIlObUmuHeQJ7gcdAPp57gsYgl04wVuVY/edit

22 R. Gallagher, 'Google staff tell bosses China censorship is "moral and ethical" crisis', The Intercept, 16 August 2018, https://theintercept.com/2018/08/16/google-china-crisis-staff-dragonfly/

23 D. Kravets, 'WikiLeaks exposes Australian web blacklist', Wired, 19 March 2009, https://www.wired.com/2009/03/wikileaks-expos/

24 J. Malcolm, 'No justification for Spanish internet censorship during Catalonian referendum', Electronic Frontier Foundation, 2 October 2017, https://www.eff.org/deeplinks/2017/10/no-justification-spanish-internet-censorship-during-catalonian-referendum

25 E. Dreyfuss, 'Facebook: too big to delete', Wired, 29 June 2017, https://www.wired.com/story/facebook-too-big-to-delete/

26 N. Kulwin, 'The internet apologizes …', New York Magazine, 16 April 2018, http://nymag.com/selectall/2018/04/an-apology-for-the-internet-from-the-people-who-built-it.html

27 M. Scott, 'Welcome to new era of global digital censorship', Politico, 14 January 2018, https://www.politico.eu/article/google-facebook-twitter-censorship-europe-commission-hate-speech-propaganda-terrorist/

28 B. Tarnoff and M. Weigel, 'Why Silicon Valley can't fix itself', The Guardian, 3 May 2018, http://www.theguardian.com/news/2018/may/03/why-silicon-valley-cant-fix-itself-tech-humanism

Selected bibliography

Ahrens, N. (2013) *China's Competitiveness: myth, reality, and lessons for the United States and Japan*, Washington DC: Center for Strategic and International Studies.

Baker, S. (2013) *Skating on Stilts: why we aren't stopping tomorrow's terrorism*, Stanford CA: Hoover Press.

Bamman, D., B. O'Connor and N. Smith (2012) '*Censorship and deletion practices in Chinese social media*', *First Monday* 17, no. 3–5, http://firstmonday.org/ojs/index.php/fm/article/view/3943/3169.

Baranovitch, N. (2003) 'From the margins to the centre: the Uyghur challenge in Beijing', *The China Quarterly* 175.

Bejtlich, R. et al. (2013) *APT1: exposing one of China's cyber espionage units*, Alexandria VA: Mandiant.

Brautigam, D. (2009) *The Dragon's Gift: the real story of China in Africa*, Oxford: Oxford University Press.

Buruma, I. (2001) *Bad Elements: Chinese rebels from Los Angeles to Beijing*, New York NY: Random House.

Callanan, C., H. Dries-Ziekenheiner, A. Escudero-Pascual and R. Guerra (2011) *Leaping Over the Firewall: a review of censorship circumvention tools*, Washington DC: Freedom House, https://freedomhouse.org/sites/default/files/inline_images/Censorship.pdf.

Chase, M. and J. Mulvenon, J. (2002) *You've Got Dissent! Chinese dissident use of the internet and Beijing's counter-strategies*, Santa Monica CA: Rand Corporation.

Chiu, J. et al. (2018) *Forbidden Feeds: government controls on social media in China*, New York NY: PEN America.

Cliff, T. (2016) *Oil and Water: being Han in Xinjiang*, Chicago IL: University of Chicago Press.

Cook, S. (2017) *The Battle for China's Spirit: religious revival, repression, and resistance under Xi Jinping*, Washington DC: Freedom House, https://freedomhouse.org/sites/default/files/FH_ChinasSprit2016_FULL_FINAL_140pages_compressed.pdf.

Corera, G. (2016) *Intercept: the secret history of computers and spies*, London: Weidenfeld and Nicolson.

Damm, J. and S. Thomas (2006) *Chinese Cyberspaces: technological changes and political effects*, Abingdon: Routledge.

Deibert, R. (2013) *Black Code: inside the battle for cyberspace*, Toronto: McClelland & Stewart.

DeLisle, J., A. Goldstein and G. Yang (2016) *The Internet, Social Media, and a Changing China*, Philadelphia PA: University of Pennsylvania Press.

Dickson, B. (2016) *The Dictator's Dilemma: the Chinese Communist Party's strategy for survival*, Oxford: Oxford University Press.

Dikotter, F. (2016) *The Cultural Revolution: a people's history, 1962–1976*, London: Bloomsbury.

Epstein, H. (2017) *Another Fine Mess: America, Uganda, and the War on Terror*, New York NY: Columbia Global Reports.

Faris, R., J. Palfrey, E. Zuckerman, H. Roberts and J. York (2010) '2010 circumvention tool usage report', Cambridge MA: Berkman Klein Center for Internet and Society at Harvard University, 14 October, https://cyber.harvard.edu/publications/2010/Circumvention_Tool_Usage.

Fish, E. (2015) *China's Millennials: the want generation*, Lanham MD: Rowman & Littlefield.

French, H. (2014) *China's Second Continent: how a million migrants are building a new empire in Africa*, New York NY: Alfred A. Knopf.

Gessen, M. (2012) *The Man Without a Face: the unlikely rise of Vladimir Putin*, New York NY: Riverhead Books.

Girard, B. (2009) *The Google Way: how one company is revolutionizing management as we know it*, San Francisco CA: No Starch Press.

Goldsmith, J. and T. Wu (2006) *Who Controls the Internet?: Illusions of a borderless world*, New York NY: Oxford University Press.

Gorham, M. et al. (2014) *Digital Russia: the language, culture and politics of new media communication*, Abingdon: Routledge.

Greenwald, G. (2014) *No Place to Hide: Edward Snowden, the NSA, and the US surveillance state*, New York NY: Henry Holt and Company.

Gutmann, E. (2004) *Losing the New China: a story of American commerce, desire, and betrayal*, San Francisco CA: Encounter Books.

Harris, R. and A. Isa (2011) '"Invitation to a mourning ceremony"': perspectives on the Uyghur internet, *Inner Asia* 13.

He, Q. (2008) *The Fog of Censorship: media control in China*, New York NY: Human Rights in China.

Herold, D. (2011) *Online Society in China: creating, celebrating, and instrumentalising the online carnival*, London: Routledge.

Hillman, B. and G. Tuttle (2016) *Ethnic Conflict and Protest in Tibet and Xinjiang: unrest in China's west*, New York NY: Columbia University Press.

Holdstock, N. (2015) *China's Forgotten People: Xinjiang, terror and the Chinese state*, London: I. B. Tauris.

HRW (2006) '*How censorship works in China: a brief overview*' in '*Race to the Bottom*': *corporate complicity in Chinese internet censorship*, New York NY: Human Rights Watch (HRW), https://www.hrw.org/reports/2006/china0806/3.htm.

HRW (2009) '*We Are Afraid to Even Look for Them*': *enforced disappearances in the wake of Xinjiang's protests*, New York NY: Human Rights Watch (HRW).

Ilham, J. (2015) *Jewher Ilham: a Uyghur's fight to free her father*, New Orleans LA: University of New Orleans Press.

Inkster, N. (2016) *China's Cyber Power*, Abingdon: Routledge.

Jacobs, J. (2016) *Xinjiang and the Modern Chinese State*, Seattle WA: University of Washington Press.

Johnson, I. (2004) *Wild Grass: three stories of change in modern China*, New York NY: Pantheon Books.

Kalathil, S. (2017) *Beyond the Great Firewall: how China became a global information power*, Washington DC: Center for International Media Assistance.

Kang, X. (2000) 法輪功事件全透視, *Hong Kong*: Ming Pao Publishing.

King, G., J. Pan and M. Roberts (2013) '*How censorship in China allows government criticism but silences collective expression*', American Political Science Review 107, no. 2, pp. 1–18.

King, G. et al. (2017) '*How the Chinese government fabricates social media posts for strategic distraction, not engaged argument*', American Political Science Review 111, no. 3, pp. 484–501, http://gking.harvard.edu/files/gking/files/50c.pdf?m=1463683069.

Kleinwächter, W. (2005) *Reforming Internet Governance: perspectives from the Working Group on Internet Governance*, New York NY: United Nations Publications.

Lagerkvist, J. (2010) *After the Internet, Before Democracy: competing norms in Chinese media and society*, Bern: Peter Lang.

Lee, K. (2011) *Making a World of Difference, self-published by* Kai-Fu Lee.

Leiner, B., V. Cerf, D. Clark, R. Kahn, L. Kleinrock, D. Lynch, J. Postel, L. Roberts and S. Wolff (1997) '*Brief history of the internet*', Reston VA: Internet Society, https://www.internetsociety.org/internet/history-internet/brief-history-internet/.

Levy, S. (2011) *In The Plex: how Google thinks, works, and shapes our lives*, New York NY: Simon and Schuster.

Li, H. (2014) '*Zhuan Falun*', FalunDafa.org.

Lindsay, J. et al. (2015) *China and Cybersecurity: espionage, strategy, and politics in the digital domain*, New York NY: Oxford University Press.

MacKinnon, R. (2012) *Consent of the Networked: the world-wide struggle for internet freedom*, New York NY: Basic Books.

McGregor, R. (2012) *The Party: the secret world of China's Communist rulers*, New York NY: Penguin Books.

Millward, J. (2007) *Eurasian Crossroads: a history of Xinjiang*, New York NY: Columbia University Press.

Morozov, E. (2012) *The Net Delusion: how not to liberate the world*, London: Hachette.

Mueller, M. (2009) *Ruling the Root: internet governance and the taming of cyberspace*, Cambridge MA: MIT Press.

Ng, J. (2013) *Blocked on Weibo: what gets suppressed on China's version of Twitter (and why)*, New York NY: The New Press.

Ownby, D. (2008) *Falun Gong and the Future of China*, New York NY: Oxford University Press.

Palmer, D. (2007) *Qigong Fever: body, science, and utopia in China*, New York NY: Columbia University Press.

Parker, E. (2014) *Now I Know Who My Comrades Are: voices from the internet underground*, New York NY: Farrar, Straus and Giroux.

Penny, B. (2012) *The Religion of Falun Gong*, Chicago IL and London: University of Chicago Press.

Perdue, P. (2005) *China Marches West, Cambridge MA:* Harvard University Press.

Pomerantsev, P. (2014) *Nothing Is True and Everything Is Possible: the surreal heart of the New Russia*, New York NY: PublicAffairs.

Roberts, M. (2018) *Censored: distraction and diversion inside China's Great Firewall*, Princeton NJ: Princeton University Press.

Ryan, F. (2018) *'Weibo diplomacy and censorship in China'*, Canberra: *Australian Strategic Policy Institute, https://www.aspi.org.au/report/weibo-diplomacy-and-censorship-china.*

Segal, A. (2016) *The Hacked World Order: how nations fight, trade, maneuver, and manipulate in the digital age*, New York NY: PublicAffairs.

Shakya, T. (1999) *The Dragon in the Land of Snows: a history of modern Tibet since 1947*, London: Pimlico.

Shambaugh, D. (2013) *China Goes Global: the partial power*, New York NY: Oxford University Press.

Shao, G. (2012) *Internet Law in China*, San Diego CA: Elsevier Science.

So, S. and J. Westland (2010) *Red Wired: China's internet revolution*, London: Marshall Cavendish.

Soldatov, A. and I. Borogan (2015) *The Red Web: the struggle between Russia's digital dictators and the new online revolutionaries, New York NY:* PublicAffairs.

Starr, S. (2004) *Xinjiang: China's Muslim borderland*, New York NY: M. E. Sharpe.

Szadziewski, H. and G. Fay (2014) *'Trapped in a virtual cage: Chinese state repression of Uyghurs online'*, Uyghur Human Rights Project.

Tai, Z. (2006) *The Internet in China: cyberspace and civil society*, London and New York NY: Routledge.

Tohti, I. (2011) *'My ideals and the career path I have chosen'*, Uyghur Online.

Toops, S. (2013) 'Where Inner Asia meets Outer China: the Xinjiang Uyghur Autonomous Region of China' in S. M. Walcott and C. Johnson (eds), *Eurasian Corridors of Interconnection: from the South China to the Caspian Sea*, New York NY: Routledge.

Tufekci, Z. (2017) *Twitter and Tear Gas: the power and fragility of networked protest*, New Haven CT: Yale University Press.

Walton, G. (2001) *China's Golden Shield: corporations and the development of surveillance technology in the People's Republic of China*, Montreal: International Centre for Human Rights and Democratic Development.

Walton, G. et al. (2009) *'Tracking Ghostnet: investigating a cyber espionage network'*, *Information Warfare Monitor*, 29 March.

Wu, X. (2005) *Chinese Cyber Nationalism: evolution, characteristics and implications*, Lanham MD: Lexington Books.

Xin, X. (2012) *How the Market Is Changing China's News: the case of Xinhua news agency*, Lanham MD: Lexington Books.

Yang, G. (2009) *The Power of the Internet in China: citizen activism online*, New York NY: Columbia University Press.

Zetter, J. (2014) *Countdown to Zero Day: Stuxnet and the launch of the world's first digital weapon*, New York NY: Crown/Archetype.

Zhu, Y. (2012) *Two Billion Eyes: the story of China Central Television*, New York NY: The New Press.

Zittrain, J. and B. Edelman (2003) '*Empirical analysis of internet filtering in China*', Cambridge MA: Berkman Klein Center for Internet and Society, https://cyber.harvard.edu/filtering/china/.

Index

Abbott, Tony, 203
acceptable criticism, boundaries of, 75
Access Now, 236
Adelaide, Australia, 206
Adkins, Heather, 169
Admiralty, camp, 19
Adobe, 170
Africa: China presence, 287–8; Huawei
    earnings, 304; internet in, 291;
    Xinhua success, 80
Agora, dark web, 100
Ahmadinejad, Mahmoud, 111
AI software, 200
Ai Weiwei, 170, 214
Albert Einstein College of Medicine, 38
Al-Assad, Bashir, 209
Al-Bashir, Omar, 291
Al-Ghanim, Mohamed Nasser, 231
Algeria, 230
Ali, Guzelnur, 195, 198
Alibaba, 200, 235, 242, 279; Alipay,
    281; Taobao online marketplace,
    210; Yahoo stake in, 67
Allawi, Ayad, 223
Alphabet, 315
Al Qaeda, 199
American Civil Liberties Union, 245
Amir-Ebrahimi, Masserat, 150
Amnesty International, 280
Andreessen Horowitz, 279
Angola, 289
Anhui province, 78
Anite, Evelyn, 303
Anonymous, 185–6, 188
Anti, Michael, 36, 93, 116
anti-Rightist Movement, Xinjiang
    avoidance, 133
anti-surveillance tools, 5
Antonov, Polina, 254–5
Antonov, Vadim, 253–4
Apple, 1990s faltering, 277
Applebaum, Jacob, 104–5

APT1, 186–7
Arab Spring, 8, 10, 264, 311
Artux, 132, 134
Asia-America Gateway, underwater
    cable system, 155
AsiaInfo, 31
Asiaweek, 54
Associated Press, 80
Aum Shinrikyo cult, 49
Australia, censorship, 315
Aximujiang Aimaiti, killing of, 146
Azat, Nijat, 157

baby formula scandal, 204
Badiucao, 175, 178–9, 184, 204–5,
    207–8, 211–12, 215; smear attempts,
    214; 'traitor' accusation, 210; Weibo
    account deleted, 206
Baidu, 4, 63, 171–2, 242, 260; Baike
    web site, 210; market share growth,
    126; party members, 235; patriotism
    boast, 124; search engine, 165
balinghou generation, 204
Bandurski, David, 212
Bardin, Valery, 253, 255–6
Barlow, John Perry, 6, 243, 246;
    utopian language, 7
Barlow, Norman, 243
Barr, Aaron, 185–6, 188
Bastrykin, Alexander, 251
Beach, Sophie, 212
Beidaihe, China resort, 47, 89
Beijing, 29; academia elite circles, 134;
    Beihang University, 234; Engagement
    Centre ICANN, 234; jamming
    signals, 107; Medical University, 37;
    Niujie mosque, 138; Youth Daily, 73
Berners-Lee, Tim, 252
Besigye, Kizza, 292–3, 295–6;
    'preventative arrest', 298; treason
    charge, 299
Big Vs, 180

Bijie, 95
Bildt, Carl, 223
Bingtuan, 134
BitTorrent, 5
Blocked on Weibo, 183
blogging, 93
Bloomberg, 80
Bluetooth, communication use, 19
Brand, Stewart, 244
Brautigam, Deborah, 290
Brin, Sergey, 62–3, 116, 119, 168, 315;
    family history, 171
Brito, Jerry, 229
broadband connection, 155
Brown University, USA, 85
Burkina Faso, 288
Burkov, Dmitry, 253
Bush, George W., 110, 246
BuzzFeed, 199

Charlie Hebdo, attacks on, 209
Callahan, Michael, 119
Cambridge Analytica, 313, 317
Cambridge University, 162
Canada, 232; Tibet Committee, 85–6
Cankao Xiaoxi, 36
Cao Guowei, 182–3
Carnegie, Dale, 117
Cartoonists, persecution of, 209
Catalonia, 2017 referendum, 316
Causeway Bay, camp, 19
CCTV International, 287
censorship: AI-based, 315; anti-tools,
    102–3; in-house, 183; manual, 75;
    software, 101
Cerf, Vint, 221, 228
CERN, 252
Chan, Connie, 279
Chen Jieren, 171
Chen, Kathy, 312
Cheney, Dick, 243–4
Cheng Jianping, 74
China, People's Republic of, 137,
    204; Academy of Sciences, 49, 51;
    Africa criticism Western hypocrisy,
    290–1; Africa investments, 305;

censorship, 27; Central Television,
181; Civil Aviation Administration,
310; courts conviction rates, 198;
cyber sovereignty doctrine, 8,
234, 292; cybersecurity law 2017,
280; Cyberspace Administration
of, 3; Democracy Party, 41–2, 92;
Development Bank, 304;domestic
security profits, 201; early internet
enthusiasm, 32; elite, 90, 117; elite
hackers, 172, 192; entertainment
industry, 215; factory sexual
harassment, 145; first commercial
internet service, 25; globalised
online influence, 212; Google
compromised, 315; high-speed rail
system, 176–7; human rights lawyers,
206; internet companies overseas
business, 236; Internet Network
Information Centre, 235; Internet
Society of, 64; Ministry of Foreign
Affairs, 165, 167; Ministry of Public
Security, 26; National Electronics
Import & Export Corporation,
303; National Defence Daily, 153;
nationalised internet, 231; Netcom
Communications, 31–2; official aid
budget, 289; PLA, *see below*; Qigong
Science Research Society, 48; Qing
Empire era, 205; social credit system,
281–3; State Council, 42, 11, 181,
241; tech firms security contracts,
200; Telecom, 30–1, 156; telecoms
buying, 30; 2008 Olympics, 180;
UN advocacy, 233; Unicom, 156; US
Embassy in, 180; -US relations, 109;
WTO joining, 91, 92; Youth Daily,
64, 172
China Digital Times, US-based, 76
ChinaNet, 30
Chinese Communist Party (CCP), CCP,
8, 42, 74, 288; internal politics, 312;
Politburo Standing Committee, 165
Chinese Golden Shield, 104
Chinese Institute of Computer
Applications, 24

Chinese People's Political Consultative Conference, 77
choke points, China internet, 29
CIA (US Central Intelligence Agency), 85, 161; Q-Tel venture capital arm, 108
circumvention tools: Tor, 101; user lack, 71
Cisco, 29, 32, 115, 119, 236, 304; basic filtering technology, 32
Citizen Lab, 159–60, 163–4, 276
Civic Square, Hong Kong, 15, 17, 20; pro-democracy rally 2014, 16
'civilized behaviour', as censorship, 240
Clarke, Ian, 99
Clinton, Bill, 43, 246; China internet optimism, 42
Clinton, Hillary, 173, 211, 264
CNET.com, 84
CNN, 56–7
Coca Cola, 187
Cohen, Jared, 111
Cold War, 106
collective action, China surveillance attention, 74
Columbia Law School, 241
Comey, James, 190–1
Comment Crew, 187
Communications Decency Act, USA, 245
Communist Youth League, 171
"Complete IT Intrusion Portfolio", 293
Confucius Institute, 288
Connaught Road camp, Hong Kong, 17
Contemporary Business News, 64
Crimea, Russian invasion, 267
CQRS, 49
Crowley, P.J., 111
Cuba, 237
Cultural Revolution, 8, 23, 24, 48, 176, 205; Xinjing avoidance, 133
'cyber-sovereignty', China doctrine, 8, 234, 237–8, 242, 250
Cyberspace Administration of China, 181

Da Cankao, 35–6, 79, 91, 93, 97; back issues, 100; defeat of, 92; first issue, 39
Dalai Lama, 84–5, 87, 160, 206, 309; office hacked, 162
Darfur, 291
Deibert, Ron, 159–60
Delta Airlines, 309
Democracy Forum, 65, 66
Democratic National Committee, Russian hacking of, 192
Demos/Relcom, Russia, 252–3, 255–6
Deng Xiaoping, 21–4, 47, 89; martial law declaration, 37
Dharamsala, 85–8, 160, 163, 276; internet, 84, 160
'digital divide', 222
Dilshat Perhat, 150
Ding, James, 30–1
DIT, Broadcasting Board of Governors, 108
Diyarim.com, 150–1, 157
Djibouti naval base, 289
domain name system (DNS), 220
Dorsey, Jack, 111
dot.com bubble, first, 84
Dourado, Eli, 228–32
Dow Chemical, 170
Dow Jones, 81
Downey, Brandon, 314
Dreazen, Yochi, 110
DropBox, 276
Drummond, David, 61–2, 171
Dunhuang, 154
Durov, Pavel, 259–63, 265–6, 268–9, 272; Dubai exile, 270; flight, 267
Dynamic Internet Technology, 104, 106–7; Broadcasting Board of Governors, 108
DynaWeb, 101–2; Foundation, 106
Dzungaria, 136

'East Turkestan', 136, 149; question of, 152
Eastern Buddhas Study Falun Dafa Association, 97

Education Computer Resource Centre, India, 86
Egypt, 230–1; Twitter, 264
Eiffel Tower, website crash, 2
Electronic Frontier Foundation, 244–6
elite, Chinese, 90, 117
email address grabbing, 35
encryption, 268–9
Epoch Times, 96–8
Epstein, Helen, 297
Ethiopia, 10, 289, 304
EU (European Union), WSIS stance, 223
Eudora, 88
Eximbank, 288

Facebook, 18, 242, 264, 282, 286, 297, 301, 303, 312–13, 317; banned, 183; censoring by, 314; Firewall blocked, 259, 278; Internet.org, 291
'fake news' panic, 311, 314
Falun Gong, 9, 28, 45–6, 49, 59, 62, 91, 96, 102, 107–8, 112, 118; anti- campaign, 48, 58; blocking of, 99; China mass detentions, 54; community, 103; CRQS withdrawal, 51; members self-immolating, 56; -neoconservatives link, 98; North America shift, 96–7; online censorship, 55; origins, 47 Research Society, 54
FalunDafa.org, 97
Fang Binxing, 249–50
FBI (US Federal Bureau of Investigations), 186, 190–1
FDC (Forum for Democratic Change, 294–6, 300
Ferzat, Ali, 209
filters, border, 29
financial crash 2008, 8, 289
FinFisher, 293, 294
FireChat, 19
FireEye, 192
foreign media coverage, importance of, 255
France, Rwanda Hutu aid, 291

Freedom House, 104
FreeGate, 95–6, 103, 105, 107–9, 110, 112–13; successful, 104; user-friendly, 102
FreeNet China, 99, 101; 2001 launched, 100
freetibet.org, 163
Friedman, Tom, 90, 246
Friendster, 260
Friends of Tibet, 308
FSB, Russia, 265–6, 269
Fuyou Street, Beijing, 45

Gaddafi, Muammar, 290
Gallagher, Ryan, 314
Gamma Group, 293
Gang of Eight, USSR, 254–5
Gauthier, Ursula, 199
George Mason University, 228
Geshe Sopa, 84
Ghost Remote Administration Tool (Gh0st Rat), 162–3; hackers, 164
Gilmore, John, 244
Github, DDos attack, 1–4, 310
global governance, cycles of, 236

Global Internet Freedom Consortium (GIFC), 102, 110; funding boom, 109; projects, 112
Global Internet Inc, 106
Global Times, 172
GoAgent, 5, 6
Golden Shield project, 26–7, 91
Goldsmith, Jack, 30, 219, 243
gongfu, Chinese martial art, 48
Google, 64, 113; 2002 blocked, 91, 2006 China attitude, 115, 2009 accusations, 167, censorship compliance, 118, censorship reversal, 172, China 'foreignness' accusation, 125, China blocked, 166, China brand, 117, China cultural errors, 126, China operating, 116, China strategy, 119, Chinese-language search engine, 62, Congressional hearing, 120, 124, cultural mistakes,

125; Dragonfly, 314, Google China, 61, 62, 165, 246;

Google Drive, 162; hacked, 168, Schrage accusation, 121, shareholder critique, 168, US criticism, 173, US media criticism, 115

Google.cn search engine, 117

Gorbachev, Mikhail, 75, 173, 252, 255–6; KGB detained, 253

Gordon, Richard, 176

Gore, Al, 31

government commentators employed, 213

Grateful Dead, 244

Great Cannon, China cyber weapon, 3–4

'Great Firewall', 5, 8, 9, 26–7, 29, 43, 46, 58, 66, 71, 90, 92, 99, 101, 107, 112, 117, 159, 199, 207, 242, 311; Cisco help, 116; costs of fighting it, 106, export of, 10; Google brief ejection, 124; international spreading of, 310; keywords detection, 28; Kremlin copy, 260; Uganda import, 287; upgrading of, 92; US components, 30

Great Hall of the People, 23

Great Leap Forward, 8, 138; Xinjiang avoidance, 133

Great Wall, historical, 25

GreatFire.org, 3–4

'Green Dam Youth Escort', 27, 98

Greenwald, Glenn, 268

Group of 77, 237

Gu Ge, name error, 125 see also NoGuGe

Guangdong, 143, 201

Guangxi, 78

Guangzhou, 29

Gulf of Aden, 289

Guo Wengui, 92

Guomindang, 49

Guonei Dongtai Qingyang, 79

Haig, Dan, 83–4, 86–8, 160

Hainan, Lingshui: signals intelligence, 164; servers in, 163

'Harmony' CCP-speak, 72

Harris, Rachel, 151

Harvard, 71, 74, 91; Law, 244

HBGary Federal, 185–6; hack, 188

He Guoqiang, 171

He Zuoxiu, 49

Hefei, anti-corruption case, 280

Hinton, Carma, 176

Hitchens, Christopher, 49

Hoglund, Greg, 186

Holder, Eric, 189

Holdstock, Nick, 137, 149

home routers, 217

Hong Kong: Admiralty, 18; Broadband, 155; Chinese University, 217; Civic Square, 15; independence discussions, 20; Internet Exchange, 217–18; parliamentary elections, 19; Science Park, 200; 2014 effect, 19; Umbrella Movement, 255

Horowitz, Michael, 107, 109

hosts.txt file, 219

HP corporation, 245

Hsu, Stephen, 108

Hu Jintao, 184

Hu Qiheng, 234

Hu Yaobang, 21

Huai Jinping, 234

Huang Cuilian, 145

Huang Shike, arrest of, 280

Huang, Alan, 102

Huawei, 251, 288; military ties, 235; Uganda censorship profits, 304

Hudson Institute, 107

Human Rights in China, New York, 76

Human Rights Watch, 147, 234

Hvistendahl, Mara, 281

IBM Nazi Germany connection comparison, 119, 122–3

ICANN see Corporation for Assigned Names and Numbers

Ilham, Jewher, 141, 195–8

images, censorship challenges, 208

India, blackouts, 87

Indiana University, 195–6

Infocom, 222; prosecution of, 223
Inner Mongolia massacre, 133
Instagram, 309, 316
intellectuals, anti-qigong, 49
International Centre for Human Rights and Democracy, 30
International Criminal Court, 299
international telecommunications, access as human right, 232
internet: access points, 28; Africa blackouts, 10; China war on, 6; Chinese characters, 31; construction control, 156; content providers government registration, 72; founders, 219; governance, 225, 228; intergovernmental control, 223; unwritten rules, 72; US control conflict, 222; utopianism, 245; workings of, 155
Internet Assigned Numbers Authority, 219, 222
Internet Corporation for Assigned Names and Numbers (ICANN), 221–5, 228, 230, 256; China influence, 234; China pushing, 237
Internet Engineering Task Force (IETF), 234
Internet Explorer browser, 169
Internet Governance Forum, 224
Internet Society of China, 234–5
IP server connection, 28, 155; addresses workings of, 154; numbers, 219
Iran, 111; Green revolution, 311; social networking blocking, 111; 2009 election protests, 110, 112, 246
Iraq: US invasion of 2003, 223; Uyghur fighters, 199
'iron rice bowl' jobs, 47
Isa, Aziz, 151
Islamic State, 199; internet use, 9; Paris attacks, 269
Islamists, 195
Israeli intelligence, 190

Jacobs, Justin, 137
Jiang Qing, 133

Jiang Zemin, 32, 78, 90–1, 184
Jiangsu province, 74
Jiao Guobiao, dismissal of, 95
Jilin, China, 47–8
Jobs, Steve, 117, 259
Jones, Roy, 307–9

Kadeer, Rebiya, China riots blame, 152
Kaifu Lee, 116–17, 124–6, 165–6, 171–2; government fights, 167; Making a World of Difference, 118
Kalathil, Shanthi, 236
Kang Xiaoguang, 54
Kapor, Mitch, 244
Kaspersky Labs, Moscow, 192
keywords, 184; Chinese language filtering, 208; detection, 28
KGB/FSB (USSR/Russia), 256–7, 265–6, 269
Kirillovich, Vladimir, 249
Kiselyov, Dmitry, 247
Kissinger, Henry, 108
Kleinwächter, Wolfgang, 223
Kot, Edward, 264–5
Kramer, Terry, 228–9, 232–3
Kremlin, deep packet inspection, 266
Kristof, Nick, 46
Krumholtz, Jack, 122–3
Kryuchkov, Vladimir, 253
Kurchatov Institute of Atomic Energy, 252, 256, 261

LAN protocols, 241
Lantos, Tom, 122
Leach, Jim, 120; censorship accusation, 121
Leavy, Penny, 186
Leo Technology, Urumqi-based, 200
letter substitutions, 107
Leung Chun-ying, 19
Leviev, Lev, 267
Levy, Stephen, 118
Lhasa, 85
Li Chang, 54
Li Changchun, 165–6, 171
Li Dongxiao, 178

Li Gang, 5
Li Hongkuan, 35–6, 38–9, 79, 91–3, 99
Li Hongzhi, 47–50, 53–6, 96–7, 99, 103; books banned, 46; teachings of, 52; USA move, 51
Li Keqiang, 240
Li Peng, 26, 42; martial law declaration, 21
Li Yuanlong, 95; son's arrest, 96
Li Zhi, 148
Li, Robin, 124–6, 172
Lin Hai, 39
Link, Parry, 73
Liu Xiaobo, 66, 198
LiveJournal, DDoS attack, 264
Lo, Kenneth, 217–18
Lockheed Martin, 187
Lokodo, Simon, 304
love bug, 161
Lu, Phus, 5–6
Lu Wei, 78, 80–1, 207, 237, 242, 249, 312; downfall of, 313; promotion, 181; rise of, 79
Luo Fuhe, 77

Ma Zhaoxu, 173
Ma, Jack, 67
Ma, Pony, 280
MacArthur Genius Grant, 76
MacKinnon, Rebecca, *Consent of the Networked*, 72
Mail.ru, 267
Makanim.com, 149
Makerere University, 295, 300
Malofeev, Konstantin, 248–51
malware, 162; specialised, 163
Mandiant, malware, 186, 188–90
Manitsme, malware family, 188
Manning, Chelsea, 229; defence fund, 186
Mao Zedong, 184, 240; Anti-Rightist campaigns, 205; death of, 23; Great Leap Forward, 89
Marczak, Bill, 3
Marriott Global Reservations Sales and Customer Care Centre, 307–8; China

apology, 309; Chinese language website, 308
Martínez, Antonio García, 317
mass mailings, 103
May Fourth Movement, 176
McLaughlin, Andrew, 117
Medvedev, Dmitry, 263
melamine, contaminated, 204
Messi, Lionel, 278
Micek, Peter, 236
Microsoft, 115–16, 119, 245
Millward, James, 133, 137
Minghui.org, 97
Ministry of Industry and Information Technology, 235–6
Minzu Iniversity, 134
Mirilashvili, Vyacheslav, 260, 267
MIT Media Lab, 243
mobile payments, 279
Moma, Google intranet, targeted, 169
Mong Kok, camp, 19
Montreal, 85
Morozov, Evgeny, 110
Mountain View Google HQ, 116, 169
Mugabe, Robert, 285, 290
Murong Xuecun, 205
Museveni, Yoweri, 285, 287, 292–3, 296–8, 300, 301–3, 305; Kampala opposition, 286; 2016 swearing in, 299
Museveni, Janet, 286
MySpace, 260

Nagaraja, Shishir, 162
Nairobi, Chinese language signs, 288
Namubiru, Lydia, 305
Nanfang Daily, 64
Nanjing, 36; University, 212
Nasa, Goddard Space Flight Center, 99
National Endowment for Democracy, 92, 108
National Reconciliation Day, 158
nationalism, Chinese, 8
Navalny, Alexei, 263–5
Negroponte, Nicholas, 243
Network Solutions, 220–1

New Tang Dynasty Television, 97
Newland, Jesse, 2
Ng, Jason Q., 183
Nigeria, 232
Noah, Trevor, 302
NoGuGe.com, 126
non-aggression, cyber pact, 251
Northrop Grumman, 170
Nossik, Anton, 257, 262
Nur Bekri, 146, 148
Nureli, 157
Nyanzi, Stella, 286–7, 303, 305;
    imprisoned, 301–2; Stella,
    persecution of, 300

Obama, Barack, 157, 165, 191, 228,
    246; 'pivot to Asia', 192
Obote, Milton, 292; overthrow of, 285
Occupy movement, 9
Office of Personnel Management
    (OPM), 190, Chinese hacked, 191
"Operation Fungua Macho", 293
Ownby, David, 55, 98

Page, Larry, 116, 168, 171
Palmer, David, 50
Palmer, Mark, 107–9
Pan Shiyi, 180–2
Pan Yiheng, 177
Panama Papers, 251
'patriotic hackers',161
peer-to-peer software, Chinese, 101
Pegasus, early email software, 86
Pentagon, the, 161
perestroika, 75
Perhat, Dilshat, 157
Pfeifle, Mark, 110
Philippines, 161; China boycotts call,
    77
Piccuta, Dan, 165–6
Pirate Bay, file-sharing website, 185
PLA (Chinese People's Liberation
    Army), 22, 37, 132, 240, 242, 251,
    312; Third Technical Department,
    164; US indictment, 189
pornography, 91, 105–6

Postel, John, 219, 221–2, 228;
    'benevolent dictator', 220
Press, Larry, 254–5
Prophet Muhammed, image forbidden,
    209
proxies: sharing of, 102; use of, 101
'public opinion channellers', 214
'public order', CCP-speak, 72
Public Pledge on Self-Discipline for the
    Chinese Internet, 64
Public Security Bureau, 149
Putin, Vladimir, 228, 247, 249, 251,
    257, 262–6; internet concern, 261

qigong, 55; enthusiasm for, 47; groups,
    50 masters' absurd claims, 49;
    opinion shift against, 48
Qin Yongmin, 42
Qin Zhihui, arrest, 182
Qing Gang, 35
QQ, 182, 277
Qzone, 182, 278

Radio Free Asia, 106, 147, 248, 311
Rajagopalan, Megha, 199
Rand Corporation, 192
Razak, Najib, 209
Reagan, Ronald, 248
Rebel Pepper, 212, 215
Red Guards, 133
Reincarnation Party, 209
Relcom see Demos/Relcom
Ren Zhengfei, 251
RenRen, 182
Reporters Without Borders, 64
Republic of China (ROC/Taiwan), 288
Reuters, 80–1
RFA, 108; 1994 launch, 107
riots, Urumqi, 148
'River Elegy', TV programme, 20
Robinson, Michael, 30–2
Roldugin, Sergei, 251
root authority, 201
rootkit.com, 186, 188
Rosenberg, Jonathan, 117
Roskomnadzor, 266, 269, 270

Ross, Alec, 264
Rossiya Segodnya, 247–8
RSA, hacked, 187
RT, TV station, 247, 311
Runet, 257, 270
Russian Federation, 10, 237; early
    years of, 256; FAPSI, 257; firewall
    urgency of, 251; internet blacklist,
    266; internet use surge, 257; liberal
    internet era, 262; Libertarian Party,
    272 nationalised internet, 231; Safe
    Internet Forum, 248; 2012 election
    protests, 251

Sadikejiang Kaze, killing of, 146
Safe Internet League, 249–50
Safe Web, Triangle Boy, 108
Sakharov, Andrei, 270
Salkin.com, 157
Samdup, Thubten, 85–6, 160
Saudi Arabia, 230
Saulsbury, Brendan, 190
Schmidt, Eric, 116, 124, 127, 168;
    China strategy support, 126; Google
    outvoted, 171
Schneider, Rick, 87
Schrage, Elliot, 120–4
'secret backdoors', 162
Seldon, Tenzin, 170
self-censorship, Google justification,
    120
self-immolation, 58
SenseTime, 200
Sha Tin New Town, Hong Kong, 217
Shambaugh, David, 233
Shanghai, 29; Cooperation
    Organisation, 251; Cyberspace
    Administration, 308; European Jews
    haven, 205; Expo 2010, 180; police
    computer security, 35
Shaoguan incident *see* Xuri Toy factory
Shchyogolev, Igor, 248, 250
Shen Yun, performance group, 97
Shenzhen, 143; public security bureau,
    surveillance division, 72–3
Shi Caidong, 51–3

Shi Tao, 64–5 67, 76, 116, 119; prison
    sentence, 66
Sichuan province, 201
Siemens BS2000 mainframe computer,
    24
Signal, encryption app, 268
Silicon Valley, 1; biggest companies, 59;
    private enterprise victory, 7
Silk Road, dark web, 100
Sima Nan, 49
Sina Weibo, 182–3, 278; censors at, 75
Sino-Soviet split, 288
Sither, Lobsang Gyatso, 276–7, 283
Smirnov, Sergei, 266
Smith, Chris, 115
Smith, Craig, 90, 309
Snapchat, 260
Snowden, Edward, 190, 268, 269;
    revelations of, 313
Sobel, David, 245
social media, companies, 7
Soldatov, Alexey, 256, 261
solidarity: surveillance attention, 74;
    threat of, 10
Solzhenitsyn, Alexander, 5
Song Zheng, 235
South China Sea: Chinese ambitions,
    192; international court ruling, 77
spammers, trading among, 39
'spear-phishing', 159, 187
'spiritual pollution', 35
Sprint, 30–1
St Petersburg: briefcase bomb 2017,
    269; State University, 260
Stanford Research Institute, 220
State Commission of Machine Industry,
    24
Steve Jackson Games, 245
Stevens, John Paul, 245
Students for a Free Tibet, 170
Stuxnet virus, 190
Sudan, 230, 290
Sullivan, Andrew, 110
Sulzberger Jr, Arthur Ochs, 89–90
supremacist ideology, Han, 133
Surkov, Vladislav, 262–3

Sweden, 232

Symantec, 108, 170

Syria, Uyghur fighters, 199

System of Operative Search Measures, Russia, 257

Taiwan *see* Republic of China

Tanzania, 288; Tan–Zam railway line, 287

Tarim Basin, 136

Tarnoff, Ben, 317

tear gas, 18

tech giants, collaboration accusation, 119

techno-libertarians, 243, 246

Telegram app, 268, 272; banned, 269; blocked, 270

Tencent, 182, 235, 279, 281–2; data hoovering, 280; leg up, 278; WeChat, 277; Weibo, 278

The Atlantic, 110

The Gate of Heavenly Peace, subtitled version, 176

The New Republic, 110

The New York Times, 3, 89–90, 100, 111, 179, 211, 223, 257

The People's Daily, 21, 79, 172, 178, 246

The Wall Street Journal, 110, 309

The Washington Post, 57, 110, 302

Third World Academy of Sciences, 24

Tian, David, 99

Tian, Edward, 30–1

Tiananmen Square, 9, 21, 25, 46, 62, 99, 175; anger, 38; crackdown, 89, 107; massacre, 22, 26, 3, 208; massacre 20th anniversary, 166; Mothers, 65; movement, 20, 76; *Papers*, 100; protests, 78; self-immolation, 56–7; Tianjin protest, 52–4

Tibet, 83–4, 98, 106, 138, 149, 210; Action Institute, 274, 276; Computer Resource Centre, 86, 161; diaspora battling cyberspies, 276; Freedom Movement fund for, 163; Institute of the Performing Arts, 85; PLA victory, 85; Youth Congress, 85

Tohti, Ilham, 132, 134, 140–1, 143, 150, 152, 158, 195, 199; detention, 157; father killing, 133; harassment experience, 135; trial of, 131, US exile, 140

Tor Browser, 100, 102

Touré, Hamadoun, 228, 231, 236

traffic spikes, websites, 2

Trivedi, Aseem, 209

trolls: Badiucao attacks, 211; pro-China government, 92, 212

Trump, Donald, 192

Tsai Ing-wen, 212

Tsang, Donald, 15

Tunis Agreement 2005, 237

Tunisia, 9; Facebook, 264

Turnbull, Malcolm, 203

Tusiime, Samson, 295–6, 304; arrest of, 300

Twitter, 111, 207, 211, 246, 296–7, 303, 307, 309, 311–12; banned, 183; blocked, 27; 'Revolution', 110

UAE (United Arab Emirates), 230

Uganda: Chieftaincy of Military Intelligence, 293; Communications Commission, 303–4; Computer Misuse Act, 300; fake wireless hotspots, 294; security services, China learning, 295, 303; Special Investigations Unit, 300; Telecom, 304; Trojan horse viruses, 294; Twitter, 300; 2016 election, 296–8; 'walk to work' protests, 292

UgandaDecides, hashtag, 297

UglyGorilla, 187–8

UK (United Kingdom), 232

Ukraine, 250

Ulhaque, Zulkiflee Anwar (Zunar), 209

UltraSurf, 102, 105, 107–10, 112; programming, 106; successful, 104

Umbrella Movement/generation, 16, 19–20

United Nations, 10, 313; 'cyber-sovereignty', concept of, 224; ITU, 225, 227–32, 236; ITRs, 225, 233; WSIS, 222
Unit 61398, 190–1; indictment of, 189
United Arab Emirates, 230
United Russia party 2011 rally, 263
University of British Columbia, 309
University of California, Berkeley, 30
University of Edinburgh, 99
University of Helsinki, 253
University of Southern California, 220–1
University of Toronto, 159; Citizen Lab, 3–4
university servers, 35
URLs: blocking of, 29; proxies, 102–3
Urumqi, 132, 136, 153–4, 201; -Beijing link, 156; Han revenge attacks, 149; internet cut-off, 151; People's Intermediate Court, 131; police attack, 148; proxies, 102–3; riots, 183; student protest, 146–7
USA: Chinese Embassy protests, 98; -China relationship, 112; Commerce Department, 222; Defense Advanced Research Projects Agency, 219; Google Congressional hearing, 122; House Subcommittee on Human Rights, 115; imperialism internet use, 112; National Security Agency, 170, 244, 268, 293, 313; Republican Party, 244; Senate Sub-Committee on Human Rights, 108; State Department, 22, 81, 109–11, 166, 298
UseNet, 253
Usmanov, Alisher, 261, 267
USSR (Union of Soviet Socialist Republics): dissolution of, 256; 1990s internet start, 252
Uyghurs, Chinese language forums, 157, dangerous vagabonds characterised, 132; discrimination against, 138–9, 152; *doppa* headgear,

132; internet, 143, 150; pervasive unemployment, 134; stereotyping of, 140; terrorism label, 140; Uyghur Online, 131, 135, 139, 151, 157; websites control, 149

Villeneuve, Nart, 159–60, 162–3
VIP Reference, 35
virtual private networks (VPNs), 9, 103, 113, 157, 299; apps, 297; users, 28
VKontakte (VK), 259–60, 262, 267; customer support, 265; groups, 270; user base growth, 261
Voice of America, 106–8, 248, 311
Voice of China, 287
Voice of Russia, 247

"Walk to Work" protests, 294
Walton, Greg, 160–3, 276
Wang Baodong, 109
Wang Dong, 188–9
Wang Lequan, 152
Wang Liming, 209, 210
Wang Yongping, 178
Wang Youcai, 42
Wang Yunfeng, 24, 25
Wang Zhiwen, 54
Wang, Jack, 188
'War on Terror', 290
WCITLeaks, 229–31, 233, 236
Weaver, Nicholas, 3
WeChat (Weixin), 207, 242, 277–8, 281–3; censorship challenge, 268; monopoly of, 278; payments system, 279–80
Weibo, 46, 177–9, 181, 184, 206–7, 210, 268, 277; failure, 215; ingenuity of, 182; microbloggers use, 180; muzzling of, 214; public offering, 182; surveillance sidestep attempts, 208; Weiboscope, 77
Weigel, Moira, 317
Weir, Bob, 244
Wen Jiabao, 79–80
Wenhui Daily, 173

Wenzhou train crash, 177, 179; internet revealed, 178
Westinghouse, 187
Wexler, Robert, 123
WhatsApp, 16, 268, 278, 296, 303, 316
Whole Earth 'Lectronic Link, 244
WikiLeaks, 104, 185–6, 315–16
Wikipedia, specific pages blocked, 27
Wired, 84, 106, 243–4
World Bank, 24
World Conference on International Telecommunications, 227; Leaks *see above*
World Internet Conference 2015, 241
World Uyghur Congress, 152
World Wide Web Consortium (W3C), 234
WSIS 10, 237; US victory, 224
WTO (World Trade Organization), 80–1; China joining, 42, 91–2
Wu, Dandan, 125
Wu, Tim, 30, 219, 241, 243
wumao, 212
wumaodang, recruited students, 213
Wuyi, Zhejiang province, 310
Wuzhen, 239–40

Xabnam.com, 157
Xi Jinping, 81, 181, 191, 203, 207, 238–40, 281, 312; internet clampdown, 78
Xia, Bill, 99–100, 102–3, 107, 112
Xiao Qiang, 76, 21
Xi'an, Shaanxi province, 154
Xinhua, 56–7, 64, 77, 78, 156, 181; commercial offerings, 80; Hong Kong bureau, 79; journalists' watchdog role, 79; official line, 148
Xinjiang Autonomous Region, 107, 131–2, 135, 140, 148, 156, 195, 199, 210, 280; Beijing terrorism lens, 152; famine avoidance, 138; internet access, 156; internet blackout, 153; new policies of control, 200; Qing Empire, 137; Shanshan county, 201; University, 150
Xu Hong, 39
Xu Wendi, 42
Xue, Charles, 180, 181
Xuri Toy Factory/Shaoguan incident, 143, 146; footage of, 151; Uyghur workers, 144–5

Yahoo, 115, 119, 170; arrest responsibility, 116; China subsidiary, 63–4, 67; informer role criticised, 66
Yanayev, Gennady, 253
Yang Jisheng, 20
Yang, Jerry, 66–7
Yanukovych, Viktor, 267
Yeltsin, Boris, 75, 254–5, 257; resignation, 261
YouTube, 167, 246, 274, 303, 314, 316; blocked, 183
Yu Jie, *China's Best Actor*, 80
Yu Wanli, 173–4, 246
Yuan Zengxin, 138

Zambia, 304
Zara, 309
Zhang Zhenhuan, 49
Zhang Jianchuan, 235
Zhang, Shawn, 309
Zhao Houlin, 236–7
Zhao Jing, 36
Zhao Ziyang, 80, 889; house arrest, 21–2
Zhongnanhai complex, 45; 1999 protest, 46, 52–3, 55
Zhou Yongkang, 171
Zhu Rongji, 53
Zhu, Julie, 62
Zhuan Falun, 50; text banned, 52
Zimbabwe, 10, 290, 304
Zorn, Werner, 24–5
ZTE, 288
Zuckerberg, Mark, 260, 312

ZED

Zed is a platform for marginalised voices across the globe.

It is the world's largest publishing collective and a world leading example of alternative, non-hierarchical business practice.

It has no CEO, no MD and no bosses and is owned and managed by its workers who are all on equal pay.

It makes its content available in as many languages as possible.

It publishes content critical of oppressive power structures and regimes.

It publishes content that changes its readers' thinking.

It publishes content that other publishers won't and that the establishment finds threatening.

It has been subject to repeated acts of censorship by states and corporations.

It fights all forms of censorship.

It is financially and ideologically independent of any party, corporation, state or individual.

Its books are shared all over the world.

www.zedbooks.net

@ZedBooks